2004

Families by Law

Families by Law

An Adoption Reader

EDITED BY

Naomi R. Cahn and Joan Heifetz Hollinger

New York University Press

NEW YORK AND LONDON

NEW YORK UNIVERSITY PRESS
New York and London
www.nyupress.org

Library of Congress Cataloging-in-Publication Data
Families by law : an adoption reader /
edited by Naomi R. Cahn and Joan Heifetz Hollinger.
p. cm.
Includes bibliographical references and index.
ISBN 0–8147–1589–3 (cloth : alk. paper) — ISBN 0–8147–1590–7 (pbk. : alk. paper)
1. Adoption—Law and legislation—United States. 2. Adoption—United States.
I. Cahn, Naomi R. II. Hollinger, Joan H. (Joan Heifetz)
KF545.F36 2004
346.7301'78—dc22 2003018166

New York University Press books are printed on acid-free paper,
and their binding materials are chosen for strength and durability.

Manufactured in the United States of America

c 10 9 8 7 6 5 4 3 2 1
p 10 9 8 7 6 5 4 3 2 1

Contents

Acknowledgments

Adoption is undergoing a dramatic transformation. Adoptive families were once understood as equivalent "in all respects" to a biologically based family, except of course for the "missing" genetic tie. Over the past several decades, this model has been challenged by alternative models that reflect the increasingly diverse faces within the several million adoptive families who now live in the United States. These new models also reflect the multiple functions adoption serves—not simply as a way for infertile couples to become parents of infants, or as a means to provide homes for orphaned children, but as a way to care for older children with special needs, protect children being raised by single or same-sex parents, and create families that cross racial, ethnic, national, and cultural boundaries.

As the policies and practices of adoption have changed, so too has the study of adoption. This reader is part of the emerging field of adoption studies, a field that now involves many academic disciplines, but that hardly existed when we both began teaching and writing about adoption in the 1980s. Although we knew and respected each other's work, we did not meet until 1998, when Jackie Parker, legislative aide to Senator Carl Levin, asked us to testify on adoption-related congressional legislation. We began talking about the need for research from different theoretical perspectives to interpret adoption laws and court decisions in relation to the changing demographics of family life and the developmental needs of children. Joan Hollinger's experience drafting model adoption laws in the context of competing demands from those purporting to speak for the interests of each member of the "adoption triad" convinced us that it is important to encourage less partisan and more intellectually rigorous analyses of the role of adoption in our society. Naomi Cahn's work in adoption history and jurisprudence, as well as her personal ties to adoption through her husband's experiences as an adoptee, similarly fostered our determination to explore adoption from multiple perspectives.

We are deeply indebted to all of our contributors for allowing us to draw upon their broad-ranging research and commentary and for sharing our belief that multi-disciplinary scholarly attention to adoption is long overdue. Thanks to our contributors, *Families by Law* is able to explore the ways the legal and psychosocial aspects of adoption have gradually outgrown their secretive, "second best" history to become more "open" by acknowledging the differences between adoptive and biogenetic families. By presenting excerpts from the work of historians, social scientists, philosophers, psychologists, and legal academics, our reader is also able to show that as adoptive families come to understand, and even celebrate, their distinctive characteristics and needs, adoption laws often retain the legal fictions of the older model. This poses challenges to those who appreciate that the needs of adoptive children for permanent and secure families do not require the fictive denial of a child's origin.

We especially thank our colleagues Anita Allen-Castellitto, Annette Appell, Nancy Dowd, Ellen Herman, Catherine Ross, Elizabeth Samuels, Molly Shanley, and Barbara Bennett Woodhouse for their advice and encouragement. At the George Washington University Law School, we were fortunate to have the assistance of Patrisha Smith, Chelsea Grimmius, Lauren Peacock, and especially Mary Dini, who has been the administrative anchor for the book.

At New York University Press, we appreciate the support of our editors Jennifer Hammer and Despina Gimbel, as well as of Niko Pfund, former editor in chief, who first encouraged us to compile this reader. Naomi Cahn thanks the George Washington University Law School and Dean Michael Young for financial, administrative, and emotional support. Joan Hollinger thanks her students at Berkeley's Boalt Hall Law School and the undergraduate Legal Studies Program for their helpful comments on earlier versions of the reader and Dean Robert Berring for his support in the final stages of our project.

Finally, we want to thank our families, who have adopted this project as their own, and each other for sustaining our mutual enthusiasm for the study of adoption and for this reader.

Families by Law

Introduction

This reader provides a multidisciplinary perspective on adoption law and policy in the United States. *Families by Law* examines the social and legal history of adoption in the United States as well as its contemporary psychosocial and cultural functions. An understanding of adoption requires analysis of fundamental and complex issues: (1) Who is a family member? (2) What are the consequences for children and adults of separating biogenetic from social and psychological parenting? (3) What is the state's role in creating families? and (4) What are the sources and scope of parental rights and obligations?

Adoptive families are the product of law, not blood. Through a highly regulated process culminating in a judicial proceeding, the state creates the status of parent and child "in all respects" between individuals who are not biogenetically related and severs the child's legal relationship to the biogenetic parents and their families. Once an adoption decree has been issued, the adoptive family replaces and becomes the legal equivalent of the biogenetic family.[1] The adoptee receives a new birth certificate with the names of her adoptive parents substituted for the names of the woman and man, if any, listed as her parents at birth. In most states, the original birth certificate is sealed and its contents cannot be disclosed except upon court order or the mutual consent of a birth parent and the adoptee, once she is eighteen or twenty-one years old.

Adoption entails psychosocial as well as legal consequences, and, until recently, was often described as the "perfect solution" to an unwanted pregnancy. Adoption enables birth parents, especially mothers, to place their children in a new family when, for various reasons, they cannot raise them on their own. It provides children for adults who are infertile or who want to extend the boundaries of their otherwise biologically connected families. It allows states to shift the high public costs of caring for dependent children to the private realm. Most important, adoption gives children the security of a loving, permanent, and "forever" family.

A substantial body of research testifies to the successful outcomes for children raised by adoptive parents. On a variety of outcome measures, adopted children do as well as children living in "intact" families with their biological parents and significantly better than children living with parents who are ambivalent about them, or children left in foster care, group homes, or other institutional settings. As discussed in part 2, love and nurture can indeed temper nature and mitigate the effects of any pre-adoptive history of maltreatment.[2]

Of the estimated six million or more adopted individuals of all ages living in the United States, 2.1 million were living in households headed by one or both of their adopted parents in 2000. Three quarters of the children in these familes—1.6 million—were under 18; only 42,000 were infants less than a year old. The proportion of all children under 18 who are adopted hardly varied from one region of the country to another—ranging from 2.4 to 2.6 percent. A significantly larger percentage of adopted children than biological children under 18 live with two married parents. Morever, adopted children live in housholds with higher incomes than either biological or stepchildren; adoptive parent-householders are more highly educated, more likely to own their own home, and less likely to live in poverty. Because so many people turn to adoption only after trying to have biogenetically related children, it is not surprising that, on average, adoptive parents are older than biological parents—43 years compared to 38 years.

An estimated 120,000 to 150,000 adoptions are now being approved each year. No more than 35 percent of these adoptions conform to the traditional model of an infant being adopted by an unrelated and infertile married couple who are "legal strangers" to the child.[3] Voluntary adoptive placements have become increasingly rare not simply because of access to contraceptives and safe abortion since the early 1970s, but because young unmarried women, for a variety of reasons, are deciding to raise their children—even as policy makers in Washington and elsewhere encourage them to relinquish their children for adoption. Because the stigma that once shadowed out-of-wedlock pregnancy and single parenthood has largely evaporated, young women are reluctant to give up their babies. They are all the more reluctant to do so if their own families or the babies' fathers are willing to help out with child care and financial support.

Although many infertile couples continue to pursue adoption, a substantial number of adoptions are not prompted by a desire to overcome infertility, but by the needs of children whose lives are disrupted by divorce, death, or the involuntary termination of a parent's rights for neglect or abuse. While the idealized nuclear family of the 1950s often remains the goal for private adoptions, the nuclear family has enjoyed a far longer run in the imagination of those who assist in the formation of adoptive families than it has had in our society as a whole or in contemporary adoptive families.

Perhaps half or more of all adoptions are by stepparents; many others are by grandparents or other relatives who, like stepparents, have become the de facto parents or state-supervised kinship caregivers of the children they adopt. In addition, since the late 1990s, as discussed in part 3, there has been a dramatic increase in the number of children adopted from foster care to nearly 50,000 a year, more than double the annual rate of the 1980s. In many states, more than two-thirds of these children are being adopted by their former foster parent(s), some of whom are building unusually large families of eight to ten or more adopted children. A number of recent federal child welfare initiatives are contributing to this increase, including the Adoption and Safe Families Act (ASFA, 1997), the Multi-Ethnic Placement Act (MEPA, 1994–96), the Family and Medical Leave Act (1993), adoption-related tax credits of up to $10,000 per adoption, and subsidies for families who adopt children with "special needs."

A small but growing number of adoptions are by adults who want to create non-traditional families that reach across racial, ethnic, and cultural boundaries, not just biological ones. These new frontiers of adoption are discussed in part 6. Adoptions by U.S. citizens of children born in other countries have nearly tripled since 1990, with more than 21,000 foreign-born adopted children likely to enter this country in 2002–2003. The 2000 Census reports that at least 13 percent of all adopted children are foreign-born. With the U.S. implementation of the 1993 Hague Convention on Intercountry Adoption, intercountry adoptions are expected to increase at an even faster rate, raising issues that are explored in parts 6 and 7. Still other adoptive families are being formed by lesbians and gays who seek to legitimate their status as the "second parents" of their partners' child or who are recruited by public agencies in many states to adopt children with special needs, as explained in part 6.

As the kinds of children being adopted, and the kinds of adults seeking to adopt, become ever more diverse, popular perceptions of adoption usually continue to focus on adoptions between an infant and "strangers." This kind of adoption may strike some raw personal and cultural nerves. "Kinship" in this society, explained the anthropologist David Schneider in his classic study, *American Kinship,* is "the fact of shared biogenetic substance."[4] From this perspective, adoption is not a "perfect solution" or a story of personal and societal gain, but a tale of loss: the "natural" parent's loss of the opportunity to raise biological offspring, the adoptive parent's loss of the opportunity to have "natural" children, the child's loss of biogenetic kin, and the state's loss of its ability to preserve "natural" families.

Adoptive families are barraged with reminders that this form of family-building is an unwelcome "last resort," an artificial and imperfect substitute for a family that might have been. As the historian Barbara Melosh notes, "[i]n the nuances of language and informal social exchange, adoption is marked as difference. We speak of adoptive families and adopted children, modifying the unmarked category of families linked by biological kinship."[5] The issues of "difference" and "similarity" are discussed explicitly by feminists in part 7, and recur throughout this reader.

Indeed, the conventional view is that adoption is a "second best" means of forming a family. Prejudice against adoptees is long-standing. In a 1952 survey, 46 percent of respondents believed that a mother should save her biological child from drowning first, before saving her adopted child; only 3 percent believed the mother should save the adopted child first.

The continuing cultural preference for biologically based families can be seen in a survey fifty years later.[6] While attitudes toward adoption were more positive, differences remained in beliefs about adoptive and biological children. While 94 percent of those surveyed believed that adoptive parents are "lucky," only 75 percent believed that adoptive parents love their children as much as they would have loved their biological children, and fewer (less than 60 percent) believed that adoptive parents received the same amount of satisfaction from raising an adoptive child as from raising a biological child.

Extrapolating from the 2002 survey data to the general population, the researchers also found that 45 percent of Americans believe that adopted children are more likely than biological children to have behavioral and medical problems. There is, then, continuing ambivalence with respect to families formed through adoption, rather than through biology, a belief that blood ties are stronger and more desirable than adoptive ties. These issues are further explored in parts 2, 5, and 7.

Biogeneticism and the companion public attitude that adoption is at best a risky "last resort" are reinforced by advances in medically assisted reproduction, which offer infertile adults the possibility of having children who are at least partially "their own." Despite the high financial and emotional costs of techno-reproduction and the uncertain outcome, many childless adults would rather pursue this route toward parenthood. Analogies between adoption and families formed through the new reproductive technologies are discussed in parts 7 and 8.

Biogeneticism is also reinforced by the venerable common law and constitutional doctrines of "parental rights" and "family autonomy," which protect the rights of individuals to rear their offspring with minimal interference from the state. A central tenet of these doctrines is the presumption that "natural bonds of affection lead parents to act in the best interests of their children." *Parham v. J.R.*, 442 U.S. 584 (1979). As explained in part 2, ever since the first adoption statutes were enacted in the 1850s, parental consent, or a legitimate reason for dispensing with the need for consent, has been an essential, albeit not a sufficient, jurisdictional prerequisite for a valid adoption. The lack of uniform state laws or policies to address the rights of unwed fathers, as well as birth mothers, to consent to or veto a proposed adoption is also discussed in part 2. In its historical overview of adoption in American law, part 1 explores the origins of these doctrines and the role of the nineteenth-century child-saving movement in the genesis of modern adoption practices.

By contrast to the protections accorded biogenetic parents, individuals who wish to parent through adoption find their personal values and most intimate behaviors subject to intense scrutiny and bureaucratic regulation. As discussed in part 2, a powerful and opinionated cast of "helping professionals" are enlisted to evaluate the "suitability" of prospective parents before they can legally adopt. Nonetheless, estimates are that 11 percent to 24 percent of couples with infertility problems take some steps toward adopting a child, and almost 40 percent of Americans claim to have considered adoption at some point in their lives. In 1995 about 1 percent of all women ages eighteen to forty-four reported that they were currently "seeking to adopt." However, only 232,000, or less than half, of them had taken steps toward adopting, such as consulting a lawyer or an agency, and only about 100,000 had actually applied to an agency, retained a lawyer, or actively pursued adoption opportunities.[7]

Concerns about the costs of adoption, the complexity of adoption laws and regulations, and doubts about the characteristics of the children available for adoption from public agencies are among the reasons childless women cite when asked what dissuades them from pursuing adoption. Those most likely to consider adoption are childless married white women with fecundity impairments and relatively high income and educational levels. There is also evidence that single heterosexual African American and white women without fertility problems, as well as gay men and lesbians, are adopting in greater numbers.

Biogeneticism and the parental rights doctrine embody an ideal to which many adoptive families aspire. This aspiration is most evident in the traditional assertion that adoptive families are a "complete substitute" for, and function "as if" they are, biogenetically based families and are entitled to the same cultural acceptance and legal protection. The goal was—and for many adoptive parents still is—to look and feel as close as possible to what they can never really have. State laws that seal adoption records, substitute the names of adoptive parents for birth parents on "certificates of live birth," and permit, even if they do not require, anonymity and strict separation between birth and adoptive families are fully consistent with the asserted-equivalence model. The legal underpinnings of, as well as critical perspectives on, the perfect substitute, or asserted-equivalence, model are discussed throughout this reader.

During the past twenty-five years, the asserted-equivalence model has been subject to mounting criticism for trivializing the psychological, social, and biogenetic differences between "natural" and adoptive families. These differences are now said by many adoptees and birth parents, as well as by ever larger numbers of adoptive parents, to be of profound importance. An alternative response to the dual influence of biogeneticism and the parental rights doctrine has emerged. As discussed in parts 4 and 5, "openness" and the acknowledgment and acceptance of difference are rapidly becoming the mantras of contemporary adoption practice.

Adoptive families continue to seek cultural acceptance and legal protection, but more of them are doing so by applauding their distinctive characteristics and not portraying themselves as mirror images of the biogenetic families they cannot be.

The attack on secrecy in adoption has prompted the recently successful demand by adoptees in a number of states for access to sealed adoption records and their original birth certificates, developments examined in part 4. Another consequence is the call for more "openness" at some or all stages of an adoption. Whether limited to an exchange of information between birth and adoptive parents at the time of a child's placement, or broad enough to include regular visitation by members of the birth family with the adopted child long after the adoption is final, open adoption is said to have many benefits. Post-adoption contact is addressed in part 5.

As the legal edifice that once so completely separated birth and adoptive families crumbles, and as the diverse faces within adoptive families belie the possibility of ethnoracial or psychosocial equivalence, where are the guideposts to assist birth and adoptive parents? The complex web of different, and often inconsistent, adoption laws and costly time-consuming procedures at the state, national, and international level is a reflection of our society's inability to achieve consensus on how to facilitate the formation of adoptive families and encourage them to thrive. It is also a major source of frustration and confusion for the millions of people who want to abide by, and work within, the legal system to achieve critical reforms in adoption policies and practices.

In the final analysis, our adoption laws should protect all the parties, and especially innocent and vulnerable children, against harm. Our hope is that in addition to being a roadmap through the most significant issues in adoption history, law, psychology, and sociology, *Families by Law* will also suggest some ways to resolve the dilemmas of contemporary adoption. Using a variety of theoretical and pragmatic materials, ranging from cases, statutes, the practice standards and ethical codes of professional organizations, and scholarly research and commentary from a wide variety of perspectives and academic specialties, this reader will challenge existing understandings of adoption. We hope that *Families by Law* will be part of an ongoing effort to encourage additional, and long overdue, research on adoption and its lifelong consequences for adoptive children and their families.

Most of the selections in this book are adapted from previously published works or are excerpted from statutes, court opinions, or other documents in the public domain. Several selections were written specifically for this reader. For full attribution of quotations, references, and other source materials, please see the original versions, citations for which are listed in the Sources section at the end of the book. Where necessary, we have added clarifications in square brackets. Suggestions for further reading and a list of relevant state and federal court opinions are posted on the New York University Press Web site.

NOTES

1. Joan H. Hollinger, ed., *Adoption Law and Practice*, 3 vols. (New York: Matthew Bender, 1988–2003); Joan Heifetz Hollinger, "Authenticity and Identity in Contemporary Adoptive Families," 3 *Journal of Gender Specific Medicine* 23 (2000).

2. David Brodzinsky, "Long-Term Outcomes in Adoption," 3 *Future of Children* 153–166 (1993); Ann E. Brand and Paul M. Brinich, "Behavior Problems and Mental Health Contacts in Adopted, Foster, and Nonadopted Children," 40 *Journal of Child Psychology* 1221 (1999). Vivian B. Shapiro, Jane R. Shapiro, and Isabel H. Paret, *Complex Adoption and Assisted Reproductive Technology: A Developmental Approach to Clinical Practice* (New York: Guilford Press, 2001).

3. Rose M. Kreider, "Adopted Children and Stepchildren: 2000" (U.S. Census Bureau, Census 2000 Special reports, August 2003). The 2000 Census is the first to include "adopted son/daughter" as one of the options for householders to select, separate from "natural born son/daughter" and "stepson/stepdaughter." Despite the unprecedented data on the ages, race and ethnicity, and other socioeconomic characteristics of adoptive family households, the 2000 Census does not tell us whether these adoptive families were formed independently or through private or public agency placements, or whether the adoptive parents were the adoptees' stepparents, grandparents or other relatives, foster parents, or previously unrelated married couples or unmarried individuals. See Kathy S. Stolley, "Statistics on Adoption in the United States," 3 *Future of Children: Adoption* (1993), at 26–27 for a discussion of the obstacles to obtaining accurate data about the numbers and types of adoption. See, for discussion of very large adoptive families, Melissa Fay Greene, "The Family Mobile," *New York Times Magazine*, August 19, 2001.

4. David M. Schneider, *American Kinship: A Cultural Account* (Chicago: University of Chicago Press, 1980), 107.

5. Barbara Melosh, *Strangers and Kin: The American Way of Adoption* (Cambridge: Harvard University Press, 2002), 2.

6. Dave Thomas Foundation for Adoption and Evan B. Donaldson Adoption Institute, National Adoption Attitudes Survey (2002), www.adoptioninstitute.org/survey/survey_summary.html.

7. Anjani Chandra et al., "Adoption, Adoption Seeking, and Relinquishment for Adoption in the United States," National Center for Health Statistics, Advance Data no. 306, May 11, 1999.

History of Adoption in the United States

In part 1 we provide a brief history of adoption in the United States. Adoption is mentioned in the Code of Hammurabi and the Hindu Sanskrit texts and was practiced in ancient Rome, where it was typically used to perpetuate the male familial line. Under the common law legal systems derived from English law, however, formal legal adoption of an unrelated child is of fairly recent origin. Although informal placements of out-of-wedlock or orphaned children with relatives or "legal strangers" was prevalent long before the twentieth century, England did not enact a general adoption law until 1926; in the United States, formal legal adoption did not appear until the mid-nineteenth century and is generally attributed to the 1851 Massachusetts statute included in this part.

Naomi Cahn's article and the other selections in this part show that adoption existed in a variety of forms before the 1851 Massachusetts legislation, even though these actions were not identified as formal adoptions.

The article by Catherine J. Ross explains how the early adoption laws arose in the context of a child-saving movement dedicated to removing children from "unsuitable" families. Mid-nineteenth-century child-saving organizations provided houses of refuge for children, and often attempted to place them with foster families, either locally or in other parts of the country. The most famous of these societies, the New York Children's Aid Society, founded by Charles Loring Brace, developed an extremely ambitious "Emigration Plan" so that poor children could move west.

The two other selections in this part explore some of the changes in the societal functions and interpretations of adoption in the first half of the twentieth century. Julie Berebitsky explains how beliefs in the heritability of personal traits influenced attitudes toward adoption, especially the willingness of prospective parents to adopt children. Regina G. Kunzel describes how unwed mothers often resisted the pressure to relinquish their children for adoption at a time when social workers began to promote, and to control, the adoption process in order to enhance their own professional esteem.

An Act to Provide for the Adoption of Children (1851)

General Court of Massachusetts

Be it enacted by the Senate and House of Representatives, in General Court assembled, and by the authority of the same, as follows:

Sect. 1. Any inhabitant of this Commonwealth may petition the judge of probate, in the county wherein he or she may reside, for leave to adopt a child not his or her own by birth.

Sect. 2. If both or either of the parents of such child shall be living, they or the survivor of them, as the case may be, shall consent in writing to such adoption; if neither parent be living, such consent may be given by the legal guardian of such child; if there be no legal guardian, no father nor mother, the next of kin of such child within the State may give such consent; and if there be no such next of kin, the judge of probate may appoint some discreet and suitable person to act in the proceedings as the next friend of such child, and give or withhold such consent.

Sect. 3. If the child be of the age of fourteen years or upwards the adoption shall not be made without his or her consent.

Sect. 4. No petition by a person having a lawful wife shall be allowed unless such wife shall join therein, and no woman having a lawful husband shall be competent to present and prosecute such petition.

Sect. 5. If, upon such petition, so presented and consented to as aforesaid, the judge of probate shall be satisfied of the identity and relations of the persons, and that petitioner, or, in case of husband and wife, the petitioners, are of sufficient ability to bring up the child, and furnish suitable nurture and education, having reference to the degree and condition of its parents, and that it is fit and proper that such adoption should take effect, he shall make a decree setting forth the said facts, and ordering that, from and after the date of the decree, such child should be deemed and taken, to all legal intents and purposes, the child of the petitioner or petitioners.

Sect. 6. A child so adopted, as aforesaid, shall be deemed, for the purposes of inheritance and succession by such child, custody of the person and right of obedience by such parent or parents by adoption, and all other legal consequences and incidents of the natural relation of parents and children, the same to all intents and purposes as if such child had been born in lawful wedlock of such parents or parent by adoption, saving only that child shall not be deemed capable of taking property expressly limited to the heirs of the body or bodies of such petitioner or petitioners.

Sect. 7. The natural parent or parents of such child shall be deprived, by such decree of adoption, of all legal rights whatsoever as respects such child; and such child shall be freed from all legal obligations of maintenance and obedience, as respects such natural parent or parents.

Sect. 8. Any petitioner, or any child which is the subject of such a petition, by any next friend, may claim and prosecute an appeal to the supreme judicial court from such decree of the judge of probate, in like manner and with the like effect as such appeals may now be claimed and prosecuted in cases of wills, saving only that in no case shall any bond be required of, nor any costs awarded against, such child or its next friend, so appealing. [Approved by the Governor, May 24, 1851.]

Society's Children
The Care of Indigent Youngsters in New York City, 1875–1903

Catherine J. Ross

Criticisms of institutional care for youngsters . . . intensified through the turn of the century. The main challenge to asylum care arose from the relative success of alternative programs which placed children in families other than their own, through indenture, foster care, or adoption. As those programs expanded, the legal and social distinctions among them clarified. The benefits of family placement, uneven and controversial as they were, cost the congregate system much of its remaining prestige, and forced the directors of institutions to reevaluate the design of the care they offered, despite their investment in it.

Proponents of the 1875 Children's Law in New York had not envisioned the establishment of a large network of publicly supported institutions. The SCAA [State Charities Aid Association] expressed the hope that asylums would "devote their efforts to the care of those children who are diseased and feeble-minded, serving otherwise only as centers of collection whence healthy children shall be speedily passed on to homes in families."

The care and training of children of all classes in families other than their own had a long history in western culture. Through indenture to persons of a similar social status, youngsters multiplied their connections, and presumably their opportunities, while they received legal protection of their physical and mental training. In America as in England, one historian has suggested, "Puritan parents did not trust themselves with their own children. . . . They were afraid of spoiling them with too much affection." In that spirit, indenture was designed for general training rather than to provide a specific skill. Girls served as part of the housekeeping staff. Boys were as likely to share in chores as they were to learn a specialized trade. By the late eighteenth century, however, indenture had disappeared among the middle and upper classes in the United States. It applied only to those children whose parents could not otherwise support them.

Colonial parents might have hoped that indenture would lessen the risk of coddling their children, but depending on the background of the specific case, indenture could ease or exacerbate the tensions that normally accompany growing up. Although nineteenth century scholars had not articulated theories about the turbulence that characterizes adolescence, many families must have experienced difficulties with their own children. The care of a stranger's child posed additional problems. Indentured youngsters faced the search for autonomy without a longstanding emotional bond to the adults who exercised authority over them. That complicating circumstance affected the chances that any given indenture would satisfy both parties.

Disregarding the potential difficulties of indenture, New York state expanded the legislative framework for it in the middle of the nineteenth century in order to encourage the placement of indigent youngsters. New laws gave an increasing variety of organizations the power to place dependent children in families other than their own. In 1855 New York revised its indenture laws so that in addition to the local overseers of the poor, "the trustees, directors, or managers of any incorporated orphan asylum" could bind out boys until age 21 and girls until age 18, if the parents had surrendered the children to the asylum. But the parent, or, in the case of orphans, the mayor, held custody. Some unincorporated asylums received similar powers through individual enabling legislation. The Children's Fold, for example, could bind out any child under the age of ten who had resided in it for one year; children over ten could be placed after only six months in the institution. Legislation of the 1870's further extended those terms.

The sponsors of the 1875 Children's Law, opposed to congregate care, also drafted a companion measure designed to facilitate placement in families. That law, passed a few months later, empowered "incorporated associations and societies . . . for the purpose of taking care of and protecting destitute infant minor children, to bind out by indenture destitute children who are in their care and keeping." One major innovation of this act lay in the assignment of custody to the asylum instead of the parents until the indenture ended. A judge had to approve the signing of the contract. The law required that the indentured child be at least eight years old and have resided for at least three months in the orphanage. More important, the legislation introduced enforceable legal rights for the child. He, or any person representing him, could sue to "recover damages if the employer failed to provide suitable and proper board, lodging and medical attendance, or . . . to perform any of the provisions" of the indenture.

The final major amendment to indenture laws in New York passed in 1878. According to that statute, institutions gained custody of any child whose parents failed to pay board for one year. A mother received sole custody of a child for the purpose of surrendering him to an asylum if the father neglected to contribute to the child's expenses for six months. Most significantly, children supported by New York City in institutions would be "considered as deserted, . . . if no inquiry had been made about their welfare and no board had been paid for the space of one year." The institution to which the city paid board could, with judicial approval, place the child for adoption or indenture.

The tradition of indenturing dependent youngsters particularly informed the work of the New York Children's Aid Society (CAS), which conducted the most extensive and widely publicized program for placing youngsters in private homes in nineteenth century America. A group of Protestant missionaries to New York's poor founded the CAS in 1853 in response to reports from the Police Chief that up to twenty thousand vagrant youths were roaming the city's streets. The ministers decided to inaugurate a program to educate and provide for that group of "street rats, . . . who cannot be placed in asylums and yet are uncared for and ignorant and vagrant." Charles Loring Brace accepted a position as the Society's secretary. The Society remained under his energetic leadership for nearly half a century, during which time it placed about 90,000 children from New York in families outside the city. . . .

The CAS approached the problem of vagrant youths in several ways. Most famous was the placing out system, which sent children to work on western farms. The CAS also sponsored lodging houses where "street arabs" could pay for shelter, dinner and breakfast. Later it founded "ragged schools" and industrial schools and established special savings banks and recreational facilities for indigent youngsters. . . .

Brace claimed that removing children to the country would decrease the crime caused by overcrowding in New York, while exposing the children to "country air, instead of the gases of sewers, trees and fields and harvests in place of narrow alleys." The child's "first circumstances," according to Brace, would then "favor his being an honest man." Equally important, the scheme would reverse the economic difficulties in city life, "for it sends future laborers where they are in demand."

Like many of his fellow reformers, Brace often confused poverty, crime and immigration with urbanization, but he was not a backward-looking visionary. Because he understood that cities would dominate American life, he devoted much of the CAS's energies to programs for youngsters who had to remain in New York, perhaps because they had families there. The city, he believed, provided an effective atmosphere for fostering positive behavior from gemmules [Brace's term for inherited traits], for it allowed weak families to disintegrate. Still, he believed that the physical benefits of rural life, combined with the informal oversight engendered by a small community, favored rural placement in a Protestant home. Brace's placement system was simple. A CAS employee traveled to a rural community with a group of 20 or more children. A local committee, established earlier, had publicized the cause, and sorted through applications for children to determine which families it considered respectable and worthy. Such families were active in their congregations, enjoyed the good opinion of their neighbors, and usually owned small farms. At a large public gathering prospective employers picked the children they wanted. Neither party signed legal documents. The employer promised to educate the child, and to give the youngster $100 when he reached maturity. Brace believed that this loose arrangement, supplemented by the committee's continuing vigilance, and occasionally by visiting CAS agents, would be more likely to encourage natural affections than would a legal indenture. Brace's system allowed both parties to back out at any point; therefore both would consistently strive to fulfill their obligations. Brace hoped that on becoming adults, the children would stay in the communities in which they had been employed.

Most of New York's orphanages also indentured or informally placed a proportion of the children who were old enough to leave the institution. Indeed, many turned some of the children over to the CAS for placement. Indentured children received benefits similar to those gained by CAS terms. While they remained in service the law guaranteed children education and medical care. When they completed their terms their employers gave each of them a sum of money, a suit of clothes and a Bible.

One institution developed a philosophy and system designed to utilize the benefits of both the CAS immediate placement of children in families and the discipline and education provided by the years in an institution. The New York Juvenile Asylum, which functioned as a reformatory as well as a shelter for the indigent, located children in western homes. But it required the children to stay in the asylum for an average period of two years, during which they learned the behavior which would enable them to adjust successfully to a middle class native American family.

Other groups recognized the advantages of the Juvenile Asylum's plan. The SCAA noted that a special class of youngsters existed, "vicious, depraved and wholly unfit for family care," who, although not criminal, required preparation for integration into normal society. Shortly after Brace's death in 1890 even the CAS established a farm school in Westchester where it instructed boys before sending them west. "We hope," it announced, "to give them a brief training which will fit them for farm life and at the same time weed out those unfitted for placing out." The scheme especially suited "the older boys who wander the streets of our city." Just as many asylums taught girls to perform household tasks, the CAS conducted an industrial school that trained girls as "ordinary house-servants." The wife of the Society's leading placement agent ran the school, which was attached to the girls' lodging house. Brace believed that "nothing is more needed . . . by the public generally" than schools for servants.

Because their training and labor seemed so crucial to successful placement children over ten years old were most likely to live in private families other than their own. Nearly 80 percent of the children who went west under the auspices of the CAS were over ten years of age. Orphanages tended to apprentice children at about age twelve. . . .

Despite symbolic efforts to respect family ties, the placing out system ordinarily severed the child from his own parents. Indeed, some reformers hoped that fear of separation would discourage poor parents from attempting to place responsibility for their offspring in the hands of outsiders. . . .

At the root of the question about whether or not children should maintain ties with their natural families lay an uncertainty about the nature of the relationship established between the child and the family in which he lived and worked. In 1900 the CAS differentiated between the 22,121 children for whom it had found "permanent homes" and the 24,601 youngsters whom it had placed in "situations at wages in farmers' families" during the preceding half-century. Many participants, the children themselves, natural parents and the families receiving children, failed to appreciate the distinction. Their confusion about the purposes of placement resulted in a wide variation of treatment for the children.

Some families took in youngsters purely for their labor as farm hands. One dissatisfied employer wrote the Juvenile Asylum that "I would not advise any man to take a boy from ten to fourteen years old and have to release him at eighteen. He will have all his trouble and expense for nothing, according to the experience I have had with my ward, but if they are apprenticed until they are twenty-one they may repay for themselves." Other farmers' wards earned more than their keep. A seventeen-year-old boy, who went west at age nine, loved his "splendid home" even though his employers were getting old:

> He is 83 and she is 77, and I do all the work. I farm sixty acres all myself. This year I mowed twenty acres of grass, and planted sixteen acres of corn and five acres of oats, and raised twenty-five hogs.

His employers, pleased with the boy's contribution, desired a girl from an asylum as well. Many adolescents on American farms must have worked just as hard as this youngster. But the employers' ages when they first brought the boy into their home suggested an element of planning for their retirement.

Many families declared that they desired only children who would perform well in their tasks. Applicants for indentured helpers often specified that the children should be old enough to work. The agencies found such requests reasonable. They reassured farmers, "these children have all been in training schools in New York for at least a year . . . they are not street children." . . .

Ample evidence of exploitation notwithstanding, some children developed close emotional ties with employers who viewed themselves primarily as guardians or substitute parents. Letters from children to placement agencies commonly mentioned "my foster parents," my "Mamma," my "aunt," or my "grandmother," with reference to their employers. The CAS instructed all families to treat the child they received "as one of their own." Many children wrote that they in fact enjoyed the same privileges and education as the natural children of their employers. Those lucky youngsters seem to have maintained life-long ties with the families they entered. Fanny S., for example, "was married from the home of her foster parents to a young farmer 'who lives three miles from papa's farm'. . ." Some children informally used their guardian's family name. Still others received totally new identities. One woman answered the CAS's inquiry about Johnny, that "having a William and a John before he came here, we have given him the name of Frederick; he is generally called Freddy. . . . I will unhesitatingly say that we surely love him as our own; and we have had visitors here for a number of days," she added, "without once thinking that he was not our own child."

The experiences of prodigal children suggested the depth of some of these loving relationships. Minnie, the daughter of a convict, went west as a small child. The Burns family agreed to care for her through the first winter until the CAS could find a permanent home for "the little waif," and, Mrs. Burns recalled, "I soon found myself loving her." The family "decided to keep her and make her our own daughter" although she was in poor health. The Burnses tried to raise Minnie well, but, they reported, she became stubborn and disobedient. Finally, like many unhappy adolescents, she ran away from home. The distraught Mrs. Burns wrote:

> She is hundreds of miles away from us and among strangers, and God only knows what will become of her. Our home is quiet and peaceful now, but there is a great vacancy. Our hearts are very sad. . . . Will she ever return? . . . see her mistake, and turn her face towards home. . . .

She signed the letter, "your loving Mamma," in the hope that Minnie might see it in the CAS bulletin. When Minnie returned from her journey, reportedly chastened and "much improved," the Burnses welcomed her.

The disparities in the treatment accorded children who emigrated to farms reflected in part the confusion about their legal status. Laws governing adoption and distinguishing it from other forms of custodial care followed the growth of placement programs. The concept of adoption in the modern sense (of children, by adults who would function permanently as the only parents in a relationship which included reciprocal inheritance rights) was foreign to British and American common law. Not since the Romans, who legalized adoption (usually of an adult, by an adult) in order to perpetuate family lines, had a western country recognized adoption.

Nonetheless, relations resembling adoption had long existed. In colonial New York orphaned or abandoned infants were indentured by contracts which bound them until age 21. When the indentured child was an infant, like Mary Huggins' two month old daughter, the arrangement must have been designed for the child's welfare and probably resembled adoption more than employment. By the beginning of the nineteenth century wealthy families sought and obtained specific enabling legislation that assured "adopted" children their share of estates.

Changing assumptions about the nature of childhood, the family, and employment converged in the nineteenth century to mandate various forms of family placement, particularly adoption. The idea that children occupied a special status in life, with unique needs for affection and care developed during the period of the early republic. Youngsters' innocence released them from responsibility for their economic or moral condition. During the closing years of the century bourgeois culture romanticized the ideal of the nuclear family. The "intense family" replaced communal social life, especially in urban areas. The family seemed a bulwark against a changing and threatening world, and a retreat from stagnant work situations. As it withdrew from "wider social circles, the family bounded the social terrain of husband and wife alike." If families were the guarantors of personal fulfillment, happiness necessitated affiliation with a family unit. Middle class American society, by imbuing the family with such responsibilities in the late nineteenth century, resembled many cultures which have perceived that families, by perpetuating traditional behavior, are "inimicable to . . . rapid social and economic change."

The economic changes which frightened many Americans also undercut the master-apprentice relationship that had long served as the legal substitute for adoption. Masters only rarely expected to teach the skills of a specific trade to their apprentices, but general skills no longer sufficed. In a labor scarce economy, young people resented serving without pay. Urban poverty exacerbated the problem of placing dependent children, in part because it made so many of them so visible. Further, the anti-urban prejudices of philanthropists led to placements far from the child's original community, which deprived the child of protective oversight.

The authors of a proposed revision of New York's Civil Code complained in 1865 that "thousands of children are actually, though not legally, adopted every year; yet there is no method by which the adopting parents can secure the children to themselves except by a fictitious apprenticeship, a form which, when applied to children in the cradle, becomes absurd and repulsive." . . .

The development of laws governing adoption provided a clearer model of the potentials of family placement. It did not guarantee equal treatment of children placed in homes other than their own, or even of all children who were legally adopted. Yet the legal changes seemed to affirm the desirability of fully incorporating youngsters into families, and of clarifying their status and rights once placed.

During the 1870's and 1880's, as the legal standing of both adoption and indenture clarified, the proponents of family placement intensified their criticism of asylum care. Although Brace had originally claimed that he was interested only in children the orphanages did not serve, he began to attack institutions for their inadequacies. The depersonalization of asylums outraged him. Orphanages, Brace wrote, designated a child as "'D' of class 43; or as 'No. 193.'" The inmate was:

> roused up to prayers in the morning with eight hundred others, put to bed at the stroke of the bell, knowing nothing of his teacher or pastor . . . treated thus altogether as a little machine, or as one of a regiment.

In his criticism of asylum life, Brace found a powerful ally in the SCAA, led by Josephine Shaw Lowell. Joined by a growing number of child welfare workers, they censured institutions on several grounds.

Orphanages, they charged, encouraged dependency at great cost to the public. Perhaps the most convincing argument to the public and to professionals concerned with poverty was the expense of institutions when compared to family placement. Brace estimated that he spent only $15 to transport children who would otherwise have cost the public about $150 each year in an asylum. Both parents and children learned to rely on public support. Parents, the SCAA suggested, "are willing to be thus temporarily relieved of the care of their children, since they can reclaim them when old enough to aid in supporting the family." Because others took care of every need, the children, like their parents, learned to expect public or private charity to provide for them. Critics claimed that orphanages taught nothing about handling money, doing household chores, or decision making. Instead, reformers urged, youngsters should grow up in an environment which resembled the one in which they would later have to function.

Even some supporters of asylums began to find such arguments convincing, but the children tended to stay in orphanages until they outgrew them, in large part because institutions had great financial investments in the continuation of congregate treatment. Endowments, physical facilities, and pride in their work mitigated against early family placement. . . .

By the opening years of the twentieth century a clear pattern had emerged in favor of family placement, or, if that proved unfeasible, of institutions that tried to simulate families by following the cottage plan. Large institutions continued to function, but the trend away from congregate care could not be mistaken. The treatment of children who lived in families other than their own varied greatly, and placement programs received the criticism they often deserved. New attitudes toward both childhood and the nuclear family lent support to the movement for family placement that the CAS spearheaded, and to the passage of laws designed to clarify and protect the youngster's position as an adopted or indentured child. The trend of attitudes and legislation, based increasingly on a greater interest in the child's welfare rather than that of either his natural or custodial parents, encouraged relationships that rested on emotional bonds instead of economic demands. Even the most avid proponents of family care usually believed that indigent children would benefit from separation from their natural parents. But increased emphasis on the family as a unit of social and emotional support would, at the turn of the century, begin to challenge that assumption, although not always for unambiguous reasons.

3

Perfect Substitutes or the Real Thing?

Naomi Cahn

III. Adoption Law in Nineteenth Century America

In 1851, Massachusetts enacted what is generally characterized as the "first modern adoption statute." The 1851 Massachusetts act was not, however, widely noted at the time, and, what recognition it did garner, appears not to have focused on its authorization of adoption. Although the statute was certainly significant, many of the deeply held beliefs about it are not supported by the legal history of adoption. The 1851 statute is claimed to have made the best interests of the child paramount, and to have made adoptive families equivalent to biological families.

These are overstated claims that tend to evade the tensions inherent in mid-nineteenth century adoption law. First, some form of adoption was recognized by various types of statutes prior to 1851, and second, modern adoption did not emerge, full-formed as a result of this statute. While the 1851 statute was a significant advance over prior statutes, the story of adoption has far more layers and texture and a much more complex historical pedigree. This [chapter] provides an overview of the different meanings and forms of adoption that existed throughout the nineteenth century, and that presaged the development of the mid-nineteenth century general statutes that authorized the judicial adoption process. The general adoption statutes that were enacted mid-century did not create the social form of adoption, although they were part of the process of clarifying and regularizing the status.

A. Adoption before 1851

Adoption existed in a variety of forms prior to the 1851 Massachusetts legislation, notwithstanding the failure to identify each of these actions as formal adoptions. First, statutes authorized individuals to adopt children; second, other statutes authorized agencies to place children for adoption; third, families practiced their own informal adoptions; and finally, indenture contracts often served to legalize functional parent-child relationships.

1. ADOPTION PETITIONS

Earlier statutes concerning adoption had been enacted in many states, although they differed from the 1851 Massachusetts act in that they were focused on individual adoptions in response to specific legislative petitions. The right to petition for individual redress was deeply rooted in early American law, and families used this action in order to effect legal recognition of a child's changed status.

This individually-focused legislation authorized name changes or other methods to ensure that children were able to inherit from their adoptive parents. Although these acts centered on inheritance rights, the underlying relationships were generally familial, rather than mercenary. For example, in 1837, the Louisiana legislature provided: "That Pierre Jean Baptiste Vidal and Felicite Blanche Power, of the parish of Orleans, be authorized to adopt a young orphan child named Adele, aged about seven years, who has been brought up by them." More than twenty years later, Adele sought to be named the intestate heir of her adoptive mother. While the lower court held that nephews and nieces related to her mother through blood were the intestate heirs, the appellate court held that adoption meant more than simply allowing an orphan to live with a family; instead, adoption meant establishing a new parent-child relationship, and thus, Adele was entitled to inherit from her adoptive mother.

Texas enacted a generally applicable statute in 1850 that was designed to protect the inheritance rights of adopted children by allowing any individual to file a statement with the court to adopt another person. In other states, the legislatures authorized individuals to change their names, acts that carried with them full inheritance rights. Between 1804 and the end of the Civil War, for example, Vermont enacted more than 300 such acts, one for each person adopted. In Massachusetts, 101 acts of private adoption were enacted between 1781 and 1851. . . .

2. CHARITABLE ADOPTIONS

A second, and early, type of legislation relating to adoption centered on authorizing charitable organizations to place children for adoption. These statutes typically envisioned that parents would surrender custody to the charitable organization, which would then place the child in an appropriate family subject to various safeguards. In 1849, New York allowed the incorporation of the American Female Moral Reform and Guardian Society. Once parents had relinquished their children to the organization, the legislation authorized the Society to: "place such child by adoption or at service in some suitable employment and with some proper person or persons . . . in every such case the requisite provisions shall be inserted in the indenture or contract of binding to secure the child so bound such treatment, education, or instruction as shall be suitable and useful to its situation and circumstances in life." Moreover, the New York statute provided for oversight of the child's treatment, requiring the approval of either the commissioners of the alms house or the surrogate of New York, all of whom were public officials.

Similarly, the 1849 act of incorporation for the Worcester Children's Friends Society allowed for the placement of "'children in the families of virtuous and respectable citizens, to be brought up in such families as adopted children and members thereof.'" Many of the Society's founding members volunteered to take in these children. . . . Within its first five years of operation, the Society had already placed 62 children who had a strong expectation of adoption within their foster families. The language of these statutes is remarkably similar to that of the Massachusetts "general adoption" statute enacted two years later: all are concerned that the child be placed with the "proper" person, and that the child be treated in a "suitable" manner.

The 1849 Massachusetts statute even specified that the adopted children should become "members" of their new families. And, all of the statutes require some public oversight to finalize a placement. Unlike the more general 1851 statute, however, the 1849 statute did not specify a precise interpretation of the effect of adoption. Nonetheless, the claim that the 1851 legislation was the first "modern" statute overlooks these prior legislative efforts, in addition to its vague and questionable meaning of "modern." Adoption as a public matter existed outside of the context of an individual petition.

3. INFORMAL ADOPTION

The final form of adoption that existed was more informal, and did not become legal—or at least public—until judicially disputed. . . . European visitors to the United States frequently commented on the ease with which children were adopted into new families, although such adoptions typically occurred by relatives upon the death of a family member. For example, in *Van Dyne v. Vreeland*, John Van Dyne claimed that, in the early 1820s, his father had consented to his being adopted by his uncle, and his uncle had promised to leave his property to Van Dyne. Van Dyne apparently did not even know that he was adopted until he was about ten years old. The uncle executed several wills in favor of Van Dyne, including one in 1843 in which he referred to him as "'my beloved adopted son.'" In reliance on this agreement of prospective inheritance, Van Dyne worked for his uncle on his farm for more than 20 years. The uncle remarried, however, and sought to deprive Van Dyne of his inheritance. The court held that Van Dyne could sue as a third party beneficiary of the contract between his father and his uncle to receive all of the entitlements as though he had been adopted, even though the uncle had never filed any formal petition.

This type of informal adoption was fairly widespread. . . . In her study of the Boston Female Asylum, Professor Susan Porter observes that some children were never formally admitted to the orphanage because, although known to the orphanage, the children had already been placed through informal adoptions.

Although there is little documentation of this practice, informal forms of adoption provided parents for children within the African-American community. Foster parents and "fictive kin" expanded the familial support available to children both during and after slavery.

A final form of informal adoption was through deed, in which children (like chattel) were deeded as property from their biological parents to their adoptive parents. In 1872, Pennsylvania legalized the existing practice of "adoption by deed," although courts continued to struggle with the meaning of this term. The practice of deeding continued until at least the early twentieth century.

4. INDENTURE

Indenture performed a variety of functions in nineteenth century America, ranging from the provision of hired help to apprenticeship within the same social class to adoption. Masters owed the indentured children for whom they were responsible many of the same duties that a parent owed a child; correspondingly, the children owed the personal services otherwise due their parents to their masters. Indenture thus served to alienate and divide parental responsibility between the biological parents and the master.

Orphaned and poor children were frequently placed out pursuant to indenture contracts, and courts typically supervised the indenture relationships. For children of wealthier families, indentureship helped inculcate cultural values appropriate to their class. Colonial wills occasionally referred to non-biological children who had been placed as servants or apprentices, and with whom the testator had developed a relationship akin to that of parent-child. Although indenture continued throughout the nineteenth century for apprenticing poor children, wealthier families abandoned the practice, in part because of the developing ideology of middle-class motherhood which required the mother to become intensively involved in raising her children.

Nonetheless, throughout the nineteenth century, indenture contracts served as a method for transferring custody of children from an orphanage or other institution to foster parents, and the early charitable adoption legislation frequently authorized the organizations to engage in both indenture and adoption. Until the adoption process became more formalized, indenture contracts were used as one of the means for transferring custody of children to a foster family for a virtual adoption. The statutes regulating placing out and indentures disrupted both the indivisibility and the inalienability of parental rights prior to the enactment of adoption laws by, for example, allowing parents to retain some rights to receive economic compensation while sharing custody with someone else. Indenture contracts clearly exemplified the possibility of dividing child custody and of allowing non-biological parents to have the same obligations as biological parents. By the early twentieth century, however, indenture had been displaced as formal adoption became more widely available and accepted.

B. The Development of General Adoption Legislation

The conventional view of adoption legislation identifies the Massachusetts statute as the first modern adoption statute. On this view, the statute enshrined the best interest of the child standard into adoption law, was designed primarily to benefit children, and provided for the complete integration of the child into her new family. Many scholars have labeled the 1851 statute as the starting point for the development of modern adoption law.

This conventional view neglects, however, the changing meanings attached to children's interests: the meaning of the children's interest under the Massachusetts statute did not necessarily mean anything but an examination to ensure that the child would not be economically exploited, although the child could certainly be asked to work within the family. Moreover, the best interest standard was not a firmly entrenched benchmark in adoption cases. While the discourse of subsequent adoption law has recognized children's interests, those interests have varied depending on broader cultural concerns. Adoptive parents sought children for their economic worth at mid-century, while also attempting to help them escape the poverty of their birth families; by the early 20th century, they sought children for their intrinsic value as well as in conformity with the larger cultural narratives of expected motherhood.

In his landmark 1971 article, Professor Stephen Presser identifies the 1851 Massachusetts statute as "[t]he first comprehensive adoption statute," although he speculates that the legislators "might not have thought of adoption as much more than a change of name for the adopted child." While the statute became a model for the adoption statutes of several other states, there was enormous regional variation in the approach to adoption. The Massachusetts statute provided that the adopted child should be generally treated as though "he had been born to [his parents] in lawful wedlock; except that he shall not be capable of taking property expressly limited to the heirs of the body or bodies of the parents by adoption, nor property from the lineal or collateral kindred of such parents by right of representation."

The 1851 statute allowed Massachusetts residents to petition the probate judge for permission to adopt a child, and required written consent to the adoption from the child's parents or guardian. The statute then provided that an adoption would be allowed if the judge was satisfied that the potential adopting parents: "are of sufficient ability to bring up the child, and furnish suitable nurture and education, having reference to the degree and condition of its parents and that it is fit and proper that such adoption should take place."

Nowhere does the statute mention the child's best interests, nor does it specify procedures for evaluating the fitness of the adoption. Indeed, it was probably the 1855 Pennsylvania adoption statute which first mentioned promoting "the welfare of the child" as a concern in allowing an adoption. And, not until the late nineteenth and early twentieth centuries did statutes begin to establish procedures for evaluating the appropriateness of the adoption.

Instead, there is a focus in the original Massachusetts legislation on the ability of the adoptive parents to provide "suitable" nurture for the child, with the suitability explicitly varying on the "degree and condition of its [sic] parents." The appropriateness of the placement thus varied according to the class and condition of the adoptee's parents. Seventy-five years later, Evelyn Foster Peck of the Federal Children's Bureau commented that this provision suggested that some children were simply not suitable, by virtue of their background, for adoption. Even the 1953 Uniform Adoption Act reflected this attitude; it provided that the pre-adoption investigation should determine whether the child "is a proper subject for adoption." Given the strong belief in heredity throughout the nineteenth and early twentieth century, that the child would turn out like her biological parents, issues surrounding the child's background were particular significant in the adoption process.

The requirement that the adopting family act suitably towards the child is also reminiscent of the much earlier laws regulating the treatment of apprenticed and indentured children. In addition, it contains overtones of class, of providing middle-class nurture and culture to a poor child. Finally, the statute specified that the adopted child would, for purposes of inheritance, custody, and "all other legal consequences and incidents of the natural relation of parents and children" be deemed to be the legitimate child of her parents.

The 1851 statute was certainly a significant step in the development of United States law on adoption. But it cannot be seen in isolation from other legal and cultural developments occurring mid-century, nor from later adoption reforms. Indeed, there are several explanations for the development of general adoption legislation. Many scholars believe that more formal methods of adoption developed because of the inability of the public child welfare system to handle all of the children who needed help; as a private child welfare system developed the practice of placing out children, it needed some method to regularize the children's situations. Not only were they placing out children in increasingly large numbers, they had also sought, and been granted, legislative authority to do so. The need to specify the terms on which they could operate may have been responsible for the early legislation.

Some scholars believe that the adoption acts served merely to recognize the gradual evolution in formation of families that was already occurring through other legal mechanisms. Parents could create a status equivalent to adoption through indenture contracts, which served as a means for transferring parental responsibilities, through wills, which ensured appropriate inheritance rights, and through private petitions to change a child's name. The existence of these legal means "made adoption a part of the legal process under the law of the Commonwealth," and "that made it possible for the General Court to enact the Adoption of Children Act of 1851."

Other scholars have suggested that the statutes provided stability to the adoptive family, ensuring that the biological parents would not seek the return of their children. Adoptive parents may have wanted a procedure to ensure that an adoption was final, not a temporary expedient—that all of the effort invested in their adopted child (and all of the labor provided by the child) guaranteed a legally binding parent/child relationship that could not be undone. And adoption may have developed to protect the expectations of children that they could stay in their new families, and inherit property from their new parents. Finally, the developing norms of motherhood, norms which became even more defined during the first half of the twentieth century, certainly influenced the creation of legislation which provided legal recognition of new parent-child relationships.

Finally, the development of general adoption statutes may itself represent the move towards judicial, rather than legislative, action in family law cases. Prior to the 1851 statute, the Massachusetts legislature had been frequently presented with petitions for name changes which it labeled as adoptions. As the legislature was confronted with increasing numbers of these petitions, a more general adoption statute may have seemed an appropriate method for handling these cases. Indeed, the movement away from private petitions towards more generally applicable legislation, shifting direct responsibility away from the legislature, as happened in adoption, was typical of nineteenth century law. In an 1873 article, the author challenged the title of the first general New York adoption statute, which was designed to "legalize" adoption: "no one can maintain that the matter intended to be legalized was ever an illegal transaction." Adoption as an individual legal action appeared well-recognized, if not universally accepted.

4

Like Our Very Own
Adoption and the Changing Culture of Motherhood, 1851–1950

Julie Berebitsky

Introduction

In 1940, the journalist Avis Carlson published an article in the *Atlantic Monthly* heralding the new array of scientific tests that could accurately measure the mental development of infants and possibly even predict the ultimate achievements their in-nate gifts would allow. These devices, Carlson contended, were especially good news for childless American couples whose only prospect for having a "family" was to fol-low the uncertain course of adoption. Although adoption was in "vogue," it also con-stituted "a real emotional upheaval for those who undertake it." These tests, Carlson believed, could allay "some of the anxiety and hesitance. . . . Foster parents who have much to offer a child in the way of cultural advantages should be able to rest quietly in the knowledge that only a superior baby will be given them. And it would be a great help during the first precious months of adjustment to their new estate if they could be free from the nagging little fear that after all the baby may not come up to their ex-pectations."

According to Carlson, to "have showered love on and centered hopes in a disap-pointing child is a bitter experience for any couple." Likewise, "to grow up in a home where more is expected of him than he has the capacity to be is one of the cruelest sit-uations any child can have to meet." This disappointment was not limited to families created by adoption; as Carlson noted, this "fundamental disparity happens some-times with the parents' own offspring." With the use of the new developmental tests, though, this situation could be avoided in adoption. In fact, Carlson maintained, "all responsible placement agencies yearn to keep it from happening in [adoptive] homes, where the fitting of child to home is not an act of God. Elimination of this element of chance should be a part of the compensation of adoption."

Magazine stories that assured prospective parents that reputable child-placing agencies now used scientific tests and rigorous screening of a child's background to eliminate the hereditarian "risk" of adoption began to appear in the 1920s. Given Americans' growing faith in science, these pieces possibly eased the fears some felt about taking an unrelated child into their home and contributed to the growing inter-est in adoption. By 1940, then, although highlighting the difference between adoptive and biological families, Carlson's article nonetheless presented adoption as a positive way to create a family that closely mirrored the biological ideal. Indeed, with the help of trained professionals, infertile couples could not only realize their dream of a family but also be ensured that their hopes and dreams for their children's future would come true. . . .

"Born of Good Parents"

For prospective adoptive parents, taking an unrelated child into their home was taking a step into the unknown. During the late nineteenth and early twentieth centuries, cultural beliefs about heredity and attitudes regarding illegitimacy compounded a prospective adopter's natural fears. These concerns were so pervasive that it is not surprising that [one] specifically requested a child "born of *good parents.*" Americans' faith in the power of heredity especially affected attitudes toward adoption. Many people, for example, assumed that characteristics such as poverty or laziness could be inherited. Some also believed that an individual's future fate lay in the moment of her or his conception; if a child had the misfortune to be conceived in the throes of drunken passion, a likely future of alcoholism or insanity awaited. In 1876, one legal commentator, referring to the new adoption laws, warned that the "fact that the subjects of adoption are so largely taken from the waifs of society, foundlings, or children whose parents are depraved and worthless; considering also the growing belief that the many traits of mind are hereditary and almost irradicable; it may be questioned whether the great luxury of the American rule is for the public benefit."

Eugenicists, whose influence increased in the early twentieth century, made their disapproval of adoption widely known. Henry H. Goddard, a leading eugenicist and author of the famous study *The Kallikak Family,* which claimed to prove that generation after generation inherited the social pathology of their ancestors, spoke out against adoption. Goddard told the story of a family who, moved by compassion, adopted a young girl to raise as their own alongside their biological children. Time passed, and the family's son fell in love with the girl. They married and soon began to have children. But the children were feebleminded. Although the girl had escaped her hereditary taint, it had appeared in a subsequent generation, and, Goddard warned, it always would.

Beginning in the late nineteenth century, a number of progressive thinkers, social scientists, and reformers began to challenge these views. Jane Addams, John Dewey, and others whom historian Paul Boyer labels "positive environmentalists" argued that people were creatures of their environment. An individual's poverty or immorality came about through his or her exposure to a degraded and immoral society, not because of an innately and irreparably defective character. Environmentalists actively worked to create better physical spaces—cleaner cities, safer workplaces, and purer amusements—in the belief that these changes would result in more moral citizens.

Adoptive parents had to put aside their fears and join this group, which argued that an environment's influence could overcome any taint of heredity. Despite the dire predictions of eugenicists and others, many people adopted children with less than ideal family histories. For example, of the twenty-one legal, unrelated adoptions of children who entered into the Board of Children's Guardians (BCG) custody between October 26, 1903, and January 25, 1906, six had parents with alcohol problems. Of the remaining fifteen, one's mother had been arrested and convicted for being a "vagrant and public prostitute," another had syphilis, and yet another lived in the Government Hospital for the Insane.

The troubled backgrounds of the children are not surprising. In the 1890s, many social reformers began to argue that authorities should remove children from their families under only the most egregious conditions. Consequently, the children who ended up in permanent BCG custody (and who were, therefore, eligible for adoption) usually came from families with such severe problems that social workers believed they could not be salvaged. Although it is possible that caseworkers or judges could have exaggerated the problems in the light of their own standards of morality, case histories indicate that the majority of BCG wards came from deeply distressed families.

These were the children available. If prospective adopters could not overcome fears about "tainted blood" or a child's previous environment, then they could not adopt. The sad case of John Hill suggests just how gripping these concerns could be. When John was one month old, his father made arrangements with a Mrs. Dwyer to care for the infant. His father had promised to pay Mrs. Dwyer board, but in seven months, he had paid her only three dollars, and it was rumored that he was now in Norfolk, Virginia. It appears that Mrs. Dwyer approached the BCG to have the child classified as dependent, entered into BCG custody, and then legally transferred back into her custody on trial for adoption. These actions would prevent John's father from returning and reclaiming the child.

These efforts to retain John imply that Mrs. Dwyer had a deep attachment to the boy. Three years later, however, when John was four, the agent noted that he was "developing transmitted vulgarity; incontinence of wine, and tainted blood inherited from father"; then the agent added, "Mrs. Dwyer [is] glad she did not adopt him." Three years later, Mrs. Dwyer returned John because she could no longer control him. We will never know if fears about John's heredity were the primary reason Mrs. Dwyer decided not to adopt the boy, but his story shows how pervasive and credible Mrs. Dwyer's concerns were—credible enough to be accepted as justification for changing her mind.

As part of their involvement in the national debate about the care of dependent children, BCG agents participated in a pioneering effort to promote family-based care sponsored by the *Delineator,* a popular, New York–based women's magazine with a national circulation of close to a million. The *Delineator*'s "Child-Rescue Campaign" . . . began in November 1907 and continued through February 1911. In its heartrending appeals, the magazine emphasized the importance of nurturance and environment over heredity in a child's development. Although it featured children from around the nation, two of the first children profiled in the series were BCG wards from Washington.

The *Delineator* reported that James, a "sturdy" white four-year-old, entered BCG custody on his mother's request in 1904 when he was only eleven months old. His mother was a laundry worker whose husband had deserted her and their three children, and she could no longer make ends meet. After relinquishing James, his mother, too, vanished. The courts then classified his case as abandonment, according to the magazine. However, more was known of James's background than the article told. James's father was an "unstable drinking man," according to BCG records, and his mother's moral reputation was in doubt. In fact, James was illegitimate. Although his mother had a long-term relationship with his father, she had never divorced her first husband, who had left her because of her "immorality." Despite the fact that many readers would have interpreted these circumstances as alarming signs of a heritable disaster, the BCG and the *Delineator* apparently did not believe that they rendered a child unfit for adoption. Or if so, they apparently did not feel obliged to pass on this information. James was quickly placed with a Massachusetts family whose only son had died five months earlier. Her heart "filled with joy" at receiving the child, James's new mother gratefully wrote to the *Delineator*. In "two years," she said, "I believe James will be as dear to us and fill the place of our own son. . . . He resembles our boy in a marked degree."

Even those who adopted from the private Washington City Orphan Asylum (WCOA)—which screened applicants to ensure that only children of the worthy poor were accepted—expressed fears about the children's heredity. In March 1901, the Widmans took six-year-old Katie Moreland and twelve-year-old Allen Rogers from the asylum. Almost immediately, the children began "constantly giving a description of their homes & of their parents," according to a letter from Mrs. Widman to the director of the WCOA. The couple was shocked by what they heard: "Almost the first information from Allen to Mr. Widman was that his mother was dead . . . that he had a colored brother[;] that his mother had this boy by a black man [and] he didn't seem to think there was anything wrong about it." Mrs. Widman continued, "You can imagine how I felt [—] I supposed every thing was spoiled." She had calmed her husband by telling him that "no doubt Allen has misrepresented his mother . . . I supposed she had a little colored fellow around the house and he thought it was a brother." But although she convinced her husband, Mrs. Widman had lingering doubts: "I still think perhaps that was the way of it," she wrote. Mrs. Widman also found Katie's background disturbing. According to Katie, her father was in jail "for stealing ice water." Despite her apprehensions, Mrs. Widman was determined to make a success of her new family and told the WCOA director that she had admonished the children, "if we ever heard another word we would punish them severely." But if the children's parents left something to be desired, the Widmans were pleased to find them "perfectly honest. Nothing in the house is locked against them. . . . There's not a drawer or pantry place of any kind not even my trunk that is locked." The Widmans recognized that the adoption of older children could bring problems, such as stealing. Although they seem to have been prepared for such imperfections, the Widmans' account shows just how alien and disconcerting a child's background could be to his or her new parents.

5

Fallen Women, Problem Girls
Unmarried Mothers and the Professionalization of Social Work, 1890–1945

Regina G. Kunzel

"Problem Girls": Docility and Dissidence in Maternity Homes

Of her stay at the Lakeview maternity home on Staten Island, a young woman wrote, "though to all this is a home, to some it is a prison as well, because we are not here of our own choice." In a sentence, she captured the ambiguity inherent in the quasi-voluntary, quasi-coercive nature of charitable maternity homes, as well as in the hierarchical arrangement of power in those homes. She was probably no less resourceful than many women who struggled to put maternity homes to their own purposes. Yet those efforts were bounded by the place unmarried mothers occupied in homes that were explicitly disciplinary and implicitly incarcerational. . . .

Telling the Story of Out-of-Wedlock Pregnancy

. . . From the moment they stepped into a maternity home or social agency, unmarried mothers were asked the question, "how did you become pregnant?" Chances were good that they would be asked to tell the "story" of their pregnancy more than once, questioned again and again by maternity home matrons and social workers eager to discern the "truth" amid omissions and outright lies. Judging from the frustrated remarks of those who worked with unmarried mothers—many of whom believed that they lied with uncommon "ease and fluency"—discovering the "true story" of out-of-wedlock pregnancy was a difficult task indeed. Social worker Anne Cohn worried that "there has seldom been any attempt at verification of the stories of impregnation as related by the girls to the case workers" and noted, "it has not always been possible to determine whether these stories were real or fabricated." . . .

While some women questioned and subtly subverted dominant discourses of out-of-wedlock pregnancy, others more openly upset narrative expectations of unmarried motherhood. When one social worker took the novel approach in 1928 of asking unmarried mothers not only to tell the story of their pregnancy but to identify its "cause," she was surprised by their responses. In contrast to the familiar list of causes assigned by social workers—broken homes, bad companions, hypersexuality, low mentality—over half of the women analyzed the cause of their pregnancy as "I liked the man," some qualifying, "at least at the time."

"Such are the deserted, despairing, cowering victims with whom we deal," the super-intendent wrote of the "unhappy girl-mothers" in the Boston Crittenton home in 1915. From the records of maternity homes and published observations of social workers that portray unmarried mothers as victimized and pathetic, one might easily conclude that evangelical matrons and social workers presided over institutions of so-cial control, where they successfully imposed middle-class standards of morality, reli-gion, and sexuality to remold unmarried mothers in their own image. And indeed, this interpretation would not be entirely wrong. Run under the slogan "every girl saved a public asset, every girl lost a public menace" by women who believed doing laundry to be a "means of grace," maternity homes were replete with controlling im-pulses. But despite the workers' easily documented efforts to control the clientele of maternity homes, those clients continued to pursue their own agendas and to put the homes to their own uses. Although constrained by unequal power relations in those homes, the mothers were not the docile subjects either of maternity home regimes or of "expert" constructions of unmarried motherhood. Keenly aware of the difference between moralism and service, many unmarried mothers managed, within limits, to get the care they needed and to avoid or escape from the rest. To greater or lesser de-grees, many maternity home residents probably shared Marjory's willingness, noted by her social worker, to "respond to an appeal to her common sense and discretion, whereas she shows an instant rebellion against anything that suggests an authoritarian tone or manner."

Case records offer abundant material for the growing body of historical work criti-cal of arguments based on social control. Yet as sources that recorded unmarried mothers' stories of out-of-wedlock pregnancy, the records raise other questions be-yond the scope of that debate that are at least as important. While shedding light on the material experience of out-of-wedlock pregnancy, they also alert us to the ways in which that experience itself was shaped by its discursive rendering, illuminating the complexity of unmarried mothers' responses to dominant meanings of illegitimacy and their interpretation of their own experiences through language and narrative.

Unmarried mothers did not speak in one voice, and the stories they told served a range of purposes. Some shaped their stories to support claims to respectability and to improve their chances of getting the help they needed, appropriating and revisiting the traditional language of melodrama to bridge the differences between themselves and evangelical matrons and to express their own sexual vulnerability. Others searched for words to voice experiences of sexual coercion or struggled with the inad-equacies of available vocabularies to speak of rape and incest. As stories of illicit sexu-ality, narratives of out-of-wedlock pregnancy offered ways of repressing, containing, or expressing sexual desire. Whereas some women told stories in which they denied sexual agency, others laid bold claim to it, some calling on narratives that allowed them to move beyond the boundaries of middle-class notions of femininity and to ar-ticulate a new, modern sexual subjectivity. . . .

"Caseworkers Have Become Necessities"

. . . At the urging of the Children's Bureau and other child welfare advocates, several states passed laws in the 1910s prohibiting the separation of a child younger than six months from its mother. Evangelical women believed that these laws affirmed a style of reform they had pioneered. Social workers' endorsement of maternity home policy, however, stemmed not from a belief that it facilitated the unmarried mother's spiritual reclamation but from their conviction that it served the best interests of the child. . . .

This tendency of social workers to privilege the interests of the child over those of the mother further distinguished them from evangelical women. Whereas evangelical women conceived of the baby virtually as a tool in the redemption of the mother—"one of the strongest incentives to right living"—an increasing number of social workers held that "the child is the client" and believed it necessary to subordinate the mother's interests to those of the baby. When social workers' assessment of the child's best interests shifted, so did their position of the disposition of illegitimate children. Increasingly critical of the policy of keeping mother and child together, social workers declared that professional objectivity demanded a case-by-case evaluation rather than a standard policy applied uniformly. Whether to keep mother and child together or to put the child up for adoption, social workers asserted, was a decision "which only can be solved upon an individual consideration of each and every case." . . .

. . . While still insisting on differential diagnosis, social workers began to sing the praises of adoption. They explained their shift by arguing that adoption served the best interests of the child. . . .

Although social workers professed a belief in the fundamental right of unmarried mothers to make their own decisions, in practice, they often pressured them to place their babies for adoption. . . .

Social workers' new interest in adoption reflected, in part, the accelerated interest in and concern for dependent and neglected children in the Progressive era. . . .

At least as important as social workers' shifting assessment of the best interests of the child in explaining their turn to adoption was their appraisal of unmarried mothers. The question of what to do with the baby, Children's Bureau officers Maud Morlock and Hilary Campbell declared, depended on "the kind of person" the unmarried mother was—"her relationships, what her life has been so far, and what she is likely to make of her future—particularly what kind of mother she would be under the most difficult circumstances for motherhood." Committed in theory to the idea that the answer to this question was "different for each mother," many social workers nevertheless believed that out-of-wedlock pregnancy disqualified women from proper motherhood. Social workers were more likely to favor adoption because they were less inclined than evangelical women to see those who bore children out of wedlock as fit mothers. . . .

Whereas evangelical women's belief in the redemptive power of motherhood led them to endorse the potentially radical notion of a fatherless family, social workers informed more by an ideology of family and motivated by a concern about "family breakdown" tended to see unmarried mothers as "mothers in name only," unfit to raise their own children. . . .

The few social workers who ventured to use the term *illegitimate family* felt compelled to justify what they feared would seem to their colleagues oxymoronic. Stuart Queen and Delbert Mann thus nervously explained their use of the term: "We are not sure that it is wholly justified, but its use is suggested by the fact that every instance of illegitimacy involves a man, a woman, and a child. In the biological sense, at least, there is a family." Social workers more concerned with the ideological meaning of the family than its biological basis, however, typically banished unmarried mothers from its circle. . . .

Unmarried Mothers and Casework

. . . The amount of ink spilled and the number of conference hours spent by social workers discovering casework to be a process in which their own ideas, desires, and preconceptions figured as strongly as those of their clients would have been ironic, even laughable, to most unmarried mothers. Social workers' revelation of their own subjectivity would hardly have been news to their clients, for whom the subjectivity of the casework relationship was usually abundantly obvious. The best indication that unmarried mothers understood casework as a forum for social workers' agendas rather than a vehicle for them to make their own decisions was the frequency with which they tried to manipulate their social workers. The social worker who "had the feeling" that her client "was trying to say all of the right things but they weren't genuine" suggested that the mothers knew that there were "right things" to say to social workers. By social workers' admission, clients were adept at discerning and maneuvering around the ideas and agendas of caseworkers. Ruth Brenner, for example, noticed that one unmarried mother explained her wish for secrecy in terms she figured to be "most acceptable to the caseworker," stressing "her parents' foreign birth, their lack of sympathy with American customs and with their American-born children, their expectations that she would give up her education to establish her own and their support." Knowing that a social agency would withhold assistance to her if they knew that she was living with the father of her child, another woman told her social worker that "she had been deserted and was in need of care." That social worker estimated that "many who know the whereabouts of their lovers denied all such knowledge."

II

Creating Adoptive Families
Legal Requirements and Psychological Consequences

Part 2 provides an overview of the adoption process, examining the role of laws, social service agencies, lawyers, and others in creating adoptive families. Several selections address the requirement of parental consent and other essential elements of a valid adoption as well as conflicting public attitudes toward birth and adoptive parents. The article by David D. Meyer examines the status of unwed fathers in adoption proceedings, while Joan Heifetz Hollinger describes efforts to enact uniform adoption laws and explains why it is so difficult to reach consensus on the goals of adoption law reform. The selections by Brian Paul Gill and Elizabeth Bartholet provide historical and critical perspectives on changing standards for choosing "suitable" adoptive parents.

The final selections in this part describe the most important legal consequences of adoption and examine the latest research on the psychological and social consequences of adoption for adopted children and their families.

A

Contemporary Standards of Adoption Practice

6

State and Federal Adoption Laws

Joan Heifetz Hollinger

The lack of coherence and uniformity in our adoption laws and practices exposes to needless risks all parties to an adoption, and, especially, the children who become enmeshed in protracted litigation about their legal status. Efforts to make adoption laws more responsive to the actual circumstances of children and their families have been persistently undermined by the difficulty of achieving a consensus on just how the legal system should address the needs of the increasingly diverse people who are now adopting or being adopted. Central to this difficulty is an ongoing, historically rooted controversy: should adoption laws, by creating a status that was allegedly "unknown at common law," be "strictly construed" so as to protect birth parents and their children from being separated from each other, or, alternatively, be "strictly"—or "liberally"—construed to recognize ties between children and the "legal strangers" who are committed to, and capable of, providing them a permanent loving family when their original parents are unable to do so.

For the most part, adoption, like other family relationships, is subject to state rather than federal laws. Yet, state adoption laws are not and never have been uniform, nor have they been consistently applied. The inconsistencies from one jurisdiction to another are particularly vexing for families involved in interstate and intercountry adoptions. Moreover, state law is not the only source of authority for creating adoptive families or determining the consequences of a valid adoption. A growing body of federal child welfare, social security, employee benefits, tax, jurisdictional, immigration and naturalization laws come into play, as well as constitutional doctrines. Except in cases that involve Indian children who are reservation domiciliaries, state courts have original jurisdiction over adoption proceedings. Federal courts are often called upon, however, to consider whether adoption proceedings comport with constitutional protections, especially with regard to the rights of birth mothers and unwed fathers to consent to, or veto, a proposed adoption.

Adoptions can be classified according to the types of people adopting or being adopted. They can also be classified according to how they originate: a direct "private" placement by a child's birth parent(s) with a prospective adoptive parent selected by the birth parent(s) with the assistance of a lawyer or other intermediary; or, alternatively, placement by a public or private agency that has acquired custody of a child through a voluntary relinquishment or an involuntary termination of the birth parents' rights. Every state permits placements by licensed private agencies, many of them affiliated with religious denominations, and by public agencies responsible for dependent abused or neglected children.

Many would-be adoptive parents are dismayed by the complexity of agency procedures and the prospect of having to wait many years before an adoptable child becomes available. They turn, instead, to the private or independent route to adoption, where they are more likely to locate a birth parent interested in placing her child, but are also likely to encounter unanticipated and costly hurdles, or become prey to unlicensed "facilitators" who hawk their child-finding services in the media and on the Internet.

All but a handful of states permit direct non-agency placements, and most domestic adoptions of infants are the result of direct placements. Moreover, the vast majority of these direct placements culminate in uncontested adoptions. If, however, the rate of voluntary placements by unwed mothers continues to remain as low as it has been since the mid-1990s—less than 2 percent of all unwed births for all ethnic and racial groups—competition by prospective parents for fewer and fewer adoptable infants and young children will become ever more intense.[1] One plausible consequence of this increasingly competitive market is that already high fees will continue their upward spiral. Another is that private agencies will either absorb more of the "private ordering" practices of the independent adoption market or risk going out of business if their practices remain unresponsive to the demands of birth as well as adoptive parents.

To date, efforts to achieve more uniformity in adoption laws and practice have faltered. The most recent effort, the proposed Uniform Adoption Act (UAA) of 1994, as more fully described below, provides more procedural protections and information about a child's background than most current state laws and insists that agencies and lawyers be held accountable for the quality of their adoption-related services and the reasonableness of their fees. Nonetheless, some of the UAA provisions have been criticized as too favorable to adoptive parents, others as too protective of birth parents' rights to place their children directly without relinquishing to an agency, and others as being insufficiently attentive to the needs of adopted individuals for access to their original birth certificates.

The only way to create a legal adoptive relationship in the United States between a child—minor or adult—and a parent is through a court order based on a finding that the essential requirements for the creation of an adoptive parent-child relationship have been satisfied and that the proposed adoption is in the best interests of the particular child.

Adoptive relationships have six principal elements, each of which is said to be a necessary legal prerequisite for, or a consequence of, adoption, or a socially and psychologically desirable characteristic of adoption. These are: (1) the necessity of parental consent from a child's original parents—usually referred to as "birth parents"—or a sound basis for terminating parental rights, as a jurisdictional prerequisite for an adoption proceeding; (2) selection of suitable adoptive parent(s) in order to serve the child's best interests; (3) the characterization of adoption as a non-contractual "gift" and not a bargained-for-exchange; (4) the "asserted-equivalence" doctrine, that an adoptive parent-child relationship replaces "in all respects" the child's relationship to her birth family; (5) the confidentiality of adoption proceedings and records; (6) the permanence and autonomy of adoptive relationships, subject to the same statutory and constitutional protections that would initially apply to a child's original family. In other words, adoptive parents have no more and no fewer rights than biological parents typically have with respect to performing or relinquishing their parental roles. In the absence of fraud or some other fundamental irregularity, adoption decrees are final and irrevocable and bind future generations as well as the immediate adoptive family.

[Because these principal elements—and the controversies surrounding them—are examined by many articles in this and other parts of the reader, only the first and third are discussed here.]

What does it mean to say that "consent" is a necessary condition for the creation of a new adoptive relationship? A court cannot approve an adoption without proof that a child's birth parents have executed voluntary and informed consents, or, alternatively, that their parental rights were terminated because of their failures to perform parental responsibilities. When a parent relinquishes a child to a licensed agency, or the agency acquires custody of the child after a court orders the involuntary termination of parental rights, the agency's consent to a proposed adoption is necessary.

The requirement of parental consent derives from the principle of parental autonomy, which, in turn, is a product of cultural traditions and theories of natural law and delegated duties that endow biological parents with superior rights to the possession and control of their offspring. Both common law and constitutional precedents incorporate aspects of these traditions and theories into the doctrine of family privacy or parental autonomy. Central to this doctrine is the presumption that parents are fit to decide how to raise their children and should be permitted to do so without interference by the state. Absent a voluntary or provable forfeiture of parental status, the state has no license to remove children from their parents in order to seek a "better" placement. Informal transfers of children to other relatives or unrelated caregivers are generally not regarded as sufficient proof of an intent to abandon parental rights.

Recent constitutional decisions recognize that a biogenetic connection to a child is not by itself sufficient to give someone the benefit of the presumption of parental fitness. When, for example, a man takes advantage of his constitutionally protected "opportunity interest" to establish a genuine parental relationship with his child, *Stanley v. Illinois* (1972); *Lehr v. Robertson* (1983), this relationship cannot be terminated without proof of unfitness on the basis of clear and convincing evidence, *Santosky v. Kramer* (1982).

Our courts and legislatures are uncertain about precisely which mothers and fathers have earned or jeopardized a right to consent to, or to block, their child's adoption. Indeed, the very meaning of "mother" and "father" is contested. Are a father's interests in establishing a parental relationship with his child so substantial that they justify requiring the child's mother to identify him, even if she fears that he will be abusive once he learns about a pending adoption? Are a mother's interests in placing her child and a child's interests in remaining with adoptive parents so substantial that they justify terminating the rights of a father who has been "thwarted" in his efforts to perform parental duties by the birth mother, an agency, or the adoptive parents? How soon after a child's birth may a parent execute a consent, and what procedures are likely to ensure that the consent is "informed" and "voluntary"? Should a birth parent have a right to separate legal counsel regardless of whether the parent relinquishes a child to an agency or places the child directly with adoptive parents? Once executed, should a consent or relinquishment be revocable, and, if so, for how long, for what reasons, and with what consequences for the custody of the child? When is a child's own consent to adoption needed, and does it override the preferences of the child's birth parents? May children initiate their own actions to protect their relationships to their foster parents or other caregivers?

Intrinsic to the debates about the appropriate procedures for obtaining a birth parent's consent are concerns about who should have custody of a child when a birth parent revokes his or her consent, or a parent's status is not properly terminated, but the child has been living with prospective adoptive parents who are eager to retain custody, even if a formal adoption is not possible.

When a contested adoption pits a birth parent or parents against prospective adoptive parents in a fight over "possession" of a child, media and popular accounts often invoke the terms of one of the standard narratives about the modern American family. According to one narrative, young unmarried women and men who are morally suspect and promiscuous, bring children into the world for whom they cannot care. Fortunately, there are hard-working, loving married couples who are ready to live the American nuclear family dream if only they are given a fair chance and an opportunity to raise children. In this narrative, the adoptive parents are the true "natural" parents, an ideal family in the making, frustrated only by the accident of infertility. By trying to disrupt an adoptive placement, the birth parents function as spoilers, as malevolent aliens who threaten the family circle built by people whose love and commitment are the stuff of which families are supposed to be made. Even if a legal flaw prevents a court from granting an adoption, this narrative supports a rule that would allow would-be adoptive parents, who have become the child's de facto or "psychological" parents, to retain custody and caregiving responsibilities instead of "returning" the child to a biological parent whom she has never known.

But this is not the only narrative in which the media and the public place the cast of characters in a contested adoption. In the second script, virtue is embodied in poor and uneducated birth parents who are made victims by a system too responsive to powerful people eager for children. When innocent birth parents marry and settle down to raise families on their own, they give credibility to the second narrative.

This second script forgives youthful transgressions, and looks favorably on men and women who must struggle to make something of themselves. It also sees through the class and cultural biases that infect the legal system. "Experts" are portrayed as favoring adoptive parents; psychologists and social workers who testify that a child will be "irreparably harmed" if transferred from her would-be adoptive parents to the birth parents who have never cared for her, are simply contributing to the war on the poor. While the first narrative applauds those who turn to the experts for advice on how to be a good parent, the second praises those who learn to parent on their own, "naturally."

Birth mothers, in the second narrative, suffer when they are convinced, often through inappropriate pressure, to give up their babies. Further, many birth fathers would like a chance to bond with their offspring if only the authorities would not create so many obstacles in their way. And "blood" is important: children separated from their "real" parents by artificial social arrangements supported by a class-bound legal and administrative order often suffer worse pains than those who are allowed, even under less than ideal circumstances, to remain with their biological parents. Ordinary people who settle down to a life of caring for each other and their children can be redeemed. Adoptive parents, in the second narrative, deserve sympathy for their efforts to acquire children, but they do not have a right to sever children's ties to their birth families. . . .

The third principal element, listed above, is the characterization of adoption as a "gift" that entails the gratuitous transfer of a child to an adoptive parent, analogous to a testamentary bequest or the donative deeding over of real property. Birth parents are said to "bestow" their children directly upon the adoptive parents, or to "surrender" them to child-placing agencies. These transactions are not supposed to generate improper financial gain, nor be tantamount to "trafficking" in children. "Solicitation" of children is deplored: no money or other valuable consideration is to be paid in exchange for a child or for the birth parent's or agency's consent. By statute or case law, all states decry "baby-selling" and most prohibit the payment of "finders fees" to agencies, lawyers, or unlicensed intermediaries.

The notion that adoption is not contractual is so powerful that it obscures the extent to which bargaining is intrinsic to a transfer of a child by a birth parent in exchange for a promise by adoptive parents or an agency to support and care for the child and thereby relieve the birth parent of these legal duties. Adoptions by stepparents, for example, often involve agreements to forgive a noncustodial parent's child support arrears in exchange for the parent's consent to the adoption. Women who are considering placing an infant for adoption prefer to deal with private agencies, or directly with adoptive parents, who will pay for pregnancy and birth-related medical and living expenses. Indeed, most states now recognize that, subject to court approval, adoptive parents may pay, and agencies and private intermediaries may charge, for adoption-related expenses, including legal and counseling fees, so long as they are characterized as "acts of charity" or compensation for professional services. These payments are not supposed to be contingent, however, on the birth parents' consent or the completion of an adoption; prospective adopters assume the risk of not being reimbursed for expenses they have paid on behalf of a birth parent who later decides not to consent to an adoption, or who revokes her consent.

When children with special needs are available for adoption, financial considerations typically run in the other direction. It is not prospective adopters who, at least indirectly, induce birth parents or agencies to place children with them. Instead, public agencies offer subsidies and medical and other support services as inducements to recruit adoptive parents for less "marketable" children who have been subject to parental neglect or abuse or have serious developmental delays.

To what extent should bargaining about financial and other aspects of an adoption be allowed to tarnish the notion that adoption is a gratuitous transaction? Upon finding that a proposed adoption involves unlawful placement activities, but is otherwise in the best interest of a child, most courts will approve the adoption and will leave the punishment of the unlawful activities to state criminal or licensing laws. In some cases, however, the illegalities may be so egregious that a refusal to approve an adoption is warranted; see, e.g., *In re Adoption of P.E.P.*, 407 S.E.2d 505 (N.C. 1991).

The traditional insistence that adoption is a gratuitous transfer is yielding to a recognition that specific birth-related, counseling, travel, and legal expenses should be compensable in order to facilitate adoptions. Yet, it remains difficult to craft a clear distinction between adoption-related services that are compensable and those that are unlawful and subject to civil or criminal penalties. . . .

Within the social context in which adoptions now take place, two of the traditional goals of adoption are less harmonious than they may have been in the past. The first of these goals is the one stated explicitly in most adoption statutes: to serve the best interests of children by providing permanent homes for those who might otherwise remain homeless. The second goal, embedded more in the social history of adoption than in specific statutes, is to provide children for childless adults. In achieving these goals, the interests of a child's biological parents and our fundamental commitment to family autonomy must somehow be reconciled. Although in theory, these two goals are not inconsistent with each other, they are sometimes in conflict with each other, and it is by no means clear how adoption laws and practices can resolve these conflicts.

NOTE

1. As tracked by the National Survey of Family Growth (NSFG), the rate of voluntary relinquishments of infants for adoption has fallen steadily since the 1950s and 1960s, when it is estimated that 30 percent or more of unwed white mothers relinquished. Even before *Roe v. Wade* (1973) legalized abortions, the rate of voluntary adoptive placements had fallen to less than 10 percent of all women, then to 4 percent in 1981, and since then has not exceeded 2–3 percent. The 1995 NSFG survey found that as it became more socially acceptable to raise a child as an unwed mother, with or without the father's assistance, the number of out-of-wedlock births soared to more than 30 percent of all births; but fewer than 2 percent of unwed white women relinquished babies between 1989 and 1995. The rate of relinquishment among African American and Latina unwed mothers has always been less than 2 percent and may now be as low as 1 percent. Anjani Chandra et al., "Adoption, Adoption Seeking, and Relinquishment for Adoption in the United States," National Center for Health Statistics, Advance Data no. 306, May 11, 1999.

7

Code of Ethics

American Academy of Adoption Attorneys

The American Academy of Adoption Attorneys hereby make and establish this Code of Ethics.

1. A Member shall be duly licensed to practice law in each state in which the Member maintains a law office, shall fully comply with the Ethical and [other Rules and Canons] of Professional Conduct . . . and shall maintain the highest standards of professional and ethical conduct. A Member shall not engage in activities which bring discredit upon the Academy.

2. (a) A Member shall assure that the Member's clients are aware of their legal rights and obligations in the adoption, and that all parties to the adoption are aware of their right to separate legal counsel. . . .

3. A Member shall not purport to represent both the prospective adopting parent(s) and one or both birth parents, where such representation is specifically prohibited. . . .

4. A Member shall actively discourage adoption fraud or misrepresentation, and shall not engage in such conduct, and shall take all reasonable measures not inconsistent with the confidentiality of the attorney/client relationship, to prevent adoption fraud or misrepresentation, withdrawing from representation where necessary to avoid participation in any such conduct.

5. (a) A Member shall assure that clients to an adoption are aware of any laws which govern permissible financial assistance to a birth parent.

(b) A Member shall not assist or cooperate in any adoption in which the Member has reason to believe that the birth parent or parents are being paid, or given anything of value, in exchange for the placement for adoption, for the consent to an adoption, for a relinquishment for adoption, or for cooperation with the adoption of his or her child, without first making full disclosure to the appropriate court. This rule does not make it improper for a Member to assist or cooperate with an adoption in which the birth parent or parents are reimbursed for reasonable and necessary pregnancy-related expenses actually incurred by the birth parent, or in which such expenses are paid directly on behalf of the birth parent, provided that such payment or reimbursement is allowed under the [state] law. . . .

6. A Member shall assure that the Member's fee arrangement with each client is carefully explained and fully understood by the client. . . .

7. A Member shall not enter into an agreement for, charge, or collect an illegal or unconscionable fee . . . [and] shall not, directly or indirectly, charge a finder's fee for locating a birth parent. . . .

8. A Member shall not possess a financial stake in the success of any adoption in which the Member is retained as counsel for any party. A financial stake in an adoption [occurs] if the Member enters into a fee agreement by which the Member is to receive a greater fee for a successful adoption than is warranted based upon the reasonable value of the services performed by the Member; or . . . a lesser fee than the reasonable value of the services performed by the Member if the attempted adoption is unsuccessful. . . .

10. A Member shall not make false or misleading claims in advertisements, nor shall a Member include client testimonials in such advertising. . . .

11. (b). . . A Member shall not induce or encourage a birth parent to change selection of prospective adopting parents unless the Member knows or has reason to believe that the proposed adopting parents cannot obtain court approval of a placement with them.

12. A Member shall not enter into any agreement with any person which would have the effect of restricting the Member's ability to exercise independent professional judgment on behalf of the Member's clients.

13. A Member may, when appropriate and/or when requested by a client, refer parties to competent and professional medical providers, legal counsel, psychological counselors, or adoption agencies. . . .

14. A Member shall be under a duty to investigate representations made to the Member by prospective birth parents and prospective adopting parents if the Member believes or has reason to believe that such representation is false. [e.g. a birth mother's claims about the whereabouts or name of the biological father]. Under all other circumstances, a Member may ethically rely upon representations made by the parties to an adoption.

8

Adoption as a Child Welfare Service
CWLA 2000 Standards

Child Welfare League of America

Adoption practice has changed significantly since CWLA's previous adoption standards were published in 1988; today, it is marked by increased openness in infant adoption, heightened awareness of the need to protect children adopted across national boundaries, and an emphasis on promptly finding adoptive families for children in care who cannot return to their birth families. . . .

In adoption practice, the child is the primary client, and the best interest of the child is paramount in decisions concerning his or her adoption. Families are viewed as potential resources for children needing adoption, rather than as an agency's primary clients. The agency's responsibility has also shifted from investigating families to educating and preparing families to meet the needs of children placed with them.

Building a family by adoption is now understood to be fundamentally different than building a family biologically, with lifelong implications for the adopted individual, the adoptive parents, and the birth parents. Increasingly, agencies have accepted the responsibility to provide continuing education, support, and counseling for all the members of the adoption triad as needed throughout their lives.

Core Values and Assumptions Underlying Adoption Services

Given the complexity of the broader societal context in which adoption practice now occurs, it is especially important to reaffirm the fundamental values that provide a framework for professional adoption services. The core values listed below form the foundation for the ethical development and delivery of adoption services.

All children have a right to receive care, protection, and love.
The family is the primary means by which children are provided with the essentials for their well-being.
The birth family constitutes the preferred means of providing family life for children.
When adoption is the plan for a child, the extended family should be supported as the first option for adoption placement, if appropriate.

Adoption as a child welfare service should be focused on meeting the needs of children to become full and permanent members of families.

All children are adoptable.

Siblings should be placed together in adoption unless serious reasons necessitate their separation.

Adoption is a lifelong experience that has a unique impact on all the parties involved.

Adoption should validate and assist children in developing their individual, cultural, ethnic, and racial identity, and should enhance their self-esteem.

All adoption services should be based on principles of respect, honesty, self-determination, informed decision-making, and open communication.

All applicants for services should be treated in a fair and nondiscriminatory manner. . . .

[The] 2000 edition of CWLA's Standards for Excellence in Adoption Service reflects a significant departure from previous adoption standards in at least two respects. First, much greater emphasis has been placed on making these standards equally applicable to both public and private, nonprofit agencies and to domestic infant, intercountry, and special-needs adoption. [In the past CWLA standards were addressed primarily to domestic private and public agencies and expressly disapproved of private non-agency or lawyer-assisted adoption.] Second, attention has been given to not only updating the standards to reflect where the field of adoption has come in the last decade, but also to developing standards that can guide the field over the coming decade.

9

Analysis of the Proposed
Uniform Adoption Act (UAA) of 1994

Joan Heifetz Hollinger

Guided by the belief that adoption is a beneficial way to build families, the Uniform Adoption Act (UAA) of 1994 ensures the integrity of adoption proceedings through rules that are attentive to the interests of birth and adoptive parents as well as to the paramount needs of children. Drafted by the National Conference of Commissioners on Uniform State Laws (NCCUSL), the UAA was recommended for enactment by state legislatures by NCCUSL, the American Bar Association, and a number of other organizations. The UAA offers a procedurally fair and constitutionally sound path through the thicket of conflicting views about the functions and consequences of adoption. Yet, precisely because the UAA does not allow genetic ties by themselves to trump the interests of children in having secure legal and psychological ties to the people who are actually parenting them, the Act is opposed by many groups that cannot get beyond the "blood and genes" view of family. Concerned United Birthparents (CUB) and the Child Welfare League of America (CWLA) criticize the Act, for example, for encouraging adoption and for not having provisions to strengthen children's ties to their birth families.

By creating a framework to accommodate different kinds of adoptive families, the UAA combines a deference to "private ordering" by the parties to an adoption with legal rules that carefully delineate the prerequisites for, and consequences of, a valid adoption. The UAA recognizes both direct or independent parent-initiated placements for adoption and placements by licensed public and private agencies. The Act aims to facilitate consensual adoptions, expedite the resolution of contested proceedings, standardize the procedures for obtaining valid parental consents or relinquishments, and bolster the finality of adoptions. Birth and adoptive parents are allowed, if they prefer, to select each other, with or without the assistance of lawyers and public or private agencies; they can decide for themselves how "open" or "closed" they want their relationships to be at the time of an adoptive placement and in later years.

The scope of the UAA is in some respects limited. First, except for its provisions requiring the recognition of valid foreign adoptions, the UAA says little about intercountry adoptions, which are regulated primarily by federal immigration laws, the laws of sending countries, and international conventions. Second, as a state law, the UAA does not and cannot preempt the federal Indian Child Welfare Act (ICWA), which is intended to promote tribal sovereignty and the survival of tribal communities. Third, because NCCUSL is an advisory rather than a legislative body, it cannot mandate the use of public funds for child welfare programs. Thus, the UAA does not deal with social services to dependent and foster children. It complements, but does not displace, federal and state child protection laws that authorize the permanent separation of children from parents who have abused, neglected, or otherwise mistreated them.

The UAA's most significant features are the following:[1]

(1) The Act protects minor children from unnecessary separation from their birth parents, placement with unsuitable adoptive parents, and delays in determining their legal status.

(2) Consistent with long-standing constitutional principles, the Act protects birth parents against unwarranted termination of their parental rights. Minor children may not be adopted without parental consent or appropriate grounds for dispensing with parental consent. Many provisions—including access to psychological and legal counseling—ensure that a decision by a parent to relinquish a minor child and consent to the child's adoption is informed and voluntary. A parent is not required to relinquish a child at any particular time; a relinquishment or consent is not valid unless signed after the birth of a child and given to a judge or comparable person whose duty is to protect the birth parent's interests. Nonetheless, once a birth parent decides to relinquish a child and properly executes the consent, the decision is considered final and, with very few exceptions, irrevocable.

Involuntary as well as voluntary termination proceedings conform to constitutional standards of due process, but an individual's biological ties to a child are not by themselves sufficient to bestow full parental rights. The UAA protects the parental status of women and men who have consistently performed parental duties. Even "thwarted" fathers, who have been prevented by the misdeeds of others from functioning as parents, may be prevented from blocking a proposed adoption of a child if there is clear and convincing evidence that it would be detrimental to the child to deny the adoption. Decisions to continue or dismiss an adoption proceeding, as well as decisions about a child's ultimate custody, focus on the needs and welfare of the child and not simply on the "rights" of adults.

For example, the UAA's protections against hasty and uninformed relinquishments would have prevented the initial adoptive placements of the infants in the notorious 1990s cases, Baby Jessica and Baby Richard, from taking place. In these cases, the fathers' identity would have been discovered sooner and their parental capabilities could have been assessed much earlier in the proceedings.[2]

(3) The UAA protects adoptive families by requiring that they receive whatever information is "reasonably available" about the child's background, including health, genetic, and social history, and by ensuring ongoing access to updated health information. It is, of course, difficult to obtain reliable information from birth mothers who may know little about their own health or genetic predispositions and who may fear that their child will not be adoptable if "unsavory" information is disclosed. It is even more difficult to learn much about "unknown" biological fathers or to keep track of the medical records of children who spend years in and out of foster care.

Nonetheless, in striking contrast to the conventional wisdom of the mid-twentieth century, adoption service providers now agree that accurate information about an adoptee's health and social history should be furnished to prospective adoptive parents at the earliest possible time. The primary reason for this new policy is the realization that nondisclosure impairs early diagnosis and treatment of serious conditions or diseases that some adoptees later develop, often with tragic consequences.[3] A second reason is that failure to advise adoptive parents of the known risks to a child's physical or mental health has resulted in disrupted adoptions when adoptive parents conclude they cannot cope emotionally or financially with a child's needs. Third, early disclosure may strengthen bonds between adoptive parents and a child because it leads to more appropriate placements. Fourth, disclosure enables adoptive families to determine their eligibility for state or federal subsidies that are not available except at the time of placement. Fifth, access to information often eases the normal curiosity about their origins that many adoptees experience during adolescence or as adults. Finally, the availability of more reliable information about adoptees' health and social histories may stem the rising tide of the hundreds of "wrongful adoption" lawsuits brought by adoptive families seeking monetary damages from agencies for fraudulent or negligent failures to disclose information about a child's pre-adoptive history or physical and mental health.[4]

(4) The UAA discourages unlawful placement activities within and across state and national boundaries by tracking minor children who are placed for adoption, defining lawful adoption-related expenses and activities, requiring that agencies, lawyers, and others fully disclose their fees and the scope of their adoption-related services, requiring judicial approval of adoption-related expenses, and imposing sanctions against unlawful activities. Although birth parents and adoptive parents may be assisted by others, the Act prohibits "placement" or "finders fees." It is unlawful to pay, request, or receive any fee or compensation for consenting to a child's adoption; but adoptive parents are permitted to reimburse a birth parent's reasonable medical, counseling, and living expenses.

(5) No one may be categorically excluded from being considered as an adoptive parent. To ensure that children have an opportunity to have two legal parents, the UAA explicitly permits "second parent adoptions" by unmarried and same-sex couples, subject to the court's finding that these adoptions are in a child's best interests. A specific individual's or couple's "suitability" to be an adoptive parent is determined through preplacement and post-placement evaluations by a reputable social worker.

Under the UAA, an individual may be found "unsuitable to adopt" only if the evaluator has well-substantiated "specific concerns" that placement of a child with the individual "would pose a significant risk of harm to the physical or psychological well-being" of the child.

(6) A child's foster, de facto, or psychological parents have standing to seek to adopt the child, subject to the particular child's needs. Agencies receiving public funds are required to actively recruit prospective adoptive parents for children who are considered difficult to place because of their age, health, race, ethnicity, or other special needs. Consistent with the federal Multiethnic Placement Act (MEPA), the

UAA prohibits the delay or denial of an adoptive placement solely on the basis of racial or ethnic factors.

(7) Prompt hearings are required for contested adoptions and a guardian ad litem or lawyer must be appointed for minors whose well-being is threatened by protracted or contested proceedings. Diligent efforts must be made to provide notice of an adoption proceeding to a parent or alleged parent whose rights have not previously been determined. Birth mothers are strongly encouraged to help locate the child's father. If, however, the court concludes that the identity or whereabouts of a possible parent are unknown, the proposed adoption can proceed without further delay.

(8) The UAA clarifies the relationship of adoption proceedings to various interstate jurisdictional and placement statutes and to federal full faith and credit requirements.

(9) The UAA supports the finality of adoptions by strictly limiting the time for appeals or other challenges. In contrast to many states that allow challenges for a year or more, the UAA provides that a final adoption may not be challenged by anyone for any reason more than six months after the decree is issued. If a challenge is begun within six months, the adoption may not be set aside unless the challenger proves with clear and convincing evidence that the adoption is contrary to the child's best interests.

(10) The UAA explicitly permits mutually agreed-upon communication between birth and adoptive families and does not prohibit separate agreements for post-adoption contact or visitation. Adoptive families are entitled to the same constitutional protections against state intervention as are birth families.

No issue was more bitterly contested by NCCUSL than the question of whether the members of birth and adoptive families should be prohibited from, allowed to, or required to know each other's identities. This issue polarizes the wide spectrum of views about adoption into two extremes. At one extreme is the view that adoption reinscribes the "natural family" by creating an impermeable psychosocial and legal wall between a child's birth and adoptive families that cannot be removed without the consent of all relevant parties. The opposing view is that, except to the extent that it creates legal rights and duties, adoption is "unnatural" and can never displace a child's birth family. In this view, without clear proof that an adoptee would be significantly harmed by contact with her birth family, access to identifying information should be the norm. Because the UAA takes a middle path between these extremes, it displeases advocates for both extremes.

(11) The UAA clarifies the legal and economic consequences of different types of adoption so that, within the formal structure of a valid adoption, the emotional and psychological aspects of adoptive parent and child relationships can take root and flourish.

NOTES

1. The UAA provisions and the controversies they provoked are more fully described in Joan Heifetz Hollinger, "The Uniform Adoption Act: Reporter's Ruminations," 30 *Family Law Quarterly* 345–78 (1996).

2. Joan Heifetz Hollinger, "Adoption and Aspiration: The Uniform Adoption Act, the De-Boer-Schmidt Case, and the American Quest for the Ideal Family," 2 *Duke Journal of Gender Law and Policy* 15 (1995).

3. See, e.g., *Burr v. Bd. of Co. Comm.*, 491 N.E.2d 1101 (Ohio 1986) (public agency intentionally misrepresented biological family history of Huntington's disease and mental illness, leaving adoptive parents totally unprepared for the child's later development of multiple neurological disorders); *Gibbs v. Ernst*, 615 A.2d 851 (Pa. App. 1993) (agency failed to disclose child's history of physical and sexual abuse by birth parents and foster parents, leaving adoptive parents unprepared to deal with child's aggressive and uncontrollably violent behavior).

4. Marianne Blair, "Liability for Misconduct in Disclosure of Health-Related Information," in Hollinger, *Adoption Law and Practice*, chap. 16; Lisa Belkin, "What the Jumans Didn't Know about Michael," *New York Times Magazine*, March 14, 1999, 42.

Family Ties
Solving the Constitutional Dilemma of the Faultless Father

David D. Meyer

II. The Emergence and Qualification of Unwed Fathers' Rights

B. Unanswered Questions and the Faultless Father

. . . [The Supreme Court's cases on unwed fathers] seem to contemplate only two models of fatherhood: the man of virtue who is integrally involved in the rearing of his children and the scofflaw who has slept on his rights while others changed diapers and read bedtime stories.[1] The Court's cases do not squarely resolve what should be done with the father who falls somewhere in between these two poles—for example, the man who has done everything he reasonably could to establish a relationship with his child but who has been thwarted by circumstances beyond his control.

There are two possible understandings of the Court's holdings in its unwed-father cases, and the choice between them will determine the extent to which fathers who have been unable to establish a substantial parent-child relationship through no fault of their own will be able to invoke the Constitution to unsettle pending or even completed adoptions.

Under one understanding, the Court made the validity of the father's constitutional claim turn solely on "the existence or nonexistence of a substantial relationship between parent and child(,)" without regard for the reasons why the relationship happened to sputter or thrive. Under this account, the only reason why the Court found that Abdiel Caban was constitutionally entitled to preserve his parent-child relationship, while Leon Quilloin and Jonathan Lehr were not, is that only Caban had succeeded in developing a substantial personal relationship with his children. . . .

Under this view, the Court's protection of the father-child relationship against state interference is effectively "child-centered," protecting the relationship only where the child would regard the man as a true and "loving father" and not merely as an abstraction or a stranger. The rule would thus limit constitutional intervention to those cases where the human relationship is most worthy of protection, recognizing that the loss of a mere opportunity to develop a relationship is less substantial than the extinguishment of an existing human bond. Limiting the scope of constitutional intervention in this way would be consistent with the Court's previous recognition that "the importance of the familial relationship, to the individuals involved and to the society, stems largely from the emotional attachments that derive from the intimacy of daily association, and from the role it plays in 'promot(ing) a way of life' through the instruction of children."[2] By this understanding, a father's claim that he cannot be faulted for the non-existence of a substantial relationship with his child is simply irrelevant. What counts, to the Court as to the child, is not the "*potential*" for a relationship furnished by conception and childbirth, but "'the *actual* relationship between father and child'" (*Lehr*). The Court is not concerned with what might have been, but examines "the relationship that in fact exists between the parent and child" (*Caban*). There being in fact no substantial relationship between father and child, there would be no basis for invoking the Constitution to protect it.

There is, however, a second plausible way of understanding the Court's holdings, and it is one that introduces a significant measure of insecurity into the adoption process. Under this view, the Supreme Court is concerned not simply with the existence or non-existence of a meaningful father-child relationship, but ultimately also with the strength of the father's *moral* claim to a relationship with his child. By these lights, the reason why the Court made constitutional rights turn on whether the claimant "act(ed) as a father toward his children" is not solely to judge whether the loss of that relationship would be substantial enough to both father and child to warrant protection, but also to judge whether the claimant has acted in a way *deserving* of protection.

To be sure, the Court's opinions in *Quilloin*, *Caban*, and *Lehr* are laden with rhetoric that can be read to reflect judgments about the moral culpability of each of these fathers. Abdiel Caban, for instance, did "act as a father toward his children" because he lived with his children for some years before he separated from their mother; he visited them regularly thereafter, took custody of them for a time, supported them financially, and, ultimately, sought to win permanent custody of them. The father in *Quilloin*, by contrast, "failed to act as a father" because he was largely absent from his child's life for eleven years, visiting occasionally but "providing support only on an irregular basis" and never seeking custody.

Jonathan Lehr, too, had no substantial constitutional claim to fatherhood because he had "never had any significant custodial, personal, or financial relationship with Jessica and he did not seek to establish a legal tie until after she was two years old." These men lost because they "had never shouldered any significant responsibility with respect to the daily supervision, education, protection, or care of the child" (*Lehr*), and having failed to "complain of their exemption from these responsibilities," had no basis for complaining that they were being deprived of "the blessings of the parent-child relationship."

When Justice White, dissenting in *Lehr*, suggested that Lehr was personally blameless for his lack of a relationship with his daughter, the majority responded in a way that seemed calculated to underscore doubts about Lehr's claims of fatherly devotion. If Lehr were genuinely interested in parenthood, the majority observed, he could have ensured himself notice of any adoption proceeding "simply by mailing a postcard to the putative father registry" (*Lehr*).

The Supreme Court itself seems torn between these competing understandings. In the Court's most recent case considering a biological father's constitutional claim to parenthood, individual Justices appeared to subscribe to both points of view (*Michael H. v. Gerald D.*, 491 U.S. 110 (1989)). . . .

Although the Court itself has yet to resolve which of these competing understandings is correct, many state courts have already embraced the view that the Constitution protects not only existing relationships, but also a parent's "opportunity interest" in establishing such a relationship. Indeed, this conclusion largely explains the decisions in the Baby Richard and Baby Jessica cases (*In re B.G.C.*, 496 N.W. 2d 239 (Iowa 1992); *In re Petition of Doe*, 638 N.E. 2d 181 (Ill. 1994)). In both of those cases, the state supreme courts regarded the fathers as blameless victims of the machinations of others and held, in effect, that the Constitution would not permit these men to suffer the loss of fatherhood when they had done nothing to warrant such a grievous penalty.

In the Baby Richard case, for example, the Illinois Supreme Court concluded, on the basis of sharply controverted evidence, that the biological mother had schemed with the couple who sought to adopt Richard in order to deprive the biological father, Otakar Kirchner, of any chance to obtain custody. The relationship between Kirchner and the child's mother, Daniella Janikova, ended suddenly during the pregnancy when Janikova suspected that Kirchner was rekindling an old flame during a visit to his native Czechoslovakia. When Kirchner returned to Chicago, Janikova's relatives informed him that the baby had died after childbirth, and Janikova thereafter hid herself and the child from Kirchner's "persistent inquiries." In the weeks that followed the birth, Kirchner searched local hospitals and the homes of Janikova's relatives in an effort to discover clues about the child's fate or whereabouts. When the child was fifty-seven days old, Janikova confessed to him that she had surrendered the child for adoption and Kirchner promptly hired an attorney and sought to block the adoption.

Based on these facts, the Illinois Supreme Court unanimously concluded that the adoption was defective and could not go forward. Although the lower courts had found that Kirchner's consent to the adoption was unnecessary because he had shown a lack of interest in the child during the first thirty days of the child's life, the Illinois Supreme Court held that finding to be unsupported by the evidence. Without Kirchner's consent and without any grounds for involuntarily terminating his parental rights, the court concluded that the adoption must be vacated.

Significantly, . . . the court ultimately sought to justify the result by pointing to the commands of the federal Constitution as well [as Illinois law]. When one year later Kirchner petitioned to enforce the 1994 judgment, the court surveyed the U.S. Supreme Court's cases dealing with the rights of unwed fathers and concluded that Kirchner constitutionally would be entitled to upset the adoptive placement of his son. Although Kirchner did not have "a substantial relationship" with his son in the same way that Abdiel Caban had, neither had he dodged his responsibilities or slept on his rights in the way the Court had attributed to Leon Quilloin and Jonathan Lehr. [Otakar Kirchner] fell somewhere in between (*In re Petition of Kirchner*, 649 N.E. 2d 324 (Ill. 1995)).

III. Legislative Responses and Incomplete Solutions

A. Statutory and Judicial Limitations

. . . [E]ven the revised Uniform Adoption Act [UAA of 1994], which contains perhaps the most expansive termination provision to date, accords significant protection to the blameless biological parent. After setting out more traditional fault-based grounds for termination, the Act broadly authorizes a court to terminate parental rights based solely on a finding that "failure to terminate the relationship of parent and child would be detrimental to the minor," UAA 3-504(d)(4). . . . Although the Act's drafters have indicated that this provision could be applied to deny rights to a "thwarted" unwed father, Comment to UAA 3-504, the Act itself significantly qualifies that resolve by directing that "detriment() to the minor" be assessed specifically with reference to the father's diligence and "the role . . . other persons (may have played) in thwarting (his) efforts to assert parental rights," UAA 3-504(e). Thus, even in attempting to redirect the focus of the termination decision to the child's welfare, the model statute mandates consideration of the father's conduct and interests.

In sum, notwithstanding recent legislative efforts to expand the grounds for terminating the rights of biological parents or otherwise excluding them from the adoption process, . . . a father who can show that he always stood ready to assume custodial duties but that he was thwarted in his good-faith efforts to establish a relationship with the child retains the legal right in almost all jurisdictions to block an adoption so long as he asserts his interests promptly upon the first opportunity.

B. Constitutional Limitations on "No-Fault" Termination

Whatever state legislatures would like to do to protect children, it appears doubtful that the Constitution permits the states to be much more aggressive in terminating the rights of fit and faultless biological parents. The United States Supreme Court has hinted strongly that the Constitution prohibits a state from extinguishing a parent-child relationship without proof of the parent's "unfitness," and, although parental "unfitness" is a broad and flexible concept, it is almost universally taken to require proof of blameworthy conduct—such as abuse, neglect, or abandonment—or incapacity on the part of the parent (*Santosky v. Kramer*, 455 U.S. 745 (1982)). If that is true, it follows that the continued expansion of the grounds for terminating parental rights cannot serve as a complete solution to the dilemma posed by the fit and faultless father who objects to the adoption of his child.

IV. Toward an Alternative Model of Adoption

Accepting the premise that the law's goal should be to promote the welfare of children to the maximum extent possible without violating the constitutional rights of others, I contend that legislatures could improve significantly the lives of children now living with non-parent caregivers by authorizing a new form of adoption that would not require terminating all of the rights of biological parents. . . .

A. Adoption without Termination of Rights: The Outlines of a New Model

In this country, it has always been considered axiomatic that adoption necessitates the legal extinguishment of all other parental relationships with the child. . . . Following an adoption, the child and her biological parents are considered, in the eyes of the law, strangers to one another. . . . It is . . . precisely this assumption that has generated the apparent legal quandary in cases like those of Baby Richard, Baby Jessica, and others. Where there is no legal basis for destroying the biological parent-child relationship, there is no legal possibility of adoption.

In recent years, many have observed that this unswerving linkage between adoption and termination of prior parental relationships sometimes has worked to the disadvantage of children. Some critics, focusing on cases in which traditional grounds for terminating the biological parents' rights exist, have argued that the linkage harms children by insisting unnecessarily upon the destruction of biological parent-child relationships in order to give children the benefits of permanency conferred by adoption. Others have focused on cases in which traditional grounds for termination do not exist, and argued that the linkage has harmed children by snuffing out beneficial relationships with non-parent caregivers. The consensus solution of these critics, however, generally has been to advocate the invention or greater use of intermediate forms of custodial rights for non-parent caregivers that stop short of adoption, such as permanent guardianships, so that a child might have the benefits of ongoing ties with both the biological parents and the non-parent custodians. . . . [This is what the UAA recommends.]

I approach the problem from a different direction. . . . I propose the creation of a new form of adoption that could be ordered, even over the objection of a fit biological parent, without terminating the biological parents' relationship with the child. . . .

This suggestion is consistent with the tentative steps by [many] states toward validating "open adoptions," in which a biological parent consents to an adoption while reserving a contractual right to visit the child after the adoption. But these jurisdictions have been careful to limit the availability of this form of adoption only to cases in which all affected adults, biological and adoptive parents alike, consent to the arrangement. Moreover, existing forms of "open adoption" typically contemplate that the biological parent will lose the legal status of parent while retaining visitation rights as a "former parent," not that the arrangement will result in a new form of multiple parenthood. This limited form of "open adoption" may well be beneficial and, because it rests on consent, neatly sidesteps any constitutional questions. But it plainly cannot serve as a solution in those cases where fit biological parents resist adoption. In those cases, a different model of adoption, one in which adoption can go forward without either the consent of the biological parents or a termination of their rights, is necessary. . . .

1. An Alternative to—Not a Substitute for—Traditional Adoption

The model of adoption proposed here . . . is offered not as a substitute, but as a supplement. It is not meant to displace traditional adoption or voluntary open adoption [both of which work well for many families], but to extend the benefits of adoption to a new class of cases where adoption is now considered impossible. Essentially, it would be available only in those cases where courts find themselves confronted with a custody contest between a faultless biological parent and a non-parent who has an established custodial relationship with the child. Courts in such cases now have available only two options: return the child to the custody of the parent (as the courts did in the Baby Richard and Baby Jessica cases) or leave the child in the custody of the non-parent, as guardian to the child, with visitation rights to the parent. This proposal would give courts a third option: leave the child with the non-parent, but transform that caregiver into a parent through a non-exclusive adoption that would leave the biological parents with visitation rights. As such, acceptance of this proposal does not require reconsidering the existing framework of statutes and rules governing traditional adoption; rather, the proposal could be accomplished as a freestanding supplement to existing law. . . .

2. Reduced—But Not Extinguished—Parental Rights for the Biological Parent

Because [this] model of adoption . . . contemplates the existence of more than one set of parents for a child, it is essential to define clearly the respective rights of each. The adoption necessarily implies that the biological parent or parents would not have custody of the child, just as biological parents currently lose custody when children are placed with permanent guardians. In many other respects, the biological parent could then be treated just like any other non-custodial parent under the law. Like all other non-custodial parents, for example, the biological parents would have the right to visit and communicate with the child. The extent and management of visitation rights could be worked out on terms identical to those applied to non-custodial parents in other contexts. If conflicts arose between the adoptive and biological parents over access to the child, courts could employ the same tools they currently use to enforce visitation rights or induce sparring parents to work out child-rearing conflicts, including contempt of court, awards of money damages, and, in appropriate cases, threatening to deprive the recalcitrant parent of custody or visitation.

Although the rights of the non-custodial parent under this model of adoption generally could mirror those of non-custodial parents in other contexts, two adjustments seem desirable with regard to the availability of modification and joint custody. First, [in order to promote the stability and security of the child's custodial placement with the adoptive parents] the biological parent should not be permitted to seek a change of custody except upon demonstration of extraordinary circumstances, such as imminent and substantial harm to the child. Under this standard, courts would be permitted to change custody upon proof of abuse or neglect, for example, but not upon the bare conviction that the child, on balance, would benefit from living with genetic family members. . . .

The second appropriate adjustment concerns the availability of joint custody. The law should make clear that full decision-making authority in matters of child-rearing lies exclusively with the adoptive parents. . . .

3. LIMITATIONS ON THE AVAILABILITY OF THE ALTERNATIVE MODEL OF ADOPTION

Two limitations upon standing to petition for a non-exclusive adoption would go a long way toward eliminating the danger of abuse. [This kind of] adoption should be confined to cases in which the petitioning adult: (1) already has custody of the child, either with the initial consent of one of the child's legal parents or under authority of a court order; and (2) is already a "psychological parent" to the child. These requirements would ensure that this relatively intrusive form of custody would be used only where the benefits to the child clearly outweigh the costs to the biological parent. The scenario under which the intrusion upon biological parents' rights seems most justifiable is the sort of case, as with Baby Jessica or Baby Richard, where the child has been living with a non-parent and regards that caregiver as a parent, and where the child's relationship with the absent biological parent is correspondingly diminished. This is the sort of case where many courts and legislators are now already prepared to grant permanent custody to a nonparent (though adoption itself, of course, remains unavailable). Imposing "psychological parent" status as a requirement for standing would ensure that biological parents are not too easily hauled into court by a social do-gooder to defend their rights to continued custody of their children. Only those relatively uncommon persons who legally had established a custodial relationship as a "psychological parent" to the child would have standing to seek adoption without proving grounds for terminating parental rights.

Permitting non-exclusive adoption only where a substantial, de facto parent-child relationship already exists with the adoptive parents would provide a significant limitation on judicial power to intrude on pre-existing parent-child relationships while ensuring that adoption remains available in cases where children would have the greatest interest in recognition of a new parent-child relationship. . . .

V. Conclusion

. . . Courts regularly, if infrequently, order the transfer of children from seemingly settled adoptive placements to the custody of biological parents who are largely or entirely unknown to the children [as they did in the Baby Jessica and Richard cases]. And, overwhelmingly, the judges and parents who populate these controversies have not been heartless or disdainful of the consequences for the children involved. The parents, on all sides, have earnestly believed they were acting on behalf of children in real peril, and the judges typically have gone to pains to insist that their decisions transferring custody were the only ones allowed by the law. Ultimately, the largest blame for these tragedies lies not with these individual actors, who mostly struggled to do the best they could for the children within the confines of an unwieldy legal regime they only dimly comprehended. Rather, it lies with a society that has clung to a legal regime built almost reflexively around notions of parental fault and entitlement and that is unable to comprehend the possibility of more than one set of caring, deserving parents. What is needed, then, is not legal reform aimed at thwarting a particular villain, the selfish parent or the callous judge, but reform that thinks sensitively about the needs of children and creatively about how those needs might be met more fully. . . .

. . . Despite recent expansions of the grounds for terminating parental rights, some biological parents still will be able to disrupt settled adoptive placements. In those cases, guardianship may prevent a traumatic transfer of custody, but it is not a panacea. Much of the research into child development and psychology that justifies avoiding a transfer of custody in these cases also justifies going further and solidifying the children's relationship with their custodial caretakers in a way that is possible only through adoption. Because it presumably would be impossible to terminate the rights of both biological parents—that is the reason why traditional adoption is not thought desirable or possible in these cases to begin with—a new model of adoption is required, one in which an adoption decree would create new custodial parents for the child without disregarding the parents who gave the child life. By fully legitimizing the familial status of the child and her caregivers and by giving their relationship the law's fullest measure of security, this model of adoption would promote their ability to develop the deepest sort of family bonds, to their great mutual benefit. At the same time, by ensuring that one or both biological parents can continue to play a meaningful role in the child's life, this model of adoption would be sufficiently sensitive to the rights of biological parents to satisfy the Constitution. Until the law, through such an innovation, confers upon these children the blessings of a fully validated family, society cannot rightfully claim to be doing all that it can on behalf of children.

NOTES

1. *Stanley v. Illinois,* 405 U.S. 645 (1972); *Quilloin v. Walcott,* 434 U.S. 246 (1978); *Caban v. Mohammed,* 441 U.S. 380 (1979); *Lehr v. Robertson,* 463 U.S. 248 (1983).

2. *Smith v. Organization of Foster Families for Equality and Reform (O.F.F.E.R.),* 431 U.S. 816, 844 (1977).

Who May Adopt
Evaluating Prospective Adoptive Parents

Proposed Uniform Adoption Act (UAA) of 1994

Determining Suitability to Adopt

Section 1-102. Who may adopt or be adopted. Subject to this [Act], any individual may adopt or be adopted by another individual for the purpose of creating the relationship of parent and child between them.

Comment

No one is categorically excluded by the Act from being considered as a prospective adoptee or as a prospective adoptive parent. Determinations concerning the availability and suitability of individuals to become each other's adoptive parent or child are to be made on the basis of the particular needs and characteristics of each individual. A specific minor will not become available for adoption, for example, unless the minor's parents consent to a direct adoptive placement or relinquish their parental rights to an agency, or unless the parents' relationship to the minor is terminated involuntarily by a court. A specific individual will not be entitled to adopt a minor unless the individual is favorably evaluated as suitable to adopt, obtains custody of a minor from a person authorized to place the minor for adoption, and is permitted to adopt by a court upon a finding that the minor's best interests will be served by being adopted by the individual. Marital status, like other general characteristics, does not preclude an individual from adopting, but, if a prospective adoptive parent is married, his or her spouse has to join in the petition.

Adoption Agencies and the Search for the Ideal Family, 1918–1965

Brian Paul Gill

Introduction: The New Selectivity in Adoption Practice

... In the nineteenth century, most of the children who were "placed out" into substitute families were old enough to begin making an immediate contribution to the family economy. Beginning around World War I, however, children were increasingly desired for reasons more sentimental than economic, generally by adults who were otherwise childless. These prospective parents wanted children who would be as fully as possible their own, beginning in infancy. The demand for babies to adopt began climbing in the 1920s, and exploded with the culture of domesticity after World War II.

Excess demand for young children gave adoption agencies a new opportunity, beginning in the 1920s, to be selective in the choice of adoptive parents. Selectivity was consistent with the interests of agency workers in the creation of adoptive families. Indeed, the professional expertise of the social worker in the adoption agency was the foundation of the worker's right to choose adoptive parents: "The only basis on which adoption agencies can ... ask for community backing of their right to make ultimate decisions about the families with which children are placed is demonstrated competence," declared Ruth Brenner, a leading adoption worker, in 1951.

To demonstrate competence, the agencies moved away from the turn-of-the-century emphasis on preventing harm to children, instead aiming higher: they began to claim a unique ability to create the "best" adoptive families. In 1951, explaining the market reality that permitted agency perfectionism, two agency workers described the caseworker's job as selecting "those couples who have the best potential as parents, recognizing the ten to one ratio of supply and demand in applicants and babies for adoption." ...

The Normal as Normative

Agencies assumed that the "best" families were those who were most "normal." A 1933 pamphlet of the U.S. Children's Bureau declared that all children should have "a chance to live in a normal family group"; a quarter-century later, the National Conference of Catholic Charities echoed that sentiment, stating that "the objective in adoption procedure is to provide a normal home life for a child." Dorothy Hutchinson, an adoption worker whose 1943 volume, *In Quest of Foster Parents,* was the most widely-read professional text of the period, maintained that "the selection of foster homes has at best been based on the assumption that although there is no such thing as a perfect home there is such a thing as a normal family." She added that "Normality is something that is hard to define, yet easy to feel and see. In it is assumed a wide range of behavior and attitude, not a narrowly fixed concept." Although Hutchinson typified the common agency position that normality was "the crux of the matter" in selecting applicants for parenthood, her assertion that it defined "a wide range of behavior and attitude" was misleading. Hutchinson and many other agency workers devoted considerable effort to defining normality narrowly.

As this essay will demonstrate, between the 1920s and the 1960s adoption agencies employed three principles in the service of creating the "best"—and most "normal"—adoptive families. First, they sought to create adoptive families which resembled biological families as closely as possible. Second, they excluded disabled children from adoption. Third, they took a new interest in the inner lives of prospective parents, aiming to choose only those who were psychologically ideal. In concert, these three principles involved the pursuit of an aesthetic ideal of the family—a pursuit which was perhaps the most ambitious program of social engineering (in its perfectionism if not in its scale) seen in twentieth-century America. Indeed, adoption agencies pursued the creation of aesthetically ideal families even when that goal was in tension with the interests of children waiting for adoption.

I. Simulating the Biological Family

The quest for normality that followed the new selectivity on the part of adoption agencies involved, first of all, a systematic effort to create adoptive families on the model of the biological family. During the Progressive Era, by contrast, agencies had sought to place children in homes that met uniform and relatively objective standards of quality, regardless of whether the merged family looked like a "normal" biological family. The notion that adoptive families ought to be as much like biological families as possible was rapidly assimilated by adoption professionals after World War I, and went largely unchallenged until the 1950s. As one agency director in 1939 argued, when a child could not be cared for by his own parents, "the best substitute for his own home would be another family home resembling as closely as possible what his home would have been." Nearly two decades later, the Child Welfare League of America (CWLA), the adoption agencies' umbrella professional organization, reaffirmed this view, arguing that the adoptive relationship ideally "approximates as nearly as possible the relationship between natural parent and child."

The agencies' efforts to simulate the biological family went unexamined and unexplained. The presumption in favor of the biological model was so persuasive that an explanation was thought unnecessary. Although they were in the business of creating non-biological families, adoption workers assumed that the biological family was the appropriate model for the adoptive family. The goodness of the biological family required no explanation because it was "natural," apparently ordained by God. When adoption workers talked about the challenges of "playing God," they assumed that their role in adoptive families resembled God's role in biological families. . . .

Matching

In practice, the pursuit of the biological family model involved an attempt to "match" characteristics of the child to characteristics of the adoptive parents. Between the First World War and the mid-1950s, adoption agencies sought to create families in which parents and child were physically, ethnically, racially, religiously, and intellectually *alike*. One agency director provided, in 1910, the definitive statement of the more general matching philosophy that would prevail in later decades, declaring that "there are first-class, second-class and third-class children, and there are first-class, second-class and third-class homes."

Florence Clothier, a psychiatrist at the New England Home for Little Wanderers and an influential adoption expert in the 1940s, justified matching by explaining that "as the child grows up and approaches maturity, it will be easier for him and for the adoptive parents if his appearance and constitutional type are not too foreign to that of the family of which he is a part." In Clothier's view, the benefits to adoptive parents and children resulting from similarity justified matching across a wide range of variables, including race: "The racial antecedents of the child and of the adoptive parents should be the same or as like as possible"; physical appearance: "physical characteristics of the true mother and father should be borne in mind when adoptive parents are being considered for a child"; and personality: "the temperaments of the child's true parents should not be in complete contradiction to the temperaments of the adoptive parents." Elsewhere, Clothier also advocated matching the intellectual capacities of parents and child. Even the national origins of the child's ancestors were relevant: Clothier suggested that "though there are no scientific data on the point, and though heredity may play but a slight role, there may be some validity to the lay concept that breeding or cultural tradition will show itself." She disapproved, for example, the placement of a light-skinned, freckle-faced boy with olive-skinned Italian-American parents.

By mid-century, matching of parents and child had become standard practice in adoption agencies nationwide. The three characteristics that received the most attention were intelligence, religion, and race. With regard to the first category, a U.S. Children's Bureau survey of ten adoption agencies in six states (conducted in 1922–23) reported that "all the agencies placed Catholic children in Catholic homes, Jewish children in Jewish homes, and Protestant children in Protestant homes." An infant's religion was defined by reference to the religious affiliation of her biological mother— and religious matching was sometimes enforced even against the wishes of the biological mother. Matching by religion remained standard adoption agency practice through the mid-1950s.

Meanwhile, the CWLA's influential Standards for Organizations Providing Foster Family Care (1933) advocated matching by intelligence, prescribing that "overplacement (placement of mentally dull or backward children with unusually intelligent and cultivated foster parents) as well as underplacement (placement of bright children in homes with little mental stimulus or cultural opportunity) should be avoided." Confronted with a limited ability to measure the child's intelligence directly, agencies sometimes simply assumed that "it is more likely that a child of superior [biological] parents will be superior than will a child of dull parents," making it "common practice" to place the child of unusually intelligent biological parents with unusually intelligent adoptive parents, according to the CWLA survey conducted in the late 1950s. At the other end of the scale, 75 of the agencies responding to the CWLA's inquiry reported "that they place children of less-than-average intelligence with parents who also have limited intelligence."

Racial matching was the most firmly institutionalized form of matching. In 1944–45, a sample of 91 agency placements in California found not a single transracial placement. A decade later, a 1965 CWLA survey reported unequivocally that "agencies are not placing Negro children in white homes or white children in Negro homes." . . .

Although religion, intelligence, and race were the most prominent of the matched characteristics, agencies hoped to match children and parents across a laundry list of other variables. . . . In 1950, for example, the regulations of the California Department of Social Welfare declared not only that "the racial background of the adopting parents and the child should be similar," that "the child shall be placed with adoptive parents whose religious faith is the same as his own or that of his parents," but also that "the personality, temperament, education, intelligence and cultural level, stature, and coloring of the adoptive parents shall be considered in relation to the personality, temperament, physical appearance, coloring, cultural background, and potential mental ability of the child." In 1956, the CWLA surveyed the adoption practices of 270 agencies which accounted for about half of all agency adoptions nationwide. The survey found overwhelming support for matching on many variables. In large majorities, the agencies reported that they considered it important to match by "religious background"; "racial background", "temperamental needs"; "educational background"; "physical resemblance to child"; "cultural background"; "nationality background"; and "level of intelligence and intellectual potential." As the director of the Boston Children's Friend Society summed up in 1950, matching was "an endeavor to have the child as nearly as possible resemble the adoptive parents." . . .

II. Excluding "Defective" Children

Adoption agencies were strongly influenced by hereditarian notions of child development. In early twentieth-century America, the "nature vs. nurture" debate was especially heated; an optimistic reform movement aimed at improving social environments coexisted uneasily with an intense public interest in eugenics. Many social workers resolved the tension between these two competing ideological views by concluding that, although "normal" people could be affected by positive environmental influences, genetics determined the fate of "defectives." This resolution had implications for professional adoption practice which would endure for half a century.

Not all of the children turned over to the agencies were matched to an approved set of adoptive parents. Before an infant became eligible for adoptive placement, the agency determined whether the child was "adoptable." It was not only would-be adopters, but also would-be adoptees, who had to meet agency approval. The agencies regarded children with disabilities as "defective," and according to eugenic theory, beyond help. Prospective adopters, by contrast, had proven themselves—by meeting agency screening standards—to be non-defective. In the view of the agencies, they were therefore entitled to non-defective children. "Defective" children did not belong in ideally "normal" families; they were therefore ineligible for adoptive placement.

From the end of the First World War until the end of World War II, agency authorities spoke with one voice against the placement of children with disabilities. . . . The 1949 regulations in California expected children available for adoption to be "suitable for adoption, from the standpoint of health, heredity, intelligence and personality." Mental disabilities were the agencies' greatest concern; children with less than "normal" intelligence were most zealously targeted for exclusion from the adoption market as "defectives."

The agencies' standards for "adoptability" could exclude a large number of children. In 1946, the New York City welfare department referred 730 children to adoption agencies, but the agencies placed only 336 of the children that year, returning 276 to the department "as unsuitable for adoption." The agencies' refusal to place disabled children belied any claim that their paramount concern was the welfare of the children. Although a few agency workers tried to argue that such children were better off in institutions than in adoptive homes, some conceded that the policy was designed not for the children, but for the prospective parents. The agencies sought to provide their customers—adoptive parents—a flawless product. As Joseph Reid, Executive Director of the CWLA, noted in 1957, it had not been long since "agencies were convinced and attempted to convince the public that they could guarantee them a perfect child; that by coming to an agency, adoptive parents could be sure that the child was without physical, emotional or mental defect, that his heredity was sound and adopting a child was a far less risky procedure than having one normally." If excluding disabled children did not serve the children's interests, it did serve the agencies' interest in creating families that met their aesthetic standards. In the view of the agencies, "normal" families did not have "defective" children.

III. Good Parenting as Psychology

Beginning in the late 1920s, the intensification of agency efforts to create "normal" families involved increased attention not only to the biological family model and to the characteristics of prospective adoptees, but also to the psychological makeup of prospective parents. For the agencies, normality meant that the applicants had to fit a psychological model defined in terms strongly reflecting the prevailing ideology of the family. . . . [A]pplicants were expected to be "normal" in age, in motivation to adopt, and in gender roles. The range of permissible eccentricity was narrow; it could include a prospective mother "who smokes and serves a cocktail," and a would-be father "who cuts the grass on Sunday attired only in shorts." Although she was willing to accept these kinds of applicants as "families with individuality and color," Hutchinson frowned on true eccentricity, opposing placement "in families regarded [in their communities] as 'queer' or too far 'off center.'"

Assessing the normality of the psychological makeup of applicants for adoption required a new attention to their private lives. One agency worker, for example, declared in 1930 that adoption agencies had a responsibility to "*know* the home—not being satisfied with the outer picture [it] . . . presents, but striving to evaluate the complex inner life which we call personality." By mid-century, the importance of "the complex inner life" of the applicants had become conventional wisdom. Strongly influenced by Freud's view of the significance of unconscious drives, adoption workers were fond of pointing out that a full understanding of personality required a look behind a client's public demeanor and stated motivations. As another agency worker argued in 1937, "some of the deepest inner aspects of intimate family life will often only be glimpsed by the worker and frequently the foster parents themselves are neither articulate about themselves nor even conscious of what motivates their actions." . . .

Psychological "Normality": Married Life and Gender Roles

Adoption professionals insisted that adoptive parents be married couples—because marriage indicated "normality," and normality was regarded as synonymous with psychological health.. . . . Freudian psychology supported the agencies' refusal to consider unmarried applicants. As Clothier explained: "To attain what we regard as psychosexual maturity in our culture, the child needs close association with both a mother and a father during the early years of life. Normal Oedipal development cannot occur in an environment in which one parent figure is lacking." Clothier went on to explain that a "boy has need of a father figure whose personality, by the process of identification, can strengthen his masculinity. He has need also of a mother figure to awaken and call up his love impulses and tenderness. His relationship to his mother will serve as a prototype of his future love relationships." In Clothier's view, a "girl, too, needs happy relationships with both a mother and a father, if she is to attain a feminine identification and, in adult life, a tender relationship with a man that is not overshadowed by fear and aggression." Indeed, she believed that girls without "wholesome father-daughter" interactions often ended up as unwed mothers. Clothier concluded by returning her focus to the single adoptive parent, arguing that "the unmarried adoptive parent is in danger of investing all her (it is usually a woman) emotional interest in the child and thus smothering its emotional growth. The role of adoptive parent is easier if there is a stable marriage as a background for the interplay of feelings."

Armed with psychoanalytic wisdom, adoption agencies from the 1930s through the early 1960s sought out couples with ideal marriage relationships. As one professional text put it in 1939, "nothing is of more importance to an agency in selecting its foster homes than the marital status of foster parents." The authors of the text added that "the relations existing between a man and his wife furnish valuable clues to the nature of homes." The 1958 CWLA Standards for Adoption Service divided "criteria of capacity for adoptive parenthood" into six categories, one of which was "quality of marital relationship." Ruth Brenner believed that the marital relationship was "of vital importance to the success of the adoption." Dorothy Hutchinson likewise decreed that "the relationship between husband and wife has crucial significance for the child to be placed." "Normality," Hutchinson added, appealing to the watchword of the era, "is what the worker is looking for."

Agencies sought out couples who fit the prevailing gender norms. . . . Short of homosexuality and divorce, perhaps the gravest sin a mother could commit against a gender norm during this period was to venture into the working world. Most of the adoption commentators did not flinch from taking their gendered view of the world to its logical conclusion: they expected adoptive mothers to stay at home. In Abraham Simon's view, for example, a major "role" that a wife should fulfill was "homemaker"; likewise, a husband should "fulfill his social role as breadwinner." Similarly, a couple consisting of an engineer husband and a homemaker wife earned Dorothy Hutchinson's praise: "Both Mr. G. and Mrs. G. accept their respective masculine and feminine roles. The division of labor between them is a normal one, and they both like being what they are—a man and a woman." A comprehensive study of adoptions in 60 agencies scattered around the United States in 1957 found that only 2% of the women approved (with their husbands) to adopt healthy white infants intended to work after receiving the child.

Family Values and Child Welfare

The agencies almost never attempted to explain why the most "normal" families were the best families. They systematically confused the descriptive and evaluative meanings of "normal." Adoption agencies drew evaluative (normative) conclusions from descriptive facts—the typical middle-class family of the postwar years was viewed as normatively good by virtue of nothing more than its typicality. Because biological children resembled biological parents, agencies assumed that adoptive children should resemble adoptive parents. Because most white, middle-class, married couples followed traditional gender patterns, agencies assumed that adoptive couples should follow traditional gender patterns.

Adoption agencies not only assumed that descriptively normal families were normatively best, but also failed to appreciate the distinction between creating "best"/"normal" families, on the one hand, and promoting positive child welfare outcomes, on the other. Their definition of the ideal family was an aesthetic one. . . .

During this period, the paramount value in agency practice was the ideally "normal" family. Mid-century adoption agencies had considerable success implementing their ideal. Applicants who did not fit the agencies' profile of ideal parents—such as career women, couples over 40, single applicants, and gays and lesbians, for example—were excluded without much difficulty. Children with disabilities (especially mental disabilities) were likewise excluded from family life, at least until the mid-1940s. And, by preventing the creation of families of mixed race and families of mixed religion, agencies also ensured that adopted children would not end up with the "wrong" parents. A study of adoptive families undertaken in the late 1950s confirmed that agencies were remarkably successful in establishing uniform national standards. The study involved adoptions sampled from placements made by 60 agencies in nine varied communities around the United States. The study found that accepted couples were remarkably similar everywhere. According to the author's "composite portrait," the typical couple adopting through an agency was married, in their mid-30s, child-less, and infertile for a clear physical reason. Neither parent had been previously mar-ried. Both practiced the same religion and were active in their local church. Both were on friendly terms with their families, and both remembered happy childhoods. Only 2% of the adoptive mothers of healthy, white infants planned to work after the place-ment of the child. The couples "seemed psychologically well within the range of the normal."

To be sure, this vision of the ideal family was not an original invention of the adop-tion agencies. Indeed, their obsession with normality suggests exactly the opposite: rather than constructing a new ideal of family, their goal was to reflect and reinforce an existing ideal.

Adoption and the Parental Screening System

Elizabeth Bartholet

Screening for parental fitness is a basic part of the agency adoption process. Both public and private agencies conduct home studies designed to assess eligibility for adoptive parenthood. . . .

Defenders of the home study system claim that screening assesses such important qualities as the capacity to love and nurture an adopted child. They also claim that the child assignment, or "matching," process involves sophisticated judgments as to which particular parent-child combinations will work best. But the fact is that the screening and matching system is extremely crude and quite inconsistent with its alleged purposes.

The system ranks prospective parents from top to bottom in terms of relative desirability, which is assessed primarily on the basis of easily determined objective factors. These factors reflect the system's bias in favor of a biologic parenting model as well as a socially traditional family model. So heterosexual couples in their late twenties or early thirties with apparently stable marriages are at the top of the ladder. These are the kind of people who could, if not for infertility, produce children, and who should, in the system's view, be parents. Single and older adoptive applicants—those in their late thirties and forties—are placed lower on the ladder, along with people with disabilities. . . .

The adoption screening system ranks and categorizes children waiting for homes, as well as parents, in order to decide how to make particular parent-child matches. The children are placed on their own desirability list, with healthy infants at the top, somewhat older and less healthy children next, and the oldest and most seriously disabled children at the bottom. Children are also classified according to racial, ethnic, and religious heritage.

In matching children with parents, the system operates primarily on the basis of what looks roughly like a market system, one in which ranking produces buying power. The most "desirable" parents are matched with the most "desirable" children, and the less desirable with the less desirable, on down the list. . . .

Those who procreate live in a world of near-absolute rights with respect to parenting. Those who would adopt have no rights. They must beg for the privilege of parenting, and do so in a state-administered realm that denies them both the right to privacy and the "civil rights" that we have come to think of as fundamental in the rest of our communal life. Differential treatment on the basis of age, race, religion, and disability has been outlawed in almost all areas of our lives. Increasingly, the law forbids discrimination on the basis of marital status and sexual orientation. It is only in the area of adoption that our system proudly proclaims not simply the right to discriminate but the importance of doing so. . . .

. . . Some voices have called for changes in the agency screening criteria, arguing, for example, that agencies should be barred from using such factors as age, marital status, religion, disability, and sexual orientation as the basis for categorically excluding certain groups from adoptive parenthood. Some have proposed that agencies be required to screen in all applicants who satisfy a minimal fitness standard, excluding only those who are found demonstrably unfit. But there is no consensus that this is the appropriate direction in which to move. In any event, these proposals would do little to change the essential nature of today's screening and matching system, which functions primarily not as a device to disqualify adoptive applicants but as a method to allocate available children to the parents deemed most desirable. . . . Reform proposals that have as their goal real changes in the system must take on not simply the eligibility cutoff determination but the entire ranking and matching setup.

An Alternative Vision

We now place an extremely high value on the right to procreate and the related right to hold on to our biologic product. We place no real value on the aspect of parenting that has to do solely with relationship. There is an essentially absolute right to produce a child, but there is no right to enter into a parenting relationship with a child who is not linked by blood—no right to adopt. Foster parents, stepparents, and others who develop nurturing relationships with children are deemed to have no right to maintain such relationships. They and the children who may have come to depend on them are subject to the whim of the blood-linked parent. . . .

Children have essentially no rights and no entitlements, although the system is supposed to operate in their best interests. Everyone knows that their best interests require nurturing homes and parenting relationships, but it is painfully obvious that children have no enforceable rights to those things.

We could flip this picture, upend the hierarchical ranking of values. We could place the highest value on children and their interests in growing up in a nurturing relationship. We could place a higher value on nurturing than on procreation, and we might choose to do so in part because it seems to serve children's interests in being parented. A less radical step would be to accord at least more significant value than we now do to the nurturing aspect of parenting.

Any such revision of parenting rights and responsibilities would lead to a very different view of the role that adoption agencies should play. It would seem obvious that their primary function should be to create parent-child relationships—to find homes for children in need of nurturing parents, and to find children for adults who want to nurture. In this new world, agencies would become adoption advocates. . . . They would encourage people dealing with infertility to consider adopting an existing child instead of undergoing treatment designed to produce another child. They would encourage those capable of procreation to consider adoptive or foster parenting instead. . . .

Quite obviously, this vision would mean abandoning the system of parental screening and matching that we know today. All who want to become adoptive parents would be presumed fit. We could create a parental licensing system based on a minimalist screening principle to disqualify those found demonstrably unfit, for such reasons as a past history of serious and persistent drug or alcohol abuse, prior child abuse, apparent incapacity to provide for a child's most basic needs, serious ill health, or advanced age. . . .

We would scrap the more extensive screening that goes on today. Adoption workers would get out of the business of ranking parental quality and lose their power to determine which kinds of children should be allocated to which kinds of parents. Prospective parents would make their own decisions as to which kinds of children to apply for and would be served on a first-come, first-served basis. Adoption workers would facilitate matches. They would seek to accommodate the interests of birth and adoptive parents as well as the interests of those children old enough to express their own preferences. . . .

What Children Have to Gain

One thing children have to gain is what they most need—homes. The current screening and matching system creates barriers that prevent many potential parents from adopting. . . . Another thing children have to gain is parents who are prepared to parent and to deal with any special issues involved in adoptive parenting.

Consequences of Adoption

Proposed Uniform Adoption Act (UAA) of 1994

Legal Consequences of Adoption

Section 1-104. After a decree of adoption becomes final, each adoptive parent and the adoptee have the legal relationship of parent and child and have all the rights and duties of that relationship.

Section 1-105. Except as otherwise provided in Section 4-103 (the parental status of a custodial parent married to an adoptive stepparent does not terminate), when a decree of adoption becomes final:

(1) the legal relationship of parent and child between each of the adoptee's former parents and the adoptee terminates, except for a former parent's duty to pay arrearages for child support; and

(2) any previous court order for visitation or communication with an adoptee terminates. [But the Act does not preclude a separate agreement by adoptive parents to allow an adopted child to visit or communicate with a birth parent or other former relative or foster parent.]

Section 1-106. A decree of adoption does not affect any right or benefit vested in the adoptee before the decree becomes final.

Adoptees' Inheritance Rights

Naomi Cahn and Joan Heifetz Hollinger

Under the common law approach to inheritance, only a legitimate, blood-related child served as the father's heir. Indeed, this principle was so strongly embedded in the law that illegitimate children were deemed to have "no" blood; they were incapable of inheriting. The early adoption statutes often provided that an adopted child was, with certain exceptions, the heir of the adoptive parents, but they could not inherit from the child.

Children's rights to inherit through their adoptive parents varied greatly. While some early statutes granted adopted children the same inheritance rights as "natural children," most did not. First, some statutes specifically distinguished between the rights of adopted and biological children to inherit from their legal parents. Second, under the "stranger-to-the-adoption" rule, an adopted child generally could not inherit through relatives who were not a party to the adoption. Third, in some states, adoptive children could continue to inherit from their biological relatives and their biological relatives could inherit from them even after the adoption. Finally, some statutes allowed the adoption agreement itself, rather than the intestacy statutes, to determine the adoptee's rights.

During the twentieth century, every state eventually amended its statutes to accord equal treatment to biological and adopted children for purposes of intestacy, class gifts, and other donative dispositions. Nonetheless, the scope of adoptees' intestacy rights remained contentious throughout the century. When the first proposed Uniform Adoption Act was drafted in 1953, for example, questions concerning an adoptee's right to inherit from collateral adoptive relatives remained unresolved. So divisive was the issue that the language in the Act that would have allowed adoptees to inherit through their parents was bracketed, indicating that states were not bound to follow this rule.

By the time the Uniform Laws Commission thoroughly revised the proposed Uniform Adoption Act in 1994, the new UAA incorporated what is now the standard rule in most states: "each adoptive parent and the adoptee have the legal relationship of parent and child and have all the rights and duties of that relationship," UAA 1-104, including, as the Comments note, the rights to intestate succession and inheritance by, from, and through each other.

Even today, however, the intestacy rights of an adopted child remain complicated, as some states cling to the principle that "Inheritance follows blood." In Vermont, for example, until changed by the 1996 case of *MacCallum v. Seymour*, an adopted child could not inherit from relatives of her adopted parents who had died intestate. In Mississippi, the rights of adoptees to inherit from collateral relatives is still unclear. In some states, depending on the phrasing of the will, an adopted child may not be able to inherit through a "class gift," or a gift that is phrased as to "my descendants" or to "my grandchildren." Nonetheless, both the current Uniform Adoption Act (1994) and the Uniform Probate Code (2002 version) treat adoptees as fully equivalent to biological children for purposes of intestacy and all donative dispositions, including class gifts, as well as for purposes of receiving wrongful death and other public or third-party benefits from the estate of an adoptive parent or collateral adoptive relative.

Many states provide an important exception for children adopted by stepparents from the now general rule that adoption severs the legal and economic ties between adoptees and their biological or former legal families. These states follow the Uniform Probate Code (UPC) provisions that a child adopted by her stepparent—the spouse of her custodial biological or adoptive parent—can still inherit from her other biological or former adoptive parent, even though all legal ties have otherwise been severed between that parent and the child, including that parent's right to inherit from or through the child. This means that the child can inherit from and through three family lines: the biological parent with whom the child and the adoptive stepparent live, the adoptive stepparent, and the noncustodial biological parent, UPC 2-114. While these statutes are intended to address some of the complexities of "blended" stepfamilies, and specifically, to protect a child's relationship with her noncustodial former parent's relatives, the assumption behind these provisions seems, nonetheless, to be based on blood—the decedent would prefer that her estate be left to a blood relative than to others.

16

Is Adoption a Risk Factor for the Development of Adjustment Problems?

Jeffrey J. Haugaard

A fairly common theme in the clinical and research adoption literature is that adoption as an infant or a child increases a person's risk for the development of adjustment problems. . . . Although there is a small but growing research base with which to assess adopted persons' risks for adjustment problems, there have been few recent efforts to synthesize the research and examine it critically. . . .

If adoption is a risk factor for adjustment problems, those involved in the adoption process should be made aware of this. Awareness of actual increased risk may allow adopted individuals and their families to reduce other controllable risks. Just as a family with a history of heart disease might be especially careful to avoid secondhand smoke, a family with an adopted child might be especially attentive to early signs of emerging adjustment problems and engage in activities known to reduce the risk of adjustment problems.

On the other hand, if adoption is not a risk factor for adjustment problems, or if only subgroups of the adopted population are at increased risk, then the continued acceptance of the link between adoption and adjustment problems could be harmful. Inaccurate beliefs about increased risk could adversely influence parenting styles, family processes, and individual expectations. For example, adoptive parents could become hypervigilant and could overreact to troublesome but normal child and adolescent behaviors. . . .

The studies using inpatient and outpatient samples suggest that there is a meaningful association between adoption and increased adjustment problems. However, results from nonclinical samples suggest that the link between adoption and adjustment problems is modest or nonexistent. . . .

Heterogeneity among Adopted Individuals

Considerable heterogeneity exists within the population of individuals who are adopted. This heterogeneity is present not only in the personal characteristics of the adopted individuals, but also in the circumstances that led to their adoption. For example, children adopted as newborns are likely to experience quite different circumstances than children who are adopted during their school-age years. If these circumstances influence risk, then research that combines children who have had disparate experiences may systematically overestimate the risk to some children and underestimate the risk to others. In addition, if the average risk is calculated for a diverse sample of adopted children, the findings may not accurately represent the actual risk to any of the children within the sample. Three characteristics of this heterogeneity are of particular importance when evaluating the research. . . .

[First], the most common form of adoption is adoption by a stepparent. The experiences of these children are likely to be quite different from those of children who are adopted by nonrelatives, particularly in the continuity of care by one birth parent. Thus, these two groups should be considered separately. Most, but not all, research does distinguish between these two groups.

[Second], the age of the child at the time of initial placement also is an important circumstance to consider. Age at placement is likely to indicate whether the child had a relationship with a birth parent and/or foster parent that was disrupted in the adoption process. Many empirical studies distinguish between children adopted as infants and those adopted in childhood. However, the age used to distinguish infancy from childhood has not been consistent between studies. If the transition to new parents is one factor that increases risk for adoptees, then research combining children of various ages at initial placement is likely to overestimate the risk for newborns and underestimate the risk for older children.

[Third], preplacement experiences of some adopted children may increase their risk for adjustment problems. Most children adopted after infancy have been removed from their birth parents because of abuse or neglect. Therefore, basic assumptions about the presence of an unhealthy family environment in the early lives of most of these adopted children can be made with some confidence. Making confident assumptions about the experiences of adopted newborns and infants is more difficult. For example, the dramatic increase in the number of newborns harmed by their mother's drug use during pregnancy has resulted in an increase in drug-exposed newborns and infants who are eligible for adoption. . . . Clearly, these children's preplacement environments are substantially different from adopted newborns who developed in a healthy fetal environment. Similarly, some infants may have been placed for adoption after good care by a young mother who eventually decides that adoption is best for her baby, while other infants will have been abused or neglected before removal from their birth parent's home. As with age at initial placement, if adopted children who experienced disparate circumstances before their adoption are evaluated together, estimates about the risk for adjustment problems for the various subgroups of adopted children are likely to be inaccurate. . . .

Research based on non-clinical samples presents a different picture [than research based on clinical samples]. Several studies found few or no differences in the mental health of adopted and nonadopted children and adolescents. Other studies found mean differences in the adjustment of adopted and nonadopted children; however, these differences were often modest and the means for both the adopted and non-adopted children's behaviors generally fell within the normal range. Longitudinal studies with non-clinical samples found differences between adopted and nonadopted children at some ages and no differences at other ages, suggesting that adjustment problems in adopted children may be transitory. This research, therefore, suggests that there may be a risk of increased behavior or adjustment problems for some adopted children, or for adopted children at certain ages, but that this risk is neither high nor widespread.

. . .

Unless one is willing to dismiss the results of either the clinically based or non-clinically based research, hypotheses about adoption and the risk for adjustment problems must account for their disparate results; . . . two such hypotheses are explored. The first hypothesis focuses on the possibility that adopted children are referred for mental-health treatment more frequently than nonadopted children with similar levels of maladjustment. The second hypothesis focuses on whether differences in the distribution of maladjustment among adopted and nonadopted children could result in both a high percentage of adopted children in mental-health treatment and few mean differences in general adjustment between the adopted and non-adopted samples.

Some researchers have suggested that parents of adopted children may refer their children for mental-health treatment more often than do parents of birth children. There are several potential influences on this pattern, including: (a) adoptive parents may be more vigilant toward the development of mental-health problems than are nonadoptive parents, . . . (b) children who were abused or neglected before their adoption may have been in mental health treatment when they were adopted, and the connection between the parents and the therapist made at this time may facilitate a subsequent return to mental health treatment, . . . (c) the beliefs of other professionals (e.g., physicians, teachers) about adopted children and adjustment problems may encourage them to recommend mental health treatment if consulted by the parent, and (d) adoptive families may be more fragile and thus react more strongly to lower levels of problems in one of the children than would nonadoptive families. . . .

One line of future research should continue the investigation of potential biases in the referral of adopted children to therapy. Understanding the size of any potential bias may help to estimate the extent to which increased referrals to therapy are a result of overall poorer adjustment of adopted children.. . . .

Future research should also expand to consider more carefully process variables that influence a child's ongoing adjustment to adoption. Some adoption researchers have done this. For example, David Brodzinsky and his colleagues have explored the development of children's thinking about adoption and how this thinking influences their adjustment. . . .

The extent to which the process of growing up as an adopted child has a negative influence on a child's development is unclear. The research that is currently available provides a confusing picture regarding adopted children's development, with clinically based studies suggesting that adoption has a significant negative influence on a child's development and many non-clinical studies suggesting that there is little or no influence of adoption on a child's development. Research on referral bias suggests that some increased involvement of adopted children in mental health treatment may be due to a greater tendency of adopted parents and juvenile justice authorities to refer adopted children to treatment. An examination of the three models for the distribution of adjustment problems in the adopted and nonadopted populations showed that adoption may have some level of negative consequences for many or all adopted children. However, equally likely was that most or all adopted children are not negatively affected by their adoption experience and that increased disturbance in adopted samples is due to factors other than the adoption that influence a small number of adopted children.

There is a strong body of research suggesting that the characteristics that some adopted children bring with them into an adoptive family place them at risk for the development of physical and/or mental problems (e.g., genetic vulnerabilities, being born with fetal alcohol syndrome). There also is research showing that the experiences of some children before their adoption place them at risk for adjustment problems (e.g., severe abuse or neglect). However, a similar body of research showing that increased risk for adjustment problems is associated with going through the process of being adopted and growing up in an adoptive family does not exist. Consequently, based on current research, it would be inappropriate to base practice or policy on the supposition that adoption itself places a child at risk for the development of adjustment problems. . . .

Within the adopted population there may be many subgroups of children who are at risk for the development of adjustment problems. Until further research on adoption and adjustment is completed, clinicians and policy makers must be careful not to generalize this risk to the entire adopted population. At some point the research literature may show that adoption is a risk factor for adjustment problems, but it does not support such a conclusion at this time.

Coming to Terms with Adoption
The Construction of Identity from Adolescence into Adulthood

Harold D. Grotevant

The important unanswered question is how the fact of adoption is integrated into one's overall identity; in what way is a coherent whole formed? Following Erikson's argument that an important aspect of identity is continuity across past, present, and future, coming to terms with one's identity as an adopted person should play an important role in the overall identity development process . . . [we need] to understand how the different domains of identity are related to one another, and particularly how domains of identity that are assigned (such as one's adoptive status) are related to those that are more freely chosen. . . .

Analyses of data from the National Longitudinal Survey of Adolescent Health do not find significant behavioral differences between adopted and non-adopted children growing up in similar households. Variables based on family and peer relationships are significant predictors of antisocial behavior, but adoption is not.

Nature and Nurture
A New Look at How Families Work

Susan Freivalds

[O]ne of the most comprehensive studies of families ever undertaken is shedding light on the adoption experience. Called the Sibling Interaction and Behavior Study (SIBS), it was launched in 1999 by the University of Minnesota's Center for Twin and Family Research. Funded by the National Institutes of Health, the SIBS study has two primary purposes: to examine how siblings interact and influence one another, and to see how family dynamics impact the psychological health of adolescents.

The SIBS study includes a significant percentage of adoptive families because of the unique research opportunity they offer. In families in which all members are related by birth, behavioral scientists cannot separate genetic from environmental influences on psychological characteristics. Scientists know that certain traits, including academic achievement, personality features, and risk of psychological disturbance, tend to "run in families." But do these reflect a common genetic heritage or do the traits reflect the fact that siblings grew up together in the same family? One way to find out is to look at families with no common genetic component and see if the effects are still there. . . .

Four hundred of the 600 families in the SIBS study were selected because they include at least one adopted child. Over half of the adopted children are from Asian countries. Findings will be important to all families, no matter their composition. But because adoptive families make up a large percentage of the subjects, researchers will be able to answer questions specific to families formed through adoption. . . .

With data in from just over one-third of the families, Principal Investigator Matt McGue has released preliminary findings. For adoptive families, the most significant are:

1. There is virtually no difference in psychological functioning between children raised in adoptive families and those raised in biological families. In measures of delinquency, antisocial attitudes, aggression, substance abuse, and other problem behaviors, the differences between adopted children and children being raised by their biological families were insignificant. Measures of well-being, identity, academic achievement, and other positive characteristics were also virtually identical.

These positive findings contradict earlier research that found adopted adolescents at greater risk for psychological problems than their non-adopted peers, SIBS researchers note. [Because] the average age of the adolescents in the study is only 15, . . . differences between adopted and non-adopted individuals may [or may not] emerge later.

2. Sibling relationships appear unaffected by adoption. Relationships were equally close and loving among all kinds of sibling pairs (adopted-adopted, adopted-bio, and bio-bio). Although bio siblings thought of themselves as being more similar, this perceived similarity did not affect the quality of relationships between adoptive and biological siblings. Birth order was much more significant in sibling relationships than was adoptive status. The older sibling was almost always more powerful in the relationship, regardless of whether s/he had been adopted.

3. In parent-child relationships, researchers identified some differences between adoptive and biological families. Parents and children felt as attached to each other in adoptive families as in biological families, but adopted children reported more conflict with parents than did biological offspring. This did not, however, result in greater behavior problems outside the home, as might have been expected.

4. Despite the absence of genetic links, adoptive siblings are psychologically similar to one another in some significant ways. As would be expected, siblings by adoption showed no similarities in the kinds of personality traits that psychologists know to be largely genetic in origin, such as being shy or outgoing. In two areas of behavior, however, researchers identified surprising similarities among adoptive siblings. First, in academic achievement, adoptive siblings turned out to have comparable IQs (although not as similar as those of biological siblings), as well as similar academic motivation and achievement levels. This is likely attributable to parental influence.

Adoptive siblings were also alike in regard to problem behaviors, such as smoking, alcohol use, and disobedience. Having an older sibling with problem behavior was highly predictive of such behavior in younger siblings. Thus, the research suggests that problem behavior is less a matter of parental influence than of sibling influence. It's too early to tell if the adoptive status of an older sibling is a factor.

How valid are these findings? SIBS is breaking ground by addressing the limitations of earlier adoption research. The designs of many previous studies, particularly those with positive results, have been criticized for including mostly volunteers from well-functioning families with few problems. The SIBS study is different in a number of ways:

1. Families are recruited for the study through adoption agencies, not by requesting volunteers. . . .

2. Study participants are interviewed face-to-face. Problem behaviors that might not be elicited through a questionnaire are more likely to surface.

3. SIBS maximizes participation by accommodating interviewees' schedules, giving incentives, and thoroughly explaining the project and its importance.

4. The inclusion of biological families in the study allows for identification of characteristics specific to adoptive families.

5. Researchers are conducting brief assessments of families who choose not to participate to see if they differ from those who do. As it turns out, no difference in problem behavior levels has appeared between families who agreed to participate in the research compared to families who declined to take part: 26% of the study families said

their adopted children had problem behaviors vs. 26.2% of non-participating families. The divorce rate, while low for both groups, is somewhat higher for study participants than for non-participants.

Thus, Professor McGue feels that the study group is fairly representative of adoptive families and that the findings will accurately portray families who adopt infants and toddlers through an adoption agency. . . . [Nonetheless, the] SIBS findings to date are based on partial data and thus may be subject to change as the full quota of families is studied. Findings are also limited by the fact that assessments are taken at a single point in adolescent life. Will these positive indications hold when children leave home? SIBS researchers hope . . . to study the same families at three-year intervals until the children reach young adulthood.

19

Nature in Adoptive Parenthood

Irving Leon

[A]doptive parenthood is essentially natural. That is, the crucial cement for the construction of parenthood is the motivation to parent and the action of parenting. The psychological achievement of parenthood is the natural response to the child's need to be nurtured—the behavioral, emotional, cognitive—in a word—social—relationship of parenting. . . . As important as reproduction is for most couples in ushering in parenthood, that act is neither necessary nor sufficient for true parental ties to be made. . . .

. . . My goals are twofold. First, I believe there are aspects of adoptive parenthood which optimally meet children's needs. The overall quality of biological parenting may be improved by incorporating some of these features of adoptive parenthood. Secondly, a positive model of adoptive parenthood is long overdue. Too often adoptive families have been told that adoption is the last resort, that adoption leaves a battalion of scarred birthmothers and wounded adoptees, that being adopted is a cultural metaphor for being different from one's family and not fitting in. A positive model for adoptive parenthood may be seen to benefit prospective adoptive parents as well as parenthood in general.

My intent is not to gloss over the very real losses and challenges that adoption presents for adoptive parents. Infertility is no easy loss to grieve. Adoptive parents must learn to attach to their child without experiencing pregnancy, the period during which that bond usually begins and grows. Adoptive families are denied the powerful joys of biological connection. . . . I am convinced, however, that most difficulties resulting from adoption are not due to the nature of adoption in and of itself, but the prejudice, often subliminal but pervasive, against it in our society. The critical issues in adoption are less, I believe, about facing inevitable loss than recognizing and challenging culturally induced shame and stigma.

Nor is my intent to be antagonistic to biological parenthood or to establish an artificial dichotomy between adoptive and biological parenting. The two are much more alike than different and how good a parent one is has much less to do with whether one is a biological or adoptive parent than with how good a parent one is. . . .

While biological parenthood should remain the norm of parenthood in our culture, how biological parenthood is put into practice can and should be challenged. . . .

[t]here is simply too much emphasis on the act of procreation rather than the ongoing process of parenting. Children should be viewed less as offspring owned by the creating couple than as developing persons whose needs should be met by competent parents. . . .

[B]ecause in our culture, being a "real" parent means creating one's child, biological parents may be inclined to believe that their genetic connection with their offspring will inevitably solidify the emotional bond with their young. It may feel a bit less important to parent when one is so assured of being the parent. Adoptive parents, not having that genetic connection, must rely on the actual parent-child bond as the principal determinant of parenthood. Attachment theory . . . and developmental/clinical theory . . . make it clear that in the eyes of a child the sense of Mommy and Daddy is based on who takes care of that child, meeting that child's needs, and knowing that child's uniqueness and individuality in moment-by-moment daily interactions. . . . Adoptive parenthood holds the potential for the development of attachments becoming the essence of what it means to be a parent. All parenthood can and should aspire to that meaning. It provides the best chance for children to develop in the most secure and productive fashion. . . .

Adoptive parents are frequently warned not to expect the similarities in styles, temperaments, talents, and so forth that are usually taken for granted in biological families. With the now constant reporting of genetic contribution to human behavior, today's adoptive parents are probably even more primed to face inborn differences with their children. As we all know, however, genetic connections work in mysterious ways. How common it is in families to have one child be the "spittin' image" of a parent and another seem, well, different. While some families comfortably tolerate differences, others do not. Might adoptive parents be more ready to accept and even enjoy these differences, assuming that has been part of their preparation for adoption? Both the readiness to accept inborn differences in one's children and the less likely tendency to invest one's self-worth in their achievements, may help adoptive parents to better appreciate their children as unique individuals in their own right.

Biological differences between men and women in the role of reproduction may reinforce our cultural values which favor women playing the primary role in parenting. After carrying a baby during pregnancy, giving birth to that child, and then being uniquely equipped to nurse that child, a mother may feel more than a leg up on being the primary caregiver. With those reproductive activities favoring the maternal role absent, adoption may enable a more equal involvement in parenting by mothers and fathers right from the outset. Fathers may become more important as parents. . . .

Adoption offers a different concept of family and community, one in which the sharing of life together matters more than the sharing of genes. It continues to be a radical idea, challenging what we usually call family. Like interracial marriage, it says the most intimate of human relationships need not be restricted to "one's own," but may reach out to embrace others to make them "one's own." . . .

Much of what I discussed is a vision of adoption . . . which says children belong to their parents, but are owned by no one. It is a vision not only of adoption but for all parenthood. It is a vision based not on the rights of adults but rather on what all children need and deserve.

III

Foster Care and Informal Adoption

Children may be placed in foster homes for what is intended to be temporary care while state and local child welfare agencies assist parents who are having difficulty caring for their children. Alternatively, children may be in foster care while agencies seek court approval to terminate their parents' rights. Until the 1980s, foster care was often sought voluntarily by parents with severe economic, health, or marital problems. Since then, most of the ever growing number of children entering foster or other out-of-home care are removed from their parents involuntarily upon a court finding of neglect or abuse. The state retains legal custody of the children while granting physical custody to foster parents whom the state selects, licenses, pays, and, presumably, trains and supervises. As Jill Duerr Berrick explains below, in many states, children are placed in "kinship care" with relatives who are sometimes subject to the same regulations as licensed foster parents, but who in many jurisdictions are not regulated or entitled to the same benefits as foster parents.

More than half a million American children were in foster care in 2002, and well over half of these children were African American, Hispanic, or members of other racial or ethnic minorities. Since the early 1980s, the total number of children in foster care has nearly doubled as drugs, physical and sexual abuse, and other ills have afflicted more and more families.

African American children, and to a much lesser extent, Hispanic children, regardless of their age when they enter out-of-home care, wait dramatically longer than white children for a permanent placement. In the mid-1990s, for example, African American children in the California child welfare system were only one-fifth as likely to be adopted as were white children. For a very large percentage of the children in state custody, the "temporary" haven called foster care has—or will—become a permanent way of life.

In 1997 Congress enacted the Adoption and Safe Families Act (ASFA), which shifts the "paramount concern" of the public child welfare system from "family preservation" to promoting a child's "health and safety." A major objective of ASFA is to move children out of foster care more expeditiously. ASFA intends to accomplish this by (1) easing procedural obstacles to achieving permanency, (2) encouraging "concurrent planning," (3) imposing strict time limits for determining whether "reasonable efforts" should be made to reunify children and their parents or, instead, whether parental rights should be terminated and "reasonable efforts" be made to place children with an adoptive family, a permanent guardian, or in "an alternative permanent living arrangement," and (4) providing financial incentives to public agencies that increase the number of finalized adoptions of children in their care.

Along with other recent federal child welfare initiatives, ASFA favors "concurrent planning" for children who enter the public child welfare system. With concurrent planning, reasonable efforts to reunify children and their parents occur simultaneously with efforts to find a permanent adoptive home for children in the event that parental rights are eventually terminated. In cases in which caseworkers believe that reunification efforts will fail, a child's foster parents or kinship caregivers are often encouraged to consider becoming the child's adoptive parents.

Concurrent planning and other child welfare practices that allow or encourage foster parents to become adoptive parents represent a fundamental departure from child welfare practices of the past half century. Nowadays, as many as two-thirds of the children adopted from public agencies are adopted by their foster parents and 15–20 percent are likely to be adopted by their kinship caregiver. A majority of those who adopt children from public agencies are married couples, but in many states, nearly one-third are single women and a smaller percentage are single men or unmarried couples.

According to data submitted by most, but not all, states to the U.S. Department of Health and Human Services (USDHHS), the number of finalized adoptions of children from foster care has increased substantially since the mid-1990s to nearly 50,000 per year (GAO Report 2002 on ASFA). Although it is not possible from these data to determine whether this sharp increase is attributable to ASFA or to other policies and practices, this trend is likely to continue.

The newly adopted children consist of roughly equal numbers of girls and boys whose median age was six to seven. Most of these children had been in out-of-home care for three or more years before their parents' rights were terminated. They typically had to wait an additional eighteen months or more before their adoptions were completed.

Although disproportionate numbers of Black and Latino children still remain in foster or kinship care much longer than Caucasian children, at least 45 percent of the children now being adopted are Black and 13–15 percent are Latino. As many as 80 to 90 percent of these children have "special needs" that qualify them for adoption subsidies.

States receive a $4,000 "incentive payment" for each finalized adoption and $6,000 for each special needs adoption that exceeds a prior year's total number of finalized adoptions. Federal law does not prescribe how this incentive money is to be used, but California and the other states that have received the largest payments report that they are using the money for post-adoption services and recruitment of more foster and adoptive parents who are willing to take on the distinctive needs of many of the children waiting for permanency.

Despite the significant increases in the number of adoptions, especially by foster parents, and the shift in public policy to concurrent planning and more expeditious implementation of permanency plans, hundreds of thousands of children remain in out-of-home care. While in some states, most children are returned to their original families, ASFA data indicate that one-third or more of children who were returned to their families in 1998 had to be removed again.

As the number of children who spend much of their childhood in "temporary" foster care grows, it is hardly surprising that many of them become attached to their foster parent(s). Many foster parents believe it is unfair for the state to disrupt their foster families, especially when children are not being reunified with their legal parents but are simply being sent to another foster home. In addition to wanting to participate in judicial reviews of a child's dependent status—a right that ASFA gives them—many foster parents want party status or "standing" to petition on their own to become the child's adoptive parent, even over the objection of the state agency that prefers a different placement. As the following excerpts from federal and state court decisions illustrate, however, most courts have been reluctant to find a constitutionally, or even statutorily, protected interest in the foster child–foster parent relationship strong enough to prevent the state from removing a child from his or her foster family. By contrast, California courts have recognized the possibility that children may possess their own liberty interests in maintaining ties to the foster or other de facto parents who have cared for them for a substantial period of time.

Finally, part 3 explores the various tensions that may arise between foster care and adoption. Marsha Garrison and Gilbert A. Holmes favor placements for dependent children that will draw upon the resources in children's extended family networks, and will not sever their personal or legal ties to their original families; by contrast, Elizabeth Bartholet argues for prompt and permanent adoptive placements for maltreated children.

20

Smith v. Organization of Foster Families for Equality and Reform (O.F.F.E.R.) (U.S. 1977)

Justice *Brennan* delivered the opinion of the Court.

Appellees, individual foster parents and an organization of foster parents, brought this civil rights class action pursuant to 42 U.S.C. § 1983 in the United States District Court for the Southern District of New York, on their own behalf and on behalf of children for whom they have provided homes for a year or more. They sought declaratory and injunctive relief against New York State and New York City officials, alleging that the procedures governing the removal of foster children from foster homes violated the Due Process and Equal Protection Clauses of the Fourteenth Amendment. The District Court appointed independent counsel for the foster children to forestall any possibility of conflict between their interests and the interests asserted by the foster parents. A group of natural mothers of children in foster care were granted leave to intervene on behalf of themselves and others similarly situated.

A divided three-judge District Court concluded that "the pre-removal procedures presently employed by the State are constitutionally defective," holding that "before a foster child can be peremptorily transferred from the foster home in which he has been living, be it to another foster home or to the natural parents who initially placed him in foster care, he is entitled to a hearing at which all concerned parties may present any relevant information to the administrative decisionmaker charged with determining the future placement of the child," *Organization of Foster Families v. Dumpson*, 418 F.Supp. 277, 282 (1976). . . . We reverse.

I

A

The expressed central policy of the New York system is that "it is generally desirable for the child to remain with or be returned to the natural parent because the child's need for a normal family life will usually best be met in the natural home, and . . . parents are entitled to bring up their own children unless the best interests of the child would be thereby endangered," Soc. Serv. Law § 384-b(1)(a)(ii). . . . But the State has opted for foster care as one response to those situations where the natural parents are unable to provide the "positive, nurturing family relationships" and "normal family life in a permanent home" that offer "the best opportunity for children to develop and thrive." §§ 384-b(1)(b), (1)(a)(i).

Foster care has been defined as "[a] child welfare service which provides substitute family care for a planned period for a child when his own family cannot care for him for a temporary or extended period, and when adoption is neither desirable nor possible." Child Welfare League of America, Standards for Foster Family Care Service, 5 (1959). Thus, the distinctive features of foster care are, first, "that it is care in a family, it is noninstitutional substitute care," and, second, "that it is for a planned period either temporary or extended. This is unlike adoptive placement, which implies a permanent substitution of one home for another." . . .

Under the New York scheme children may be placed in foster care either by voluntary placement or by court order. . . .

. . . Foster parents, who are licensed by the State or an authorized foster-care agency, provide care under a contractual arrangement with the agency, and are compensated for their services. The typical contract expressly reserves the right of the agency to remove the child on request. Conversely, the foster parent may cancel the agreement at will.

The New York system divides parental functions among agency, foster parents, and natural parents, and the definitions of the respective roles are often complex and often unclear. The law transfers "care and custody" to the agency, but day-to-day supervision of the child and his activities, and most of the functions ordinarily associated with legal custody, are the responsibility of the foster parent. Nevertheless, agency supervision of the performance of the foster parents takes forms indicating that the foster parent does not have the full authority of a legal custodian. Moreover, the natural parent's placement of the child with the agency does not surrender legal guardianship; the parent retains authority to act with respect to the child in certain circumstances. The natural parent has not only the right but the obligation to visit the foster child and plan for his future; failure of a parent with capacity to fulfill the obligation for more than a year can result in a court order terminating the parent's rights on the ground of neglect. . . .

Children may also enter foster care by court order. The Family Court may order that a child be placed in the custody of an authorized child-care agency after a full adversary judicial hearing . . . if it is found that the child has been abused or neglected by his natural parents. . . . The consequences of foster-care placement by court order do not differ substantially from those for children voluntarily placed, except that the parent is not entitled to return of the child on demand. . . .

B

The provisions of the scheme specifically at issue in this litigation come into play when the agency having legal custody determines to remove the foster child from the foster home, either because it has determined that it would be in the child's best interests to transfer him to some other foster home, or to return the child to his natural parents in accordance with the statute or placement agreement. Most children are removed in order to be transferred to another foster home. The procedures by which foster parents may challenge a removal made for that purpose differ somewhat from those where the removal is made to return the child to his natural parent[, but none of these procedures requires an adjudicatory hearing]. . . .

C

Foster care of children is a sensitive and emotion-laden subject, and foster-care programs consequently stir strong controversy. . . .

The extent to which supposedly "voluntary" placements [especially of minority children from impoverished families] are in fact voluntary has been questioned . . . it has been said that many . . . placements are in fact coerced by threat of neglect proceedings and are not in fact voluntary in the sense of the product of an informed consent. Mnookin I 599, 601. Studies also suggest that social workers of middle-class backgrounds, perhaps unconsciously, incline to favor continued placement in foster care with a generally higher-status family rather than return the child to his natural family, thus reflecting a bias that treats the natural parents' poverty and lifestyle as prejudicial to the best interests of the child. . . .

. . . The District Court found as a fact that the median time spent in foster care in New York was over four years. 418 F.Supp., at 281. Indeed, many children apparently remain in this "limbo" indefinitely. Mnookin II 226, 273. The District Court also found that the longer a child remains in foster care, the more likely it is that he will never leave [quotation omitted]. It is not surprising then that many children, particularly those that enter foster care at a very early age and have little or no contact with their natural parents during extended stays in foster care, often develop deep emotional ties with their foster parents.

Yet such ties do not seem to be regarded as obstacles to transfer of the child from one foster placement to another. The record in this case indicates that nearly 60% of the children in foster care in New York City have experienced more than one placement, and about 28% have experienced three or more [citations omitted]. The intended stability of the foster-home management is further damaged by the rapid turnover among social work professionals who supervise the foster-care arrangements on behalf of the State [citations omitted]. Moreover, even when it is clear that a foster child will not be returned to his natural parents, it is rare that he achieves a stable home life through final termination of parental ties and adoption into a new permanent family. . . .

. . . Our task is only to determine whether the District Court correctly held that the present procedures preceding the removal from a foster home of children resident there a year or more are constitutionally inadequate. To that task we now turn. . . .

II

A

... Our inquiry is ... narrowed to the question whether the [foster parents and children's] asserted interests are within the "liberty" protected by the Fourteenth Amendment.

The appellees' basic contention is that when a child has lived in a foster home for a year or more, a psychological tie is created between the child and the foster parents which constitutes the foster family the true "psychological family" of the child. See J. Goldstein, A. Freud, & A. Solnit, Beyond the Best Interests of the Child (1973). That family, they argue, has a "liberty interest" in its survival as a family protected by the Fourteenth Amendment. Cf. *Moore v. City of East Cleveland,* 431 U.S. 494. Upon this premise they conclude that the foster child cannot be removed without a prior hearing satisfying due process. Appointed counsel for the children, appellants in No. 76-5200, however, disagrees, and has consistently argued that the foster parents have no such liberty interest independent of the interests of the foster children, and that the best interests of the children would not be served by procedural protections beyond those already provided by New York law. The intervening natural parents of children in foster care, appellants in No. 76-5193, also oppose the foster parents, arguing that recognition of the procedural right claimed would undercut both the substantive family law of New York, which favors the return of children to their natural parents as expeditiously as possible, see supra, at 2099, and their constitutionally protected right of family privacy, by forcing them to submit to a hearing and defend their rights to their children before the children could be returned to them. ...

It is, of course, true that "freedom of personal choice in matters of ... family life is one of the liberties protected by the Due Process Clause of the Fourteenth Amendment." *Cleveland Board of Education v. LaFleur,* 414 U.S. 632, 639–640, 94 S.Ct. 791, 796, 39 L.Ed.2d 52 (1974). There does exist a "private realm of family life which the state cannot enter," *Prince v. Massachusetts,* 321 U.S. 158, 166, 64 S.Ct. 438, 442, 88 L.Ed. 645 (1944), that has been afforded both substantive and procedural protection. But is the relation of foster parent to foster child sufficiently akin to the concept of "family" recognized in our precedents to merit similar protection? Although considerable difficulty has attended the task of defining "family" for purposes of the Due Process Clause, [citations omitted], we are not without guides to some of the elements that define the concept of "family" and contribute to its place in our society.

First, the usual understanding of "family" implies biological relationships, and most decisions treating the relation between parent and child have stressed this element. ... A biological relationship is not present in the case of the usual foster family. But biological relationships are not exclusive determination of the existence of a family. The basic foundation of the family in our society, the marriage relationship, is of course not a matter of blood relation. Yet its importance has been strongly emphasized in our cases. ...

... No one would seriously dispute that a deeply loving and interdependent relationship between an adult and a child in his or her care may exist even in the absence of blood relationship. At least where a child has been placed in foster care as an infant, has never known his natural parents, and has remained continuously for several years in the care of the same foster parents, it is natural that the foster family should hold the same place in the emotional life of the foster child, and fulfill the same socializing functions, as a natural family. For this reason, we cannot dismiss the foster family as a mere collection of unrelated individuals. Cf. *Village of Belle Terre v. Boraas,* 416 U.S. 1 (1974).

But there are also important distinctions between the foster family and the natural family. First, unlike the earlier cases recognizing a right to family privacy, the State here seeks to interfere, not with a relationship having its origins entirely apart from the power of the State, but rather with a foster family which has its source in state law and contractual arrangements. . . . While the Court has recognized that liberty interests may in some cases arise from positive-law sources, [citation omitted], in such a case, and particularly where, as here, the claimed interest derives from a knowingly assumed contractual relation with the State, it is appropriate to ascertain from state law the expectations and entitlements of the parties. In this case, the limited recognition accorded to the foster family by the New York statutes and the contracts executed by the foster parents argue against any but the most limited constitutional "liberty" in the foster family.

A second consideration related to this is that ordinarily procedural protection may be afforded to a liberty interest of one person without derogating from the substantive liberty of another. Here, however, such a tension is virtually unavoidable. Under New York law, the natural parent of a foster child in voluntary placement has an absolute right to the return of his child in the absence of a court order obtainable only upon compliance with rigorous substantive and procedural standards, which reflect the constitutional protection accorded the natural family. . . . Moreover, the natural parent initially gave up his child to the State only on the express understanding that the child would be returned in those circumstances. These rights are difficult to reconcile with the liberty interest in the foster family relationship claimed by appellees. It is one thing to say that individuals may acquire a liberty interest against arbitrary governmental interference in the family-like associations into which they have freely entered, even in the absence of biological connection or state-law recognition of the relationship. It is quite another to say that one may acquire such an interest in the face of another's constitutionally recognized liberty interest that derives from blood relationship, state-law sanction, and basic human right, an interest the foster parent has recognized by contract from the outset. Whatever liberty interest might otherwise exist in the foster family as an institution, that interest must be substantially attenuated where the proposed removal from the foster family is to return the child to his natural parents.

As this discussion suggests, appellees' claim to a constitutionally protected liberty interest raises complex and novel questions. It is unnecessary for us to resolve those questions definitively in this case, however, for like the District Court, we conclude that "narrower grounds exist to support" our reversal. We are persuaded that, even on the assumption that appellees have a protected "liberty interest," the District Court erred in holding that the preremoval procedures presently employed by the State are constitutionally defective.

21

In re G.C. (Pa. 1999)

Zappala, J.

The sole issue before us on appeal is whether foster parents have standing to seek or contest awards of custody concerning their foster children. The Superior Court held that they do not have standing. We affirm.

On July 24, 1992, G.C. was born to Amy Pursel and Travis C. On September 21, 1992, G.C. was admitted to Geisinger Medical Center suffering from trauma, bruising around his left eye, a torn upper frenulum and a displaced left parietal skull. On the same day G.C. was admitted to the emergency room, Northumberland County Children and Youth Services (CYS) received anonymous information indicating that G.C.'s injuries were a direct result of serious child abuse. This allegation was later confirmed by a CYS investigation and independent medical evidence. Five individuals were named by the anonymous source as possible perpetrators of the abuse; one of the named individuals was G.C.'s maternal grandfather, David Pursel.

On September 25, 1992, upon his release from the hospital, G.C. was placed in the care of Appellants, foster parents approved by CYS. G.C. was adjudicated dependent and legal custody was awarded to CYS pursuant to the Juvenile Act, 42 Pa.C.S. § 6351. Following G.C.'s placement with Appellants, supervised weekly visits were scheduled at their home with G.C.'s natural parents and with his maternal grandfather, David Pursel. In March of 1993, David Pursel petitioned the court to place G.C. with him. This request was denied but G.C. was permitted to visit with David Pursel and his wife at their home beginning in September of 1993.

G.C.'s natural parents, without the consent or knowledge of CYS, asked Appellants if they would adopt G.C. and Appellants agreed. On February 4, 1994, CYS requested that Amy Pursel voluntarily relinquish her parental rights and she agreed to do so on the condition that Appellants be permitted to adopt G.C. CYS refused the condition and further decided that G.C. would not be placed with Appellants. On May 24, 1994, David Pursel filed a petition seeking physical custody of G.C. Appellants filed their own petition to retain physical custody of G.C. After hearings, at which Appellants were granted provisional standing in order to develop an adequate record, the court granted physical custody of G.C. to David Pursel; legal custody remained with CYS. Appellants appealed this decision. . . .

The Superior Court has addressed the issue of foster parent standing in a number of cases in a number of different contexts. In determining whether foster parents have standing, the court's primary focus in all cases has been on the nature of the foster parent/child relationship as established by the Legislative scheme. In *In re Adoption of*

Crystal D.R., 480 A.2d 1146 (1984), the court addressed the issue of whether foster parents have standing to file petitions for the termination of parental rights. . . .

In rejecting the argument made by the foster parents that they stood *in loco parentis* to the child, the court, generally, addressed the nature of the foster parent/child relationship. The agency, while transferring physical custody to the foster parents, remains responsible for the care of the child, and may at any time be required by the child's interests to regain physical custody and terminate the foster parent's relationship to the child. . . .

The Legislature has further defined the nature of the foster parent/child relationship by setting forth how the agency is to supervise the performance of the foster parents. Before a child may be placed in a foster home, the home must be approved by the agency. If their home is approved, the foster parents are paid for providing care for the child. The agency supervises the placement, which entails enforcing regulations governing the child's health, safety, and discipline, and in appropriate circumstances the agency may remove the child from the foster home. . . .

Based on the foregoing, the court in *Crystal* observed that "[t]he Legislature has provided that the relationship between the foster parents and the child is by its very nature subordinate both to the relationship between the agency and the child and to the relationship between the child and the child's parents." . . . The *Crystal* court further noted the following:

> [F]oster parents may not by pleading their love for the child escape their legal status. For in defining the foster parents' status as subordinate both to the agency's and to the child's parents', the Legislature has in no sense acted arbitrarily. Quite to the contrary, the foster parents' status reflects the Legislature's conviction that if possible, a child should grow up with its parents. . . . When foster parents enter into their relationship with the child, they know that the relationship is temporary; the agency has the authority to remove the child; and that the parents have the right to visit the child.

. . . Thus, the court held the foster parents lacked standing to petition for the termination of parental rights. . . .

By its very nature, the foster parent/child relationship "implies a warning against any deep emotional involvement with the child since under the given insecure circumstances this would be judged as excessive." . . .

We are persuaded by the overwhelming analysis of the [lower courts] regarding the uniquely limited and subordinate, state-created, agency-maintained, foster parent/child relationship established through the Legislative scheme, that foster parents lack standing to seek or contest custody of their foster children.

22

Rodriguez v. McLoughlin (S.D.N.Y. 1999), Reversed (2d Cir. N.Y. 2000)

U.S. District Court Opinion (1999)

Wood, J.

This action arises out of Cardinal McCloskey Children's and Family Services' ("McCloskey") removal of a former foster child, Les Andrew Kelly ("Andrew"), on an alleged emergency basis from the home of his former foster, now adoptive, mother, Sylvia Rodriguez, on March 18, 1994. Sylvia Rodriguez, individually and on behalf of her son Andrew, alleges under 42 U.S.C. § 1983 that the removal of Andrew violated their right to procedural due process guaranteed by the Due Process Clause of the Fourteenth Amendment because (1) the circumstances of Ms. Rodriguez's foster children . . . did not justify an emergency removal, and therefore she was entitled to notice and an opportunity to be heard prior to their removal, (2) Ms. Rodriguez was not provided with either adequate post-removal notice or opportunity to be heard to contest the removal, and (3) Ms. Rodriguez was not provided an adequate opportunity to be heard to contest the denial of her request to visit Andrew. Defendants move to dismiss the complaint with prejudice . . . or, in the alternative, for summary judgment. . . .

[This case] presents the Court with a series of novel and difficult questions concerning the scope and character of the procedural protections of the Due Process Clause of the Fourteenth Amendment in the context of an alleged emergency removal of a child from a New York foster mother who was in the final stages of adopting her foster child, whom she had cared for continuously since his first weeks of infancy. . . . [T]he Court holds that there is a constitutionally protected liberty interest in the stability and integrity of the relationship between such a foster mother and foster child. Further, the Court also holds that the delay in providing Ms. Rodriguez with notice and an opportunity to be heard to contest (1) the removal and (2) the denial of Ms. Rodriguez's request to visit Andrew for approximately three months following the removal violated the Due Process Clause's fundamental requirement that an aggrieved party be provided with an opportunity to be heard "at a meaningful time and in a meaningful manner." However, the Court grants defendants' motion for summary judgment as to plaintiff's claims that there was no basis for emergency removal. . . .

Procedural Due Process

LIBERTY INTEREST IN PRE-ADOPTIVE FOSTER CARE RELATIONSHIP

Plaintiff asserts that she has a constitutionally protected liberty interest in the integrity and stability of her pre-adoptive foster care relationship. Specifically, plaintiff argues that there is a constitutionally protected liberty interest in the continuity of a foster care relationship where, as here, the foster parent has cared for the foster child for several years continuously from the child's infancy, the foster child had not known any other parent, the biological parents' parental rights over the child were terminated, and the foster parent had applied to adopt the foster child. . . .

The instant case presents difficult issues of whether due process protection extends to a parent-child relationship that has its origin in state law and contract, but in which emotional and psychological ties hoped for in biological families, as well as an expectation of permanency, have developed. [See *Smith v. O.F.F.E.R.*]. . . .

. . . Ms. Rodriguez's relationship with Andrew seems to present a relatively strong case for the recognition of a liberty interest in a foster parent's relationship with her foster child. . . . [U]nlike the foster parents in decisions subsequent to *O.F.F.E.R.* that have found that foster parents do not have a liberty interest in their relationships with their foster children, as a prospective adoptive parent who had entered into an Adoptive Placement Agreement, Ms. Rodriguez cannot be said to have expected her relationship with Andrew to end. By entering into the Adoptive Placement Agreement, the State (through McCloskey) expressed its interest in Andrew's adoption by Ms. Rodriguez, so long as McCloskey continued to view adoption as in Andrew's best interest. Hence, while Ms. Rodriguez's expectations as to Andrew at the outset of her relationship with him were not necessarily permanent, by the time that she entered the Adoptive Placement Agreement, such intentions and expectations of permanency had formed.

Second Circuit Court of Appeals Opinion,
Reversing the District Court (2000)

Kearse, J.

On appeal, all defendants contend principally that the district court erred in ruling that plaintiffs have a cognizable liberty interest. . . . For the reasons that follow, we conclude that Rodriguez and Andrew did not possess a liberty interest in their foster-parent-and-child relationship, and we therefore reverse the judgment and order of the district court and remand for dismissal of the complaint.

A liberty interest may arise from either of "two sources—the Due Process Clause itself [or] the laws of the States." [Citations omitted.] Among the liberty interests that may arise under the Due Process Clause itself is "freedom of personal choice in matters of . . . family life." *Smith v. O.F.F.E.R.* . . .

... [T]he reasoning [in *O.F.F.E.R.*] leads us to the conclusion that any liberty interest arising in the preservation of a biologically unrelated foster family would arise, if at all, only under state law and not under the Due Process Clause itself. Accordingly, we turn to the question of whether plaintiffs had a liberty interest created by New York law.

Mere expectations do not necessarily give rise to a state-created liberty interest protected by the Due Process Clause. [Citations omitted.] "[T]he most common manner in which a State creates a liberty interest is by establishing 'substantive predicates' to govern official decisionmaking . . . and, further, by mandating the outcome to be reached upon a finding that the relevant criteria have been met." [Citations omitted.] . . .

Further, the search for specific substantive directives to the decisionmaker is context-specific. . . . Finally, the fact that a state has established procedures to be followed does not mean that it has created a protectable liberty interest.

. . . We see in [the New York statutory provisions relied on by the district court] no language providing substantive predicates for, or substantive limitations on, the exercise of official discretion with respect to matters of removal or visitation. The provisions . . . confer on foster parents certain procedural rights—the rights to intervene in a custody proceeding, to petition for adoption, and to receive notice that a child in their care has been made available for adoption or freed for adoption. But, under the principles discussed above, the establishment of these merely procedural requirements—even if they purported to govern visitation matters, which they do not, or to govern removal unrelated to possible adoption proceedings . . . do not suffice to create the liberty interests asserted by plaintiffs. [The provisions] give foster parents a "preference" or "priority" over another applicant seeking to adopt a child if the child has been in the foster parents' custody for at least 12 months. While these provisions doubtless encourage foster parents to adopt their foster children, they do not purport to deal with, much less create substantive rights with respect to, a foster child's removal, return, or visitation. . . .

Finally, [the] provision . . . which affords an adoption subsidy for children who are "hard to place," undeniably gives an incentive for potential adoptive parents to become foster parents as a means to adoption, and thereby helps to implement New York's policy favoring foster parenting as a precursor to adoption. But, despite its reference to a "separation from the foster parent(s)," it imposes no relevant substantive limitations on official discretion with respect to matters of removal and visitation. We cannot conclude that [this provision] gives a subsidy recipient the liberty interests claimed by Rodriguez.

Plaintiffs also cite a State regulation that provides that "efforts to remove a child from the care and custody of his biological parent, adoptive parent, or legal guardian shall be undertaken only when it is clearly established that such action is in such child's best interest." . . . Although Rodriguez falls within the regulations' definition of "adoptive parent" . . . as including "a person with whom a child has been placed for adoption", she cannot avail herself of [this regulation] because, as the Adoptive Placement Agreement makes clear, Andrew was not in Rodriguez's custody. Custody remained with McCloskey, and thus the regulation governing removals of a child from a parent or guardian's "care and custody" was inapplicable to Rodriguez.

In sum, none of the statutory or regulatory sections called to our attention contains any substantive predicates or explicitly mandatory language giving directives to decisionmakers as to the cohabitation or visitation rights of a foster mother and child in the wake of an emergency removal of the child from the foster home. We cannot conclude that these provisions are sufficient to give plaintiffs the liberty interests they assert.

Finally, we are unpersuaded that a protectable liberty interest was created by the fact that Rodriguez and McCloskey had entered into the Adoptive Placement Agreement. Though the district court found that that Agreement created in Rodriguez expectations of permanence, the terms of the Agreement made clear that adoption was not a foregone conclusion and that the agency retained both custody of Andrew and discretion to determine whether his best interest would be served by effectuating the adoption or by removal from the foster home. . . .

Thus, the Agreement was explicit that the agency, not Rodriguez, was Andrew's legal custodian and would remain so until the adoption was finalized. We see no contractual provisions placing substantive limitations on the agency's judgment as to whether adoption or removal would be in the best interest of the child. We cannot conclude that the State's standard form Adoptive Placement Agreement so augmented the statutory and regulatory provisions as to give plaintiffs a liberty interest in the foster relationship prior to the adoption's finalization. . . .

We have considered all of plaintiffs' arguments on this appeal and have found in them no basis to conclude that plaintiffs have shown a liberty interest protected by the Due Process Clause. The judgment is reversed and the matter is remanded for dismissal of the complaint.

23

In re Jasmon O. (Cal. 1994)

Mosk, J.

Jasmon O. is now seven and a half years old. She has resided with her foster parents, who wish to adopt her, since she was an infant of six months. Her natural father asserts that it is in Jasmon's best interests not to terminate his parental rights but to transfer Jasmon's custody to him.

A court hearing an action to terminate parental rights . . . must consider, when a child has been in an out-of-home placement . . . for a year, whether "return of the child to the child's parent or parents would be detrimental to the child" and whether "the parent or parents have failed during that period, and are likely to fail in the future, to maintain an adequate parental relationship with the child." We conclude that there was sufficient evidence in this case to support the trial court's conclusion that detriment to the child and parental inadequacy warranted termination of the father's parental rights. . . . Finally, we conclude that the Court of Appeal erred in holding that a court . . . may not find that the child's best interests require the setting aside of an earlier juvenile court order on the basis of evidence that the child will suffer long-term, serious emotional damage if the bond with foster parents is severed. Accordingly, the judgment of the Court of Appeal is reversed. . . .

We have no quarrel with the assertion that the existence of a successful relationship between a foster child and foster parent cannot be the sole basis for terminating parental rights or depriving the natural parent of custody in a dependency proceeding. The evidence here was of a different order. It established that the severing of the bond with the foster parents would do serious, long-term emotional damage to Jasmon. . . .

. . . [A]fter a lengthy period of foster care initially made necessary because both parents were quite unfit to care for their child, evidence that the attempt to transfer custody from the foster parents to the natural parent has caused the child to develop serious mental illness may establish that it is not in the child's best interests to be returned to the natural parent. Although courts determining a child's best interests . . . should carefully evaluate whether a child's distress in severing a temporary bond is simply situational, and not base their decisions on a transitory problem, courts may place great weight on evidence that after a substantial period in foster care, the severing of a bond with the foster parents will cause long-term, serious emotional damage to the child.

We reach this conclusion because we are of the opinion that when a child has been placed in foster care because of parental neglect or incapacity, after an extended period of foster care, it is within the court's discretion to decide that a child's interest in stability has come to outweigh the natural parent's interest in the care, custody and companionship of the child. (*In re Marilyn H.,* 5 Cal.4th at pp. 307–309.)

The parent has a fundamental right to maintain the parent-child bond and to the care, custody and companionship of his or her child. [Citations omitted.] However, the right is not absolute and may be abridged when it is necessary to do so to protect the welfare of the child. . . . Thus, in this case, no one would dispute that it was necessary to abridge the natural father's right to the care and companionship of his child when she was placed in the foster home, and for an extended period thereafter, because the father was unable to care for the child.

Children, too, have fundamental rights—including the fundamental right to be protected from neglect and to "have a placement that is stable [and] permanent." [Citations omitted.] Children are not simply chattels belonging to the parent, but have fundamental interests of their own that may diverge from the interests of the parent.

Our task is to interpret the statutory scheme as a whole in a manner that balances the interest of parents and children in each other's care and companionship, with the interest of abandoned and neglected children in finding a secure and stable home.

24

Parents' Rights vs. Children's Interests
The Case of the Foster Child

Marsha Garrison

[T]he case of the foster child . . . is an interesting case because, in contrast to the general emphasis on relationship protection that has characterized advocacy on behalf of children, advocates have here argued in favor of faster and easier termination of the parent-child relationship. . . . In divorce, the child's relationship with a noncustodial parent is almost invariably described as a positive factor in her development that should be encouraged and facilitated; termination of the parental relationship is approved only in extreme cases where the parent threatens the child's health or safety. In foster care, however, the noncustodial parent is typically seen as a threat to the child's relationship with her foster parent or her opportunity to obtain adoptive parents; termination of parental rights is urged whenever the child's return home cannot be accomplished quickly.

Termination vs. Preservation of Parental Contact:
Which Serves Children's Interests?

. . . Parents whose children enter foster care are less likely to exhibit capable parenting than those who divorce, but the available evidence does not suggest that parental capacity affects the strength of the parent-child relationship. . . .
. . . [W]hile foster care and divorce are clearly different and we lack research providing direct comparisons, there is much to suggest that, from the perspective of the child, these two situations present more similarities than differences. In each case, a parental attachment must be maintained through visitation rather than day-to-day contact. . . .

Why Has Adoption Been Preferred to Alternatives
That Preserve the Parent-Child Relationship?

One reason for preferring adoption over continued foster care is their comparative cost. Foster care is expensive. If the child is adopted by parents who can afford to pay

his keep, he costs the state nothing, and even subsidized adoption is cheaper than foster care. But while the savings that adoption can achieve have undoubtedly contributed to its popularity, both open adoption and foster guardianship could achieve
these same results.

Traditional adoption is a widely recognized legal concept while open adoption and
foster guardianship are new approaches, with less certain procedures and results. . . .

A more important reason why traditional adoption has been preferred to its alternatives, I suspect, is its greater appeal to prospective adoptive parents. . . .

The comparative costs of adoption vs. foster care, the altered adoption market, and
the interests of prospective adoptive parents undoubtedly have an interactive effect.
Most of the adoptive parents who might save the state money want a child that is exclusively their own. Termination of parental rights followed by adoption thus meets
both the fiscal needs of the state and the desires of a well-organized and sympathetic
adult interest group.

In addition to serving confluent state and adult interests, adoption offers powerful
symbolic benefits to children. An adoption order provides a legal rebirth—complete
with a new name and identity—into a new family. The child who is adopted is thus
legally reincarnated. Because adoption symbolically grants the child the good parents
and good life she previously lacked, that legal reincarnation has a redemptive quality
not unlike a baptismal or conversion experience.

The symbolic benefits conferred by adoption are magnified by the stigma attached
to foster care status. Foster care is a form of public assistance that denotes family failure and entails ongoing state supervision. The parents of children in foster care placement are almost invariably from the bottom of the socioeconomic ladder, while adoptive parents are typically middle-class; intact, two-parent families are almost as common among adoptive parents as they are rare among those whose children go into
placement. Adoption thus offers a permanent improvement in socioeconomic status
in a socially preferred family structure. . . .

It is natural that children's advocates should wish to confer these benefits—a sense
of belonging, the right to feel part of the family, a symbolic rebirth into a happier,
more secure life—upon deprived children. It is these intangible, and generally unexamined, aspects of adoption that have, in my view, ensured its appeal. . . .

Because the symbolic benefits of adoption have been largely intuited, their cost and
consequences have been largely ignored. Indeed, children's advocates have not even
noted that these symbolic benefits derive from the same notion of parental rights as
property-like entitlements that they ordinarily wish to disavow. After adoption, the
child belongs to a new set of parents, who have the right to curtail his contacts with
his former family. The state of belonging implies emotional certainty; but it also implies ownership. The current preference for adoption over alternatives that preserve
the parental relationship thus serves to preserve and replicate the same rigid, exclusive
definition of parentage that children's advocates have elsewhere disfavored.

Conclusion

. . . [T]he symbolic benefits conferred on foster children through adoption have been purchased at a very considerable price and have obscured the very real benefits conferred on both the state and adult adoptive parents. The denigration of foster care contributes to the widespread acceptance of cheap foster care alternatives that subject children to more risks than they prevent and to rigid, abstract decision making that ignores the realities of many foster children's lives. Obtaining the symbolic benefits of adoption also requires the sacrifice of children's real emotional needs, a tragic choice that we do not impose on the more privileged children outside the foster care system. Perhaps we can do no better, but certainly we should not congratulate ourselves that the current approach represents what is best. It is preferable to make tragic choices consciously than to pretend that there is no tragedy and no choice.

25

When Children Cannot Remain Home
Foster Family Care and Kinship Care

Jill Duerr Berrick

Foster care is designed to provide temporary care, supervision, and support to children who cannot live at home because they have been abused or neglected by their parents.... As the number of families reported to child welfare authorities has rapidly increased [to more than one million a year since the mid-1990s], so has the number of children requiring substitute care. The substitute care population increased from 276,000 children in 1985 to approximately 494,000 children a decade later.

When children are removed from their homes, they may be placed in a variety of settings. In many states, foster family care has been the predominant form of substitute care for several decades....

A growing proportion of children in the foster care system are cared for by their relatives. Relatives have no legal obligation to become children's caregivers, but kin are increasingly likely to exercise their responsibility to their extended family members. In some states, child welfare authorities recognize kin as foster caregivers within the child welfare system only if they participate in training and become licensed in the same manner as foster parents. In other states, preferences for kin have been written into legal statutes. In California, the preference encompasses kin who have not been licensed or trained by child welfare authorities. These differences in philosophy and policy result in great variability in the use of kinship care among states....

Changing Attitudes

... Traditionally, child welfare workers and judges have harbored significant ambivalence about placement with relatives, concerned that the maltreating parent's parenting practices were learned through interactions with members of a dysfunctional immediate or extended family. More recently, increasing numbers of child welfare workers have embraced the philosophical shift that values placement within the family, and that focuses on the strengths, rather than the deficits, of family members. Enthusiasm for kinship foster care has paralleled an overall trend in child welfare services toward more family-centered, community-based services to families. . . .

Financial Incentives

. . . [T]he introduction of payments for kinship caregivers may have profoundly changed child welfare placements. When a child whose family was eligible for cash assistance (formerly Aid to Families with Dependent Children, or AFDC) is placed in foster care, the caregiver receives federally funded foster care payments to help offset the costs of maintenance and care of the child. . . . In 1979, the U.S. Supreme Court ruled that kin should be eligible to receive these payments under specified conditions similar to those imposed on non-kin foster parents. Interpretations of this ruling have led to different financial reimbursement policies in various states: in some, kin receive these payments only if they meet the same licensing standards as nonkin foster parents. Other states have developed more lenient approval standards for kin. . . .

. . . The difference in monthly payments may be great, depending upon the number and ages of the children in care, and whether the kinship caregiver qualifies for welfare as an adult. . . .

. . . Many states have lower welfare benefits, and there the difference between AFDC [now Temporary Assistance to Needy Families (TANF)] and the foster care subsidy is even greater. This disparity spawns concerns that the foster care payment system may act as an incentive for a troubled family to seek a formal agency-supervised placement with kin rather than sharing child-rearing responsibilities informally with the same relatives. . . .

New Practice Issues

Because kinship foster care has expanded so rapidly, it has changed child welfare practice in important ways. Child welfare workers have learned to negotiate the complex family dynamics between parents and caregivers; they have developed new service strategies guided by family preservation principles; and they have expanded conventional notions of what constitutes a permanent home to include long-term foster care with kin. Nevertheless, many children in kinship foster care are treated inequitably by the child welfare services system.

Evidence from a number of sources suggests that kinship foster parents receive less support, fewer services, and less contact with child welfare workers than foster family parents receive. These differences are problematic because kin foster caregivers are less advantaged than nonkin caregivers to start with. Studies show that kin are, in general, older and less financially stable; they are more likely to be single parents, and they have less education and poorer health. . . .

As kinship foster care grows rapidly across the nation, it bears close examination as a placement resource for children. . . .

Kinship Care and Child Protection

... One study set out to identify the characteristics associated with maltreatment in out-of-home care by studying a sample of foster homes. In about one-sixth of the homes, reports of maltreatment had been confirmed. The researchers discovered that nonkin foster parents were twice as likely as licensed kinship foster parents to have a confirmed report of maltreatment. These findings can be explained several ways. Maltreatment might be more readily discerned in nonrelative foster homes than in kinship homes because the former receive more services, and so are more often observed by child welfare workers. On the other hand, the children in the two types of homes might differ in ways that provoke different treatment from their caregivers. As the researchers note, "Selection could account for the results. Kin may choose to care for less disturbed children leaving for placement in regular care the most disturbed." While no child should be maltreated while in out-of-home care, it would not be surprising if those who cared for the most troubled children were also to find it most difficult to provide a safe and nurturing home.

Whether children in kinship care are less behaviorally or emotionally disturbed is a subject of some debate. Several studies that reviewed the characteristics of children placed in kinship foster care and nonrelative foster care found similarities among the children in health status, educational needs, and behavioral problems. However, other studies suggest that children placed with nonrelatives arrive in care with more severe developmental and behavioral problems. Kin may choose not to care for these children when asked to do so, because of their own age or health status. Such choices exercised by kin would reduce the proportion of especially challenging children found in kinship settings, and would make it less meaningful to directly compare rates of maltreatment in kin and nonrelative foster homes.

In addition to the fundamental measure of children's exposure to maltreatment while in out-of-home care, there are other indicators of protection from harm. ... The kin homes [in two studies] provided a similar level of safety, support, and supervision to children as did the nonrelative homes. Nevertheless, perhaps because of their relative poverty, inadequate access to resources, and insufficient training, the kinship foster parents were less likely to have materials or skills that would assist them in an emergency. ... Non-kin foster parents provided somewhat more desirable caregiving environments, although the care in both settings fell in the "average quality of care" range. ...

Kinship Care and Support for Families

If kinship foster care protects children's safety, does it also support families? By offering kinship care, the extended family serves as a resource during periods of family distress as it has during its long history in the United States and many other countries. Informal shared living arrangements between children and their extended families have been particularly prevalent within the African-American community. ...

Kinship care arranged informally by families therefore dwarfs the number of children placed in kinship foster care by government authorities.

Since a large number of children in the United States are reared by their relatives and kinship foster care mirrors this informal system, it is easy to assume that kinship foster care, by definition, is supportive of families. Certainly, kinship foster care can, as one author put it, "provide continuity, lessen the trauma of separation, preserve family ties, and offer growth and development within the context of a child's culture and community." And when the kinship caregiver selected for the child is a known and trusted relative, the child's extended family ties have indeed been maintained. The majority of kinship caregivers are grandmothers, who often already have close relationships with the children in care. Of course, blood relationships are not always meaningful to children, particularly to infants removed in the first months of life, whose conception of *family* is formed through relationships and over time. Notions of whether kinship care supports family ties should be considered from the child's perspective, as well as the parent's and relative's.

Kinship care is not the right answer for all families. For some kin, the burdens associated with child rearing represent a significant sacrifice at a time in the life cycle when additional supports and services are needed, but may not be available. One study found that kin caregivers were visited and called less frequently by caseworkers than other foster parents, and another discovered that more than one-quarter of kinship foster parents had had no contact with a caseworker in the previous year. Child welfare workers sometimes justify the inequities in service provision between kinship and foster caregivers by arguing that kin prefer fewer intrusions into their personal family lives. However, the disparities between kin and foster caregivers described above suggest that kin caregivers have an equal, if not greater, need for services and assistance.

26

Taking Adoption Seriously
Radical Revolution or Modest Revisionism?

Elizabeth Bartholet

This [article] is about the children who are growing up without true families—without, that is, families that are functioning to provide the kind of care and nurture that is essential to well being. It is about victims who are the children of victims. It is about children born to parents who are themselves the products of inadequate parenting, of poverty and unemployment, of drugs and alcohol, of violence at the hands of their mates or of strangers. It is about black children and white children, Latino, Native-American and Asian children. It is about children growing up in homes in which they are physically brutalized or sexually exploited. It is about children born damaged by drugs and alcohol used during their mothers' pregnancies, children in need of very special parenting to overcome the damage, but who are sent home to parents whose first love is their drug. It is about children who grow up parenting themselves and their siblings as best they can because the adults in their home are not mentally or emotionally capable of parenting. This [article] is about the children left to grow up in inadequate homes, but also about the children removed only to be placed in inadequate foster or institutional care. It is about those who will spend the rest of their childhood in state custody, and about those who will spend it bouncing back and forth between foster care and their homes of origin. These are Nobody's Children.

This [article] is also about the culture that makes it possible to see children as Nobody's, or Somebody Else's, and certainly Not Ours. It tells the story of how our child welfare policies came to place such a high value on keeping children in their families and communities of origin without regard to whether this works for children. It envisions a new culture in which the larger community assumes responsibility for the well-being of its children, a culture in which we understand children born to others as belonging not only to them, and not only to their kinship or racial groups, but to all of us. . . .

The Race/Class Problem

. . . [T]here's a problem in looking to the entire community to take care of all its children. We live in a society in which that community is segregated along race and class lines. The local villages are often black or Latino or white villages. The families in trouble, in which children are threatened with abuse and neglect, and from which children are removed to foster care, are disproportionately poor, and they come disproportionately from racial minority groups. If the state, representing the larger community, steps in to protect children, it intrudes on the lives of those already oppressed. If the state takes their children away, it takes the only thing many of these families feel they have in this world. If the state moves children from impoverished minority race families to families in the larger community, families outside the local village, families which may be in a better position to parent because they enjoy the luxury of decent jobs and housing and schools, is this the larger community stepping in to provide help? Or is this the ultimate form of exploitation? Is this class and race warfare?

There's another problem also. In a class and race segregated society, how do you get the well-off groups to care about the children who most need care—children it may be easy to think of as foreign "others." How do you get funds devoted to programs designed to prevent child maltreatment? How do you get people to step forward to offer their homes and their hearts, to become foster and adoptive parents to the children in need?

Race and class issues dominate policy in this area, although the issues are rarely addressed honestly in a way that illuminates for onlookers their power. Change is impossible unless we can face up to the issues. Debate has been silenced, and potential actors paralyzed, by fear of opening up wounds and triggering rage, fear of proposing or taking action which would victimize already victimized groups, and fear of being accused of racism and classism. . . .

The starting point for honest and meaningful debate has to be recognition that racial and social injustice is the problem at the core of child abuse and neglect. The parents who treat their children badly are themselves victims, and if we want to stop the vicious cycle, we need to create a society in which there is no miserable underclass, living in conditions which breed crime, violence, substance abuse and child maltreatment.

But at the same time we need to recognize that children who are abused and neglected, children who are growing up in foster and group homes, are also victims. Like their parents, they are often black and brown skinned victims, and they are generally poor. Keeping them in their families and their kinship and racial groups when they won't get decent care in those situations may alleviate guilt, but it isn't actually going to do anything to promote racial and social justice. It isn't going to help groups who are at the bottom of the socio-economic ladder to climb that ladder. It is simply going to victimize a new generation. Moving those children into nurturing homes will give them, at least, a chance to break the cycle. . . .

. . . Encouraging people who are in a position to provide good parenting to step forward, without regard to race or class or membership in the local village, encouraging them to see children born to others as children they feel responsible for, can be painted as a form of vicious exploitation. But that's not how I see it. It seems to me that if more members of the larger community thought of all the community's children as their responsibility, we'd have a lot better chance of creating the just society that is our goal.

Blood Bias and Family Autonomy Politics

At the core of current child welfare policies lies a powerful blood bias—the assumption that blood relationship is central to what family is all about. Parents have God-given or natural law rights to hold on to their progeny. Children's best interests can be equated with those of their parents because parents have a natural inclination to care for their young. These beliefs are deeply entrenched in our culture and our law. And they are common to the thinking of people from one end of the political spectrum to the other, although left and right may articulate different concerns. Some speak of children's rights to their roots and heritage. Others speak of adult rights to procreate and of parents' rights to guide and control the children they produce. But most share a deep sense that those children "belong" with and to their biological parents.

Also at the core is the related idea that the state must be kept from interfering with parent-child relationships and family privacy. Again left and right tend to agree on the overriding goal, while emphasizing different reasons, and motivated by different issues. Those concerned with poor and minority group interests are afraid that state intervention will discriminate against these groups, resulting in even greater oppression. Those concerned with women's interests are concerned that state intervention will discriminate against women, as they do most of the parenting. They welcome state intervention to protect women and children against violence by adult males, but oppose state intervention that might interfere with women's authority over their children. They promote women's privacy rights to protect against state intervention in the parenting arena as in the pregnancy arena, and for many of the same reasons.

Those concerned with individual liberty rights see state intervention in parenting relationships as a threat to individual autonomy. But just as left and right have joined in supporting the current system, individuals and groups from all parts of the political spectrum have come together in recent years to promote change, questioning the supremacy of family preservation policies, and promoting adoption as an important option for children. . . .

New Directions for the 21st Century? The Apparent Seachange

There has been an apparent seachange in attitudes toward family preservation, adoption and related issues of children's rights, in these final years of the 20th century. . . .

. . . Policy-makers in some states and localities have begun to introduce changes designed to free more children from abusive families and move more children stuck in foster limbo on to adoptive homes. Leading scholars in the child welfare research community have made a powerful case for limiting the excesses of family preservation and for placing a higher priority on children's developmental needs, and on permanency and adoption as the way to meet those needs.

Most dramatically, the federal government has passed legislation radically changing the rules of the game. The Multiethnic Placement Act, known as MEPA, was passed in 1994 with the goal of eliminating the racial barriers that stood in the way of placing black children in need of foster and adoptive homes. The MEPA was strengthened in 1996 to prevent federally funded agencies from using race at all in foster and adoption decisionmaking. Given that the near-universal policy and practice throughout the nation had been for child welfare agencies to place children with same-race families if at all possible, this law was truly revolutionary in concept.

Even more significant is the Adoption and Safe Families Act (ASFA) enacted in 1997. . . . The ASFA seems designed to create a new regime that places a much higher value on protecting children against abuse, and on giving them a permanent nurturing home at the earliest possible point in time. The ASFA tells child welfare agencies that they must make reasonable efforts not only to preserve families, but also to move children to permanency when preservation is not appropriate. The Act says, for example, that in certain egregious cases of torture or other extreme forms of abuse, and cases where parents have murdered a sibling, no efforts to preserve the family need be made, and states must file actions to terminate parental rights. It also creates strict time deadlines designed to limit the period children can be held in foster care for family reunification efforts, before they are moved on to adoptive or other permanent homes. The ASFA also creates a new emphasis on adoption as a positive option for children. It offers states financial bonuses for increased adoption rates, and it threatens them with financial penalties if they fail to live up to its various new rules.

Adoption is enjoying new popularity, and family preservation is under attack from a variety of different directions. But it remains unclear as we enter the 21st century whether the seachange is more apparent than real, and whether child welfare policies will actually undergo fundamental rather than cosmetic change.

27

The Extended Family System in the Black Community
A Child-Centered Model for Adoption Policy

Gilbert A. Holmes

[I]t was 1973 and I was a practicing attorney working for legal services in Brooklyn, New York. I represented birth parents in termination proceedings, and adoptive parents as well as birth parents in adoption cases. My clients were people of color—primarily African-American, and occasionally Hispanic. From the beginning, many clients and I felt that the system of termination and adoption was not operating correctly in providing stable homes for children. I worked with birth parents who knew that they had not or could not care for their children but were reluctant to surrender them. I saw children as young as four years old who had been abused and neglected by their birth parents and yet wanted to live with them. I represented birth parents (mainly fathers) who thought that the adoption of their children might be best because the mother had remarried, but who wanted a continuing relationship with their children, particularly when the children got older. However, neither legal doctrine nor policy had an adequate response for my clients.

At the same time, I was living with the impact of Flora and Claude Hall, my maternal grandparents. They became foster parents in the mid-1940s. I knew most of their foster children because I had grown up with them or they had come to visit my grandparents after they left the house. They were known to me as cousins or aunts and uncles, depending on their age. I also knew some of their birth parents because my grandmother, contrary to social services regulations, contacted the parents and allowed them to visit their children and our family, particularly during holidays. After my grandparents died, I purchased their house from my family, and these "cousins" and their children came to visit because both the house and I were part of their family. Additionally, some of the foster children became part of our family and attended family rites such as weddings and funerals. As a result, my view of family was always multi-adult/multi-parent, with children knowing their birth origins as well as their foster/adoptive family. Thus, when a judge said, in effect, "parental rights terminated, child freed for adoption," the result did not conform with reality—neither the reality of my, and many of my clients', experiences, nor the reality of the child's perception of who is in her family.

. . . Recognition of adopted children as part of a complex family structure raises questions about the propriety of current adoption policy that uses the simple nuclear family as its model. . . .

. . . I propose a child-centered adoption policy that acknowledges adopted children's place in a complex family structure that includes their adoptive and birth parents and their relatives, thus avoiding the inadequacies of existing policy regarding adopted children's adoptive and birth relationships. This article looks to the child rearing aspects of the extended family system in the Black community as a model of how a complex family structure operates. . . .

The Extended Family Experience in the African-American Community

The use of extended family members to support and enhance individuals, families, and cultures has a rich and diverse history. An extended family is one in which individual relationships extend beyond the conjugal family—spouses and children—and include daily interaction with, and responsibilities for, other family members such as aunts, uncles, grandparents, and cousins. The concept of the extended family is not unique to African-based communities. . . .

In studies on the extended family systems in African-based communities in general and African-American communities in particular, sociologists have identified three significant components affecting child-rearing: fostering of children with kin and non-kin households, expanding the family through fictive kin, and sharing parenting and child-rearing responsibilities for the betterment of children. Through these child-rearing components, African-based family systems viewed children as part of complex families in which multiple adults adopt parenting positions and children are aware of their birth origins. As a result, some sociologists have identified the Black extended family experience as particularly child-centered due to its emphasis on the survival of the child for the survival of the community.

These three child-rearing components of Black extended family systems promote the idea that children can benefit from numerous family relationships in as expansive a family as permissible. The inclusion of multiple kinship groups in children's lives provides a greater opportunity for growth and development through additional role models and more responsible parental/adult guidance. Sociologists have also studied the extended family experience in African-American communities because of the unique history of Africans in America, who have suffered through slavery, Jim Crow, de facto and de jure segregation, and discrimination in housing, employment, and education. These studies indicate that the complex family composition of the child-oriented extended family system in the Black communities in the United States significantly contributed to the survival and advancement of the children despite the social and political obstacles placed before them. . . .

. . . The slavery system often caused children to lose their parents. The loss could be temporary, through the voluntary or forced return of runaways, imprisonment, or the leasing out of slaves. Children could also lose their parents permanently, through runaways who never returned or through the sale or death of their parents. As a result, children often did not have parents who were able to provide direct and consistent care. When separations between parents and children occurred, other adults in the slave community who were in a position to rear and care for the child stepped in to assume the parental role. These adults were often related to the parents, but sometimes were not. These foster or surrogate parents who shared or assumed the child-rearing responsibilities generally acknowledged the role and responsibility of the birth parents, if they were available, to play a significant part in the rearing of the child. The magnitude of such shared child-rearing and the relative ease with which adults engaged in the conduct was a direct result of the common family experiences among enslaved Africans. During the sharing of the parental and child-rearing responsibilities, both the birth parent and the surrogate parent understood each other's roles. The acknowledgment of children's birth parents and family would also involve teaching children about their existing and pre-existing birth kinship group that was no longer available to them due to a permanent loss of the birth parents and families.

The African-based complex family system that provided care and maintenance to children continued as part of the Black community after slavery. In the post-slavery period, the Black extended family system continued practicing fosterage, using fictive kin to expand the family, and educating children regarding their birth kin regardless of who was actually raising them. In the rural South and through the urbanization of the northern cities, Black communities continued the African-based child-centered family traditions, using grandparents, aunts, uncles, and other relatives, both real and fictive, as needed to raise the children. . . .

A Child-Centered Adoption Policy and Its Implications

. . . A child-centered adoption policy, in general, is one that acknowledges the reality of an adopted child's family relationship structure as including adoptive and birth kin and avoids forcing adopted children into an adult-perceived legal fiction that is inconsistent with that reality. . . .

. . . A policy that does not consider adopted children's complex family composition creates a void in their lives in a manner similar to the way slavery created a void in the lives of enslaved African children and families. That void requires recognition and resolution, or it hovers like a ghost over the lives of adopted children. The void can affect a child as seriously as raising questions about genetic medical history or as lightly as mere curiosity about potential relatives in the world. A child-centered adoption policy acknowledges children's reality and refrains from imposing the void of ghost kin on children. In its approach to the adult-child relationships surrounding adoption, a child-centered policy would permit contact between adopted children and their birth kin. For birth parents, post-adoption contact could involve written communication about their children or include regular visitation and telephone contact. For adopted children, post-adoption contact could involve as little as obtaining information about their birth origins or as much as face-to-face visitation.

A child-centered adoption policy thereby offers children the full benefits of adoption. Children gain the stability of being in an intact family, the self assurance of knowing about their birth origins, and the long range benefits of security and trust between adopted children and their adoptive families, that comes from accepting the differences between adopted and non-adopted children.

IV

Adoption and Confidentiality

This part examines one aspect of the secrecy that surrounds adoption: the circumstances under which adoptees who have reached adulthood, and other members of adoptive and biological families, may obtain access to identifying information about each other from sealed records.

During the twentieth century, adoption became an increasingly secret process in this country. In most states, all court and agency records pertaining to the adoption process were sealed. Access was eventually denied, even to those who participated in an adoption, except upon a court order granted only for "good cause." The original purpose for sealing records, however, was not to prevent those involved in the adoption itself from having access to information, but to protect against the public's seeking access to these files to determine whether a child was born outside marriage. The early statutes were intended to keep the press and the general public from prying into court records, but did not bar birth or adoptive parents, or adoptees, from access to court or agency files. The 1917 Minnesota statute excerpted here was perhaps the first of these statutes; it restricted access to adoption court files to the "parties in interest and their attorneys and representatives of the state board of control."

Between the early twentieth century and the late 1960s, as explained in the articles by E. Wayne Carp and Elizabeth J. Samuels, there was a shift toward a more comprehensive sealing of records against access, even by adoptive parents, adoptees, and birth parents. Most states also issued new birth certificates for the adopted child that listed only the names of the adoptive parents and the child, and sealed the original certificates that contained the names of one or both birth parents.

Since the 1970s, many adoptees and their birth parents, along with a growing number of adoptive parents, have been challenging the confidentiality restrictions through judicial and legislative action and in the media. These challenges have prompted a dramatic shift in the policies of many adoption service providers. The excerpts in this part from the revised standards of the Child Welfare League of America exemplify these changing policies.

Adult adoptees cite health-related, medical, and psychological reasons for wanting to know the identity of their birth parents. Many are searching to fill in what they claim are missing parts of their identity, for an explanation of why they were relinquished for adoption, or to reassure their birth parents that they are well. Adoptees who seek information about their birth parents are generally not estranged from their adoptive families; indeed, in recent years many adoptive parents have supported their children's search efforts.

Every state now allows for the release of nonidentifying information to adoptees and their adoptive parents, thereby providing some recognition of the needs of adoptive parents for medical and other background material about their children.

In addition, in the final decades of the twentieth century, states established a variety of procedures for allowing some contact between adoptees and their birth families, based on evidence of mutual consent to disclosure. These procedures typically take one of two forms: first, voluntary registries, where information is released when a birth parent and an adoptee, after her eighteenth or twenty-first birthday, both file consent forms; or second, confidential intermediary systems, through which, if an adoptee or biological parent requests identifying information, the state has an affirmative obligation to search for and to request consent from the other party to the release of the information. In general, however, these procedures are cumbersome and underutilized, and fall short of the more direct access desired by many adult adoptees.

Only a few other states have joined Alaska and Kansas in allowing adoptees when they are eighteen or older to access their original birth certificates, even for adoptions completed decades ago. Several other states now permit access to original birth certificates for adoptees whose adoptions were completed since the late 1990s. According to a study of four states that recently began to allow adoptees access to their original birth certificates—Alabama, Delaware, Tennessee, and Oregon—within four years, more than fifteen thousand adult adoptees requested their birth records and an overwhelming number of birth parents—especially mothers—agreed to be contacted.

For older, foreign-born, and transracial adoptees, an insistence on complete replacement of birth families through a completely revised birth certificate makes the least sense. These adoptees apparently do best over time when their different heritages are acknowledged and accepted, as indicia not of second-class status, but of a welcome and prized diversity. The legal status of adoption does not erase the history of prior relationships from the memories of older children, nor does it resolve, by itself, the psychosocial conflicts these memories generate or perpetuate. Despite the growing awareness that adoptive relationships build upon, but do not displace, a child's heritage or previous experience, obstacles to learning about a child's background remain.

The debate over whether to allow access to original birth certificates and sealed adoption records is heated, as illustrated by the position papers of the National Council for Adoption, on the one hand, and of Bastard Nation (in the article by Janine Baer et al.), on the other. Allowing unrestricted access to birth records is often justified as allowing adoptees the same rights as any other individual to obtain an original birth certificate; opponents often claim that it violates the privacy rights of birth parents.

The materials in this part explore the rationales for sealing and opening birth records, together with the opportunities and challenges that arise when records are unsealed.

Adoption and Change of Name
General Statutes of Minnesota (1917)

7151. Adoption—Petition and consent—Any resident of the state may petition the district court of the county in which he resides for leave to adopt any child not his own. If the petitioner be married the spouse shall join in the petition. . . . A person of full age may be adopted.

7156. Decree—Change of name—If upon the hearing the court shall be satisfied as to the identity and relationship of the persons concerned, and that the petitioners are able to properly rear and educate the child, and that the petition should be granted, a decree shall be made and recorded in the office of the clerk, setting forth the facts, and ordering that from the date thereof the child shall be the child of the petitioners. If desired, the court, in and by said decree, may change the name of the child.

7157. Status of adopted child—Upon adoption such child shall become the legal child of the persons adopting him, and they shall become his legal parents, with all the rights and duties between them of natural parents and legitimate child. By virtue of such adoption, he shall inherit from his adopting parents or their relatives the same as though he were the legitimate child of such parents, and shall not owe his natural parents or their relatives any legal duty; and in case of his death intestate the adopting parents and their relatives shall inherit his estate, as if they had been his parents and relatives in fact.

7159. Records of adoption—The files and records of the court in adoption proceedings shall not be open to inspection or copy by other persons than the parties in interest and their attorneys and representatives of the state board of control, except upon an order of the court expressly permitting the same.

The Sealed Adoption Records Controversy in Historical Perspective

The Case of the Children's Home Society of Washington, 1895–1988

E. Wayne Carp

The central issue igniting the Adoption Rights Movement in 1971 was the inability of adopted persons to gain access to information about their birth families contained in adoption case records. Institutional custodians of adoption records—courts, hospitals, and adoption agencies—citing state statutes, some more than a half century old, refused to divulge any family information to adopted persons or birthparents searching for their biological kin. As early as 1917 Minnesota enacted legislation closing adoption records to public inspection, and other states soon followed. By 1943, spurred on by reformers wanting to protect the child born out of wedlock from the stigma of illegitimacy, 23 states had passed similar legislation sealing adoption records. By the early 1970s, sealed records had become a standard, if not universal, feature of the adoption process, but they had also achieved a seeming immutability that belied the past from which they emerged.

Not surprisingly, adoption rights activists assume that adoption records have always been sealed and that adoption agency officials have always been uncooperative in providing members of the adoption triad—adoptive parents, birthparents, and adopted persons—with family information. . . . But in fact, none of these assumptions is historically accurate. This article provides new information about a historical past that is all but unknown to historians, social workers, and proponents of unsealing adoption records. . . .

Data and Method

This article uses for the first time the confidential adoption case records of a twentieth-century adoption agency: the Children's Home Society of Washington (CHSW or Society). The records run consecutively from 1895 to 1973 when, because of the shortage of Caucasian infants, the Society all but ceased placing children for adoption. One out of every ten of the CHSW's 21,000 adoption case records has been examined for evidence of its administrative policies toward releasing family information. (Data that the Society has added to the case records on postadoption contact has been examined through 1988.) The study's sample yielded 463 cases, comprising 479 individuals who returned to the Society 599 times in quest of information about themselves, siblings, or birthparents. Thus, almost a quarter of all cases in this sample included postadoption contact. The case records have been supplemented by the Society's disorganized and incomplete minutes of supervisors' meetings, personnel files, and annual reports, dating mostly from the 1950s and 1960s.

This article is a case study. But corroborative evidence from the Child Welfare League of America (CWLA) and geographically diverse child placement agencies lends strong support that the CHSW's policies were not unique. . . .

The Society's Clients and Their Motivations for Postadoption Contact

Among its many tasks, Society officials provided returning clients with family information. Throughout the twentieth century, birthparents, adult adopted persons, and adoptive parents regularly contacted the Society for information about their birth families. The most frequent seekers of information were adult adopted persons, who constituted 51% of the sample, followed by birthmothers (19%), siblings of adopted persons (13%), adoptive parents (8%), birthfathers (4.5%), and birth relatives of the adopted child such as grandparents or aunts and uncles (4.5%).

Members of the adoption triad returned to the Society for different purposes. Adopted persons returned to the Society for three main reasons: to obtain copies of their birth certificates, to receive background and genetic information, and to contact members of their biological family. Of those requesting background or genetic information, the median age was twenty-three, and almost two-thirds were women. All birthmothers who contacted the Society wanted to know about their child's welfare: they asked about the baby's health or the character of the adoptive parents or requested the child's photograph. Birthmothers' median age when relinquishing their child was 20 years, and they usually returned to the CHSW within three years of placing the child for adoption. Siblings wanted to know the whereabouts of their brothers or sisters. Birthfathers and relatives, like birthmothers, sought information about the child's welfare. Adoptive parents returned to the Society seeking a birth certificate for their adopted child or information on the child's background and medical history. . . .

The Society's Postadoption Policy toward Adoption Triad Members

. . . The most notable aspect of the Society's policy toward birthparents before World War II is the openness with which it responded when they requested the whereabouts of their *grown* children. When dealing with a request about adoptees, Society officials acted as though they had a responsibility to reunite birthparents with their grown children. This was manifested in a number of ways. Sometimes, Society caseworkers facilitated reunions by personally conducting detailed searches for the adult children of birthparents. More commonly, however, the Society functioned with birthparents as a passive adoption disclosure registry. Case workers would inform birthparents that they would keep their letters of inquiry on file and if their child contacted the Society they would "be very happy to put him in touch with his mother."

Adult Adopted Persons

. . . Adult adopted persons were the primary beneficiaries of the CHSW's policy of freely divulging family information. As late as 1969, Society case workers gave *identifying* family information to adoptees upon request. . . .

Society caseworkers also eagerly assisted reunions of siblings who had been separated when young, though they made a sharp distinction between adult and underage siblings. . . .

Yet for all of its willingness to release family information and arrange reunions, the Society's policy toward adoptees was not one of "open records." The term is simply anachronistic before the era of the Adoption Rights Movement. Although social work experts asserted the child's right to family information, they never intended that adoptees should be allowed to read their own files. Nor were they prepared to reveal everything in the record. Even the most progressive social workers such as Grace Abbott, the Children's Bureau chief, counseled her compatriots that in certain circumstances professional social workers were responsible for *withholding* family information.

The Society's caseworkers adhered to professional social work principles by devising various strategies to limit the kind of information triad members received. They tried to prevent curious adoptees from discovering "unpleasant" truths about their birth families. Social workers also sought to protect birthparents, especially birthmothers, from being discovered by the children they had placed with the Society. Society case workers sometimes tried to stall or discourage young adoptees—usually those eighteen to twenty years of age—who were searching for their birthparents or siblings because of the potential embarrassment.

The most common tactic Society case workers used to prevent some adoptees from finding out "unpleasant" truths and the one recommended by adoption experts, however, was simply not to tell them. Throughout most of its existence, the Society paternalistically omitted telling a small number of adoptees about the circumstances of their birth (i.e., that they were illegitimate), their parents' medical background (i.e., that there was a history of insanity or venereal disease), or their parents' racial background (i.e., African-American or American Indian). A sincere wish to spare the individual from painful emotions or, as they saw it, from social stigmatization motivated these omissions. For example, in 1939, caseworker Mary Lehn did not tell nineteen year-old Gloria D., an adopted woman searching for her birthparents, that her mother was confined in an institution for incorrigible women, nor that her father was in prison for sodomizing her nine year-old sister. Instead, Lehn told Gloria only "the positive things I knew, leaving out the very negative which are certainly in the record." In emphasizing the strategies of adoption workers for withholding "unpleasant" truths from adoptees, we must not lose sight of the far more historically significant point that before the mid-1960s they gave *identifying* family history to most clients who requested it.

An Explanation of the Society's Postadoption Policy

How does one explain the Society's relatively open and sympathetic postadoption policy toward birthparents and adoptees? The answer lies in the matrix of record keeping, social work professionalism, the crisis of the family in the first quarter of the twentieth century, and the particular pre–World War II demographic make-up of birthmothers and their children. All of these factors worked to counteract the trend toward secrecy that had begun to surround the adoption process.

Record Keeping and Social Work Professionalism

The Society's careful maintenance of records was crucial to the ability of birthparents and adoptees to obtain family information, whether identifying or nonidentifying. These family histories—or case records, as they were called by professional social workers in the early twentieth century—functioned as the data base from which adoption workers could "scientifically" determine their clients' needs, train new social workers, undertake research, and educate the public as to the value and purpose of their profession.

More importantly, at least for the history of postadoption contact, professional social workers by the early 1920s compiled detailed family histories because they believed that children had a right to that information when they grew up. Social workers believed that it was crucial "to conserve somewhere the information which may be of vital importance to the child." They repeatedly deplored any failure to keep accurate records on dependent children. . . .

Crisis of the Family

Cultural and demographic changes at the turn of the century strengthened the Society's resolve to give family information to birthmothers and adoptees. These changes led many Americans to believe that the traditional family was in a state of crisis. The signs of decay were everywhere: the upsurge in the number of divorces; the drop in the nation's birthrate among native-born, Anglo-Saxon whites; and the dramatic change in traditional sex roles, with young women pursuing a college education, working outside the home, agitating for women's rights, and engaging in premarital sex that resulted in an apparent epidemic of unwed mothers. An alarmed America responded to the perceived crisis of the family by attempting to strengthen it. In the three decades before World War II, physicians, social workers, and adoption specialists, glorifying parenthood and the importance of maintaining "natural" families, counseled unmarried mothers to keep their "illegitimate" children. These injunctions to preserve "natural" families found expression in the Child Welfare League of America's 1932 *Standards For Institutions Caring For Dependent Children,* which stated that "contacts with members of the child's own [i.e., birth] family should be maintained by correspondence and visits, safeguarded when necessary to protect the child and the foster family, and the tie between child and his own family should be fostered and encouraged." . . .

Demographics

Most importantly, the demographic profile of the Society's clientele provided a material basis for its relatively open policy on postadoption contact. Before 1946—and the end of World War II marks a very clear dividing line—a dramatically high percentage of birthmothers seeking postadoption contact had been married at the time of the child's conception. Before 1946, 65% of children relinquished by these birthmothers were born to married parents compared to *virtually none* afterwards. Most of these prewar birthmothers placed their children for adoption as a result of poverty caused by divorce or desertion. The median age of the children they relinquished was four and one-half years. The advanced age of these children permitted strong bonds to develop between birthmothers and children before relinquishment and gave birthmothers a privileged claim to family information.

New Restrictions in the Society's Policies

Birthmothers and Birthparents

Beginning in the 1950s, the Society's attitude and policy toward birthparents and adult adopted persons who requested information slowly became more rigid and less forthcoming. . . .

What accounts for the Society's change in attitude and policy on releasing information to birthmothers and adult adopted persons? The answer lies in the matrix of social workers' increasing commitment to professional secrecy, demography, and psychoanalytic theory. The difficulties that birthmothers and adult adopted persons experienced in obtaining family information were exacerbated by the Cold War and social workers' growing adherence to the principle of client confidentiality and the importance of professional secrecy in general. In the 1930s, as casework dealt increasingly with emotional and psychological problems, social workers began to emphasize their responsibility not to reveal client-entrusted communications to other social agencies or caseworkers. . . . Both the value and precariousness of the principle of confidentiality were made evident to social workers with the passage in 1951 of the Jenner Amendment to the Social Security Act, which permitted state governments to open their hitherto confidential welfare records to public scrutiny. . . .

Demographic Change

Ironically, it was in this context of increasing concern about client confidentiality that birthmothers were the first to be affected by the Society's restrictive policy. . . . Postwar birthmothers' youth, their children's illegitimacy, and the quick separation of mother and child eroded their special claim to receive family information. At the Society, the changing demographic profile of birthmothers and their adoptive children was one important factor in the evolution of its increasingly restrictive policy of releasing family information. . . .

Psychoanalytic Studies and the Unmarried Mother

Concomitantly, psychoanalytic studies of unmarried mothers, which depicted them as neurotic at best, psychotic at worst, strengthened adoption workers' resolve to deny birthmothers information about their children. In the first quarter of the twentieth century, under the guise of "scientific" casework, social workers reacted sympathetically to the plight of unwed mothers. Their analysis stressed the underlying causes of heredity and environment, including the responsibility of the father and the community for the child. Social workers' treatment emphasized keeping birthmothers and their children together and recommended adoption only as a last resort. Between 1928 and 1935, social casework methodology shifted, with momentous consequences, from Mary Richmond's environmental perspective to a more psychoanalytic orientation using the work of Sigmund Freud, Otto Rank, and Alfred Adler. Between 1939 and 1958, as psychoanalytic theory came to dominate casework, social workers' interest in environmental factors waned, and they began to take their cues from psychiatric research conducted on unmarried mothers. These studies left little doubt that unwed mothers were psychologically unhealthy. One early investigation of 16 unmarried mothers in 1941, citing the work of the Freudian psychoanalyst Helene Deutsch, concluded that "these pregnancies represent hysterical dissociation states in which the girls act out their incest fantasies as an expression of the Oedipus situation." . . . But it was the prolific Florence Clothier, a psychiatrist affiliated with Boston's New England Home for Little Wanderers, who brought the more technical psychiatric research to the attention of social workers. In a series of articles appearing between 1941 and 1955, Clothier repeatedly stated that unmarried motherhood represented "a distorted and unrealistic way out of inner difficulties—common adolescent phantasies (rape, prostitution, and immaculate conception or parthenogenesis) and is comparable to neurotic symptoms on the one hand and delinquent behavior on the other." . . .

Origins of the Society's Restrictive Policy toward Adult Adopted Persons

Changing Definitions of Social Work Professionalism

A somewhat different set of social circumstances accounts for the Society's change in policy on releasing information to adult adopted persons. One factor may have been changing definitions of professionalism and increasing bureaucratization. As we have seen, social workers during the Progressive era advocated keeping records to conduct scientific casework and because the child had a right to know his family history. After the Second World War, the CWLA's *Standards for Adoption Service* continued to recommend these twin objectives to member agencies, though the child's right to family information was clouded by the ambiguous injunction that the agency should preserve family history "which can be made available when needed." By 1969, however, Society officials had dropped the emphasis on providing the client with information. Following Gordon Hamilton's authoritative *Principles of Social Case Recording* (1946), they viewed case records only as illustrative of "the process in a particular adoption," and as an "aid to the supervisor in working with the social workers and to administration in reviewing and assessing the services of the agency." In practice, this meant the Society emphasized keeping detailed records on the care given to unmarried mothers, the prospective adoptive parents' interview, and the child's placement, as well as specific administrative responsibilities such as raising money, plant construction, hiring staff, and meeting payrolls. But the institution's duty to preserve family information *for the child* had disappeared from the CHSW's mission.

Freudian Family Romance Theory

Psychoanalytic studies conducted on adopted children and adults also strongly influenced the Society's increasingly restrictive policy toward releasing family information after World War II. Society adoption workers began interpreting adult adopted persons who searched for their birthparents as "very disturbed young people" and "sick youths," a perspective grounded in the psychoanalytic concept of the family romance fantasy. First articulated by Sigmund Freud and then transmitted to psychiatric social workers by Otto Rank in his *Myth of the Birth of the Hero*, this concept received special emphasis in the psychology of adopted children developed by psychotherapists Helene Deutsch and Florence Clothier. According to Freud, the family romance is a common fantasy of most small children who, when sensing that their affection for their parents is "not being fully reciprocated," imagine they are a "stepchild or an adopted child." Wishing to be free of his parents, the child develops a fantasy in which he is the child of "others, who, as a rule, are of higher social standing." . . . In normal child development, the fantasy of being adopted subsides quickly. . . .

Summary and Conclusions

Throughout the twentieth century—well before the birth of the Adoption Rights Movement—adult adopted persons and birthparents returned to adoption agencies for answers to questions about themselves and their birth families. They did so for the same reasons as individuals do today: to obtain genetic background information, to satisfy their curiosity about the circumstances of their birth, and to search for biological family members. This historical analysis of the Children's Home Society of Washington reveals a past that is unknown to historians, social workers, adoption rights activists, and members of the adoption triad. It is clear that Society officials and caseworkers, often despite laws to the contrary, adhered to cultural values and professional ethics stressing family preservation. These ethics encouraged them to release identifying information to adult clients. Reinforcing their belief in family preservation was the demographic circumstances of the Society's pre–World War II clientele: older, married, impoverished birthmothers who had already bonded with their older children before relinquishment. These biological ties and memories, broken by circumstances beyond the control of family members, gave birthparents and adoptees a special claim to family information. In keeping with their own professional standards, which gave them enormous discretion, however, Society caseworkers would not reveal to birthparents the location of adopted children and refrained from conveying "unpleasant" truths to adult adopted persons, a minority of whom had been born out of wedlock or had a medical history or racial background that was thought to be stigmatizing.

For several reasons, adoption agencies became more restrictive in releasing identifying information after the Second World War. First, social workers slowly shifted their primary emphasis from providing postadoption clients with family information to concentrating on the adoptive process itself and agency administration. Second, the Cold War and the concomitant growth of professional secrecy, along with changing demographic circumstances, encouraged the Society to accept the findings of psychiatric research, which in turn reinforced the CHSW's restrictive policy. As birthmothers became younger and relinquished infants born out of wedlock, Society adoption workers convinced themselves that birthmothers had not bonded with their children, who in turn did not remember their mothers. Under these dramatically altered conditions, case workers accepted both a body of psychiatric research that medicalized the issue of illegitimacy by identifying unmarried mothers as borderline psychotics and a variant of Freudian family romance fantasy theory that viewed adopted adults' requests for identifying information as evidence of psychological maladjustment. It is somewhat ironic that the Adoption Rights Movement has placed its faith in psychoanalysts, such as Robert Jay Lifton and Arthur D. Sorosky, who claim that the identity problems of adopted persons in late adolescence and young adulthood would be solved by opening the records, when it was a previous body of psychiatric research, emphasizing the behavioral and emotional problems of unmarried mothers and adopted children, that contributed to closing the records in the first place. Adoption rights activists, in their quest for their biological families, incorrectly assume that they are demanding the opening of records that have *always* been sealed and fail to understand the multiple factors responsible for sealing adoption records. A longer historical perspective reveals instead a more complicated—but more usable—past.

30

We Have a Long Way to Go
Attitudes toward Adoption

Ellen Herman

In the first comprehensive national survey of Americans' attitudes toward adoption, scientific polling techniques confirmed the endurance of popular belief that blood is thicker than water. How else to explain the remarkable growth of the infertility industry in recent years, except as evidence that adoption is second best to having children of one's "own"? According to the survey, half of all Americans feel this way. This is a tragedy that denies the most elemental kind of attachment to countless children and adults. Sadly, it is nothing new. The equivalence between blood and belonging has been no less tenacious for being a cultural prejudice rather than a fact of nature. Throughout the century, popular and professional views have been ambivalent about the "risks" involved in adoptive kinship, a terrible irony in light of what we know about the violence that destroys too many families created the "normal" way.

Early in the century, the incipient child welfare establishment insisted that unmarried mothers and their babies would be better off if they stayed together. Moral disapproval of illegitimacy, anger at predatory male sexuality, and eugenic fears of feeble-mindedness combined to cast a pall over adoption. Before the 1930s, social workers directed their efforts toward distinguishing "adoptable" from defective children in hopes that unsuspecting adopters might be protected from taking in genetic lemons.

By midcentury, when nurture temporarily eclipsed nature and demand for children increased dramatically, professionals embraced a more positive vision of adoption. By carefully "matching" parents and children, professionals hoped to prove that adoption was no flimsy substitute. As long as it was held up to the mirror of nature, adoption could produce families almost as real as the "real thing."

Sealing records, altering birth certificates, and respecting the impassable borders of racial and ethnic difference were all practices based on the premise that authenticity required sameness, or at least its appearance. The practices backfired. By surrounding natal origins with a poisonous cloud of mystery, they denied what has always been one of the most obvious things about adoption. It is a different way of making a family.

In recent years, the resurgence of genetic determinism has revived the slogan that "blood will tell," recalling the formative years of modern adoption. Reformers have sharply criticized the benevolent intentions of the "matching" paradigm, arguing that secrets and lies cannot produce love and security. They are right. Unfortunately, solutions such as opening records and encouraging reunions may end up reproducing adoption stigma if they reinforce the entirely conventional view that birth parents are real, adopters artificial, and identity incomplete and inferior without benefit of blood.

Many survey respondents expressed strong support for confidentiality in adoption, which suggests that realness resides in replacing one family with another that is just as exclusive. Americans today are deeply divided about the wisdom of contact between adoptees and birth parents. Open adoption, because it acknowledges that love is divisible and that a child may have more than one mother and father, is one tangible sign that adoptive kinship is different.

No matter how hard our culture has tried to erase adoption's distinctiveness, the process of bringing children who need parents together with adults who want children still advertises hope. Families—and not only adoptive families—can be created on purpose. When more Americans are persuaded that intentional kinship holds the keys to child welfare and family love, we will not need surveys telling us that adoption remains a last resort. Blood, at long last, will have lost its baleful power to tell us the only story that matters about who people are and with whom they belong.

31

The Idea of Adoption
An Inquiry into the History of
Adult Adoptee Access to Birth Records

Elizabeth J. Samuels

I. Introduction

. . . The widely accepted account of when adoptions in America became cloaked in secrecy goes something like this. Early in the twentieth century, states began moving toward protecting the privacy of participants in the adoption process by closing court
records to public inspection. Then, in the 1930s, 1940s, and early 1950s, virtually all
states took the further step of imposing a unitary regime of secrecy under which
adopting parents and birth parents who were unknown to one another would remain
unknown and under which adult adoptees could never learn the identity of their
birth parents . . .

In fact, as late as 1960, some forty percent of the states still had laws on the books
recognizing an unrestricted right of adult adoptees to inspect their original birth certificates. It was only in the 1960s, 1970s, and 1980s that all but three of those states
changed their laws to close birth records to adoptees. At the same time that those
states were closing birth records, a growing national advocacy movement for greater
openness in adoption was encouraging many states to establish passive and active registries through which adult adoptees and birth parents could attempt to seek information about and establish contact with one another. . . .

. . . In the 1940s and 1950s, a variety of expert voices advised states to seal court and
birth records but to recognize in adult adoptees an unrestricted right of access to
[their own] birth records. The reason given . . . was to protect adoptive families from
possible interference by birth parents. In contrast, no reason was generally offered in
. . . support of the closings of birth records to adult adoptees that did occur from the
1930s through the 1960s. . . . The early closings may have been, in no small part, the
consequence of . . . the social context in which they occurred. Adoption was beginning
to be perceived as a means of creating a perfect and complete substitute for a family
created by natural childbirth. Over time, as legal rules established a nearly universal
regime of secrecy with respect to all persons' access to court records and all persons'
except adult adoptees' access to birth records, the regime of secrecy itself inevitably
influenced social attitudes and understandings. Actions once thought natural, such as

attempts by adoptees to learn information about their birth families, came to be so-cially disfavored and considered abnormal. Such attempts acquired negative social meanings: they were the psychologically unhealthful product of unsuccessful adop-tions that had failed to create perfect substitutes for natural families created by child-birth, and they indicated adoptees' rejection of and ingratitude toward adoptive par-ents. Eventually, lifelong secrecy would be viewed as an essential feature of adoptions in which birth and adoptive parents did not know one another. . . .

. . . Adoptees' interest in birth families came to be seen as imperiling their birth parents' interests.

Today, this [perspective] is being challenged as we are deluged with newspaper and magazine articles, television shows, movies, and books that spotlight or refer to adoptee and birth parent searches and reunions. Nevertheless, . . . only a handful of states currently recognize the once universal right of adult adoptees to unrestricted information about their origins. . . .

II. Chronology of Adult Adoptees' Access to Birth Records

In the mid-1920s, there were virtually no confidentiality or secrecy provisions in adoption law. . . .

By the mid-1930s to the early 1940s, there were more state provisions for confiden-tiality with respect to the general public's access to court records, but still few provi-sions for secrecy among the participants. By the late 1930s, fewer than a third of the states accorded court records any degree of confidentiality; of those that did, most still permitted access . . . to "parties in interest." These parties would always include adoptive parents if not adoptees as well. A 1935 summary of legislation on adoption reported a high volume of legislation in the preceding decade, thirty-nine states hav-ing either "enacted new legislation or amended repeatedly their laws upon the subject of adoption." . . .

Court records, of course, may contain a variety of types of information about the parties in investigative reports as well as in pleadings and briefs and in testimony and other evidence. . . . Birth certificates . . . usually contained only . . . facts about the birth; the mother's name, maiden name, age, birthplace, address, and earlier pregnan-cies; the father's name, age, birthplace, and occupation; whether the child was born to married parents; and the name of the person or persons who attended and certified the birth. Before 1930, birth records were not amended when a child was adopted. During the 1930s states began to provide for new birth certificates with the adoptive parents' names substituted for the birth parents' names.

With respect to court records, . . . by the late 1940s and early 1950s a significant, if not a dramatic, shift had occurred: court records . . . were apparently closed in many states to all persons. For original birth certificates, however, . . . the provisions that were developing were . . . different, usually limiting access to the public but not to the adult adoptee. . . . In 1953, at proceedings in which a draft of the [first] Uniform Adop-tion Act was presented to the National Conference of Commissioners on Uniform State Laws, the committee chair expressed the view that the act's provision for making adoption court records available only by court order was commonplace and non-controversial and that many states, as recommended by the act, both provided for the issuance of new birth certificates and permitted access by adult adoptees to original birth records. . . .

A significant shift in birth records policy had in fact occurred by 1960, the year every state reported its statutes and procedures. . . . Of the forty-nine reporting states and the District of Columbia, twenty-eight reported that original birth records were available only by court order. Wisconsin provided for inspection "at the discretion of the State registrar or upon order of a court of competent jurisdiction," and New Hampshire "at the discretion of the State registrar or the town clerk who has custody of the original birth record" or by court order. But twenty states . . . indicated that as of 1960, original birth certificates could be inspected by adult adoptees and otherwise by court order. Four of the twenty states did not specify that the adopted person had to be an adult in order to inspect the records. Seven of the twenty states also permitted adoptive parents to inspect the records. Virginia, until 1977, permitted adult adoptee access to court records but not to birth records. In Colorado, court records were available to the parties; however, these records were closed to them in 1967. In California, complete court records were available to adoptive parents under a law that is still in effect but that at present may be inconsistently applied. Similarly, of course, in all states in independent adoptions, at least the adoptive parents' attorneys knew and had records that indicated the identity of birth parents.

Of the twenty states in 1960 with laws that permitted adoptees access on demand to original birth records, two—Alaska and Kansas—have never closed these records. In South Dakota, both these records and court records appear to have always been available on demand, although it became necessary to make the demand to a court and obtain a court order. Of the remaining states, four changed their laws in the 1960s, six did not do so until the 1970s, and seven did so only after 1979. . . .

III. Social Policies and Adoptees' Access to Birth Records

. . . With respect to telling children they are adopted, there were debates about how and at what age to tell, but most social service and other social science literature recommended telling, and much of it recommended telling at a very young age. As a 1958 U.S. Children's Bureau pamphlet for prospective adoptive parents explained, the child should be told, "[f]or someday, somehow, he'll learn. So you be the one to tell him first. He loves and trusts you. If he first learns from an outsider, it may seriously affect his feelings toward you. Let him know from the beginning." The pamphlet went on to advise: "As he grows up he will want and need to know some of his own family history. Agencies will help with this if you wish." During this period, professional literature "tended to accept as a given that the adoptee would never know the true facts or identity of the birthparents." The notion of a search by an adoptee "was usually viewed as fantasied or symbolic rather than literal." A book of advice for adoptive parents, for example, simply reassured them not to become "needlessly concerned" because sometimes an adopted adolescent may ask where his birth parents are. All children sometimes feel that they are misunderstood, the authors explained, and that "somewhere in the world there must be the ideal parents." Parents with biological children see this "as a very unreal, passing, momentary thought," while adoptive parents can mistake it for reality and think that their child is yearning for his biological parents. . . .

With respect to secrecy and the desires of unmarried mothers, there are indications in the social service and other social science literature in this period that unmarried mothers sought a measure of confidentiality. . . . [T]he kind of protection they urgently sought . . . was not protection from the discovery of their identity by their surrendered children as adults. . . .

They sought arrangements that would conceal their pregnancies from their parents or from other members of their communities, or from both, rather than arrangements that would necessarily conceal their identity from adoptive parents, or by extension, from their surrendered children when those children reached adulthood. . . .

IV. Social Contexts and Adoptees' Access to Birth Records

It is difficult, in sum, to find through the 1960s expressions of specific reasons for closing original birth records to adult adoptees. . . .

The specific rationale for closing records to the parties was to prevent the possibility of birth parents interfering with adoptive families. But as most states proceeded to tie the stigma of illegality to the availability of adoption records to birth parents, adoptive parents, and minor adoptees, the states may also have affected social attitudes and understandings associated with adult adoptee access to records. The act by an adoptee of expressing interest in his or her birth family began to acquire negative social meanings. . . .

B. From the 1960s

The understanding that lifelong secrecy was an essential feature of adoption continued to gain currency even as a social revolution was occurring, a revolution that challenged both lifelong secrecy and the understanding of adoption as a perfect and complete substitute for creating a family by childbirth. . . .

The social revolution that challenged and threatened to undermine lifelong secrecy has included a lessening of the stigma of illegitimacy and a greater acceptance of single-parent and other non-traditional types of families. With respect to attitudes about adoption, white unmarried motherhood is no longer equated with mental disorder or an ability to recover easily from surrendering a child for adoption. A large majority of birth parents are reported to be open to or actually desire contact with adoptees. Adoptive families have come increasingly to be seen as having unique qualities and challenges. Thinking on human development has shifted back toward a greater emphasis on nature. Adoptees searching for information about or contact with their birth families have become familiar figures and are no longer assumed to be suffering from a mental disorder. Whether adoptees' expressed desires for identifying information is in any sense innate or instinctive, as some have argued, or is simply culturally constructed, substantial and increasing numbers of adult adoptees since the 1960s have sought information about their birth parents. A nationwide advocacy movement seeking greater openness in adoption, including adult adoptee access to birth records, has grown steadily from its beginnings in the late 1960s and has involved both litigation and legislative advocacy. In the courts, individuals have sought to establish good cause for opening records, and both individuals and groups have argued, without success to date, that closed records violate their constitutional rights. Mutual aid networks of searching adoptees and birth relatives have also proliferated, expanding in recent years through the Internet. . . .

In the 1970s, authoritative voices began characterizing adoptees' interest in their birth families as both normal and perhaps even important to satisfy. . . .

Despite these changing popular and professional views of adoptees' seeking information, the social understanding of lifelong secrecy as an essential feature of adoption persisted and states continued to close birth records to adult adoptees. . . .

In the reported opinions concerning secrecy in adoption that began appearing in the 1970s, the courts also wrote in terms of birth parents' "right to privacy" and "statutory guarantee of anonymity and confidentiality." . . . As a Rhode Island court [wrote]: lifelong secrecy gives the birth parent "assurance that his or her identity will not become public knowledge" and "an opportunity to restructure his or her life after a most traumatic episode." It allows adoptive parents to raise the child "free from interference from the natural parents and without any apprehension that the birth status of their child will be used to harm themselves or the child." It "protects the adoptee from any possible stain of illegitimacy and permits the formation of a relationship with the new parents . . . free of the threat of outside interference" of a birth parent.

Rejecting adoptees' constitutional challenges to sealed records, some courts suggested, to the contrary, that the states' important interest in protecting the privacy of birth parents might itself be "compelling" in constitutional terms. . . .

The courts also faced the difficult task, with essentially no guidance from state legislatures, of divining what might constitute good cause for revealing information in sealed records. . . . [W]hen many of the record-sealing laws were passed, legislators neither sought to remedy problems associated with adult adoptee access to identifying information nor specifically considered whether or why adult adoptees would seek or should be entitled to information. . . . In the absence of any standard, courts interpreted statutes as requiring good cause. A few statutes supplied other types of minimal guidance, such as providing that records may be inspected or information disclosed "only . . . when the court is satisfied that the welfare of the child will thereby be promoted or protected," or if it is in "the best interest of the child or of the public" to do so. The courts themselves did not develop many more concrete guidelines. . . . [Most] courts . . . uniformly rejected "mere curiosity," however keen, and found few specific reasons that did or might constitute good cause. Among the reasons a small number of appellate courts accepted were a psychological need to know, or more commonly, severe psychological problems caused by lack of information; a right to inherit from natural relatives; and a religiously based need to trace ancestors. . . .

. . . [T]here has been discussion since the 1960s about promises or assurances made by agencies to unmarried mothers that identifying information about them would not be revealed in the future to the children they surrendered for adoption. . . . A 1975 Child Welfare League survey of adoption agencies asked what should be done if a choice had to be made between a "biological mother's right to anonymity" and an "adult adoptee's right to know who was his or her biological mother." Fifty-seven percent of the agencies said they would consider the mother's right paramount, while 27% would consider the adoptee's paramount, and 16% "didn't know." Respondents were more divided on the normative question of whether agencies ideally should conduct a search for biological parents on the adoptee's behalf (14% usually, 53% sometimes, 19% never), or simply give the adoptee identifying information (9% usually, 40% sometimes, and 34% never). . . .

The fact that states have moved so cautiously toward opening birth records . . . is likely due in part to the power and persistence of the social understanding about lifelong secrecy and its affiliated meanings. . . .

V. Conclusion

. . . Although the movement of the states toward greater openness has been slow and cautious, it has been nationwide and its pace has been accelerating sharply in recent years. The numerous passive and active registries are being supplemented or supplanted by the growing number of states opening all records, re-opening records not closed at their inception, opening records prospectively, or opening all or some records subject to disclosure vetoes by birth parents. These changes both reflect and foster the difficult process of deconstructing lifelong secrecy. It may be expected that one day the number of states opening birth records will reach a critical "tipping point," a point after which a majority of states will reject lifelong secrecy as expeditiously as they once embraced it.

Doe v. Sundquist (6th Cir. Tenn. 1997)

Engel, J.

Two birth mothers (Promise Doe and Jane Roe), an adoptive couple (Kimberly C. and Russ C.), and a nonprofit organization licensed by Tennessee as a child-placing agency (Small World Ministries, Inc.) appeal the district court's denial of their motion for a preliminary injunction to block the enforcement of Tennessee's new statute governing the disclosure of adoption records. The plaintiffs allege that the statute violates both the U.S. Constitution and the Tennessee Constitution. We affirm the district court's denial of the preliminary injunction, and on the merits of the case, we dismiss the federal claims and decline to exercise jurisdiction over the state claim.

From 1951 to 1996, sealed adoption records were available in Tennessee only upon court order that disclosure was "in the best interest of the child or of the public." Tenn.Code Ann. § 36-1-131 (repealed). Under a recently enacted statute that was to go into effect July 1, 1996:

> (A) All adoption records . . . shall be made available to the following eligible persons:
>   (i)   An adopted person . . . who is twenty-one (21) years of age or older . . . ;
>   (ii) The legal representative of [such] a person. . . .
> (B) Information . . . shall be released . . . only to the parents, siblings, lineal descendants, or lineal ancestors, of the adopted person . . . , and only with the express written consent [of] the adopted person. . . .

Id. § 36-1-127(c)(1). The new law also provides for a "contact veto," under which a parent, sibling, spouse, lineal ancestor, or lineal descendant of an adopted person may register to prevent contact by the adopted person. *Id.* § 36-1-128. The contact veto also can prohibit the adopted person from contacting any spouse, sibling, lineal descendant, or lineal ancestor of the person registering the veto. *Id.* § 36-1-130(a)(6)(A)(i). A violator of the contact veto provision is subject to civil and criminal liability. *Id.* § 36-1-132. Before disclosure of the identity of an adopted person's relatives is made, the state "shall conduct a diligent search" for the relatives to give them a chance to register for the veto. *Id.* § 36-1-131. In any event, the relatives of an adopted person can veto only contact, not disclosure of their identities.

Doe's birth child is approximately six years old. One of the adoptive children of Kimberly C. and Russ C. is no older than six, and the other is no older than two. Small World started in 1985, and apparently none of the children it has placed will turn twenty-one within the next few years. Roe's birth child is over twenty-one and has tried to ascertain her identity. Six days before the statute was to go into effect, the plaintiffs filed this suit in district court. . . .

The plaintiffs claim that the new law violates their right of privacy under the United States and Tennessee Constitutions. They argue that the "zone of privacy" established in *Griswold v. Connecticut*, 381 U.S. 479, 85 S.Ct. 1678, 14 L. Ed. 2d 510 (1965), now encompasses familial privacy, reproductive privacy, and privacy against disclosure of confidential information and that the new statute violates each of these three. . . . [F]irst we note our skepticism that information concerning a birth might be protected from disclosure by the Constitution. A birth is simultaneously an intimate occasion and a public event—the government has long kept records of when, where, and by whom babies are born. Such records have myriad purposes, such as furthering the interest of children in knowing the circumstances of their birth. The Tennessee legislature has resolved a conflict between that interest and the competing interest of some parents in concealing the circumstances of a birth. We are powerless to disturb this resolution unless the Constitution elevates the right to avoid disclosure of adoption records above the right to know the identity of one's parents.

First, the plaintiffs cite *Meyer v. Nebraska*, 262 U.S. 390, 43 S.Ct. 625, 67 L.Ed. 1042 (1923), as protecting familial privacy. Dicta in *Meyer* noted that the Due Process Clause guarantees the right to "marry, establish a home and bring up children." *Id.* at 399, 43 S.Ct. at 626. Nothing in the Tennessee statute infringes on that right. Under the new scheme, people in Tennessee are still free not only to marry and to raise children, but also to adopt children and to give children up for adoption. We find that if there is a federal constitutional right of familial privacy, it does not extend as far as the plaintiffs would like.

Second, the plaintiffs claim that their right to reproductive privacy, as established in *Roe v. Wade*, 410 U.S. 113, 93 S.Ct. 705, 35 L. Ed. 2d 147 (1973), and its progeny, is violated by the Tennessee statute. The freedom to make decisions about adoption, they argue, is sufficiently analogous to the freedom to decide whether to carry a baby to term to justify an extension of *Roe*. Even should it ultimately be held some day that the right to give up a baby for adoption or to adopt a child is protected by the Constitution, such a right would not be relevant to this case. Because the challenged law does not limit adoptions, cases striking down laws restricting abortions are not analogous. And even assuming that a law placing an undue burden on adoptions might conceivably be held to infringe on privacy rights in the *Roe* realm, much as laws placing "undue burden[s]" on abortions are unconstitutional under *Planned Parenthood v. Casey*, 505 U.S. 833, 874–79, (1992), § 36-1-127 does not unduly burden the adoption process. Whether it burdens the process at all is the subject of great dispute in two briefs submitted to this court by amici curiae. Any burden that does exist is incidental and not "undue." See *Casey*, 505 U.S. at 878, 112 S.Ct. at 2821 (equating "undue burden" with "substantial obstacle").

Third, the plaintiffs claim that the law violates their right to avoid disclosure of confidential information. They rely on a dictum in *Whalen v. Roe*, 429 U.S. 589, 97 S.Ct. 869, 51 L.Ed.2d 64 (1977), that describes one type of privacy right as "the individual interest in avoiding disclosure of personal matters." *Id.* at 599, 97 S.Ct. at 876. This right has not been fleshed out by the Supreme Court. The plaintiffs' argument that it should be extended to cover this case runs counter to our decisions in *J.P. v. DeSanti,* 653 F.2d 1080 (6th Cir. 1981), and *Doe v. Wigginton,* 21 F.3d 733 (6th Cir. 1994). . . . As discussed above, even if a court were someday to recognize adoption-related rights as fundamental, such recognition would not be relevant to this case because the challenged part of the new Tennessee law does not directly regulate when, how, or by whom a child may be adopted.. . . .

The element of public interest also weighs against enjoining enforcement of the Tennessee statute. The statute appears to be a serious attempt to weigh and balance two frequently conflicting interests: the interest of a child adopted at an early age to know who that child's birth parents were, an interest entitled to a good deal of respect and sympathy, and the interest of birth parents in the protection of the integrity of a sound adoption system. It is an issue of peculiar relevance to the primary police functions of the state as reserved to Tennessee under the Tenth Amendment. See *United States v. Lopez,* 514 U.S. 549, 115 S. Ct. 1624, 1634, 131 L. Ed. 2d 626 (1995). Another aspect of public interest favoring the defendants' position is the interest of comity between states and federal governments, including the interest of the state in having the first opportunity to construe its own constitution and laws. . . .

. . . We are particularly sympathetic to the plight of the *Roe* birth mother, whose identity may be disclosed imminently to her biological child if the statute is upheld. The likelihood of irreparable harm does not, however, control completely; other factors must still be weighed. Here the plaintiffs' ultimate chance of success on their federal claims is so slim as to be entirely ephemeral. We must observe also that the plaintiffs have always had the opportunity to present their state claims to the Tennessee courts, and if there is any danger of loss in their having failed earlier to pursue that avenue, the cause of it lies in their own hands. . . .

For the foregoing reasons, we *affirm* the district court's denial of the plaintiffs' motion for a preliminary injunction. On the merits of the case, we *dismiss* the plaintiffs' claims insofar as they rely on federal law, and we decline to exercise supplemental jurisdiction over the claims insofar as they rely on state law. The stay pending appeal is *vacated* and the case is *remanded* to the district court for dismissal of the complaint and other proceedings consistent with the decision of this court.

State Legislation and Mutual Consent Registries

National Council for Adoption

State Legislation

State Legislation is a priority for the National Council For Adoption. NCFA is encouraging states to file and pass legislation similar to that passed in Texas creating Safe Havens for Newborns. In addition, NCFA is also encouraging states to file and pass legislation on Mutual Consent Registries and opposing legislation to open records of adopted children and their birth parents.

Mutual Consent Registries

Mutual Consent Registries are designed to help and protect both adopted adult persons and their birth parents. NCFA will continue to fight to:

1. Protect children born and women who bore children out-of-wedlock from public scrutiny.
2. Protect the integrity of the adopted family as a legal family.
3. Be consistent with all other social services which hold confidentiality as a predominant principle of ethical practice.
4. Protect all parties to an adoption from unsolicited or unwanted interference from other parties.
5. Facilitate the grieving process for birth parents by providing closure.

NCFA is opposed to Open Records legislation because it believes that privacy should not be removed from the adoption process unless all parties agree. If adults (adopted persons and birthparents) wish to waive their right of privacy and meet each other, neither the state, nor anyone else should prevent it. The argument used that open records are essential for medical and social history are [sic] just untrue. This information can be shared without divulging personal information about the birth parents. Currently, Tennessee, Oregon, Alaska, Kansas and Delaware permit persons who were adopted to have access to their original birth certificates. Although some of these states purport to contain safeguards for birth parents like contact or disclosure veto, they offer essentially no protection at all.

The Basic Bastard

Janine Baer et al.

Adoptee birth records are sealed because of an attitude of shame towards adoption. The language in the original laws which sealed adoptee birth records specifically stated that it was to protect adoptees from the shame and embarrassment of their illegitimate (i.e. Bastard) status. The later justifications we hear for adult adoptees' birth records being sealed are: (1) They are sealed to protect the birthparent (unspoken assumption—from the shame of the unwanted birth coming back to haunt her); (2) They are sealed to protect the adoptee (unspoken assumption—from the shame of being reminded that one was born of an unwanted pregnancy); and (3) to protect the adoptive parents (from the shame of their infertility). In reality there shouldn't be anything shameful about adoption. Sealed records preclude that possibility.

Bastard Nation explodes the myth of shame by reclaiming the word "bastard" and all of society's myths and fears regarding adoption. We make fun of the unspoken shame, joke about illegitimacy, tell the untold tales of our sisters and brothers which the media have not been willing to tackle. We give adult adoptees a place to come and express themselves, share their experiences, read about others like (and unlike) themselves, find search and reconnection resources and learn how to fight for their rights as adult adoptees. . . .

. . . Bastard Nation has redefined the adoptee rights struggle in terms of civil rights, empowerment and tactical activism. . . .

I. Open Records: Why It's an Issue

Adult adoptees in most of the advanced, industrialized nations of the world have unrestricted access to original birth records as a matter of right. In contrast, adult adoptees . . . in the U.S. are [generally] forbidden access to their original birth certificates, unlike non-adopted adult citizens. . . .

In Scotland, adoptee records have been open since 1935, and in England since 1975. Sweden, The Netherlands, Germany, South Korea, Mexico, Argentina, and Venezuela are only a few of the many nations which do not prevent adult adoptees from accessing their own birth records. Why are they still sealed in most of the U.S.?

Well-funded lobbies representing certain adoption agencies and lawyers have a vested interest in keeping adoptee records closed. . . .

While many adoptees search for their biological relatives to discover the answers to questions regarding medical history, ethnicity, and family heritage, the majority do not search, for one reason or another. Nevertheless, all adoptees should be able to exercise their right to obtain the original government documents of their births and adoptions. At issue is not search and reunion, but the civil rights of millions of American citizens. To continue to abrogate these rights is to perpetuate the stigmatization of illegitimacy and adoption, the relegation of an entire class of citizens to second-class status. . . .

VII. Do Birthparents Have a Right to Privacy?

. . . Our nation's courts have spoken clearly that the right to privacy does not extend to withholding birth information from the very person to whom it primarily pertains—the adoptee.

Despite the finding that birthparent privacy rights do not extend as far as keeping their names secret from adoptees, opponents of open records have continued to claim that some birthparents, particularly women, would be harmed emotionally if they were to be contacted by a relinquished child who reached the age of majority. In addition, some reproductive rights advocates believe that sealed birth records should be an option for pregnant women who choose not to raise a child.

In reality, their adult children, raised by others, are not the enemies of birthparents. Our laws and policies should not deprive one group of their rights in order to protect others from possibly having to face the consequences of their past choices. In the event that an adoptee chooses to contact a birthparent, both people should consider the feelings and concerns of the other. When birth records are opened to adult adoptees, a woman who relinquishes an infant will have 18 to 21 years to decide how to answer a possible phone call from that adult child. Even today, with records still sealed in most states in the U.S., birthparents must consider their responses to being found, since a network of search consultants has arisen to circumvent sealed records. Most birthparents are happy to be contacted by their adult children. A right to privacy that prevents the disclosure of birthparents' names to adult adoptees does not exist, in law or in the real world.

VIII. Open Records Does Not Equal Higher Abortion or Lower Adoption Rates

Many opponents of open records for adult adoptees have claimed, with no basis in fact, that young, pregnant women would choose abortion over adoption if their relinquished children would be able to discover their birthmothers' names in eighteen years' time. They also claim that open records would lead to a decline in adoption rates, as potential adoptive parents would be discouraged by a system in which their children would no longer be permanently denied their own birth records. Both these claims belong in the realm of myth and propaganda, and may be countered by statistical evidence to the contrary. While there are many factors that determine abortion rates in various states and countries, and it cannot be claimed that open records bears a causal relation to lower abortion rates, it can, however, be shown that abortion rates are not higher, and are in fact lower, in open records states than in states with sealed records. It can likewise be shown that states and countries with open records have not seen a decline in adoption rates.

The abortion rates for Alaska and Kansas (states which unconditionally grant adult adoptees access to their original birth certificates) were both *lower* in 1996 than the rate for the United States as a whole—14.6 and 18.9 abortions, respectively, for every 1000 women between the ages of 15 and 44, while the national abortion rate was 22.9 [citations omitted]. Data compiled by the Alan Guttmacher Institute showing the number and rate of abortions in England and Wales by years for 1961 through 1987 indicate a continuous increase in abortions and abortion rates from 1961 through 1973. In 1974 through 1976, when the opening of adoption records was discussed in Parliament and put into effect, abortions and the abortion rate *decreased*. . . .

The New South Wales [Australia] Adoption Information Act 1990, which became fully effective on April 2, 1991, made original birth certificates accessible as of right to adoptees. . . . Prior to the unsealing of adoption records in 1991, adoptions had declined from 4,564 in 1972 to 688 in 1990, a decline of 85 percent. The rate of decline after 1990 shows no significant change from the previous decline, and indicates that the opening of adoption records had no measurable effect on the numbers of adoptions.

Annual adoption figures for England and Wales for the years 1960 through 1984, taken from official publications of the United Kingdom Registrar General and the United Kingdom Office of Population Censuses and Surveys, for non-parental (i.e non–step-parent or interfamilial) adoptions by couples in England and Wales declined continuously from a peak of 14,641 in 1968 down to 1984, which appears to be the last year for which these data were published. From the start of the decline in 1968 until 1976, when adoption records were unsealed, the relevant adoptions declined from 14,641 to 4,777, a decline of 67 percent in eight years; in the following eight years, after the records were unsealed, these adoptions declined to 2,910, a decline of only 39 percent. If the unsealing of adoption records had any effect in England and Wales, therefore, it was to reduce the decline in adoptions, i.e. to increase adoptions over the numbers that it otherwise would have obtained.

35

CWLA Standards
Policy Changes, 1973–2000

Child Welfare League of America

CWLA 1973 Standards

2.3. Confidentiality

Services to natural parents should preserve confidentiality and keep knowledge of each other's identity from the natural and the adoptive parents.

5.2. Protection for Adoptive Parents

The professional service of a social agency should afford the following protection: the natural parents have made a sound and lasting decision to relinquish the child; the child is legally separated from his natural parents; the natural parents will not know with whom the child is placed; and the child is one for whom adoption is a suitable plan.

7.3. Birth Records

When a child is adopted, a new birth certificate should be made out with the names of the adoptive parents entered as parents and the new name of the child, if given, after adoption, and filed in the state of birth. The original certificate should then be sealed. . . .

The inclusion of a legitimacy item in a privileged, detachable medical-health section of the birth certificate and the reporting of this information to the National Center for Health Statistics are considered essential for the protection of the out-of-wedlock child and mother, and for the assessment of incidence and trends of the problem of illegitimacy.

CWLA 1988 Standards

4.27. Disclosure of Identifying Information about Birth Family to Adopted Adults

Within relevant statutes, child welfare agencies should assist adopted persons who have reached the age of majority in their search for information about, or their wish to establish contact with, birth parents, siblings, or other members of their birth family, provided that these persons are willing.

Agencies should advocate the development of state and provincial laws that permit adopted adult individuals to be given all identifying information, with the birth parent(s) consent, or after an unsuccessful diligent attempt has been made to locate the birth parents, as prescribed by law.

6.34. Compilation of Case Records

The child welfare agency should maintain a case record of each child accepted for care, of the family, and of each adoptive applicant, from the time of the application for service through the completed legal adoption and termination of child welfare agency service.

6.35. Content of Case Records

Case records should include a narrative or summary of the services provided and a compilation and necessary documentation of the pertinent facts. . . .

It should also include statements by the birth and adoptive parents regarding the type of information to be exchanged and the contact desired after preplacement and legal adoption. Any letters, updated material, or information, received from the birth parents after the adoption is legalized also should be contained in the case record.

6.36. Confidentiality of Records

All child welfare agency records concerning adoption should be treated as confidential.

Information should be provided to other agencies only when it is in the best interests of the child. Access to adoption records should be restricted to authorized professional staff of the child welfare agency, cooperating agencies, and adoption resource exchanges, and to such other persons whom the child welfare agency has approved to engage in research projects.

Information should be provided to birth parents, adoptive parents, or other individuals only when it is authorized by the person concerned or so ordered by the proper court. . . .

7.30. Birth Records

When a child is adopted, a new birth certificate should be made with the names of the adoptive parents entered as parents and if given, the new name of the child after adoption, and filed in the state or province where the child was born. The original certificate should then be sealed, unless the statute or written agreements between birth and adoptive parents provide otherwise.

CWLA 2000 Standards

2.6. Disclosure of Background Information Regarding the Adoptive Family to the Birth Parents

In those cases in which the birth parents are not involved in selecting the adoptive family for their child, the agency providing adoption services should provide the birth parents with background information about the family who will adopt their child prior to the child's placement.

The information provided to the birth parents should help them understand the family who will rear their child and should respond to any specific concerns or questions that the birth parents may have. . . .

2.7. Disclosure of Birth Parents' Identifying Information to Adopted Individuals

The agency providing adoption services should advise birth parents who are making a plan for the adoption of their child that information related to their identities may be disclosed to the child at some point in the future.

Many birth parents may express an interest in having their identities disclosed to the child whom they place for adoption at the time the child reaches adulthood. The agency providing adoption services should obtain, in writing, the birth parents' interest in having such information provided and should retain the birth parents' written statement in the adoption record.

Some birth parents, at the time they make the decision to place their child for adoption, may express a desire to have their identities withheld from their child. The agency providing adoption services should advise the birth parents that under current law in all states, courts may order the opening of sealed adoption records and allow adopted adults access to identifying information.

Laws sealing adoption records are being re-examined in many states, and the possibility exists that adopted adults may have increased access to identifying information in the future. As a result, agencies should assist birth parents in understanding that it is not possible to assure them that their identities will be protected from the children they place for adoption.

The birth parents' desire to have their identities shared or withheld from the child they placed for adoption may change over time. The agency providing adoption services should inform the birth parents that they may at any time communicate to the agency any changes in their desires in this regard.

6.21. Access to Nonidentifying Background Information

The agency providing adoption services should respond to the request of adopted individuals for *nonidentifying* information about themselves and their birth families that is contained in the agency's records by providing the information fully. . . .

Although counseling should be available and encouraged, it should not be required as a prerequisite to granting access to nonidentifying information. . . .

6.23. Counseling and Support Services in Search and Reunion

The agency providing adoption services should make counseling available to each adoption triad member, as requested. When an adopted adult requests identifying information and/or seeks to search for birth relatives, counseling and all information that is legally available should be provided. If state law prohibits the agency from providing the requested identifying information, the agency should advocate for legislative changes to such policies.

36

Adoption, Identity, and the Constitution
The Case for Opening Closed Records

Naomi Cahn and Jana Singer

Introduction

... The continuing controversy over the confidentiality of adoption records illustrates the inadequacy of existing constitutional law doctrine to address issues involving children and their families. . . . As they mature, adoptees often seek information about their biological families, including their original birth certificates. Constitutional law has proved to be an awkward vehicle for articulating and evaluating the claims of adoptees to information about their biological families. Courts have unsuccessfully attempted to balance the rights of adoptees against those of their biological and adoptive parents, rather than recognizing and attempting to mediate the overlapping identity issues at stake. . . .

A. The Early Claims for Opening Records

Beginning in the 1970s, adoptees sought legal access to their original birth records. They challenged the continuing secrecy of their birth certificates and pressured states to disclose the certificates, complete with the names of their biological parents. Although adoptees articulated four different sets of constitutional claims—privacy rights under the Fourteenth Amendment's Due Process Clause, informational access rights under the First Amendment, equal protection claims under the Fourteenth Amendment, and anti-slavery rights under the Thirteenth Amendment—we will focus here only on the due process claims. This constitutional issue reappears in contemporary litigation about the confidentiality of birth records, but in an ironic transformation, it is the biological parents invoking the Fourteenth Amendment privacy claims to protect the continuing secrecy of birth records against states' efforts to unseal them.

The due process privacy claims dramatize the conflicting rights that courts believe are at issue in the open records cases. In discussing the meaning of the zone of family privacy, courts pose the issue of what is a family and whose rights within the family should be protected. In discussing the adoptees' interests, the courts invoke differing meanings of privacy—is privacy confidentiality, or is it identity-formation? Is identity based on individual development, or is it relational and contextual? By declining to find confidentiality protections for either the biological parents or for the adoptees, the courts continue to articulate these conflicting privacy interests—and definitions of privacy—for members of the adoption triad. The analysis in these cases reveals the shortcomings of applying traditional due process doctrine to claims by and involving children.

In the most widely cited case brought by adoptees [*Alma Soc'y Inc. v. Mellon*, 601 F.2d 1225 (2d Cir. 1979)], the Second Circuit rejected the adoptees' claim that their "personhood" entitled them to open birth records. The plaintiff adoptees argued that the New York statutes providing for sealed adoption records violated the Due Process Clause because the adoptees were constitutionally entitled to the information contained in the records. . . . The court noted that the adoptees' requests implicated the interests of two "families," the biological family and the adoptive family. Drawing on Supreme Court cases addressing the importance of an intact family, notwithstanding the claims of a biological father, the Second Circuit recognized significant interests of the adoptive families which might be "adversely affected" through disclosure of the names of the biological parents. . . .

The court acknowledged that some birth and adoptive parents might not object to release of the information, but suggested that the state legislature had balanced the different relationships in allowing a hearing to show "good cause" as to why the records should be unsealed. . . .

Although there is no Supreme Court doctrine that squarely addresses the interrelated aspects of privacy and adoption . . . [t]he marriage cases are perhaps [somewhat comparable] to the adoption records cases: both concern issues created by a state-conferred status and both concern the rights of individuals to choose a particular family form. But unlike cases involving access to marriage, the adoptees' claims of access to birth records may affect previous familial choices made by adoptive and biological parents. . . .

B. Approaches to Opening Records

Following their failure in the courts, adoptees turned their efforts toward enacting legislation that would provide them with access to information about their birth families. These legislative efforts have met with some success. Most states now allow for the release of non-identifying information to adoptees and adoptive parents. In addition, over the past twenty years, states have established a variety of procedures designed to allow for contact between adoptees and their biological relatives when both parties agree to meet. These procedures typically take one of two forms: mutual consent registries and confidential intermediary systems. In general, however, these efforts fall short of the openness desired by many adult adoptees because the methods are flawed and underutilized. Only a few states have moved toward completely open records. . . .

III. Opening Records

As a policy matter, we believe that records should be opened for adult adoptees. Adult adoptees have a strong interest in having access to information about their biological origins. This information may be critical to an adoptee's sense of identity. Moreover, the sealed and self-contained nature of the adoption process has never accorded with the realities of the experiences of adoption triad members, who often feel strong emotions about the secrecy of the process. Finally, although opening records of completed adoptions may disrupt the expectations of biological and adoptive parents who have relied on continued secrecy, adoption remains a state-sanctioned process that is subject to legislative change. . . .

A policy of unsealing birth records is not uncontroversial, however. As applied to adoptions that have already occurred pursuant to a sealed records regime, there may be retroactivity problems. Moreover, allowing access could be viewed as promoting "genetic essentialism," that is, the view that people are merely the sum of their genes. Additionally, some have argued that unsealing records may undermine adoption by discouraging prospective adoptive parents. . . .

While we advocate disclosing the identity of biological parents, we do not justify such disclosure based on the genetic information that disclosure will provide. Instead, we believe that having the same genetic heritage creates the opportunity for a connection and knowledge that the State should not foreclose. Further, we do not believe that acquiring this genetic information will allow an adoptee to predict or explain all of her personal characteristics and traits.

Ironically, adoption law increasingly mandates extensive disclosure of non-identifying genetic information, while resisting the calls for disclosure of identifying information. This practice of fully disclosing anonymous genetic information, with corresponding secrecy of the identity of the person, seems itself to be an example of genetic essentialism. A primary rationale for requiring disclosure of non-identifying genetic information is to enable prospective adoptive parents to guard against any dangers that might be posed through "faulty" genes. By contrast, the purpose of disclosing the identity of biological relatives is to aid adoptees and parents in their personal and emotional development, though providing genetic information may be a by-product. Knowing the identity of her biological parents may help the adoptee in her identity development, but it is certainly not the only factor in that development. . . .

[Nor does] the available evidence suggest that open records regimes compromise the integrity of the adoption process. Indeed, as Professor Joan Hollinger observes, more than 80% of the biological mothers who have relinquished children for adoption in Michigan since 1980 have consented to the disclosure of their identity when their children become adults. . . . Moreover, whatever constitutionally protected interests adoptive parents may have in controlling a child's access to information while the child is a minor weakens considerably once a child reaches majority.

V

─────────────────────

Adoption with Continuing Contact
"Open Adoption"

This part examines the issues raised when birth families, adoptive families, and adoptees attempt to maintain some form of contact after an adoption has been finalized. As indicated elsewhere in this reader, the view that adoption is a discrete legal event that creates a new and exclusive family for a child, while completely extinguishing the child's birth family, is being challenged. Adoption is increasingly understood to be a dynamic, lifelong process that entails the acknowledgment by both adoptive and birth families of each other's existence and role in the lives of adopted children. "Openness" has become the mantra of contemporary adoption policy and practice.

In addition to the efforts described in part 4 to "open" sealed adoption records and original birth certificates, an even more significant response to the openness mantra is the prevalence, particularly in domestic adoptions, of formal as well as informal agreements for some kind of ongoing contact between adoptive and birth families. Open adoption may be limited to the exchange of information between the families at the time of placement and the sending of an occasional photo or letter, but may in some cases be much broader, including regular visitation by members of the birth family with the adopted child long after the adoption is final.

The selections by Joan Heifetz Hollinger and Annette Ruth Appell analyze the ways adoption laws and procedures are accommodating—and resisting—the removal of the wall of secrecy that once separated adoptive and birth families. The Child Welfare League's revised standards exemplify the current emphasis of most adoption service providers on encouraging various kinds of open adoption. The selection from the U.S. Children's Bureau guidelines governing permanence explains why open adoption arrangements are recommended for older children leaving foster care. The excerpt from the Massachusetts Supreme Court decision *In re Vito* emphasizes the importance of protecting adoptive parents' legal rights to act in the best interests of their adoptive children and the difficulty of assessing which foster children would actually benefit from continued contact with a birth parent.

In their article, the psychotherapists Annette Baran and Reuben Pannor describe why they were among the earliest critics of secrecy in adoption and have since become outspoken advocates for more openness in every aspect of adoption. In the final selection in this part, the anthropologist Judith S. Modell draws upon her interviews and observations of all three members of the "adoption triad" in her brilliant interpretation of how open adoption is transforming notions of biological and adoptive kinship in contemporary American culture.

37

Overview of Legal Status of Post-Adoption Contact Agreements

Joan Heifetz Hollinger

Open adoption is said to provide many benefits. It allegedly enables birth parents—especially mothers—to diminish their sense of loss, children adopted as infants to possess the piece of themselves missing from their otherwise secure adoptive family relationships, older children and children adopted from foster care to continue existing, albeit troubled, relationships with a birth parent, and adoptive parents to have access to information vital to their capacity to respond to their children's developmental, medical, and emotional needs. The prospect of ongoing contact with a child may encourage some birth parents to relinquish voluntarily rather than face an adversarial termination of rights proceeding. Openness may even reinforce adoptive parents' sense of entitlement to parent and enable them to empathize with birth parents. Longitudinal research on children adopted as infants suggests that ongoing contact with a birth parent contributes to their overall well-being as they grow up; but it is by no means clear that, without such contact, these or other children, including foreign-born adoptees who may never know their birth families' identities, would fare differently over the course of their lives.

Among the factors contributing to the prevalence of open domestic adoptions is the rarely noted shift in power from adoptive to birth parents. As the competition among would-be adoptive parents has intensified because of the steep decline since the late 1960s in the number of healthy infants who are voluntarily relinquished for adoption, a more distinctive "seller's market" has emerged. Birth parents, and especially birth mothers, are not only choosing the individuals who will parent their children, but often expect to retain a role in the life of the new adoptive family. Prospective parents who harbor doubts about meeting, or maintaining contact with, birth parents may be less likely to end up with a child to adopt.

Despite some resistance to these developments, a great many private and public agencies, lawyers, and social workers have become willing agents of the new ways of exercising control over adoptive parents. Indeed, Grotevant and McRoy report that many agencies are concerned that if they do not accede to birth parents' requests for open placements, they will go out of business (Harold D. Grotevant and Ruth McRoy, *Openness in Adoption: Exploring Family Connections* [Sage 1998]). The biblical tale of Pharaoh's daughter adopting the infant Moses after rescuing him from the bulrushes, but allowing his "real" mother to be his wet-nurse, is in some respects emblematic of the ambiguities and realignments of power within contemporary adoptive families.

Not all prospective adoptive parents are willing to pay what they believe is too high a price to acquire a child. They want to be parents with the same constitutionally protected autonomy and privacy as other legal parents enjoy, not long-term caregivers of a child whose destiny is ultimately determined by the biogenetic family.

Although most prospective parents now prefer, and even demand, greater "openness" when it means access to the medical and psychosocial histories of the children they adopt, and may also be willing to meet with one or both birth parents at the time of an adoptive placement, many are uneasy [as Judith S. Modell suggests, below] when continued contact with birth parents goes beyond annual exchanges of photographs or letters and encompasses visitation or other entanglements that raise the spectre of shared parenting. Barbara Yngvesson has also noted this concern: "The 'choosing' birthmother is easily incorporated into more familiar concepts of individualism and voluntarism, in ways that the visiting birthmother, whose 'choice' is not simply to identify the adoptive parents for her child but to become part of their lives, is not" ("Negotiating Motherhood Identity and Difference in 'Open' Adoptions," 31 *Law & Society Rev.* 31 [1997]).

The inconclusive research to date on the long term consequences of ongoing contact between birth and adoptive families suggests that, for all the problems with the asserted-equivalence or "as-if" model of adoption, the alternative model of maintaining contact with a child's birth family may also not be appropriate for every adoptive family. While privately negotiated "open adoption" agreements based on mutual trust between adoptive and birth parents should certainly not be prohibited, there may be sound reasons to question whether the trend toward enforceable post-adoption contact [discussed below and in *In re Adoption of Vito*] may be as beneficial for adopted children as allowing adoptive parents, and when they are older, the children themselves, to decide whether to have any communication or visitation with a birth parent.

While informal open adoption agreements have become more and more widespread in the past twenty-five years, state adoption laws have generally not permitted judicial recognition or enforcement of these agreements without explicit statutory authorization, except, perhaps, in a stepparent or intrafamily adoption. An agreement by adoptive parents for continued contact with a birth parent, or a "reservation" by a birth parent of a "right" to visit a child, is often presumed to be inconsistent with the "essential meaning" of adoption—the complete transfer of all the rights and duties of the child's original parents to the new adoptive parents; see, e.g., *In re Adoption of a Child by W.P. & M.P.*, 748 A.2d 515 (N.J. 2000) ("An adoptive family must be given the right to grow and develop as an autonomous family, and must not be tied to the very relationship that put the child in the position of being adopted. Any other ruling would relegate the adoptive parents to 'second-class' status").

Although some courts acknowledge that the well-being of children, especially older and special needs children, might be promoted by continuing contact with a birth parent, they either refuse to enforce post-adoption contact agreements while upholding an adoption, or set aside adoptions upon concluding that these agreements vitiate the birth parents' consent to the termination of their parental rights. A few courts have allowed birth mothers to revoke their consent by claiming they were fraudulently induced to give up a child for adoption by promises of post-adoption visitation that agencies or adoptive parents never intended to keep; see, e.g., *Vela v. Marywood*, 17 S.W.3d 750 (Tex. App. 2000) (agency breached its duty of full disclosure to birth mother that her relinquishment for adoption extinguished any rights she had to visitation with her child).

Since the mid-1990s, however, many state laws have acknowledged the possibility that an open adoption arrangement may be compatible with a full legal adoption. By 2003, more than twenty states had enacted statutes that expressly permit adoptive parents to enter into a post-adoption contact agreement with their adopted child's biological parent, and, in some states, with other members of the birth family. These agreements are subject to court approval during the adoption proceeding and may be enforced in a court proceeding once the adoption is final. The statutes further provide that the basic validity and finality of an adoption is not affected by the existence of an open agreement or by any dispute over its terms.

Most of these recently enacted statutes incorporate a version of Section 3-707 of the proposed Uniform Adoption Act (1994) that "the validity of a decree of adoption . . . may not be challenged for failure to comply with an agreement for visitation or communication with an adoptee."

These statutes generally provide for a civil action to specifically enforce or modify contact or visitation agreements until an adoptee's 18th birthday, subject to a "best interests" standard. Although a few statutes authorize courts to order post-adoption contact even over the objection of adoptive parents, most require that the adoptive parents and the child, if over the age of 12 or 14, voluntarily agree to maintain contact with the child's birth parent or other relative in order for post-adoption contact to be enforceable.

The "best interests of the child" standard applies to judicial decisions to approve, modify, or enforce post-adoption contact or visitation agreements. Some statutes require the court to consider the strength and quality of any existing relationship between the child and a birth parent or other person who seeks contact as well as the effect of continuing contact on the stability and autonomy of the adoptive family.

Beyond these common features, the statutes vary greatly (see Appendix 13B–C, *Adoption Law and Practice*). Some apply to all adopted children, whether placed privately or through the public child welfare system; others apply only to older children adopted from foster care or by relatives. Some require the consent of the agency and the child's Guardian ad Litem (GAL) as well as of the adoptive parents. Several favor mediation in the event of a dispute and provide for the recovery of costs, including attorneys' fees, by a prevailing party; but most are silent about the procedures applicable to enforcement actions.

Despite the substantial body of law review and child welfare articles advocating post-adoption contact for older children adopted from foster care, there is little empirical research on the short or long term consequences of open adoption for children whose biological parents agreed to resolve a contested adoption in exchange for a promise of continued contact, or whose biological parents had their parental rights terminated for child abuse or neglect.

The Grotevant and McRoy longitudinal study of open adoptions, referred to above, is not about older children adopted from foster care or by relatives, but about children adopted as infants during the late 1980s from private agencies by predominantly white middle and upper middle class couples. Most of the families were involved in a semi- to fully-disclosed adoption with varying degrees of continued contact with birth parents; none of these informal arrangements were court-approved or judicially enforceable. With their interviews now spanning 13 years, Grotevant and McRoy report mostly favorable reactions to open adoption arrangements, especially from those involved in the most "fully disclosed" adoptions. Their findings have little if any bearing, however, on the question of whether court-enforced open adoption agreements are beneficial for either the children or their birth or adoptive parents. Because their work focuses on children adopted as infants, and on birth and adoptive parents who had no prior contacts with each other, it is also not clear what relevance their research has to open adoptions of older or foster children who may have had difficult relationships with their birth parents prior to their adoption.

In contrast to the states with laws that expressly authorize courts to approve and enforce agreements for post-adoption contact, many states recognize non-binding informal agreements. Others neither permit nor prohibit them, thus exposing families to the risk that an adoption may be set aside if an agreement for continuing contact is deemed to contradict the "essential meaning" of adoption; see, e.g., *In re Adoption of C. R. Topel*, 571 N.E.2d 1295 (Ind. 1991).

Post-Adoption Visitation by Grandparents

By statute or case law, nearly every state allows grandparents to seek court-ordered visitation when their grandchild is adopted by a stepparent. A few states also allow grandparents to seek visitation when a grandchild is adopted by another grandparent or close relative. The grandparent(s) who are authorized to seek visitation are the parents of the grandchild's parent whose parental status terminates when the child is adopted by the other parent's spouse. In some states, the only grandparent(s) who may seek visitation are the parents of the grandchild's deceased parent whose surviving spouse remarries someone who later adopts the child.

While most states now recognize the ties children may have to grandparents who are not related to the child's custodial parent and adoptive stepparent, there are few precedents for court-enforced visitation by grandparents whose grandchild is adopted by "legal strangers" unless the adoptive parents affirmatively agree to such visitation.

The U.S. Supreme Court's decision in *Troxel v. Granville*, 530 U.S. 57 (2000), casts doubt on the constitutionality of many state grandparent or third party visitation statutes. The plurality held that a fit custodial parent's childrearing decisions are presumptively in the child's best interests and are entitled to "special weight" as against third party visitation claims. The Court did not spell out what "special factors" might overcome this parental "special weight," but implied that a child's actual and substantial ties to a third party, including a grandparent, might constitute such a "special factor" in specific cases. The practice of permitting grandparents to continue visiting with their grandchildren after a stepparent adoption has continued, even post-*Troxel*.

38

Perspectives on Open Adoption

Annette Baran and Reuben Pannor

We believe that confidentiality and anonymity are harmful and that adoptions should be open. This perspective was developed during more than 40 years of practice as psychotherapists and researchers. We have counseled thousands of birthparents, adoptees, and adoptive parents, following many of them over decades. As we developed our practice, it became evident that little attention had been paid to the psychological needs of adult adoptees and that no studies had been done to examine the feelings and attitudes of birthparents years after they had relinquished their children for adoption. Beginning in 1974 we, with Arthur Sorosky, began to report our observations that some of the psychological problems observed in adolescent and adult adoptees, birth parents, and adoptive parents appeared to be related directly to the secrecy, anonymity, and sealed records aspects of adoption. These observations were later expanded in our book, *The Adoption Triangle.* . . .

Psychological and Emotional Effects of the Closed System

[We have found that] requiring anonymity between birthparents and adoptive parents and sealing all information about the birthparents from the adopted child has damaging effects on all three parties. . . .

Effects on the Birthparents

Relinquishment of a newborn child may be profoundly damaging to birthparents and cause lifelong pain and suffering. Even when relinquishment is a carefully considered and chosen option, birthmothers—and often birthfathers—may suffer from a heightened sense of worthlessness after giving away a child. They may feel guilty about their actions. These birthparents may believe that their offspring will not understand the reasons for the relinquishment and that these offspring will blame and hate their birthparents for rejecting and abandoning them. The birthparents may want their children to know that they continue to care about them and, in turn, may wish to learn about the kind of people their children have become. No matter how many children they may have subsequently, birthparents may still desire knowledge and contact with the one they gave up.

In traditional closed adoptions, such knowledge and contact is not possible. . . .

Effects on the Adoptees

Adopted children also frequently suffer from the secrecy imposed in closed adoption, particularly during adolescence when they often experience greater identity conflicts than members of the non-adopted population. The process of developing an individual identity is more complicated for adoptees because they live with the knowledge that an essential part of their personal history remains on the other side of the adoption barrier. In closed adoptions, any desire on the part of an adopted child to learn more about the birthparents is blocked, often leading to fantasies and distortions. Easily escalated, these may develop into more serious problems. In our studies, we described these adoption-related identity conflicts as resulting in "identity lacunae," which can lead to feelings of shame, embarrassment, and low self-esteem. In addition, adoptees may experience a deep fear of loss and separation. Many adopted children feel that they were given away because there was something wrong with them from the beginning.

We observed that, in late adolescence, negative feelings and questions about being adopted increased. In young adulthood, plans for marriage may create an urgent desire for specific background information, particularly about family history. For adopted adult women, pregnancy and the birth of a child may raise fears of possible unknown hereditary problems. Becoming a parent may also trigger intense feelings in the adoptee toward his or her own birthmother. These feelings may include not only empathy for her difficult emotional situation, but also anger and disbelief that she could have given up her own child. The feelings frequently create a need in adoptees to search for birthparents and the hope for a reunion to bring together the broken connections from the past. . . .

Effects on the Adoptive Parents

Finally, closed adoption can also have negative psychological and emotional effects on the adoptive parents. With no knowledge of or contact with the birthparents as real people, they may be unable to answer truthfully their adoptive children's inevitable questions about why they were given up, what their birthparents were like, and what happened to these parents in later life. The ghosts of the birthparents, inherent in the closed system, are ever present, and may lead to the fear that these parents will reclaim the child and that the child will love these parents more that the adoptive parents.

Definition of Open Adoption

An open adoption is one in which the birthparent(s) at least meet the adoptive parents and may even participate in selecting them. . . . [O]pen adoption includes the exchange of identifying information and the making of agreements regarding future contact and communication. The frequency and extent of this contact and communication will vary and may need to be renegotiated at different times in the lives of the individuals involved, depending upon their needs and desires and the quality of the relationship that evolves. . . .

Misconceptions about Open Adoption

As open adoption became more common in the 1970s and 1980s, several popular misconceptions were challenged. They deserve further scrutiny.

Couples will not adopt children unless they can be guaranteed anonymity and secrecy. Such guarantees, we now know, were never ironclad. The adoptees' reform movement spawned a nationwide network of search groups that often successfully located birthparents and nullified guarantees of secrecy and anonymity given by adoption agencies to these parents. Furthermore, experience in adoption during the past decade, when fewer newborns were available, has clearly demonstrated that couples, eager to parent children, are willing to adopt under a variety of circumstances. Although once only healthy babies were considered adoptable, now children with disabilities, from mixed racial backgrounds, and in sibling groups are being welcomed by families. . . . At present open adoption is accepted by many adoptive parents and this practice appears to be increasing particularly in independent adoption.

Birthmothers want and need anonymity to move forward in their lives and put the experience of pregnancy and relinquishment behind them. This misconception was fostered by maternity homes and adoption agencies. It was sustained, in part, because some adoption social workers found it difficult to deal with the continuing pathos and misery of the birthmothers in the post-relinquishment period. Our studies of birthmothers in the 1970s indicated that, when they contacted agencies regarding their relinquished children, they often were made to feel emotionally unstable and at fault for carrying this experience with them. . . . These observations were contrary to the belief that birthmothers had emotionally resolved giving up a child, recovered from the trauma, and wished to remain hidden. These birthmothers had not been advised or counseled about the possibility that they might have lifelong anxiety and distress. Even those birthmothers who had not revealed their past to husband and children indicated that, if it were possible to protect themselves, they would want to know and meet their offspring. Not to know whether their children were alive or dead was a continuing source of sadness for some.

Adoptees will be confused by contact with their birthparents and may become emotionally disturbed as a result of being aware of and dealing with two mothers during their developmental years. Our experience has led us to conclude that closed adoptions did not protect adoptees from emotional disturbances. On the contrary, it is our belief, based on years of work with adoptees of all ages, that some of them are particularly vulnerable because of feelings of loss and abandonment, exacerbated by the secrecy and anonymity of closed adoptions. However, because open adoption placement is still comparatively new, we cannot state conclusively what effects it has on adoptees. Long-term studies on the adjustment of adoptees to open adoption are few in number and vary in quality. . . .

Benefits of Open Adoptive Placements

There are several important benefits to open adoptive placements. First, the birthparents assume more responsibility for the decision to relinquish, and as full participants in the placement and entrusting of the child to a known family, they are better able to cope with feelings of loss, mourning, and grief. If contact with their birthchild is permitted, they are able to further ameliorate these feelings.

Next, adoptees' feelings of rejection by the birthparents also can be greatly diminished. A realistic understanding of the problems that led to adoptive placement permits acceptance of the situation. The continuing link with the birthparent dispels the notion that the children were abandoned and forgotten. In open adoption the need for search and reunion is eliminated. Important background information—including genetic and medical histories—is readily available.

Finally, for adoptive parents, knowing the birthparents of their children can prevent the fears and fantasies that might otherwise have a negative effect on their relationships with their adopted children. Knowing the birthparents will enable adoptive parents to provide their children with background information based on first-hand knowledge and direct contacts. . . .

Conclusion

In conclusion, our decades of experience lead us to believe that open adoption is the best approach. It minimizes emotional and psychological harm, and it allows all parties to meet their continuing responsibilities to each other.

There is, however, more to be done. More research on the effects of open adoption is needed. Also, we must be vigilant to potential abuses. Scanning want-ad columns in newspapers across the country or the Yellow Pages of phone books in any of the major cities reveals the extent to which adoption has become a business and the degree to which open adoption can be used to expand that business. . . . The possibility of open adoption is frequently used to encourage relinquishment, particularly with young teenagers who are led to believe that they will have all the benefits of knowing their babies with none of the risks or responsibilities. Deceit of this kind unfairly encourages relinquishment and offers promises that often are not kept after the adoption occurs.

Thus, the central question today is not whether adoption shall be open or closed. . . . Rather, the challenge, in our view, is to ensure that open adoption continues to evolve in the best way possible. Every effort must be made to prevent abuse. The respective roles of birthparents, adoptive parents, and extended family in promoting the success of open adoption deserve careful consideration. However, in the final analysis, it is the adoptee whose well-being is central.

39

In re Adoption of Vito (Mass. 2000)

Marshall, C.J.

This appeal arises from the denial of a petition to dispense with parental consent to adoption. The case concerns a child who tested positive for cocaine at the time of his birth in January, 1992, and who has lived with his foster parents (also his pre-adoptive parents) since he was discharged from the hospital one month after his birth. Vito has never lived with his biological mother. He is now eight and one-half years old. . . .

We vacate the judge's order denying the petition to dispense with parental consent to adoption. The judge's conclusion that the mother is unfit is not challenged. [Father did not object to termination of his rights.] With respect to the judge's denial of the petition based on failure to provide for postadoption contact in the adoption plan, we hold that a judge may order limited postadoption contact, including visitation, between a child and a biological parent where such contact is currently in the best interests of the child. The judge has the authority to ensure that such contact in the best interests of the child is maintained during an appropriate transitional period.

Judicial exercise of equitable power to require postadoption contact is not warranted in this case, however, because there is little or no evidence of a significant, existing bond between Vito and his biological mother, and no other compelling reason for concluding that postadoption contact is currently in his best interests. Vito has formed strong, nurturing bonds with his preadoptive family; and the record supports little more than speculation that postadoption contact will be important for his adjustment years later, in adolescence. . . . Accordingly, we remand the case to the Probate Court and direct that a decree enter granting the department's petition to dispense with the biological mother's consent to Vito's adoption.

I

. . . In 1990 Vito's biological mother began using crack cocaine, which she continued to do until 1995, with occasional periods of nonuse. . . . [S]he had been trading food stamps and using public welfare benefits to purchase crack cocaine. Her children were often left at home alone. When Vito tested positive for cocaine at birth, an abuse and neglect report concerning him was filed two days after his birth, alleging his positive cocaine screen and his mother's failure to obtain prenatal care. The report was substantiated . . . and he was placed in the temporary custody of the department.

Vito was discharged from the hospital one month after his birth and was placed in the home of his foster parents; his siblings had been placed in other homes. . . . From

[that] time on, his biological mother visited Vito only once. During that ninety-minute visit, Vito responded minimally to his biological mother, withdrew from her and attached himself to his foster mother. . . . [His] mother agreed to visit Vito again on his first birthday, but although the foster mother and Vito arrived for the birthday visit, the mother failed to attend; she did not telephone to cancel the visit. Following the failed January, 1993, birthday visit, the biological mother made no request for a visit with her son for the remainder of 1993. During 1994 there were no visits with Vito, and little contact between the biological mother and the department; she told the department she had relocated to Florida.

In 1995, while back in Massachusetts in prison on shoplifting charges, Vito's mother signed a department service plan, entered a drug rehabilitation program and began visits with Vito and his siblings. Vito's mother was released from prison in October, 1995. The judge found that the mother's visits with Vito have been generally consistent since March, 1995, and that she has attended monthly supervised visits since her release. The judge found that Vito and his biological mother have "no emotional sharing" between them and remain dissociated, despite pleasant play and conversation. The judge found that Vito did not show any genuine interest in his biological siblings and did not appear to have formed any emotional attachment to his biological mother; he did not appear to be excited to see her and separated from her with no difficulties or emotional overtones. The judge nevertheless made an ultimate finding that Vito had formed "a positive relationship" with his biological mother that has developed since visitation began when she was incarcerated. The judge found that Vito's mother, however, had not fully complied with the department's service plan tasks, and concluded that Vito's biological mother cannot now resume care and custody of Vito because "she has not secured adequate stable housing, has not adequately addressed her issues of lengthy substance abuse history and has not acquired any meaningful parenting skills training." She also concluded that Vito's mother's drug abuse and resultant neglect "was severe and of a lengthy duration," although she had improved in the last two years.

In contrast, the judge found that Vito is "fully integrated into his foster family both emotionally and ethnically." The judge found that it was "important" to Vito to belong to his foster family "because that was the only family he had known," and that "the foster parents are invested in adopting [Vito]; they perceive him as their own son." She found that Vito "has a significant attachment to his foster family," and that separating Vito from his foster family could result in a range of negative responses, from severe depression to less severe trauma.

The judge concluded that, by clear and convincing evidence, Vito's mother is currently unfit to parent him. . . . Her unavailability to Vito . . . resulted in Vito's "life-long placement with [his foster] family, to which he is now attached." Despite the fact that the biological mother "cares deeply for and has good intentions toward the child," however, "good intentions . . . are insufficient to establish fitness to parent a child."

The judge further determined that "racial issues may at sometime in the future" become a problem for Vito. She found that Vito's relationship with his biological mother is "crucial" for his "racial and cultural development and adjustment," that his best interests will be served by continued "significant" contact with her after any adoption, and that under the department's adoption plan Vito would have limited or no connection to his African-American family or culture. She found that the department's plan is not in Vito's "best interest so long as it does not provide for significant ongoing contact with [his] mother and [biological] siblings."

II

A

. . . A judge's equitable power to order postadoption contact, however, is not without limit. . . . This equitable authority does not derive from the statutory adoption scheme, but it must necessarily be attentive to the policy directives inherent in that scheme, as well as to constitutional limitations on intrusions on the prerogatives of the adoptive family. The adoption statute contemplates, for example, that after an adoption decree, "all rights, duties and other legal consequences of the natural relation of child and parent . . . shall, except as regards marriage, incest or cohabitation, terminate between the child so adopted and his natural parents." G. L. c. 210, § 6. . . . [I]n ordinary circumstances adoption is meant to sever most enforceable obligations involving the biological parent with the child. . . . This statutory language is not a bar to judicial orders for postadoption contact, however, because an order for postadoption contact is grounded in the overall best interests of the child, based on emotional bonding and other circumstances of the actual personal relationship of the child and the biological parent, not in the rights of the biological parent nor the legal consequences of their natural relation. [citations omitted.]

We determine that postadoption contact is not warranted here, for example, because there is little or no evidence of a significant, existing bond between Vito and his biological mother, and no other compelling reason for concluding that postadoption contact, even for an appropriate transitional period, is warranted.

At a pragmatic level, unnecessary involvement of the courts in long-term, wide-ranging monitoring and enforcement of the numerous postadoption contact arrangements could result from too ready an application of the court's equitable power to issue contact orders. The postadoption contact arrangements contemplated by the judge in this case were both long term and wide ranging, and necessarily would have involved the court in ongoing arrangements between the biological mother and the adopting family for many years to come. But courts are not often the best place to monitor children's changing needs, particularly the needs of young children. What may be in Vito's best interest at the age of five says little about his best interests at age ten or fifteen.

We also recognize the concern raised by the department and the amici that untrammeled equitable power used to impose postadoption contact might reduce the number of prospective parents willing to adopt. Any practice that potentially reduces the pool of prospective adoptive parents raises grave concerns. We note that there are mechanisms to review the adoption plan and reassess it if a particular postadoption contact requirement might be delaying adoption. . . .

Where, as here, the child has formed strong, nurturing bonds with his pre-adoptive family, and there is little or no evidence of a significant, existing bond with the biological parent, judicial exercise of equitable power to require postadoption contact would usually be unwarranted. On the other hand, a judicial order for postadoption contact may be warranted where the evidence readily points to significant, existing bonds between the child and a biological parent, such that a court order abruptly disrupting that relationship would run counter to the child's best interests. . . .

Transitional provision for post-termination or postadoption contact in the best interests of the child, however, is a far different thing from judicial meddling in the child's and adoptive family's life, based not on evidence of the emotional ties and current dynamics between the child and the biological parent, but on speculation concerning some hypothetical dynamic between parent and child several years hence, later in adolescence, for example. Parental and familial autonomy cannot be so lightly cast aside. In Vito's case the probate judge apparently favored postadoption contact because she was concerned about Vito's future racial and cultural development and adjustment, presumably based on the guardian ad litem's testimony that transracial adoptees, generally speaking, often have adjustment problems that emerge in adolescence. The judge appears to have inappropriately relied on the guardian ad litem's speculation as to the future need of Vito to have contact with his mother in order to secure his identity years later, in adolescence. That is a matter that is properly left to the wise guidance of Vito's new family. . . .

Looking at the evidence of the actual circumstances of Vito's life and relationships, testimony of the guardian ad litem made clear that Vito's monthly visits with the biological mother had little or no impact on Vito's sense of identity. Rather, the judge's findings reveal that Vito strongly identified with his preadoptive family, emotionally and ethnically. In the wake of her incarceration, there was evidence that the biological mother "cares deeply for and has good intentions toward" Vito. But there was powerful evidence that there was little or no emotional bonding between them, hardly surprising where Vito has spent his entire life living with, being nurtured and loved by, and identifying with his foster family.

There was also little in the record before us to suggest that Vito's relationship with his biological mother was likely to become important to Vito's adolescent identity. There was evidence of some possible future significance of the relationship in the guardian ad litem's acknowledgment that, generally, adolescence may be a time when a transracial adoptee may experience adjustment problems, and that Vito would have little connection to an African-American family or culture living with his adoptive family. Generalities about what may be in the best interests of some children, without more, cannot be the basis of judicial orders concerning postadoption contact of a particular child; the best interests of the child standard is one grounded in the particular needs and circumstances of the individual child in question. . . . Assuming that it was proper to use racial grounds for determining Vito's best interest, there was no evidence in the record that showed Vito would be deprived of all African-American contacts in his adolescence if regular visits with his biological mother were not mandated. While Vito's foster family "currently" has no significant contacts with the African-American community, that fact says little, if anything, about contacts that his adoptive family might develop in the future, if this becomes important for their son. We discern no support for a determination that Vito's relationship with his biological mother is "crucial" for his "racial and cultural development and adjustment." Moreover, here the judge found that Vito "is a typical Latino child growing up in a Latino family . . . [and who] describes himself as Latino," who was "fully integrated into his foster family both emotionally and ethnically," and whose physical appearance was not strikingly different from his foster parents. His primary language is that of his foster family, not his biological mother. The judge found Vito "did not manifest any genuine interest in his biological siblings" and did not have an "emotional attachment" to his biological mother.

We conclude, therefore, that, although the probate judge had a statutory mandate to review the department's adoption plan to determine whether the best interests of the child would be served by a termination decree with that plan, and although the judge had equitable authority to order postadoption contact, including visitation, the judge's determination that such postadoption contact was required was clearly erroneous in this case. . . . Here, the evidence clearly revealed a strong bond to the preadoptive family, the only family Vito has ever known, and little to no attachment by him to his biological mother or his biological siblings. In such circumstances it was inappropriate to stall Vito's adoption at the hurdle of termination proceedings, based on speculation about Vito's need for contact with his biological mother to facilitate his adjustment later in adolescence to his racial identity.

40

Guidelines for Public Policy and State Legislation Governing Permanence for Children

U.S. Children's Bureau

3. Post Adoption Contact Agreement

We recommend that State law authorize a court terminating parental rights or granting adoption for a child in foster care to approve an agreement by the adoptive parent or parents to allow post-adoption contact between the child and a birth parent, sibling, grandparent, or other relative or individual who has a significant emotional tie to the child. . . .

Commentary

Without protective legislation, post-adoption contact is purely voluntary and rarely enforceable in court. Although a court might decide to exercise its equitable powers to enforce an informal agreement in extraordinary circumstances, another court might decide to set aside an adoption if it believes that ongoing contact with the birth family is inconsistent with the severance of all legal ties to the birth family, which is the traditional consequence of adoption. Despite these uncertainties, informal voluntary arrangements for post-adoption contact may be appropriate for some children, especially when adoptive and birth families already know each other and have a high degree of mutual trust. Legislation is needed, however, to protect the benefits of voluntary arrangements by specifically providing that the validity of a voluntary relinquishment, a judicial termination of parental rights, or a decree of adoption is not subject to challenge because of an agreement for post-adoption contact or because of any failure to comply with the agreement. . . .

Many foster children have psychological connections to their birth families, siblings, and other significant persons, such as foster parents, so that it would be in the child's interest to maintain some sort of contact even after adoption. The child may need to know and understand his or her ethnic background and heritage. There may be a need to share medical information and health histories. Preservation of an emotional tie may be beneficial to the child. Continued contact may relieve an older child's guilt or concerns about the birth parent. Contact may help the child come to terms with his or her past. A connection with a biological parent may be a positive, yet limited, influence, and may prevent the child from running away or disrupting a new placement where the child desires continuing ties. Continued contact may avoid the trauma of contested and prolonged termination of parental rights proceedings. Children generally benefit from contact with siblings. These needs may be recognized and agreed to by the new parents and approved by the court. The contact could be as simple as exchanging photos each year without any physical contact, but the arrangements could leave a door open for future relationships *when helpful to the child.*

Post-Adoption Contact
CWLA 2000 Standards

Child Welfare League of America

4.12. Preparing Families for Various Levels of Openness in Adoption

Education about and consideration of the benefits and challenges of openness in adoption should be an integral part of the homestudy and preparation process for all adoptive applicants.

Adopted individuals, birth families, and adoptive families are best served by a process that is open, honest, and supportive of the concept that all information, including identifying information, may be shared between birth and adoptive parents.

The degree of openness in any adoption should be arrived at by mutual agreement based on a thoughtful, informed decisionmaking process by the birth parents, the prospective adoptive parents, and the child, when appropriate. Educating applicants during the homestudy process about the range of openness in adoption provides them with time to explore their attitudes and possibly expand the level of openness with which they will be comfortable in adoption.

Increasing Options to Improve Permanency
Considerations in Drafting an Adoption with Contact Statute

Annette Ruth Appell

. . . Cooperative adoption is a form of open adoption in which the birth relatives and adoptive parents collaborate before and after completion of adoption to provide an agreeable level of postadoption contact between those relatives and the adoptive parents or the child. Adoption with contact refers to an adoption with enforceable rights of contact arising out of a cooperative adoption agreement.

Proponents of openness in adoption believe that it meets the needs of each member of the adoption triad. Foremost, openness in adoption can serve a number of adoptee needs. First, it may provide a conduit for birth family information that the adoptee may seek throughout various stages of life. Second, it may assist in identity formation by allowing adoptees to integrate birth relationships or knowledge about those relationships into their developmental process. Third, it may enhance the likelihood and stability of adoptions by (a) decreasing children's resistance to adoption arising out of loyalty to birth parents or siblings before and after adoption, (b) decreasing birth parents' resistance to the adoption, and (c) helping to de-escalate adoptees' behavioral problems, particularly during adolescence.

Openness in adoption provides a mechanism for the adoptive family to meet or correspond with the birth family. It enables adoptive parents to obtain information about their child's birth parents and about their adopted child's background or heritage, information which may assist adoptive parents to better meet the unique challenges of parenting adoptive children. Research suggests that postadoption contact decreases adoptive parents' anxiety that the birth parents will attempt to reclaim the child. For birth parents, openness permits them to relinquish their child without losing the ability to learn how their child is developing, and for some to come to terms with the grief of relinquishment.

Openness is not, however, without risks and limitations. Postadoption contact can lead to disappointment and confusion when some members do not meet the other members' expectations. It also can be problematic in those adoptions in which ongoing contact would be unduly disruptive or threatening to a child who is fearful of the birth parents or insecure about the permanency of the adoptive placement. Too much openness may also have negative ramifications for other members of the birth and adoptive families. Another concern is that postadoption contact blurs boundaries among the triad members. Cooperative adoptions in particular may be difficult or impossible to plan in child protection cases when parental rights are terminated in one proceeding to which the adoptive parents are not parties and adoption occurs in another proceeding to which the birth parents are not parties. . . .

[Other concerns involve the child's interests. First, it may be difficult for the child to have a voice in the agreement, particularly when he or she is too young to express or form a position on the contact. Second, the child's needs may evolve, so that what seemed to be a desirable level of contact when the adults made the agreement may no longer be, as the child reaches different developmental stages or circumstances in the child's life change. Third, if the birth relatives and adoptive parents do not respect each other or become acrimonious, forced contact could place the child in an untenable situation of conflicting loyalty.]

In light of its benefits and despite its risks, states are passing adoption legislation that recognizes varying levels of openness. . . .

. . . Adoption with contact's chief strength is the autonomy and respect it gives the parties who will be living with the agreement. Thus the key players—the adoptive parents, relatives, and perhaps the child—decide on the type and amount of contact that is most comfortable or desirable for them. After all, because they know the child, they are typically in the best position to make that decision and to determine what is best for the child. The major weakness of adoption with contact is that the parties do not always know each other, particularly when the termination of parental rights proceeding is separate from the adoption proceeding or when there is a significant time gap between the two. Another problem is that the parties may not have the sophistication or strength to recognize when postadoption contact would be best for the child.

Court-imposed postadoption contact has the inverse strengths and weaknesses. Its strength is that the court views solely the child's needs and interests, from an arguably dispassionate and objective viewpoint. Courts can also fill the gap between termination of parental rights proceedings and adoption, thereby preserving the child's important ties should no subsequent adoption materialize or until such time as the adoptive parents meet those persons important to the child. On the other hand, the adoptive parents' agreement with the contact plan may be crucial to their need for parental autonomy in building their new family, as well as their comfort with the contact. Adoptive parents may resent the court's intrusion into what is traditionally a parent's decision—the persons with whom their child will have contact. This intrusion may also limit their ability to develop a needed sense of entitlement to the child.

Perhaps the best scheme is for state legislatures to provide courts with the flexibility to encourage, approve and uphold postadoption contact agreements and to intervene when the circumstances do not enable the parties to forge a postadoption plan for the child on their own.

43

Kinship with Strangers
Adoption and Interpretations of Kinship in American Culture

Judith S. Modell

A New Kind of Kinship: The Implications of Change in American Adoption

. . . Openness alters the relationships established by adoption; given the link between fictive and real, open adoption could also revise the role of biology in cultural interpretations of kinship. . . .

. . . The "made" relationship [of adoption] delineates the terms of the natural relationship: a child born of two parents, the product of their sexual relationship. Fictive kinship tells participants that real kinship means "blood ties." These determine the structure of a family and also the emotions of its members: the feelings of *being* a parent and a child.

For people whose kinship is fictive, however, blood also represents what is missing. It is this dimension of "non-reality" that makes an adoptive relationship different, paradoxical, and in need of work—a self-conscious kinship. It takes work to maintain the "fiction" of being a childless parent, a parent without having given birth, and a child who lacks a "genetic map." The spurt of consciousness-raising in the 1960s and 1970s altered the content of this work, bringing out the deceptions of an as-if axiom and prompting the changes in adoption . . . which themselves are only beginning.

The symbolism of blood dominates interpretations of kinship in American culture, subsuming references to sexual reproduction and to biological ancestry. In an as-if relationship, blood is the model for conduct and for emotion, representing the unconditional love and enduring solidarity of a parent-child relationship. As a model, too, blood transforms the contracted relationship into a seemingly reproductive link; the child is as if a product of the parents' union, deserving the attention and care any such child would receive. Furthermore, with blood as the model, adoptive parents are "re-gendered," after having started off "running in the same place." The adoptive family is as traditional as the stereotypical biological family: father, mother, and children—"the natural setting for a child," as the CWLA [Child Welfare League of America] tells its member agencies [CWLA 1988 standards].

The symbolism of blood sustains the fiction of adoption, but it also lends the transaction a fatal flaw—an inevitable comparison with "real" blood ties. "Blood" is a reminder that adoption is a *paper* kinship. The application forms filled out by adoptive parents, the surrender papers signed by a birthparent, and the amended birth certificate all assert the fictive in this kind of kinship. And fictive here connotes "unreal" rather than "created." A paper parenthood cannot compare with the "physical realities" of conception, creation, gestation, and birth, not in American culture anyway. "I felt as if I had kidnapped a baby," an adoptive mother said to me, revealing a fear that the contract she signed was not a true bond. Nor was she reassured by the birthparent's signature on a piece of paper . . . "blood had primacy, and nature had rights." . . .

On their side, birthparents expressed astonishment at the presumption that signing a paper would erase the memory of having had a child. For them, blood was an enduring and unbreakable bond; a signature did not make it go away. Thus, papers *did* and did *not* redo parenthood, creating the ambiguous status both parents in the triad experienced: one a childless mother and the other a "birthless" parent. For the adoptee, papers play a perhaps even more powerful role, producing a "juridical rebirth." The adoptee is granted a new birth certificate, his social parents listed as if they were his biological parents, in lawful wedlock. The paradox embedded here is that the child is as-if-begotten but not *born.* In one sense, then, an adoptee's birth certificate is a profound lie. In another sense, however, it is true; with adoption, the legal parent completely (and absolutely) replaces a parent by birth. An amended birth certificate stands for the transformation adoption achieves and, simultaneously, asserts the significance of "blood" in the parent-child relationship. A social relationship makes no sense without the reference to a genealogical relationship.

In the mid-1960s, the inherent ambiguity of an as-if birth became oppressive at least to some adoptees and, supported by one another, they claimed the right to a real birth, represented by an unamended birth certificate. . . .

One could say the adoptee demand for "facts" begins with growing up adopted and comparing two parents, one who gave away and one who took a child: an unknown and a known parent; a bad and a good mother. The comparison focuses on the mother and virtually excludes fatherhood from the equation. This is true for several reasons: not only are adoptees more likely to think about the mother who gave away and the mother who took a child but also, as adoption illustrates, "mother" comes to represent "parent" more generally in American culture.

Discussing the experience of growing up adopted, adoptees reversed the conventional contrast and portrayed the birthmother as good and generous, the adoptive mother as selfish and stingy—and said they had done so as children. The birthmother, then, not the adoptive mother, fits the cultural interpretation of motherhood: loving, emotionally giving, and sexual—*productively* sexual. By contrast for the adoptee (even those who grew up happily), the adoptive mother was rigid, materialistic, emotionally cold, and unsexual—or sexually *unproductive,* and not exactly a real parent. This reordering of the conventional dichotomies effectively uncovers the paradox in American adoption: the *natural* mother—the conventionally (and often legally) ideal parent—loses her child to a parent who meets criteria and is judged *worthy.* The interests of the child are translated into a calculation of advantage that contradicts the kinship basis of the exchange. This is the knot adoption law and policy have not successfully untangled in over a hundred years. Birthparents put it in their way: those who "love" lose to those who are "well-off."

The birthparent analysis adds another level to the critique of fictive kinship. If adoption is impossible in a genealogical culture without reversing the values attached to "parent," it is also impossible without commercializing the exchange—or so the birthparents' "storied" experiences indicated. Birthparents, like adoptees, drew the contrast between a selfish adoptive parent and a generous birthparent; one greedily took and kept another person's child, while the other lovingly and altruistically gave away her child. For birthparents, the intervention of experts truly distorted the exchange, by introducing "objective criteria" into the delegation of parenthood. In this view, the *selection* of a parent turned relations of kinship into relations of capital; calculation of comparative worth intruded upon a familial transaction. Capability and performance, rather than the appropriate dimensions of nurturance and commitment, qualified a parent in this transaction. If somewhat self-serving, the birthparent critique is a cogent comment on child exchange in the United States—an exchange that cannot, it seems, be "right."

But it might be right, the implication is, if "blood" were acknowledged, not just as a model for the parent-child attachment or a symbolic reference to nature, but as an aspect of any kind of kinship. By this logic, if "blood" dominates cultural interpretations of kinship, then blood kin exist. By this logic, too, birth relatives exist, no longer a threatening presence in the child's past, but part of an ongoing family constellation—of some sort. Birthparents, then, are not the "kids" who "had babies right and left," or the natural mother with a natural right to the child: they are the parents by birth to a child others have by law. Focused on opening documents and unsealing records, the effect of reform is to bring every part of the child's ancestry—the child's biological and social collectivity, in the Eriksonian phrase—forward. The slippery categories of fictive and real—"and when I say my real parents, I mean my adoptive parents, ok?"—are suspended by "birth" and "legal" parents. As one adoptee said about those who know both sets of parents, "If you say, 'who is your mother and father?'" they know which is which.

Fictive can also take on another meaning. Rather than referring to "not real," as it currently does, fictive can connote made, created, and crafted. The problem with this, as my research shows, is the sharp discordance between a crafted kinship and cultural notions of parenthood. The experience of all three members of the triad argue for the awkwardness—the discomfort—of a made parent-child relationship. When it comes to the parent-child relationship in American culture nature prevails, not "contrivance." And so, by one strategy or another, adoption in the United States—an *opted-for* kinship—has simulated a destined parenthood. "Falling-in-love" and "meant-to-be" convey the inevitability of the adoptive relationship—as if natural. Birthparents present the "other" inevitability: "she still has my blood running through her."

But if the initiation of a parent-child relationship ought not be "crafted," its evolution can be *worked* through. . . . Yet the emphasis on work implicitly recognizes the contrivance in this kind of kinship—the "made" aspect of fictive—without relinquishing the "rush" of feeling that cements the bond. . . .

"The Winds of Change"

. . . No longer able to be as-if-genealogical, to forget the background of the child, or to be sure of having the child forever, adoptive parents stand at the edge of a new kind of kinship.

"Confidentiality cannot be guaranteed in any adoption, even the so-called closed or traditional adoption. Laws governing confidentiality are changing and may continue to change to permit greater openness; courts can issue orders to open adoption records, and members of the triad may establish contact even when existing laws support confidentiality," stated the Task Force report of the moderate CWLA, not without sympathy for this development. The end of confidentiality represents the opening of adoption—hard to accept, but not as hard as a completely open adoption, in which birth and adoptive parents know one another, arrange the transfer of the child, and continue to have contact after the transaction has been completed. Open adoption polarizes people who participate in, and think about, adoption more than has anything else in recent decades.

Why is it so disturbing? Open adoption ought to be appealing: the concern of parents about a child brings them together in love and in generosity. This is the way adoption is understood and practiced in other societies—and in some subcultures of our own society. Nor are love and generosity inconsistent with the attitudes presumed to be part of any adoption in the contemporary United States. In addition, the dangers of secrecy in a closed adoption, of hiding his or her "facts of life" from a child, and of disguising the terms of a relationship are generally recognized. Still, the idea of open adoption strikes a chill—especially in adoptive parents, but in the public as well. Open adoption is not greeted with the fascination and appreciation that a reunion between long-lost kin is, even when those kin were not supposed to know one another. Reunions are perceived as re-activating existing natural bonds, whereas open adoptions are seen as permitting people to construct "unnatural" bonds, on purpose and from the very beginning. Above all, open adoption is disturbing because it does not allow adoptive kinship to be just like biological kinship.

Opposition to open adoption, then, represents more than selfishness on the part of adoptive parents who want a child "of their own" or desperation on the part of birthparents who want to "keep" the children they relinquish, or jealousy on the part of social workers who want to control the placement of children. These elements influence the arguments against open adoption, but what really is troublesome is that open adoption threatens deeply held assumptions about the American family. By dismantling the biological premise, open adoption exposes the entailments of that premise: biology represents permanence, stability, and exclusivity—the core of parenthood. . . .

. . . It is not that open adoption makes biology less significant. Rather, open adoption puts biology in the "wrong" place—not a model for the adoptive parent, but another presence in the adoptive family. . . .

. . . Open adoption, then, exposes the weakness in an assumption that "papers" can make kinship equivalent to blood; it is just paper: that a contract is not as binding as birth in a parent-child relationship is a strong cultural convention. But it is a convention, and as a convention it can change. Paradoxically, open adoption also indicates the strength of "papers." In an open arrangement, a paper kinship can be as strong as a blood kinship for the very reason that it does not replace (or substitute for) the blood kinship; rather, the contract establishes a *parallel* legal kinship. Open adoption introduces not "alternative parenthood" but alternative parents, and the distinction is not trivial. One parent is not "real," the other "unreal"; one is not "natural" and the other "fictive."

Open adoption is radical enough to have disturbed almost everyone I met—even those who eagerly entered reunions. But open adoption does not call for a total revolution in notions of kinship or in the purposes and principles of adoption. Blood remains central; adoption is still in the best interests of the child. It is "well" for the child to know all his or her parents, even if the arrangement confuses the parents. But advocates also argue that open adoption serves the interests of the parents. The exchange is conducted by the participants, a form of self-determination that disappeared from adoption in the twentieth century. "Consider the paradox," the executive director of the CWLA said in 1985, "that while we entrust adoptive parents with the lives of adopted children, we too often do not trust them with all the information we have on the child's family background." She added, "the same staff will not allow these 'superior' [adoptive] parents who wish it to have contact with the bioparents." Rather than letting people make their own decisions, we "commit social work on them" [citations omitted].

In open adoption, people make their own decisions, whether through an agency or independently. . . .

Choice violates the cultural assumption that a parent-child relationship is a *necessary* relationship. Adoptees implied this when they complained about being told they were "picked out" to belong to a family. So did adoptive parents when they complained about the "laundry-list" of agency adoptions; selecting a baby introduced the possibility of returning a child. A parent-child relationship should happen, without calculation of the conditions. . . . What emerges from the debate over open adoption is not an imperative of motherhood so much as the imperative of a relationship between parent and child. The bond is inevitable, however initiated. And so advocates of open adoption also talk about fate, destiny, and God's will: the parent-child relationship "had to happen." . . .

Open adoption is currently betwixt-and-between. The arrangement offers its participants choice, yet the choice is constrained by the notion of an inevitable relationship. The difference in interpretation of choice in adoption and choice in marriage underline the distinctiveness of the parent-child relationship in American culture. (Or, one might say, because of the difference between these two contracted relationships, "choice" comes to mean different things in each.) If adoption were too much like marriage, there would be divorce—and in American culture, children and parents do not divorce one another. Permanency is as strong a core of kinship as is the genealogical principle with which it is intertwined. But permanence, like genealogy, is a cultural convention, not a fact of nature. . . .

. . . But despite its shying away from choice in favor of fate, open adoption does create an alternative model for chosen parenthood. A direct exchange between participants is not the same as an exchange arranged by a social worker or a lawyer. Supporters of open adoption use the word *gift* to describe the transaction: a child, freely given and received, who creates a bond between the adults. Once more there is ambiguity: in one respect, a gift model radically restructures American adoption. In forming a bond, a gift eliminates the distance between giver and taker; they are united by the "item of value" they share. Behind a vocabulary of love and generosity, then, the linchpin of American adoption is pulled out: if birthparent and adoptive parent are close to one another—even like (in both senses of the word) one another—why should an adoption occur at all! In addition, the closer an adoptive parent and a birthparent are, the less can adoption serve its function of social control—redistributing children from an "unprepared" to a "prepared" parent. In open adoption, the exchange is just that: an agreement between individuals about the place of a child, unsupervised and free of external judgements of comparative worth.

And so open adoption is more radical than it looks, or sounds, at the moment. . . .

"The Counterhegemonies They Contrast"

. . . [O]pen adoption . . . has the potential not only to alter practice but also to undermine the structures and ideologies that have sustained a *fictive* kinship in American culture. The direct exchange of a child eliminates the sharp evaluative differentiation between a birth and an adoptive parent, between a person who "just has" a child (the stereotypical "kids in the mall") and a person who is "qualified" to be a parent. Moreover, the degree of choice offered by open adoption cuts at deep-rooted convictions about the inevitability, the *imperative,* of parenthood. Carried to a logical end, open adoption "opens" concepts of parenthood, of mother and father, and of family—thus of kinship altogether. If people who are unrelated, and not otherwise "bound" to one another, share a child, what does that do to the notion of being a parent? If "mother" includes the woman who bears but does not raise a child and, with equal significance, the woman who raises but has no birth tie to the child, then "mother" is no longer absolute—or absolutely linked with nature. A family composed of people with a common interest in a child, a *blended* family, is not the same as a family extended by genealogy and by marriage. . . .

By making kin terms problematic, open adoption is more subversive than its rhetoric implies. For those who support it, openness is not a breakdown but a restoration of values—putting adoption back on course, away from the commerce and calculation that have come to characterize this transaction in kinship. Inserting love and generosity into the exchange of a child, however, has the effect of making the transaction seem anarchic—if *sentimentally,* then not *sensibly* appropriate to the "extreme act" a legal adoption (still) represents in American culture. Opponents of open adoption do not trust parents any more than did charity societies in the late nineteenth century or social workers in the early twentieth century.

"A New Kind of Kinship"

I am not sure that open adoption is the ideal adoption. It is not easy to contemplate sharing parenthood with someone who is in other ways a stranger or releasing the transfer of a child from experts and noninterested criteria for parenthood. But it is clear that openness is "swaying" adoption policy and practice—and not because laws make it necessary, but because people choose to transact parenthood that way. Resistant to being judged by experts and held to standards of parenthood no one else has to meet, adoptive parents and birthparents are taking action to alter the existing modes of child exchange. Both agency and independent adoptions have changed accordingly. Most agencies support some form of openness: a meeting between parents without identifying information; an ongoing exchange of letters; visits by a birthparent; a complete file for the adoptee. Independent adoptions also involve more communication and contact between birth and adoptive parent.

This mode of change has characterized adoption history all along. . . .

Adoption has been curiously left out of discussions of the American family, whether these discussions lament the collapse of the family, support its flexibility, or analyze its rules and roles. This is partly because adoption has been considered a version of the normal family, forgotten after the transaction is completed. Alternatively, and simultaneously, adoption is seen as too marginal to merit attention; it is not central to the evolution of the American family or to interpretations of kinship. My argument, of course, is that it is central: as a mirror of the "real" parent-child relationship and as a statement of how people should be related. Every time a child is severed from blood kin, given to strangers, and accorded a new birth certificate, the lineaments of kinship are drawn. Adoption "shows" what kinship is supposed to do. And adoption has been ignored partly for this reason: inscribing the conventional kinship arrangements of an era, adoption seems a stable—conservative—backdrop to the "real" shifts in family, marriage, and modes of childbearing. Adoption is not dramatic, unless it is treated as a powerful interpretive tool, not only for observers but also for participants in this kind of kinship. In both capacities, I have tried to show how adoption interprets American kinship.

And up to now, it has interpreted kinship as "genealogical." In the conventional form I have described, adoption upholds the biological basis for parenthood and the gender assumptions that go with that model. As long as artificial kinship inscribes the natural relationship, "blood" remains the central symbol of being related. But, as I have also shown, . . . individual actors in adoption are currently redesigning the *fiction* of their kinship. Reunions, openness, and blended families form the basis of a new kind of kinship, in which genealogy is only one way of constructing parenthood. If genealogy is no longer the core of kinship, American culture itself will be different.

VI

The Frontiers of Adoption

In recent years, the "frontiers" of adoption law have expanded to accommodate the needs of many different kinds of children in the United States and around the world. Although many of the would-be parents of these children are prompted by infertility, they are also motivated by a desire to build families across racial, ethnic, and cultural boundaries and, if they are same-sex couples, to ensure that their children's legal status is protected. This part explores these new "frontiers" of adoption, highlighting their fluid boundaries and their role in enabling our society to understand and resolve basic conflicts over individual and communal rights, identity, and family ties.

Adoption within and across
Racial and Ethnic Boundaries

44

The What and Why of the
Multiethnic Placement Act (MEPA)

Joan Heifetz Hollinger

The Multiethnic Placement Act of 1994, as amended by the Interethnic Provisions of 1996 (MEPA), 42 U.S.C. § 1996(b), is one of several recent federal initiatives and laws aimed at removing the barriers to permanency for the hundreds of thousands of children who are in the child protective system, and especially, for the African American and other minority children who are disproportionately represented in out-of-home care, and who wait much longer than others for permanent homes.

MEPA's specific goals are to decrease the length of time that children wait to be adopted, facilitate the recruitment and retention of foster and adoptive parents who can meet the distinctive needs of children awaiting placement, and eliminate discrimination on the basis of the race, color, or national origin of the child or the prospective foster or adoptive parent.

To achieve these goals, MEPA contains two basic prohibitions and one affirmative mandate:

(1) It prohibits states and other entities (e.g., adoption agencies) that are involved in foster care or adoptive placements and receive federal funds, from delaying or denying a child's foster care or adoptive placement on the basis of the child's or the prospective parent's race, color, or national origin;

(2) It also prohibits denying to any individual the opportunity to become a foster or adoptive parent on the basis of the prospective parent's or the child's race, color, or national origin; and

(3) It requires that, to remain eligible for federal funds, state child welfare agencies must *diligently recruit* foster and adoptive parents who reflect the racial and ethnic diversity of the children in the state who need foster and adoptive homes.

MEPA makes it clear that children in state custody are not exempt from the antidiscrimination principles embodied in our constitutional jurisprudence and in Title VI of the 1964 Civil Rights Act.

What Kinds of Agency Policies or Practices Violate MEPA?

MEPA prohibits policies and practices that had become routine in most states since the mid-1970's, including

- setting a specific time period during which only searches for a racially or ethnically matched placement will occur;
- placement preferences based solely or primarily on racial or ethnic factors;
- requiring caseworkers to justify transracial placements but not requiring any justification for same race placements;
- other procedures that directly or indirectly delay placements before or after termination of parental rights in order to find a racially or ethnically matched family for a child.

Can Race, Color, or National Origin Ever Be Considered in Making Placement Decisions?

- The race, color, or national origin of a child or foster or adoptive parent may not be routinely considered. Caseworkers should be alerted to the risks of serious harm to children whose placements are delayed because of stereotypical assumptions about race or ethnicity that may have no bearing on children's actual needs.
- Any consideration of race or ethnicity must pass the "strict scrutiny" test: Does a particular child's distinctive needs require consideration of these factors? Is it necessary to consider these factors in order to achieve a "compelling state interest"? In a few specific cases, the "best interests of the child" test may require attention to racial or ethnic factors and, if narrowly tailored to the needs of the particular child, may meet the strict scrutiny test—for example, when an older child who has lived all her life in racially matched homes requests a similar permanent placement.

Child welfare workers should ask: What are the distinctive needs of this particular child? Are any of them based on racial or ethnic factors? Can these needs be documented?

Can any distinctive and documented needs be met by a foster or adoptive parent who does not share the child's racial or ethnic background? Can they be met only by someone from a similar background?

MEPA does not require transracial placements; nor does MEPA prohibit same-race placements. Instead, MEPA requires decisions that focus on and promote the best interest of each individual child. MEPA does not alter the federal Indian Child Welfare Act (ICWA) and its recognition of tribal rights with respect to the placement of Indian children who are subject to ICWA.

What Factors May Be Considered in
Making Placement Decisions for a Child?

Federal law allows preferences to be given to a child's adult relatives [kinship care], provided they meet all relevant suitability and child protection standards.

Other factors to consider include

• length of time with current caregiver and depth of child's attachment to this caregiver;
• child's age, sex, cognitive capacities, special talents, educational needs;
• child's religious preferences, if any, and linguistic or other cultural needs;
• child's physical condition, health and dental needs;
• child's emotional and psychological condition, specific developmental needs as related to personal experience of abuse, neglect, or other maltreatment;
• geographical proximity to parents if reunification services are being provided;
• the caregiver's ability to maintain contact between child and siblings.

What about Culture?

• Neither MEPA nor constitutional cases treat "culture" as a suspect category; in other words, they do not prohibit consideration of a child's cultural background and personal experience in making placement decisions.
• However, "culture" needs to be defined carefully and cannot be used simply as a proxy for unlawful consideration of race, color, or national origin [USDHHS 1998 MEPA Q&A, ACYF-IM-CB-98-03].
• Agencies should not rely on standard assumptions or stereotypes about a person's cultural needs based on the color of the person's skin or the person's ethnicity. Children are not born with a culture; they acquire one as they grow up; it is not racially or ethnically determined, but is a product of their ongoing interactions with their immediate families, their peers, and the various sociocultural communities they encounter.
• Agencies should not assume that foster or adoptive parents have to share a child's cultural experience in order to develop the child's awareness and appreciation of that culture.

Can Agencies Honor a Birth Parent's Placement Preferences?

• An agency cannot honor a birth parent's placement preferences if they are based solely on racial or ethnic factors, but it can honor preferences based on other factors.
• An agency can honor a parent's request for placement of a child with a relative, or with someone of the same religion as the parent or child, so long as they are otherwise suitable.

Do Prospective Adoptive Parents Have a "Right"
to Adopt a Particular Child?

• An opportunity to be considered as a prospective adoptive parent without regard to race, color, or national origin is not equivalent to a "right" to adopt a particular child.
• No one has a right to adopt a particular child, regardless of whether the child is of the same or different racial or ethnic background.
• Agencies must evaluate *all* applicants' capacities to raise children, including children with special needs, and cannot limit this evaluation to applicants of certain racial or ethnic backgrounds.

Meeting MEPA Requirements for Diligent Recruitment
of Foster and Adoptive Parents

• Agencies should develop comprehensive, flexible, and welcoming recruitment plans based on the characteristics of waiting children.
• Recruitment and retention strategies may be targeted to different racial and ethnic communities, so long as prospective parents outside targeted communities can participate.

MEPA Presents an Opportunity to Improve Child Welfare Practices
and Create Permanent Families for More Children

MEPA is a compromise between those who believe that the best way to reduce the delays in the placement of African American and other minority children is to permit, and perhaps even to encourage, transracial adoption and those who believe that the best way to reduce the delays is to increase the recruitment and retention of racially and ethnically diverse adoptive parents. MEPA is also a compromise between those who believe that the primary causes of problems within the child welfare system are the legal procedures that delay decisions to terminate parental rights and those who believe that the main problems are the race-based decisions of child welfare workers at all stages of the process. Moreover, MEPA is a compromise between those who believe that any permissible consideration of race will encourage child welfare workers to go on practicing "business as usual" to the detriment of the children in need of permanent families and those who believe that it is detrimental to children to make "color-blind" placement decisions.

In at least two critical respects, however, MEPA is not a compromise. First, virtually everyone involved in the debates about racial and ethnic matching is eager to reduce the numbers of children in out-of-home care. Second, MEPA is based on a growing sensitivity to the difference between policies based on stereotypical and categorical assumptions about race or ethnicity and policies that acknowledge the value of taking account of racial or ethnic factors only in specific and distinctive cases.

Nonetheless, many of those who are being called upon to implement MEPA in their own states and agencies have difficulty understanding why it is unlawful—and harmful to children—to routinely use racial or ethnic factors when selecting foster and adoptive parents. MEPA thus provides a unique opportunity to reexamine the principles and practices that drove public adoption services during the final decades of the twentieth century, and to refine our understanding of how to ensure safe, permanent, and loving families for children through more individualized assessments of the characteristics and needs of each child.

45

"Are You My Mother?"
Conceptualizing Children's Identity Rights in Transracial Adoptions

Barbara Bennett Woodhouse

Adoption and the Clash of Rights Perspectives

Adoption law in the United States, depending on whom you ask, is either at a turning point or hopelessly gridlocked. Many issues seem to defy consensus. . . . Many of the most volatile adoption issues are couched in terms of rights: the birth mother's right to confidentiality; the adoptive parent's right to be treated equally without regard to race, ethnicity, religion, or sexual orientation; the rights of a racial, ethnic, or national community to custody and control of children born into that community; the adult adoptee's right to information about her origins; the right of unwed fathers to veto the birth mother's adoption decision, and so on. . . . These clashes of rights highlight the tensions between claims of blood and nurture, biological and social connection, and individual and communal definitions of self.

Of all the debates, the furor over racial matching in adoption is perhaps the most problematic for American legal culture. . . . [T]he Multiethnic Placement Act (MEPA) has become a battleground for competing visions of individual and group identity and has revived longstanding controversies about what role, if any, children's community of origin should play in adoptive placements. The very notion of preserving children's cultural or ethnic identities seems to conflict with liberal conceptions of parents' and children's individual rights, ideals of color-blind equality, and a peculiarly American kind of liberty embracing the freedom to reinvent oneself as a new citizen of a new world.

Missing from the debate, however, is a coherent schema for articulating children's rights to preservation of their identity in adoption. Perhaps this is partially because we think of children not as subjects claiming rights under law, but as objects of lawmaking who have relatively nebulous and indeterminate "interests."

[I propose to] shift the focus from adults' rights, whether those of parents or of cultural and ethnic communities, to the continuing task of developing a schema of children's rights to preservation and support of their identity. . . . I will suggest a fluid conception of identity rights reflecting children's own evolving capacities and developmental concerns as well as their need for family and group ties. . . .

. . . [I]n a rights-oriented legal culture, children need more than the weak reed of a claim to "interests" if they are to make their needs and voices heard. . . .

. . . For example, Article 8 of the United Nations Convention on the Rights of the Child recognizes "the right of the child to preserve his or her identity, including nationality, name and family relations." In the United States, at the federal level the principle of group identity or consciousness is present in civil rights remedies like affirmative action, and in laws which discourage placement of Native American children outside their tribe. . . . [M]any jurisdictions use kinship preferences in adoption and foster care or racial, religious, or ethnic matching to maintain children's identification with family and culture.

This recognition of a communal identity conflicts with interpretations of individual rights and equal treatment provided by modern constitutional jurisprudence. It is also unclear how such identity rights apply to children who have lived apart from their family, group, or nation of origin and have developed their own social and psychological identities through interactions with their environment. The nature of adoption—creation by the state of a new, nonbiological family—forces us to raise questions about children's individual identity versus group identity. In addition, adoption requires us to examine how we conceptualize children's relationship to community and state, their individual and collective past, present, and future. Does consideration of race or ethnicity violate the prospective adopter's equal protection rights? Does it violate the child's rights to equal protection or to the "best" available placement? And how does the passage of time, during which children grow and evolve, acquiring and shedding identities, affect these conflicting rights and interests? . . .

A. Thinking about Identity

. . . [C]hildren have often figured as passive objects whose identity (like title in property) can be transferred with a stroke of the pen from one to another name, family, and group. But children, scientists tell us, are not blank slates. They arrive in the world with a lively genetic heritage and become active participants in construction or reconstruction of those internal frameworks that constitute identity. Although the role of biology is still under investigation, most studies agree that genetic heritage shapes not only physical appearance, but also personality. On the other hand, psychologists tell us that children begin to construct and enact their own "personal identity" from a very early age, through attachments to caregivers and through interactions with their family environment. At six months of age, children (through the lens of social interaction) have already begun to recognize their "native" tongue (the one they hear from infancy) and identify their "parents" (the people who care for them). They grow as individuals, but in relation to the people and the cultures around them.

A child's identity, moreover, is far from a static concept. We parents know that children play an ongoing role in the evolution of their own identities, in constant dialogue with their surroundings. Children evolve and their needs change. For young children, who experience self, family, and community in highly concrete terms, continuity and stability of their attachments to intimate caregivers may be of paramount importance in forming a coherent sense of self. As children mature and their capacities for understanding evolve, they are able, and often appear driven, to integrate more complex understandings of their own identity and of their membership (attributed and chosen) in biological, social, and cultural families and groups. . . . [A] child-centered perspective would suggest that the right to preservation of a group identity of origin is best analyzed as a right of the child, and a responsibility or trust of the group.

B. Competing Definitions of "Best Interest"

. . . Proponents of transracial adoption argue that acquiring racial identity and coping skills is not contingent on being raised by same race parents but on the parents' sensitivity to the child's needs and on healthy early attachments. Critics of transracial adoption argue that children must struggle, sometimes unsuccessfully, to acquire a positive racial identity when neither parent can provide a same race role model. They argue that children of color need to be raised by parents of color in communities of color in order to acquire the "coping skills" necessary for survival in a racist society.

Having followed the many studies that purport to measure transracially adopted children's well-being, I am certainly not persuaded . . . that transracial adoption creates a serious risk of harm to children, especially when the alternative is prolonged delays in placement and foster care drift. Nor am I persuaded by those who believe that considerations of race and culture should be banned as a form of racial separatism and as irrelevant to the adoptee's interests. My uneasiness with policies advocating either relentless race-matching or relentless race-blindness goes beyond the obvious difficulties of gathering data and creating scientifically sound techniques of measurement that might prove conclusively that one or the other policy is in children's best interest. . . . [T]here simply is no easy empirical answer to the question whether transracial and transcultural adoptions are "good" or "bad" for children. In an objective sense, it is impossible to say that a child has acquired a "good" or "bad" self concept or acquired a "healthy" or "unhealthy" individual, racial, or cultural identity without also making tacit judgments about relative values of sameness and difference, individual and group, independence and interdependence. . . .

. . . My premise is that race and culture of origin, no matter how hard to define with satisfying logic, do matter to children and therefore should matter in adoption law. They may well be contingent and socially constructed, but children's awareness of race and group identity indicates that they are "real" for the purposes that matter here—the fostering and protection of children's identity. . . .

Children's Stories and Children's Rights

I use the classic story of *Horton Hatches the Egg* to provide a visual metaphor for the social and psychological relationship that forms between a child and the adult who faithfully cares for her. Horton was "faithful one hundred percent" to an egg that had been left in his care by a certain irresponsible Mayzie bird who promptly flew off to Palm Beach. When the egg hatched, out came an elephant-bird.

Children love this story about the elephant who hatches the abandoned bird's egg. They know that the story is about them and their survival, and they know that the egg would not remain warm and intact long enough to hatch without Horton's sitting on it. The elephant-bird's trunk and tail are tangible proof that Horton has become the baby's social parent; he earns his parenthood through nurturing care. It seems inevitable that the creature who hatches from the egg should be visibly related to Horton. When the baby elephant-bird rides off into the jungle on Horton's trunk, readers of all ages accept as right that Horton's faithfulness created a real and tangible relationship as significant to both the baby's identity, and to Horton's parenthood, as the biological relationship.

. . . [What I call] a "generist perspective," as exemplified by Horton, recognizes nurture of the next generation as paramount. A generist perspective views adults' relationship to children as one of responsibilities of trusteeship rather than rights of ownership. Adults' competing "rights" to control and maintain custody of children should be replaced by the less adversarial notions of obligation to provide nurture, authority to act on children's behalf, and standing to participate in collaborative planning to meet the child's needs. . . .

. . . [There is another half to] the story of adoption, and it is equally important to a theory of children's rights. In the book *Are You My Mother?* a baby robin hatches and falls out of the nest while her mother is gone. The baby bird wanders from one to another unlikely mother figure plaintively asking the question that provides the book's title. As readers, young and old, we worry when the baby attempts to bond with a dog, a cat, a cow, an airplane, and finally a huge and snorting earth moving machine, asking each of them "Are you my Mother?" We are delighted, on turning the page, to see that the steam shovel, instead of crushing the bird in its jagged teeth, has lifted the baby back into her original nest at the top of the tree. It seems appropriate, as a matter of children's rights, that the author, like the current rules of law, should prefer reunification with the family of origin. He puts the baby robin back in the nest from which she fell, so she can be raised by the parent who laid and hatched her. . . .

. . . [This is] a compelling story about displaced children's dual needs for appropriate care and for continuity with their origins. Although this intuition is not universally shared, one need not be anti-adoption to join the fairly broad consensus that children "belong" with their biological families and are served, barring serious perils, by rules that protect their stability and continuity in their families of origin.

This intuition is matched, however, by another. If the alternative were to leave the baby bird wandering indefinitely in physical peril and developmental limbo in search of mother, we would be equally delighted to see the steam shovel place her in the nest of some other appropriate mother who could speak her language and meet her needs for worms and attention—if not a robin, then perhaps a sparrow, a finch, or even the rather large hen she earlier tried to adopt as her mother.

This story, of course, is not offered as logical argument. Any skeptic would be quick to point out, for example, that people of all colors, unlike sparrows, robins, and hens, and obviously unlike cats, dogs, and steam shovels, are members of the same species and can and do produce offspring. Nevertheless, it embodies the widely shared principle that the first and best choice for children generally is to preserve and protect the child's biological family and community of origin from disruption. Unfortunately, sometimes these "biological" connections have already been ruptured by a foster or adoptive placement or the child's safety makes removal and the state creation of a new "social" family unit necessary. In our society, as in children's stories, there are few absolutes and we manage the best endings we can, given the available story elements. . . .

I have argued that out of children's needs we can develop a theory of children's rights, including rights to protection of identity. When we place children for adoption across cultural, ethnic, and political frontiers, children's needs must dominate. . . .

Examining Children's Rights-Based Solutions

Transracial adoption combines some of the most potent dilemmas of modern America—relationships of race and class and gender, as well as generational conflicts between parents' rights and children's rights. . . .

The lines between discrimination and sensitivity to a child's needs, between racial separatism and respect for pluralism, are notoriously difficult to delineate. The United States Supreme Court in *Palmore v. Sidoti* held, in the context of a child custody dispute, that the Equal Protection Clause of the United States Constitution precludes courts from considering the effects of racial prejudice, no matter how real, in determining a child's best interest. . . . [T]he underlying principle—that [allowing the state to give] legal effect to racial or ethnic factors in evaluating children's interests impermissibly perpetuates racial separatism and bias—is at the heart of liberal concerns about racial and ethnic matching.

Looking at Kinship through Children's Eyes

Returning to Horton's story, one perspective sees primarily the ears and the tail. The other sees the wings and the feathers. . . .

. . . [A]dopting the child-centered perspective I have proposed above might help mediate the disputes between discussants who seem at present entrenched in polarized positions. A child-centered perspective would provide a halfway point between these poles, and would shift the focus to children's needs-based rights defined through the lens of children's experiences. Adopting the generist, child-centered perspective which is reflected in modern trends such as the Children's Act in England and the 1989 U.N. Convention on the Rights of the Child, one would start with the proposition that biological and adoptive parents, communities of color, and political communities should not compete for ownership, but should share in a trusteeship of children. Rather than asserting rights in children, we should focus on articulating responsibilities: (1) an obligation to meet children's needs; (2) authority to act on their behalf; and (3) standing to participate in planning for children's care on their journey to adulthood. As trustees, we are obligated to make every effort to create social systems that allow children to grow up secure in their families and communities of origin. Both adoption and foster care are important tools. Their purpose, however, is not to give adults equal rights to acquire the children of their choice, but to provide families for children when the family of origin is not available or presents a serious threat to the child's safety.

46

The Color of Desire
Fulfilling Adoptive Parents' Racial Preferences through Discriminatory State Action

R. Richard Banks

The intense and protracted race-and-adoption controversy has centered on the practice of race matching. Race-matching policies require that children be matched to adoptive parents on the basis of race; black children are placed only with black parents and white children only with white parents. . . . Race-matching proponents argue that it is in a black child's best interest to be placed with a black family and that placing black children without regard to race therefore subverts the best-interests-of-the-child standard, the guiding principle of child welfare policy. Proponents of transracial adoption, in contrast, argue that adoption agencies should accord less importance to race and should be willing to match children and parents across racial lines. They claim that race-matching efforts harm black children by denying or delaying their adoptive placement. They also note that race matching represents race-based state action, which is presumptively unconstitutional.

Both proponents of race matching and proponents of transracial adoption contend that their chosen policy is best for the children involved. Yet the best-interests-of-the-child standard is of remarkably little use in defining the role of race in adoption. The meaning of the standard with respect to race is itself a matter of race politics insofar as different determinations regarding the significance of race in adoptive placement reflect divergent ideological visions of the "proper" role of racial identity in socialization. As long as ideological differences remain significant, so will varied interpretations of the best-interests-of-the-child standard.

Both supporters and opponents of race matching often assume that putting an end to the practice would make adoption policy colorblind. The race-and-adoption debate, then, is framed as a contest between those who believe that race-conscious state action (race matching) furthers the interests of black children, and those who believe that colorblind state action (transracial adoption) does so. Contrary to the assumptions that underlie the debate, however, race matching is not the only form of race-based state action that structures the adoption process.

Adoption agencies' classification of children on the basis of race facilitates and promotes the exercise of racial preferences by prospective adoptive parents. I term this practice "facilitative accommodation." When engaged in by public agencies, facilitative accommodation, like race matching, is an instance of race-based state action. In both cases, adoption agencies racially classify children. Through race matching, the state mandates the placement of children with parents on the basis of race. Through facilitative accommodation, the state's racial classification promotes the race-based decisionmaking of prospective adoptive parents by framing the choice of a child in terms of race, encouraging parents to consider children based on the ascribed characteristic of race rather than individually. In both cases, a court, in finalizing the adoption, validates the actions of the adoption agency.

As a result of facilitative accommodation policies, most black children in need of adoption are categorically denied, on the basis of race, the opportunity to be considered individually for adoption by the majority of prospective adoptive parents. This could not occur were it not for current policies of facilitative accommodation. The racial classification on which facilitative accommodation practices rely is the type of harm prohibited by the Equal Protection Clause.

Worse, facilitative accommodation reinforces and legitimizes the type of race-consciousness that produces unjustified racial inequality, both in adoption and throughout American society. Adoptive parents' racial preferences dramatically diminish the pool of potential parents available to black children relative to that available to white children. The pool of parents available to black children is also of lower average quality than that available to white children, in part because many of those whites who adopt black children do so because they are considered by agencies to be among the least desirable parents for white children. The severity of the social inequality produced by adoptive parents' preferences is made starkly clear by a fact too often accepted as inevitable, albeit lamentable, rather than as a predictable outcome of our own preference-promoting policies: Black children are simply worth less than white children.

Yet not one legal analyst has argued that public adoption agencies cannot (as a matter of law) or should not (as a matter of policy) promote adoptive parents' racial preferences through facilitative accommodation. This is especially noteworthy in the case of proponents of transracial adoption, many of whose criticisms of race matching are applicable to facilitative accommodation as well. Moreover, consideration of facilitative accommodation follows logically from consideration of race matching (that is, once one determines that the state should not place children on the basis of race, one must consider whether it should encourage parents to choose children based on race). Yet a federal statute [MEPA] that prohibits race matching by adoption agencies that receive federal funding says nothing about accommodation. Thus, current adoption policy allows both facilitative accommodation and the exercise of the racial preferences that it presupposes. The asymmetry in the scholarly and public policy analysis of these two instances of race-based adoption policy is [an] anomaly. . . .

Analysts assume that adoptive parents' racial preferences cannot or should not be altered and accept without question that parents should be able to choose the race of the children they adopt. Yet there are alternatives to facilitative accommodation. The alternative that this Article embraces challenges white same-race preferences, in adoption and elsewhere. I propose a strict non-accommodation policy that not only ends current practices of facilitative accommodation, but ultimately seeks to rid adoption of the racial preferences that systematically produce racial inequality in contemporary

American society. This approach assumes that personal racial preferences are not natural, but rather are products of the ways in which legal rules and social policy have shaped racial identity and race-consciousness. Strict nonaccommodation is part of the broader project of confronting the white same-race preferences that create racial inequality in contemporary American society and reorienting our national debate about racial inequality.

My goal is to recast racial preferences as expressions of social phenomena rather than merely individual choices. Only if racial preferences are denaturalized can they be seen as something other than self-evidently innocuous and individual choices, as the embodiments of the same sentiments and sensibilities that give rise to racial inequality in a variety of contexts. White adoptive parents' racial preferences for white children are emblematic of the race-consciousness that serves as the linchpin of racial inequality. . . .

Facilitative accommodation flourishes through lack of prohibition because it is deeply embedded in the institutional practices of adoption agencies. To promote suitable matches, adoption law is strongly oriented toward fulfilling the preferences of adoptive parents. Adoption agencies attempt to ascertain and fulfill the preferences of adoptive parents as a means of determining and creating an appropriate placement. Prospective adoptive parents are generally allowed to express preferences in a wide variety of areas. Health, age, sex, appearance, and prior experiences are all areas in which parents may say what type of children they want. Race is recognized as one of many reasonable preferences parents are likely to hold.

The only laws that proscribe the consideration of race in adoption apply to race matching. At the state level, laws regarding race matching vary from one jurisdiction to another. At the federal level, the Multiethnic Placement Act [MEPA] prohibits race matching by agencies that receive federal funding for adoption or foster care. Although the MEPA has been widely discussed as an effort to make the adoption process nondiscriminatory, the Act does nothing to prohibit facilitative accommodation by adoption agencies that receive federal funding. . . .

The prevalence of race matching has masked the significance of facilitative accommodation. Nearly all of the cases involving race and adoption have involved challenges to race matching. No court has had the opportunity to rule on the constitutionality of current policies of facilitative accommodation.

Harm of Facilitative Accommodation

The first step in evaluating the constitutionality of facilitative accommodation policies is to identify the harm that the practice causes. The harm of current facilitative accommodation policies, in short, is that they enable adoptive parents to consider children by racial group, rather than individually. Thus, they allow, indeed encourage, parents summarily to exclude from consideration an entire race of children in need of adoption. This could not occur in the absence of facilitative accommodation.

Although facilitative accommodation applies whether parents prefer black children or white children, its apparent symmetry is more the semblance than the substance of equality. Because most adoptive parents are white, and because most potential adoptive parents prefer to adopt children of their own race, most black children are categorically excluded from the opportunity to be considered individually for inclusion in the families of many adoptive parents. The denial of individual consideration made possible by adoption agencies' policies of facilitative accommodation is significant because that harm is precisely the type of harm that the Supreme Court has previously identified as an evil of racial classification. Racial classifications are wrong, according to the Court, because they promote the treatment of citizens on the basis of the groups to which they belong rather than as individuals.

The widespread policy of accommodating adoptive parents' racial preferences burdens a subgroup of black Americans—namely, black children placed for adoption—who are uniquely powerless, isolated, and unrepresented in the political process. The group that current facilitative accommodation policies most burden does not include white children. Although white children are harmed by facilitative accommodation, they are not harmed to the same degree that black children are. White children are categorically excluded on the basis of race from consideration for inclusion in those families that state preferences for black children, but the magnitude of this injury is not as great as the respective harm to black children given the racial composition of the pool of adoptive parents. Because black parents (who typically want black children) constitute only a small portion of the total pool of adoptive parents, white children as a group are categorically excluded from only a small portion of adoptive families. Current facilitative accommodation practices do not result in an overwhelming majority of adoptive parents who decline, on the basis of race, to consider any white child for adoption.

Moreover, facilitative accommodation does not burden blacks generally because black adults and black children not placed for adoption are unaffected by it (at least directly). Black prospective adoptive parents are offered the same right as white parents to express a racial preference. Whether facilitative accommodation legally burdens the biological parents of black children placed for adoption is uncertain, in that those parents retain no legally cognizable interest in their biological children's welfare after relinquishment of their parental rights. A more generalized and diffuse harm of current facilitative accommodation policies is that they promote and reflect racial bias to the extent that they arise from the desire to allow adoptive parents to shield themselves from the social disapproval that might accompany the parents' adoption of a child of another race. The Supreme Court has held that state actions may be unconstitutional if they take account of race in such a manner as to promote, reflect, or further racial bias. As the Court announced in *Palmore v. Sidoti*: "Private [racial] biases may be outside the reach of the law, but the law cannot, directly or indirectly, give them effect," 466 U.S. 429 (1984). . . .

My proposal is a simple one: Adoption agencies that receive any government funding should not accommodate adoptive parents' racial preferences. Beyond ceasing the classification of children by race in order to facilitate the satisfaction of adoptive parents' racial preferences, adoption agencies should make clear to prospective adoptive parents that their racial preferences are to play no role in the parents' selection of a child to adopt.

My vision of strict non-accommodation consists of two elements. First, prospective adoptive parents would generally be prohibited from discriminating on the basis of race in their selection of a child to adopt, and birth parents who participate in the selection of adoptive parents would generally be prohibited from discriminating on the basis of race in doing so. Prospective adoptive parents and birth parents would be informed at the outset that the adoption process is not one in which racial discrimination is allowed. Parents would be encouraged to withdraw from the process if they did not think that they could abide by that rule, and adoption agency officials would have the authority to remove parents from the process if they determined that the parents in fact were discriminating on the basis of race. Parents could even be asked to sign a nondiscrimination agreement just as do other parties who do business with or enter a relationship with the government. Admittedly, this approach runs the risk of unintentionally underscoring the importance of race by constantly proclaiming that it must not matter. Nonetheless, the extent to which race currently matters in adoption suggests that mere governmental blindness to race would not decrease its significance.

Second, the general principle of nondiscrimination is qualified by my goal of promoting the maintenance of particular groups in the interest of cultural pluralism. Notwithstanding the law's focus on the rights of individuals and the primacy of the individual rather than the group in liberal political and social theory, our society has an important interest in maintaining cultural diversity. In American society, racial identity for minority groups is linked, though not identical, to a distinctive set of cultural characteristics, a nomos. To the extent the nomos is race-linked, racial minorities would be allowed to choose a child on the basis of race as a means of furthering that nomos. If one embraces cultural pluralism and accepts the inevitability of the state's either suppressing or promoting such communities (given the impossibility of neutrality), then such racially identified choices should be promoted in principle. The claim of contributing to the cultural pluralism of American society through their own race-consciousness is a claim that blacks and other racial minorities, but not whites, can make. The nomos of whiteness as a racial identity is nothing more than a historically generated and self-perpetuated set of privileges, expectations, and entitlements that are implemented through and reflected in the dominant norms, processes, rules, and structure of American society. There is no white race-based culture separate from mainstream American culture. In principle, then, strict non-accommodation should allow fulfillment of the racial preferences of racial minorities, but not those of whites.

The demands of race politics, however, may make it difficult to enact a policy that allows blacks, but not whites, to choose a child of their own race. Whites might argue that such an asymmetry is unfair, perhaps even unconstitutional, a conclusion the Supreme Court might adopt as well. Even as it strives to undo the most pernicious race-consciousness, such a policy might itself be decried as a pernicious type of race-based treatment. More debate might ensue about the justice of the asymmetry than about the idea of non-accommodation itself. If the merits of the policy were obscured by contentious debate about whether groups should be treated differently, I would advise the practical solution of not allowing any expression of same-race preference.

47

Private Race Preferences in Family Formation

Elizabeth Bartholet

Richard Banks questions whether private racial preferences for same-race children, and state agency practices accommodating and encouraging such preferences, should be accepted as legitimate. Why are so many people so ready to assume that it is . . . appropriate to think in racial terms in the intimate family context? I agree with Banks that it is important to question this assumption. . . . [T]here is a connection between these private racial preferences and the public racial preferences that are generally condemned as "discrimination." I agree that private racial preferences are not inherent, unalterable conditions of humankind, but rather products of our social conditioning . . . and . . . that it would be good to take steps to change the way people think about race in the family context. [Racial matching] policies not only prevent the formation of transracial families, but also condition people to think badly of racial intimacy.

But if we are to think seriously about the problem of racial preferences in the intimate family context, we need to look at the arenas in which these preferences are operating most significantly and to address decisions about romantic and sexual relationships, marriage, traditional procreation, and the production of children through reproductive technology and surrogacy arrangements. . . .

By trying to force a fit between his racial theory and the transracial adoption debate, Banks mischaracterizes both the nature of that debate and the nature of the problem facing black children. He describes the debate as if it involved a group of whites defending transracial adoption and facilitative accommodation arrayed against a group of blacks defending race matching. He portrays the white position as based on a classic liberal conception of the autonomous individual, and as placing greater value on the white parent's autonomy interests than on the black child's equality interests. He claims that the white position promotes white group interests while the black position promotes black group interests, although he says the white position is purportedly race blind.

But black and white groups and interests do not stack up so neatly in this debate. There is enormous support among whites, especially those in the child welfare system, for race matching. At the same time, polls demonstrate very little support among blacks in the general population for the 1970's National Black Social Workers Association's position supporting race matching. And leading black intellectuals like Professor Randall Kennedy at Harvard Law School have joined with whites in challenging race-matching policies. . . .

Banks finds it an "anomaly" that those of us opposing state-imposed barriers to transracial adoption have not addressed the issue of "facilitative accommodation," as though we were not aware that the phenomenon exists. Of course it exists, and of course it could be legally challenged. The issue, however, is whether it would be a good idea to try to eliminate private preferences with the coercive measures that Banks suggests, arguing that the state should not allow prospective adopters to consider race. . . .

. . . I do place some value on autonomy, and do not think the state should get in the business of limiting choice in marriage, procreation, or adoptive relationships, unless absolutely necessary. And although I think that it would be good for more people to cross racial and other lines of difference in the formation of their families, I do not think that it is so clearly bad if many others form families on the basis of similarities in racial, religious, ethnic, and national heritage. Banks argues that his proposals will help alleviate the plight of many African-American children now held for long periods in foster care, [but] if his proposed system were ever implemented it might hurt the life chances of the very children he wants to help. In reforming the role race plays in adoption, the logical place to start is with the elimination of state-imposed barriers to transracial adoption. . . . MEPA may someday have a significant impact but, for now, race matching by the state [remains] alive and well [and] there is no way of knowing how much of a problem private race preferences would pose if those barriers were actually eliminated. Banks purports to describe a world in which private preferences are operating to deny black children adoption opportunities, but this is a hypothetical world. We do not know whether private preferences would have a significant negative impact on black children's adoption opportunities if state-imposed barriers that now exist were eliminated. We do know, however, that a significant percentage of prospective adopters on public agency waiting lists show an interest in adopting across racial lines. [I]n the private agency world, where state barriers do not exist, many transracial adoptions take place and black children are generally placed promptly. We might, therefore, very well solve the problems of the black children in foster care waiting for adoptive homes by simply implementing MEPA's mandate and eliminating state-imposed racial barriers.

Banks's "strict nonaccommodation" would risk making things yet harder on the children in foster and institutional care who need adoptive homes. What would it mean for children awaiting adoption to be considered individually, rather than being excluded categorically, by prospective parents who do not want a child of another race? Most children awaiting adoption are old enough to realize that they are being considered for adoption by the adults invited to meet them individually or in groups. Most of them have already been overwhelmingly battered by life. Many are born damaged as a result of alcohol and drug use by their mothers. Most suffer serious abuse or neglect before entering foster care, and then years of institutional abuse and neglect as they bounce from foster home to biological home and back again, or from one foster home to another. Once these children are finally freed for adoption, do we want to put them through more sessions of individual rejection than we need to? Do we want to put pressure on prospective parents to adopt a black child, even if they do not wish to do so?

Banks recognizes that his proposal might drive many prospective adopters from the public adoption system into the private agency and independent adoption worlds, where two-thirds of all adoptions already take place. But he argues that those who will exit will be white prospective adopters without any interest in adopting transracially and that therefore no harm will follow to the black children waiting to be adopted, or to the white children for whom he claims there is an overabundance of waiting white parents. I think Banks is wrong on both counts. First, many prospective parents who might be interested in children of another race, if given the chance to think about it, will simply refuse to enter the public adoption system if it limits their choices even more drastically than does today's system. Second, given the terrible damage, both psychological and physical, suffered by many children in foster and institutional care, we need an overabundance of prospective adopters in order to have a chance of finding the needed homes. . . .

Our public adoption system already drives away many prospective adopters, black and white, by virtue of its negative, restrictive, bureaucratized nature. They flee to the private adoption world where, along with children and birth mothers, they are treated much better. In that private world, many seek to adopt on a same-race basis, but many others adopt across racial lines. Yet others go abroad for international adoption where they typically adopt across a variety of lines of difference—racial, ethnic, religious, and national. We should be drawing prospective parents into our public adoption system, not driving them away, if we want to advance the goals that Banks and I share: improved life prospects for black children and a different understanding of the role race should play in our private lives.

48

Racial Geographies

Sally Haslanger

In the contemporary academic context, there is much controversy about the reality of race. Anthony Appiah, for example, argues that race is not real and that we should stop employing racial categories.[1] If race is not real, however, and we follow Appiah's proposal to stop categorizing by race, then it would appear that categorizing adoptions as transracial or same-race would have to go too. And with this would go controversies over whether transracial adoption is good or bad policy.

On Appiah's view, however, racial *identity* is real, even if (usually) misguided. He suggests that individuals have a racial identity by virtue of incorporating into their self-understanding an intentional agency, a label—such as "Black" or "Asian-American"—that has a history associated with racial essences (81). So I have a White racial identity insofar as I identify as White and act intentionally *as a White person*. Such identities, he argues, are optional: "So here are my positive proposals: live with fractured identities; engage in identity play; find solidarity, yes, but recognize contingency, and above all, practice irony" (104).

Within Appiah's framework, debates over transracial adoption could be replaced by debates over "trans–racial-identity" adoption; the question would be whether an individual available for adoption should be placed with adoptive parents with a different racial identity. Given that one is not born with a racial identity in Appiah's sense, and may never develop one (in his sense), the issue would only arise for prospective parents and prospective adopted persons who have a developed racial identity.

If one accepts Appiah's recommendations, it would seem that there should be no principled objection to such adoptions, for they might, in fact, provide an excellent context for identity play, fracturing of identity, and so on. Of course, whether in a particular case this would be desirable would depend on the ego strengths and structures of the parties or the implications of such fracturing in the immediate social context. But what we now think of as transracial adoption might provide a fine opportunity to create the sorts of "fractured" identities Appiah applauds.

It is significant that on Appiah's account, the term "race" (and particular racial classifications) is either a vacuous term or a label employed in the framing of one's intentional action. I've argued elsewhere that these two options are not sufficient to understand what race is and how it works; in particular, this account obscures how race also functions as a social structure of privilege and subordination.[2] It also obscures the impact of living in and among racially marked bodies. This impact is a powerful reality for those living on the color line, including many of those in transracial adoptions. This sort of experience reveals, I believe, that there are aspects of identity that are more deeply and unconsciously embodied than Appiah's account of racial identity acknowledges. And this, in turn, suggests that there is more at stake in the debates over transracial adoption than his account would suggest.

I am a White parent of two African American children in open adoptions. Loving across this color line has both made visible and disrupted what some theorists have called the "racial social geography." Charles Mills suggests that "Conceptions of one's White self map a micro-geography of the acceptable routes through racial space . . . imprinted with domination."[3] Our internalized racial maps "dictate spaces of intimacy and distance"; violation of these borders risks punishment. Yet, in the context of transracial adoption, a parent cannot continue to live according to her old racial maps. A parent's love for the physical being of her child, her attuned responsiveness to the child's needs, and her subtle communication through body language all require transgression of racial boundaries. Most of these boundaries are, until they are violated, unconscious, unintentionally adhered to. Yet they have a profound effect on how we live our bodies and on day to day interracial interaction.[4]

In transracial adoption, the parents' love for their child can also disrupt the dominant society's "somatic norm image" (Mills 61). In the contemporary United States the somatic norm is undoubtedly White (also, e.g., able-bodied, young, physically fit). But in loving another it is not uncommon to see the individual's body as if saturated with their personal beauty. Although it is compatible with the racist aesthetic of the contemporary United States to find certain kinds of nonwhite bodies beautiful (exotic, powerful), loving the physical presence of one's child, when this presence is marked as racially different, can shift one's somatic norms to embrace different shapes, sizes, colors.

Racial "identity" also involves a responsiveness to group norms. Sometimes these norms are fully conscious, but internalized norms may work on us in subtle ways. Norms for appearance and behavior are typically race-specific; depending on context, they include dress, hairstyle, gait, vocabulary, tone and/or volume of voice, physical gestures of recognition or acknowledgment, and much more. Groups enforce their own norms; and norms are also enforced from "outside." In internalizing the norms that apply to my children, I feel anxious at not meeting the standards, and I judge others by them. If my daughter's hair is not neatly braided, my son's hair not recently cut, I am uneasy and apologetic.

My sense of community has also changed. I am often anxious around large groups of White strangers; in parent meetings at school I sit with the families of color. When I want to talk about my kids, their future, our family, including the extended birth families, there's a lot that my White friends and family don't understand.

Some of these reflections seem to support the idea that my identity is racially "fractured" or "fragmented," and that transracial adoption can create the kinds of identities that Appiah recommends. However, I raise these points not to agree with Appiah but to emphasize that race and racial identity are not as cognitive and intentional as Appiah's account suggests. Our current social structure divides us by race; we are socialized within racially specific somatic, perceptual, emotional, and normative frameworks; these frameworks structure not only our conscious lives, but also subconscious habits and skills, preconscious recognitional abilities, and tacit understandings. More important, these frameworks are "imprinted with domination." As a result, in order to understand racial identity and to overcome racism, we cannot simply change our language or engage in "identity play," for racism is embedded in many dimensions of our lives beyond our conscious thoughts and intentional actions.

Once we take the social and physical reality of race into account, however, there are questions that must be re-raised for those interested in transracial adoption; for example, will the prospective adoptive parents be in a position to love across a color line? To find their child beautiful? To overcome their racial bias? To make connections with racial communities in which they are in the minority? To understand racially specific norms and educate their children so they will be able to negotiate them? These are not new questions, and answers to them do not rule in or rule out transracial adoption; much will depend on what other options are available. Nonetheless, they are questions that seem to fall between the cracks when one looks at adoption from certain contemporary perspectives on race. Transracial adoption provides good opportunities for racial fragmentation, but it must also be kept in mind that racial fragmentation may be needed in order to do justice to the challenges of such adoptions and to the individuals who grow up in them.

NOTES

1. K. Anthony Appiah, "Race, Culture, Identity: Misunderstood Connections," in *Color Conscious: The Political Morality of Race,* ed. K. A. Appiah and A. Gutmann (Princeton: Princeton University Press, 1996), 30–105. Subsequent page references are included in the text.

2. Sally Haslanger, "Gender and Race: (What) Are They? (What) Do We Want Them to Be?" 1 *Nous* 34 (2000). See also Sally Haslanger and Charlotte Witt, eds., *The View from Home: Feminist and Philosophical Issues in Adoption* (Ithaca: Cornell University Press, forthcoming).

3. Charles Mills, *The Racial Contract* (Ithaca: Cornell University Press, 1999), 52.

4. Sharon Rush, *Loving across the Color Line: A White Adoptive Mother Learns about Race* (Totowa, NJ: Rowman and Littlefield, 2000).

49

Does a Child Have a Right to a Certain Identity?

Anita L. Allen-Castellitto

Adults who regard themselves as morally responsible for the upbringing of children commonly view themselves as having an obligation—at minimum—to feed, clothe and educate. Such adults also view themselves as having an obligation to ensure that their children, or their families, friends or communities' children, have suitable identities.

What is thought to constitute a "suitable" or appropriate identity for a child? Perhaps the clearest example is gender identity. Most parents assume that male children ought to be brought up to think of themselves as men rather than as women. Many parents teach masculine gender identification through frequent overt references to "my little boy," to "boy's clothes," to "what boys like" and to "taking it like a man." However, male gender identification can be and probably is taught through more subtle social practices as well, such as half-consciously encouraging sons to emulate their fathers and forming gender-segregated play groups for very small children.

I make these general empirical observations toward suggesting another, namely that the common understanding in most Western societies is that children ought to be brought up in such a way that they will have, not only *an* identity but *a certain* identity. Thus it is supposed that a male child should come into the identity of a male and not a female; and that a female child should come into the identity of a female and not a male. A parent or guardian or public school official who permitted or encouraged a male child to view himself as a female, or a female child to view herself as a male, would be regarded with disdain as negligent or even malicious and abusive.

Gender identification, the disposition to view oneself as male or female, and to display appropriately gendered affects, is only one type of identification with which responsible adults typically concern themselves. There is similar concern for ethnic, racial, national and religious identification. In terms comfortable to those whose political outlook is liberal, children are presumed to have a moral and political right to a certain identity or a certain set of identities: the identity or identities that reflect what they really are. In terms that may be preferred by the international human rights community, children are thought to need, and therefore to have as a human right that civilized nations are bound to respect, a certain identity or set of identities.

On this pervasive view about children's rights and needs, a male of African-American descent born and living in the United States, is owed the identity of a male and a black. To rear him in a way that permitted him to have the self-identity of a white female would be condemned widely as cruel and immoral. And in some quarters, to rear him in a way that permitted him to have the self-identity of a white male would garner similar condemnation. . . .

. . . I am skeptical of the assumption that children have a right, or morally important need, to a certain identity simply because of their ontological reality. It seems to me that the popular assumption that a child is owed a specific identity reveals as much or more about the needs and privileges of adults than about the needs, rights or ontological reality of human young. In particular, this assumption reflects adults' own socially created needs for contexts that do not deeply threaten their own wishes for communities of like-minded persons who can share and appreciate their identities.

That adults have such needs may be something more than a contingent fact of human history. But whether the need for the sharing and appreciation of identity is mainly nature or mainly nurture, it seems clear upon reflection that any plausible explanation for why the needs take the particular forms they take in modern life includes the social fact that we adults tend both to impute *and* to transfer similar needs to our young.

None of this points toward an argument against rearing and educating children about what society will call "their" genders, races, religions, etc. The adult world is structured so that social life can be full of peril for someone who fails on the internal and/or external level to be what he or she is supposed to be. It is social, rather than ontological, reality that is most importantly behind any practical duties adults have to ensure that the children for which they are responsible have certain identities.

Yet some of what we do in the name of prudentially or morally assuring that children will have certain identities is foolish. It may do individual children more harm than good. In the United States, it appears, for example, that the political power struggles between both blacks and whites and Native Americans and whites are being fought, inhumanely, over the backs of little children whose childhoods are all but ruined by well-intended adult efforts to place them in homes where their cultural and racial identities are most likely to be preserved. . . .

Transracial adoption in the United States is one context in which to think about the complex imperative to bring children up to have the appropriate identities, and in which to see its problematic character. In the United States some categories of identification are treated as essential (e.g., gender), while others are treated as not essential (e.g., religion). Officially, under progressive "color blind" civil rights laws, race is supposed to be treated like religion—a weak factor to consider in matching children to families. In practice, according to Elizabeth Bartholet, race is treated as being nearly as important as gender; that is, non-whites virtually never adopt whites, and whites adopt non-whites with difficulty, mainly in response to scarcity. (There are currently very few American-born healthy white infants available for adoption.)

Transracial adoption is much more controversial than trans-religious adoption. (But religion is sometimes an explosive issue in divorce/child custody cases. From time to time it emerges as an issue for the criminal law, as it did in February of 1993, when a member of a strict Jewish sect was arrested in New York after kidnapping a child he believed would not be reared in the customs of his faith.)

One curiosity of the transracial adoption controversy is that many of the "black" children who are adopted by "white" families are in fact bi-racial or racially mixed.

The segregationist rule of the Old South that "one drop" of "black blood" makes a person black has given rise to an ultimately arbitrary labeling system that potentially makes opposition to the placement of racially mixed children with whites look silly. Yet the experts agonize over the placement of black-ancestry children for good reason. Even for blacks (defined by the "one drop" rule) who look white, the fact of African ancestry, if disclosed, can negatively affect social and economic prospects. For all blacks, of all hues and social classes, there are special problems and concerns for which white parents may be less able than black parents to prepare their children, less able to explain, and less able to endure. This has led to the "transmission of survival skills" argument for preferring black parents for black children. Among the survival skills are comprehending discrimination in historic terms and knowing enough about black social rituals to fit in. The latter may include manifesting certain external, public indicia of identity in the senses outlined earlier. Whites may be unable to see to it that their black children have the public traits that lead other blacks to conclude that they share or at least appreciate others' internal, private black identities. To fit into the black community, and to become one of its respected leaders, a black person may need an identity whites cannot provide.

Closely related to the "transmission of survival skills" argument against transracial adoption is the "cultural genocide" argument, according to which the distinctiveness of black culture will be lost if blacks are adopted by whites; and there is also the "community self-determination" argument, which says that the aggregate of blacks—not whites—should be permitted to take responsibility for the welfare of blacks orphaned by poverty, drug abuse, or death. Arguments analogous to these are heard in battles over the fates of children in other settings: would it not be the end of culturally distinct, self-determining French Quebec if children were not compelled to learn the French language?

The aforementioned arguments against transracial adoption are too strong when marshalled to explain why a few black children each year should not be permitted white parents. The truth of the matter is that the demand for black children by whites is too low to pose a significant threat to black community self-determination and cultural survival.

The "survival skills" argument requires separate comment. One wants children to have "survival skills." It is true that blacks reared by whites, however kindly brought up and well-schooled, may fail to fit into traditional African-American culture. Blacks' ability to be a part of black culture may be impaired by a "white" upbringing. (I will ignore the fact that it can also be impaired by living with black parents in a majority-white neighborhood and going to a majority-white school.)

If one believed that a black child had a right to a black identity one might have to oppose transracial adoption on the ground that whites may be unable to see to it that their black children have a black identity in either the internal or external senses. One might prefer foster care, or group homes among blacks, to adoption by whites. Yet, in the abstract, it seems indefensible to conclude, as very many people do, that a black child will be, along every relevant educational, psychological and social dimension, all things considered, automatically better off if he or she is not reared by whites. A white family may be better in particular instances than foster care, group homes, and adoption by available blacks, despite the consequences for identity formation. (And some white children might be better off reared in black families than in the best available white families.)

I contend that having a family of one's own is more important to a child than having any particular racial identity. In making this assertion, the clear implication is that I reject the idea of children having a strong right to form a certain racial identity. I reject the idea because I think it is largely a surrogate for another idea, one I find more plausible—that adults have a right to respect for their identities.

50

Intercountry Adoption
A Frontier without Boundaries

Joan Heifetz Hollinger

The number of adoptions of children from other countries by United States citizens has increased nearly threefold since the 1980s and is expected to exceed 21,000 in fiscal year 2003–04.[1] Nearly half of these children are from China and Russia. The U.S. is primarily a "receiving" country, reporting a far larger number of adoptions of foreign born children than all other "receiving" countries combined. In addition, a number of children born in the U.S. are being adopted by residents of other countries—an out-migration that has until now not been subject to much scrutiny or regulation.

Among the reasons why so many U.S. citizens are turning to intercountry adoption are: (1) the sharp decline in the number of infants available for private adoption within the United States; (2) a fear—however unfounded it may be—of being involved in a contested domestic adoption; (3) frustration with the delays and bureaucratic hurdles associated with public agency adoptions; (4) doubts about raising older or special needs children from the U.S. foster care system who are assumed to be much more difficult to care for than, in fact, many of them are; and (5) in some cases, skepticism about ending up with a domestic adoption that entails ongoing contact with birth parent(s). While most U.S. citizens who seek foreign-born adoptees are motivated primarily by their own infertility, a great many are also motivated by a desire to raise children whose lives would otherwise be profoundly marred by poverty, disease, war, homelessness, or discrimination in their countries of origin based on their ethnoracial background or religion.

In their eagerness to adopt, many prospective parents are susceptible to the allure of intercountry adoption, as promoted in the hundreds of commercial advertisements and unregulated websites claiming "prompt" and "uncontested" foreign adoptions of healthy young children. The process that actually awaits would-be parents, however, is more bewildering and onerous than what many had anticipated. To complete a valid intercountry adoption, U.S. citizens have to navigate through an extraordinarily complex, time-consuming, financially and personally costly process that involves at least three separate governments, each with their own laws and procedures relevant to adoption and immigration: (1) the child's country of origin; (2) the U.S. government, specifically, the Bureau of Citizenship and Immigration Services (BCIS) [formerly the Immigration and Naturalization Service (INS)], and the State Department; and (3) the state where the adoptive parent(s) reside. Prospective parents have to rely on domestic and foreign agencies, lawyers, and facilitators, who may or may not be competent or trustworthy and who have generally been able to insulate themselves against any liability for their inadvertent or intentional misdeeds. Even when prospective parents and their agents adhere conscientiously to all the rules, no government or other entity can guarantee them an adoptable child who will satisfy their perhaps unrealistic expectations.

Since the 1980s, intercountry adoption has become a lucrative, largely unregulated multinational industry, producing tens of thousands of, for the most part, stable adoptive families, but also generating ever higher profits for thousands of adoption "service providers" and facilitators, and in some countries, wreaking havoc on children and families whose well-being is threatened by systemic corruption. Based on a conservative estimate that the average intercountry adoption costs $10,000–15,000, in addition to the cost of mandatory home studies, travel, and "contributions" to foreign children's institutions, U.S. adoptive parents spent more than $250 million in 2001–02 for adoption-related services.[2]

The characteristics of the children available for intercountry adoption vary greatly from one country to another. Some countries will not permit their healthiest or most robust children to emigrate; others will not disclose accurate information about children's health. Conditions in Guatemala, South Korea, and the Ukraine, which have, in addition to China and Russia, become major sending countries, are not a reliable gauge of conditions in other southeast Asian, South American, former Soviet and Eastern European countries that are now releasing large numbers of children for intercountry adoption. Cultural differences are often more important than children's ages or medical histories in explaining why some children end up in "orphanages" and others do not. In China, for example, strict population control policies, endemic poverty, and cultural traditions that favor sons over daughters have led to the abandonment of hundreds of thousands of infant girls, with the healthiest often made available for adoption by foreigners.

Prospective parents are increasingly determined to learn as much as possible about the physical and psychological health of children they are considering for adoption. Some critics of intercountry adoption complain that this manifests a narcissistic desire for "custom-made" children. Yet, an effort to obtain reliable medical and other background information is often the most reasonable thing prospective parents can do in order to assess their own capacity to raise different kinds of children.

In the U.S., state and federal adoption and medical assistance subsidies are generally not available to foreign-born adoptees. Eligibility for these subsidies is limited to some of the children with "special needs" placed by public agencies in the U.S. in the context of abuse, neglect, or dependency proceedings. There is no consensus in this country as to whether foreign-born adoptees with severe physical, cognitive, or emotional disabilities should be eligible for the kinds of public or other financial assistance programs that children adopted from domestic public agencies may obtain.

How do intercountry adoptees fare? Longitudinal studies of intercountry adoptees indicate they function as well as most other adoptive and biologic families in similar socioeconomic circumstances. Even children who suffered from untreated illnesses and severe neglect in their early lives have been able to recover and flourish. Moreover, the prospects for a healthy and stable life for intercountry adoptees are infinitely greater than for the hundreds of thousands, if not millions, of children in their countries of origin who are left to roam the streets or consigned to institutional care.

Despite the mounting evidence of remarkably positive "outcomes" for foreign-born adoptees, some commentators continue to decry intercountry adoption as exploitative of poor families and as destructive of children's "proper" individual and ethnoracial group identities. While having a multicultural upbringing does indeed raise complex issues of what it means, for example, to be Chinese, Russian, Ukrainian, Vietnamese, Peruvian, Korean and American, there is no evidence that having a multicultural identity is detrimental to the children or their adoptive families. Hundreds of country-specific adoptive family support groups have sprung up around the country that maintain e-mail listservs and sponsor informational meetings, "culture camps," travel and educational tours to children's countries of origin, and other activities for adoptees and their families.

For many adoptive families, the initial legal and bureaucratic hurdles are more challenging than the lifelong challenges of being a multicultural family. Under current laws, which vary considerably from one sending country to another, some adoptions can be completed in the sending country, but others have to be completed in the adoptive parent's home state within the U.S. In addition to the requirements of a child's country of origin, federal immigration and naturalization laws and regulations determine whether a child adopted in a sending country, or to be adopted in the United States, may be brought to the United States for the purposes of living here with her adoptive parents and becoming a U.S. citizen. The BCIS regulates the procedures for adoptive parents seeking to obtain an entry visa for a foreign-born child they have adopted or intend to adopt. Along with relevant state laws, BCIS regulations also determine the eligibility and suitability of applicants to adopt "orphan" children from other countries.

Since 2000, children whose U.S. citizen adoptive parents have completed a "full and final" adoption in the sending country are entitled to "automatic" U.S. citizenship. Children entering to be adopted or re-adopted in the U.S. become citizens as soon as their U.S. adoption is final. Under the new citizenship laws, these children immediately qualify for U.S. passports, and for Social Security and other federal and third party benefits that depend on citizenship status, thus eliminating some of the remaining vestiges of unequal treatment between foreign-born adoptees and biological or U.S.-born adopted children. Child Citizenship Act of 2000, Pub. L. No. 106-395.

The much-heralded Intercountry Adoption Act (IAA), Pub. L. No. 106-279, 114 Stat. 825 (2000), will eventually enable the U.S. to join the fifty or more other countries who are parties to the Hague Convention on Intercountry Adoption with its new rules for handling adoptions both from, and to, other Convention countries. Within the U.S. State Department, the Office of Children's Issues will be responsible for carrying out the principal functions of a "Central Authority."[3] Prospective parents seeking to adopt from another Convention country will have to work exclusively with a new category of "accredited non-profit agencies" or "approved persons" as well as satisfying stringent, time-consuming, and expensive requirements for being deemed eligible and suitable to adopt.

If services actually improve, the cost of an intercountry adoption is likely to become even higher. As more agencies get into the business of offering pre-placement "training" for adoptive parents along with a range of post-placement services, families will be paying adoption-related expenses for many years. An industry that already dissuades people of modest means from participating may, over time, be better able to provide high-priced and high quality services to an ever more well-to-do, but quite limited, segment of our society. Federal tax credits for an intercountry adoption are now as high as $10,000 for each adoption and easier acquisition of "automatic" citizenship for most foreign-born adoptees may enable more adoptees to qualify for Medicare and Social Security benefits if seriously ill or disabled. Still, the costs of intercountry adoption, as well as some of the requirements for home studies, background investigations, and travel, will continue to dissuade lower income families from seeking to adopt abroad.

Some aspects of intercountry adoption are likely to improve once the U.S. fully implements the IAA and the Hague Convention. For example, the IAA provides that all records pertaining to a Convention adoption be preserved, including information, if available, about a child's birth family, and that these records be disclosed to the adopted individual or the adoptive parents under applicable federal law, which includes, of course, the federal Freedom of Information Act and other laws that allow fuller disclosure of INS records than may be possible for the records of state court adoption proceedings. In addition, Convention adoptions will immediately be subject to full recognition in the U.S. Moreover, the IAA broadens the definition of "admissible child" for purposes of Convention adoptions, making it possible for more foreign-born adoptees to be eligible for prompt entry into the U.S. The IAA will also regulate and keep track of adoptions of U.S.-born children by residents of other Convention countries.

NOTES

1. U.S. Department of State, Office of Children's Issues, International Adoption, http://travel.state.gov/adopt.html. The Bureau of Citizenship and Immigration Services (BCIS) has taken over the functions and responsibilities previously performed by the Immigration and Naturalization Services (INS), which has been divided into various bureaus within the new U.S. Department of Homeland Security, created in 2002. Immigration and visa requirements for intercountry adoption are available at www.bcis.gov and www.bcis.gov/graphics/publicaffairs/factsheets/adoption.htm.

2. Testimony of Cindy Freidmutter, Executive Director, Donaldson Adoption Institute, U.S. Congress, House Committee on International Relations, Hearing on International Adoptions, May 22, 2002.

3. The function of the new U.S. Central Authority under the IAA, as well as other aspects of the IAA and the Hague Convention on Intercountry Adoption, are discussed in Joan H. Hollinger, ed., *Adoption Law and Practice* (New York: Matthew Bender, 2003), chaps. 10–11.

B

The Indian Child Welfare Act and the
Adoption of Indian Children

51

Who Are Indian Children within the Scope of the Federal Indian Child Welfare Act (ICWA)?

Joan Heifetz Hollinger

Whenever a proposed adoption involves an "Indian child," the federal Indian Child Welfare Act (ICWA) overrides any contrary state adoption laws. ICWA's primary goals are to promote the security and stability of Indian tribes and families by encouraging the exercise of tribal jurisdiction over dependency and adoption proceedings pertaining to the tribes' most valuable "natural resource," their children, and by discouraging the break-up of Indian families, 25 U.S.C.A. § 1901 et seq. (1978). A determination of whether or not a child is an "Indian child" under ICWA is a necessary prerequisite to the exercise of tribal rights to intervene in a state proceeding and to request that the child be placed, according to the Act's preferences, with a member of the child's Indian family or tribe, instead of with a non-Indian who may have been selected by the child's birth parent(s). This paper examines the complex interplay of political, cultural, racial, and constitutional factors that influence the determination of who is an Indian child.

ICWA defines an "Indian child" as an unmarried person under eighteen who is either (a) a member of one of the more than 550 federally recognized Indian tribes *or* (b) the biological child of a member of an Indian tribe *and* eligible for membership in the tribe, 25 U.S.C.A. § 1903(4). If a child is eligible for membership in more than one tribe—as, for example, when his mother and father each belong to different tribes—the tribe with which the child has "the more significant contacts" will be entitled to whatever rights the Act recognizes for the child's tribe, 25 U.S.C.A. § 1903(5). . . . For a child to be eligible for membership in any tribe, the legal status of the child's mother and father, as "parents" and as tribal members, has to be established.

A "parent" under ICWA is any biological parent of an Indian child, whether or not that parent is himself or herself Indian, or any Indian adoptive parent of an Indian child, who was adopted under state law or under tribal law or custom. However, an unwed father whose paternity has not been acknowledged or established is specifically excluded from the category of "parent," 25 U.S.C.A. § 1903(9). A child's birth mother is a "parent," as is the biological child's father, if he is married to the mother at the time of the child's birth. As with most state adoption statutes, the father of a child born out of wedlock is not a "parent" under ICWA unless he takes certain affirmative steps to establish his legal paternity. ICWA does not indicate how or when an unwed father must establish or acknowledge his paternity. Presumably, he would have to abide by the statutory requirements of the state in which he resides, or by tribal rules, if he is a member of a tribe.

Because the blood relationship has historically been "the very touchstone of a person's right to share in the cultural and property benefits of an Indian tribe" (1978 U.S. Code Cong. & Admin. News 7530, 7543) the Act excludes some children who have been raised as Indians, while including some who have had no prior contact with Indian society. For example, children whose Indian parents are not eligible for a particular tribe's membership because they do not have that tribe's requisite quantum of Indian blood are not covered by the Act, even though they may have been brought up on a reservation or in an Indian community. Children whose mother belongs to one tribe and whose father belongs to another may not be eligible for membership in either parent's tribe because they do not meet the blood quantum requirements of either tribe, and may therefore be outside the scope of the Act. By contrast, children of Indian parents who have never resided on or near an Indian community, are covered by the Act if the quantum of their Indian blood qualifies them for membership in a particular tribe. . . .

The Bureau of Indian Affairs (BIA) Guidelines say that tribal or BIA determinations of membership are "conclusive," and ICWA § 1911(c) requires courts to accord full faith and credit to certain tribal actions. Yet, because the Guidelines are not official regulations, they are not necessarily binding on courts. If a tribe is itself uncertain about a child's status, or has not completed its findings at the time of a dependency or adoption hearing, the trial court has to make an independent determination of the child's status. This may be an unreasonable burden to impose on trial courts. If the tribe is uncertain, how is the court to resolve the uncertainty without interfering with the tribe's authority to determine its own membership? If the tribe is unable to make a timely determination, the trial court may conclude that ICWA does not apply, thus leaving itself vulnerable to a later tribal challenge to its ruling. . . .

In deciding if a child is within ICWA, a court should be guided by ICWA's goal to prevent the unwarranted break-up of families who are perceived by themselves and others to be "Indian families." However, ICWA does not have an explicit goal to create Indian families where none had previously existed. Indeed, tribal determinations of membership based solely on a small quantum of tribal blood may be constitutionally suspect as a race-based classification if no other indicia of tribal affiliation are present. Moreover, ICWA's full faith and credit provision is qualified by the statement that courts must defer to tribal actions only "to the same extent" they would defer to similar actions by official entities in other jurisdictions. In deciding how much deference to accord the tribes, state courts should keep in mind the warning of the highly regarded scholar of Indian law, Felix Cohen, that the "right of expatriation" from an Indian tribe is an important human right: "[It] is an answer not only to federal oppression but to tribal oppression as well. It would be remarkable if the development of Indian self-government failed to give rise to dissatisfied individuals and minority groups who considered their tribal status a misfortune. History shows that nations lose in strength when they seek to prevent such unwilling subjects from renouncing their allegiance" (Felix Cohen, *Handbook of Indian Law,* p. 178 [1942 ed.]).

When does the determination of the child's status have to be made? Most courts that have addressed this question find that the child's status as an "Indian child" has to be settled before a final order of termination or adoption is entered. This means that the question remains unsettled until either order is entered. A proceeding that begins with a good-faith assumption that a child is not subject to ICWA may be challenged as not meeting ICWA requirements if, at any time before its completion, the child is determined to come within ICWA. . . .

ICWA permits a parent to petition to invalidate a state court dependency proceeding for failure to determine a child's Indian status, and may even excuse a parent's failure to raise an ICWA objection during the trial; but the Act should not be used to excuse a parent's delay in objecting until well after the disputed action is final.

The "Existing Indian Family" Doctrine May Limit Scope of ICWA

Since ICWA's enactment in 1978, state courts have developed three ways to construe ICWA's definition of "Indian child" that have had the effect of excluding certain children from ICWA. The first approach shows up in decisions that the biological child of a man who is a tribal member is not an Indian child unless the father also meets the Act's definition of "parent," as discussed above. The second approach is manifest in decisions that the Act does not apply unless a "court knows or has reason to know the child is an Indian," 25 U.S.C.A. § 1912(a). The third approach is based on a particular judicial construction of what is meant by ICWA's goal of preventing the destruction of Indian families and tribal communities by putting an end to "unwarranted removals" of children from their Indian families. This approach is based on the belief that if a child, albeit an Indian, is not part of a "genuine" or "existing" Indian family, the Act should not apply.

What is referred to as the "existing Indian family doctrine," suggests that voluntary placements of a child by a birth parent who has no significant cultural, social, or political ties to a tribe should be beyond the reach of ICWA. It also suggests that involuntary dependency proceedings should not be within ICWA unless the parent from whom a child is being removed was affirmatively affiliated with a tribe or a tribal community and the child can benefit from the additional procedures and services ICWA can offer. According to this doctrine, the "discovery" of Indian ties in order to defeat a finding of parental unfitness is inconsistent with the Act's goals of protecting authentic Indian families against the loss of their children and ensuring the survival of tribal sovereignty over tribal members.

The "existing Indian family" doctrine has shown up primarily in circumstances where a child, born out of wedlock to a non-Indian mother and Indian father, has lived since infancy with the mother in a non-Indian community and has had little, or no, contact with the father or the father's tribal relatives. When the mother places her child for adoption without notifying a tribe, she argues that her individual parental rights would be violated if the child's tribe is able to block her decision and impose its own and the Act's placement preferences. The doctrine can also arise in cases where both parents are Indian and the child is technically eligible for tribal membership, but the parents are non-reservation domiciliaries and have not established or maintained any political or cultural ties to a tribe until they are threatened with the loss of their own parental rights in a dependency proceeding. . . .

Congress has not amended ICWA either to expressly permit or preclude use of the "existing Indian family" doctrine to determine whether a child or a child's immediate family is within the scope of the Act. . . . Courts have therefore been free to determine for themselves whether to abide by the strict language of ICWA, which appears to preclude any limitation to existing Indian families, or to decide as a matter of statutory construction that the doctrine is consistent with ICWA's purposes. Several California Appeals Courts have concluded that the doctrine is warranted not simply as a matter of statutory construction, but in order to protect ICWA against certain constitutional "impediments" (e.g., *In re Bridget R.*, 41 Cal. App. 4th 1483, 49 Cal. Rptr. 2d 507 (1996) review denied, Cal. Sup. Ct., May 15, 1996; cert. denied, *Cindy R. v. James R.* 117 S.Ct. 693 (1997)).

Although the U.S. Supreme Court's opinion in *Mississippi Band of Choctaw Indians v. Holyfield*, 490 U.S. 30 (1989), does not deal with the definition of "Indian child" or "Indian family," a number of state courts have concluded that the Court's reasoning in *Holyfield* implicitly requires that the existing Indian family doctrine be rejected. . . . According to these courts, limiting ICWA to situations in which a child is removed from an Indian family is an inappropriate "judicially created exception," intended to circumvent the "mandatory protections" of tribal decision-making authority and the "minimum evidentiary standards" of the Act.

In contrast to these opinions, the Washington Supreme Court and several other state appellate courts have concluded that *Holyfield* is not inconsistent with the existing Indian family doctrine. (*In re Adoption of Infant Boy Crews*, 825 P.2d 305 (Wash. 1992)). According to appellate courts in Kentucky, Louisiana, Missouri, and Oklahoma, for example, it is appropriate for a trial court to inquire whether "the policies and purposes" behind ICWA are served by applying the Act to cases in which a child is within the statutory definition of Indian child, but neither the child nor the birth parents have ever had any ties to a tribal community or Indian culture. These courts read *Holyfield* as reinforcing the right of tribal courts to exercise jurisdiction in cases in which a child's Indian parents are clearly tribal members and reservation domiciliaries, but not as requiring state courts to apply ICWA to situations in which a parent is of Indian ancestry, but never had, or no longer maintains any residential or sociopolitical ties to a tribal community.

In 1996, the California Court of Appeal ruled that the existing Indian family doctrine is constitutionally necessary to protect ICWA against creating suspect classifications of children as Indian solely on the basis of their blood quantum or genetic heritage. *In re Bridget R.* involved twin girls born in November 1993 to an unmarried couple, neither of whom were affiliated at that time with any federally recognized tribe, and both of whom were eager to place the twins for adoption without involving their own extended families.

In relinquishing their parental rights to a California adoption agency, the birth parents deliberately withheld information concerning the father's partial Indian descent from the agency as well as from the adoptive couple from Ohio whom they had personally selected and who took physical custody of the twins when they were a few days old. Several months later, the paternal grandparents learned of the placement and convinced their son and the birth mother to challenge the adoption as violating ICWA. The grandparents, who like the birth parents, had never lived on or near a reservation, claimed that the twins were eligible for membership in the Pomo Indian tribe by virtue of their lineal descent from historically recognized tribal members. They further claimed that as "Indian children," the twins should not have been placed with a non-Indian adoptive family and should be "returned" at once to their extended Indian family.

At the heart of this and other cases that have discussed the existing Indian family doctrine are fundamental questions about children's identity. To what extent should the destiny of children be determined by their racial or genetic heritage, their affiliation with various ethnic, cultural, or tribal communities, their birth parents' voluntary placement decisions, or, when they grow up, their own choices concerning their individual or group identities?

In *Bridget R.*, the California court concluded that ICWA does not apply to the voluntary adoptive placement of a child of Indian lineage unless the child is part of an "existing Indian family" in which one or both parents have a "significant social, cultural, or political relationship" with a federally recognized tribe. Unlike the other decisions discussed above which have construed ICWA as limited to children whose birth families are actually threatened with destruction, the California Court went beyond policy justifications for the existing Indian family doctrine to insist that the doctrine is necessary to protect ICWA against various constitutional "impediments." ICWA's legitimate, often compelling purposes should be served through procedures and substantive rules appropriately tailored to achieve those purposes, the Court concluded. Without some tailoring, ICWA is vulnerable to attack for impermissibly burdening the due process and equal protection rights that the Court says are guaranteed to all children under the 5th and 14th Amendments. Tribal interests must yield, said the court, to the interests of children, who were never part of a recognizably Indian family, in remaining with the non-Indian adoptive families to whom they were voluntarily relinquished in accord with valid state laws.

What is most significant about the California Court's opinion in *Bridget R.* is its unflinching focus on the perspective of the children caught in disputes about their individual, familial, and communal identities. This is manifest in the Court's understanding that much of our constitutional jurisprudence on parental rights is the counterpart of the state's reliance on parents to support, raise, and nurture their children. If a birth parent's rights and duties are transferred to others with the expectation that the transfer will be permanent, it is appropriate, as the Court says, to treat any remaining parental rights as "subordinate" to the children's substantive liberty interest in being raised by the individuals who are committed to adopting and parenting them. Similarly, tribal claims—which are not based on any constitutional imperative, but on federal statutory law—should not be invoked to challenge a valid state adoption, unless the challenge serves a compelling interest threatened by the adoption. Although the interest in not breaking up a genuine Indian family is arguably compelling, an interest in interfering with an adoptive placement of a child who was never part of an existing Indian family is clearly not compelling.

To cast the Court's analysis in somewhat different terms, children have substantive due process rights to remain with the adoptive families voluntarily selected by their birth parents. These due process rights cannot be limited unless a tribe can show that ICWA does not pose a threat to the children's equal protection rights. Such a threat arises when a tribe stakes a claim to children solely on the basis of one component of their genetic makeup. By contrast, if the tribe invokes ICWA to rekindle and preserve a sociocultural and political tie that previously existed, the children's classification as Indian would not run afoul of the equal protection clause. Application of ICWA to children whose families have significant ties to tribal communities is consistent with the many other federal Indian laws that have withstood equal protection challenges because they are rationally related to an essentially political—and not predominantly race-based—classification of individuals. By contrast, application of ICWA to children who lack such ties is an unwarranted burden on the children's substantive due process rights. Thus, inquiry into whether the children's birth parents are part of a genuine Indian family, with tribal ties based on more than blood quantum, is necessary to protect ICWA against constitutional challenge.

The California Court's focus on children's interests culminates in its discussion of situations in which children are clearly within the scope of ICWA and ICWA requires that their adoption be set aside. In these situations, any remedies intended to rectify the wrongs suffered by parents and tribes who were deprived of ICWA's statutory benefits must take account of children's due process rights. In many instances, these rights would be impermissibly burdened if children were precipitously removed from their stable custodial environments in order to be "returned" to individuals who are socially and psychologically strangers to them. Instead, as other courts, including tribal courts, have concluded, and as the proposed Uniform Adoption Act (1994) recommends, a decision to deny an adoption must be followed by a custody hearing to determine where the children should reside. At this hearing, the court could decide that the children should remain with their would-be adoptive parents while having some contact over time with members of their extended Indian family.

As explained by the Court, such a custody hearing should not be based on a simple "best interests" test but on an "avoidance of detriment" test. It should give due regard to the reasonable expectations of the parties at the time of the initial placement as well as to the harms likely to be suffered by children removed from a stable or long-term custodial environment.

It remains to be seen whether other appellate courts, or the U.S. Supreme Court, will agree with the California Court that children have an equal protection right *not* to be classified on the basis of blood alone and to similarly avoid being "protected" against adoptive placements that pose no threat to their sociocultural identity. Do children also have rights to avoid being claimed retroactively as Indian tribal members simply for the purpose of challenging an otherwise valid adoption under state law?

Some tribal advocates argue that the California Court draws too bright a line between ICWA's commitment to preserving tribal connections that already exist and

ICWA's goal of ensuring long-term tribal survival. From the tribes' perspective, their survival depends on being able to reach out to current and future generations of children of partial Indian descent whose initial tribal ties may be nonexistent or quite attenuated. From the perspective of children whose immediate families have grown apart from or actively disavowed tribal culture, it may or may not be beneficial to establish or re-establish a tribal connection. We are still a long way from achieving what Justice Stevens refers to in his *Holyfield* dissent as "the delicate balance between individual rights and group rights," 490 U.S. at 55.

. . . [T]he "existing Indian family" doctrine could significantly decrease the number of dependency or adoption proceedings that are subject to ICWA. Most likely to be affected by the doctrine are voluntary adoptive placements of Indian children by non-Indian parents who have lived outside a reservation and have not maintained much, if any, affiliation with tribal culture. Also likely to be affected by the doctrine are children subject to state welfare or dependency proceedings who are racially and ethnically mixed and whose parents do not have any strong allegiance to any particular racial or ethnic community. Indeed, for some racially mixed children, ICWA and the federal laws removing barriers to interethnic and transracial placement may be on a collision course with each other.

Unlike the tribal advocates who want to broaden the scope of ICWA, many birth parents who are themselves not Indian, or who have repudiated an earlier tribal affiliation, would prefer to remain beyond the reach of ICWA. They believe that their own and their children's individual constitutionally protected rights are in conflict with the claims of tribal communities towards which they feel no social or cultural allegiance.

52

Pigs in Heaven
A Parable of Native American Adoption under the Indian Child Welfare Act

Christine Metteer

[T]he jurisdictional scheme of the ICWA reflects the fact that "because child custody arrangements are heavily laden with cultural and social tradition, the choice of forum as between a state and tribal court can fundamentally affect the outcome of a custody dispute." (Barbara A. Atwood, "Fighting over Indian Children: The Uses and Abuses of Jurisdictional Ambiguity," 36 *UCLA L. Rev.* 1051, 1057 (1989).) The jurisdictional provisions are therefore "at the heart of the ICWA," reflecting the spirit of the Act that "where possible, an Indian child should remain in the Indian community." *Mississippi Band of Choctaw Indians v. Holyfield,* 490 U.S. 30, 37 (1989). In fact, "the broad grant of jurisdiction to tribes and the narrowing of state authority were aimed at preventing the . . . evils" set out in . . . the Act.

State courts, however, often wrestle with the spirit of the Act in determining jurisdiction, which depends upon how the courts choose to define the Act's terms. The term most often in question in determining jurisdiction is the "domicile" of the child. As might be expected, state courts seeking to retain jurisdiction define the term narrowly to mean the child's physical presence "within the territory set aside for the reservation." With such a definition in place, the "heart" of the ICWA, the "broad grant of jurisdiction to the tribes," can easily be set aside, and individuals can dictate jurisdiction simply by changing the child's domicile at the time of a custody proceeding.

The clear focus of such a definition is on the primacy of the wishes of the parents (rather than on "tribal primacy"), who, when wanting to place their child for adoption . . . typically argue for an interpretation of the rules of domicile that permits state court jurisdiction. Despite the fact that such a definition's "receptivity . . . to [the] non-Indian placement of an Indian child is precisely one of the evils at which the ICWA was aimed," *In re Halloway,* no less than three U.S. Supreme Court justices have embraced the view that:

> . . . allowing the tribe to defeat the parents' deliberate choice of jurisdiction would be conducive neither to the best interests of the child nor to the stability and security of Indian tribes and families. . . . By allowing the Indian parents to "choose" the forum that will decide whether to sever the parent-child relationship, Congress promotes the secu-

rity of Indian families by allowing the Indian parents to defend in the court system that most reflects the parents' familial standards. . . . No purpose of the ICWA is served by closing the State Courthouse door to them. *Holyfield*, 490 U.S. at 60–61, 63 (Stevens, J., dissenting).

Such a definition of domicile, however, defeats the clear intent Congress embodied in § 1911 by removing the tribe as the preferred forum, and similarly defeats the spirit of the Act, which is to protect the interests of the tribe in determining "who will have the care and custody of its children." As the court in *Halloway* found, "to permit [parents] to change . . . domicile as part of a scheme to facilitate . . . adoption by non-Indians . . . weakens considerably the tribe's ability to assert its interest in its children . . . which is distinct from but on a parity with the interest of the parents." The majority in *Holyfield* agreed, and held that "the law of domicile Congress used in the ICWA cannot be one that permits individual reservation-domiciled tribal members to defeat the tribe's exclusive jurisdiction by the simple expedient of giving birth and placing the child for adoption off the reservation." 490 U.S. at 53. Such a definition, in the Supreme Court's opinion, "would, to a large extent, nullify the purpose the ICWA was intended to accomplish." Id. at 52. The Supreme Court therefore found that Congress intended a uniform definition of the term "domicile," not subject to individual state law's interpretations.

The Supreme Court's broad construction of the term "domicile" for purposes of determining jurisdiction under § 1911 caused the *Holyfield* case to be heralded as "good news for proponents of a broad reading of the Act." While some state courts have indeed found that "'*Holyfield* also carries the clear message that [the ICWA] would be read liberally, perhaps creatively, to protect the rights of the tribe even against the clearly expressed wishes of the parents . . . ,'" *In re Baade*, 462 N.W.2d 485, 489–90 (S.D. 1990), others have refused to read *Holyfield* expansively, limiting the case to its own facts and narrow issue, *see, e.g., In re S.C.*, 833 P.2d 1249, 1254 (Okla. 1992); *In re Infant Boy Crews*, 825 P.2d 305, 310 (Wash. 1992). And although *Holyfield* called for a uniform definition of key terms of the Act, state courts' individual definitions of another provision of the Act's jurisdictional scheme, "good cause" not to transfer proceedings to the tribal court, have also plagued the liberal application of the Act as envisioned by Congress. . . .

Barbara Kingsolver's novel, *Pigs in Heaven* (1993), essentially concerns the opening of doors into each other's cultures that must occur to successfully balance the best interests of both the child and the tribe. The novel's central metaphor involves the different views of "Heaven" held by whites and Indians. First, "Heaven" is the name of the Oklahoma town on the Cherokee Reservation where much of the story takes place. When the Indian child's adoptive grandmother, Alice, comes to the tiny, impoverished town to meet with Annawake Fourkiller to discuss the best interests of the child, she asks how the town got its odd name. She is told:

> Well, that's for the blue hole. A great big water hole down in the crick where the kids love to go jump in and fish and all. . . . It's the best place around. They used to call it "The best place" in Cherokee, and when they went to turn it into English somebody thought

people was talking about Heaven. But they wasn't, they just meant the best place around here. (*Pigs in Heaven* at 191.)

This recognition of cultural differences and their impact on an Indian child custody proceeding is at the core of the ICWA and its broad grant of jurisdiction to the tribes. Such recognition is also imperative in balancing the interests of the parents and child and those of the tribe when determining good cause not to transfer a case to tribal jurisdiction. . . .

Interestingly, once cases have been transferred to tribal courts, the tribal court decisions reflect many of the same concerns for the child that state courts have enumerated. Neither the *Halloway* nor *Holyfield* court removed an Indian child from the adoptive parents with whom the child had bonded. In *Halloway*, the Navajo Tribal court decided that "a full-blooded Navajo youngster will continue to live with the white Mormon couple who adopted him six years ago. . . . [He] will become the permanent ward of his white, adoptive parents. . . . But legally he will be the son of his biological Navajo mother . . . and she will have specified visiting rights." In *Holyfield*, the tribal court went even further and "granted adoption of the children to Ms. Holyfield . . . after deciding it was in the children's best interest that they remain with her." Thus, the tribal decisions in both *Holyfield* and *Halloway* show that the tribal courts have the "experience, wisdom, and compassion" necessary to fashion what the state courts consider "an appropriate remedy." . . .

. . . [Metteer goes on to criticize the judicially developed "existing Indian family" exception to ICWA.] . . . The problem with the existing Indian family exception is that it first calls into question both what it means to be an Indian child and an Indian family, and then applies the definition of white, "civilized society" to answer these questions. By its own terms the Act applies to the Indian child on the basis of his or her tribal membership or eligibility and the tribal membership of the biological parent. However, raising the first question, the courts, instead of relying on the Act's definition of an Indian child, have fashioned . . . levels of "Indian-ness" to try to manipulate their use of the existing Indian family exception . . . [which] becomes a second litmus test for "Indian-ness" [including] such notions as: 1) ties to the tribe, 2) Indian cultural setting, and 3) length of time in an Indian home—effectively adding a new requirement or redefining an "Indian child." . . .

The courts tend to define "Indian-ness" by evaluating whether the child lives in an "actual Indian dwelling," apparently thinking of a teepee, hogan, or pueblo. However, "limiting the Act's applicability solely to situations where nonfamily entities physically remove Indian children from actual Indian dwellings deprecates the very links— parental, tribal, and cultural—the Act is designed to preserve." *In re Crystal K.,* 276 Cal. Rptr. 619, 625 (Ct. App. 1990).

Despite a broad reading of *Holyfield* which allowed the North Dakota Supreme Court to find its use of the existing Indian family exception "incorrect . . . fail[ing] to recognize the legitimate concerns of the tribe that are protected under the Act," the California court in *In re Bridget R.* similarly considered "Indian-ness" in determining the Act's applicability. The court found that "it does not follow from *Holyfield* that ICWA should apply when neither the child nor either natural parent has ever resided or been domiciled on a reservation or maintained any significant social, cultural, or political relationship with an Indian tribe." *In re Bridget R.*, 49 Cal. Rptr. 2d. 507, 536 (Ct. App. 1996). The court then remanded the case so that that factual determination could be made. . . .

The twins' Indian family, however, "is bitter over having to prove how Indian" they are. The birth parents argue that "questions about their lineage and commitment to their culture are insulting and should be left to Native Americans themselves." [One] attorney likened such determination of "Indian-ness" to "trying to determine who is a good Catholic or a good Jew. The function of the government is not to assess those things." The twins' grandmother explains, "it's not how many activities you go to . . . it's something you feel." The Indian father's tribe agrees that "it only takes one gene, one piece to make them [Indian]. . . . We don't want to lose a single one of our children. They are our heart and soul." (quotes from James Rainey, "Court Blocks Return of Adopted Twin Girls," *Los Angeles Times*, June 16 at B8 and July 7, 1995, at B1.)

Following such reasoning, one court has held that "where the mother is a Native American Indian, the mother and child, at least presumptively for purposes of initiating ICWA inquiries, constitute an 'Indian family,'" *In re Adoption of Child of Indian Heritage* (NJ 1988), despite not living on a reservation. And if the Indian mother and child constitute an Indian family despite not living on the reservation in an "actual Indian dwelling," it must be on the basis of the child's "Indian-ness" under § 1903(4)— its eligibility for tribal membership, that is, its essential affiliation with the tribe.

Extending such reasoning, if the child is part of an Indian family because of its affiliation with its tribal "family," then even the consent of the mother to place the child outside the tribe for adoption may not be a valid reason to do so. "The concept that a mother has the right to remove her child from its extended family and community, thereby depriving the child of its heritage, and the community of its valued member, is foreign to American Indian cultures." Thus, the New Jersey court found that even if the Indian child's mother seeks non-tribal adoption of her child, consideration must also be given to the rights of the child's father and Congress' belief that, whenever possible, it is in an Indian child's best interests to maintain a relationship with his or her tribe. . . . "For these reasons, we decline to follow the interpretation of the ICWA . . . which would preclude its application to voluntary private placement adoptions, and we decline to do so even where the child has never lived with an Indian family or in an Indian environment," 543 A.2d 925, 932 (N.J. 1988).

[Various] examples of the fluidity of family show why the California state courts' requirement that the child be removed from an existing Indian family, which it defines as the "nuclear family . . . parents and offspring," harkens back to the "evils" preceding the enactment of the ICWA. The ICWA was enacted to prevent the break up of Indian families "by the removal, often unwarranted, of their children from them," and to recognize "the essential tribal relations of Indian people and the cultural and social standards prevailing in Indian communities and families." According to Indian definition, the larger family is broken up any time a child is removed from the tribe of which it is eligible to be a member. Therefore, the judicially-created existing Indian-family exception is in direct violation of the spirit, and quite probably the letter of the law.

Single, Gay, and Lesbian Adoptive Parents and Their Children

53

Second Parent Adoptions Protect Children with Two Mothers or Two Fathers

Joan Heifetz Hollinger

One of the most controversial domains on the frontier of adoption is populated by lesbian and gay couples who are turning to adoption laws to legitimize and protect their status as the parents of the children they are raising. For these couples, adoption is generally a response not to infertility but to their inability to establish legal ties to their children through other means, such as private contracts or marriage.

Second or co-parent adoption is a legal procedure that allows a same-sex co-parent to adopt his or her partner's biological or adopted child without requiring the partner to relinquish parental rights. Many thousands of same-sex couples have sought this kind of adoption in order to ensure that their children will have two legal parents, each equally responsible for the children's care and support. Second parent adoption also protects the rights of the co-parents, by ensuring that the "second" parent will continue to have a legally recognized parental relationship to the child if the couple separates or if the "first" parent dies or becomes incapacitated.

Second parent adoptions usually involve a female couple in which the first parent is the biological mother through donor insemination or has previously adopted a child as a single parent. In many, but not all, states, a man who donates sperm through a licensed physician to a married or unmarried woman is not treated as the resulting child's legal father—he is barred from claiming any parental rights and relieved of any parental obligations. These adoptions may also involve a male couple in which one partner has already adopted as a single parent or is the legal father of a child through an agreement with a surrogate gestator who waived her parental rights. Many of these adoptions involve a single adult who adopts a foster child with special needs from a public agency and later seeks to add his or her partner as the child's second parent.

A child acquires a second legal parent when, with the first parent's consent, that parent's same-sex partner adopts the child through a process analogous to an adoption of a child by a stepparent who is the spouse of the child's first parent. Unlike an adoption by two "legal strangers," when a child is adopted by a stepparent or same-sex co-parent, the first parent retains parental rights and duties. The consequence of a stepparent or co-parent adoption is, thus, the addition of a second legal parent to the child's family, not the complete legal substitution of the adoptive for the original biological family as occurs in other adoptions.

In most of the households in which same-sex couples seek a co-parent adoption, there are two highly motivated and committed prospective parents who plan to have a child together, cooperate in the child's conception and birth, and then jointly raise the child from birth on. Because same-sex couples are not currently permitted to marry, a co-parent adoption may be the only way they can establish a secure legal relationship with their child. In fact, children raised from birth by same-sex parents are more likely to have families that function as "model" nuclear families than do children in typical stepparent families where the stepparent joins a household by marrying someone who already has a child from a prior marital or nonmarital relationship with the child's other parent.

Just as a stepparent adoption is more difficult to achieve when a child's noncustodial parent refuses to consent to the custodial parent's request that his or her new spouse be permitted to adopt, a co-parent adoption is not possible when a lesbian, gay, or bisexual parent has custody of a child from a previous heterosexual relationship, unless the parent's former spouse or partner is willing to consent and relinquish his or her parental rights or is subject to an involuntary termination of parental rights. Similarly, co-parent adoption is more difficult where a woman has had a child through donor insemination and the sperm donor is a legal father, unless the donor is willing to consent to the adoption by the woman's partner and relinquish his parental rights.

The Census Bureau estimates that in 1998 there were nearly two million same-sex partnerships in the United States, more or less equally divided between two-male and two-female couples. Because it is difficult to get an estimate of the number of single gay or lesbian adults raising minor children, the actual number of minor children living with a gay or lesbian parent, with or without a partner, is believed to be considerably larger than the 170,000 couples that reported they had children aged fifteen or younger living with them. Moreover, preliminary reports from the 2000 census suggest a very sizeable increase in the overall number of same-sex couples as well as in the numbers living with their biological or adopted children or interested in adopting children from this or other countries.

Social science research has consistently shown that children raised by lesbian and gay parents do as well on standard measures of adjustment, health, and cognitive and emotional development as children raised by heterosexual parents in comparable socioeconomic circumstances. See, e.g., the American Psychological Association's 1995 review of the longitudinal studies [and the article by Judith Stacey and Timothy J. Biblarz included in this reader].

Every major children's advocacy and professional organization with expertise in child development and family dynamics strongly supports the view that no one should be categorically excluded from consideration as a prospective foster or adoptive parent because of his or her sexual orientation or marital status, and that children being raised by gay or lesbian parents deserve the psychological security of having their ties to their parents legally recognized. See, e.g., the analyses and recommendations of the Child Welfare League of America, the National Association of Social Workers, the American Academies of Pediatrics and Family Physicians, and the national professional associations of psychologists, psychiatrists, and psychoanalysts. In all but the handful of states like Florida and Utah that bar adoptions of foster children by gays or lesbians, public agencies willingly accept gay or lesbian applicants to adopt children with special needs—older minority children, sibling groups, and children with physical or mental disabilities.

The validity of second parent adoptions under prevailing statutes has been recognized by appellate courts in at least eight jurisdictions: California, Illinois, Massachusetts, New Jersey, New York, Pennsylvania, Vermont, and the District of Columbia. Trial courts in as many as twenty other states have also routinely approved these adoptions as well as joint adoptions by same-sex couples of children who were previously unrelated to either prospective parent. These courts are aware that adoption by same-sex couples was not contemplated at the time most state adoption laws were enacted. But they note that their state's adoption statutes permit unmarried as well as married adults to adopt, requiring only that all prospective parents have a favorable evaluation or home study, and that, if an applicant is married, both spouses join the petition to adopt.

For these courts, the most difficult statutory construction issue is not whether a single adult is eligible to adopt, but whether a child's original legal parent must always be relieved of parental rights when a child is adopted by someone other than that parent's spouse. [As manifest in the case excerpts included in this part,] the conclusions these courts reach often depend on whether they favor "strict" construction in the interests of avoiding any kind of adoption that is not expressly authorized in the state law, or, alternatively, "strict" or "liberal" interpretation of the statutes in order to promote the well-being of children who might otherwise not have two legal parents.

Most of these courts treat a second parent adoption by a same-sex partner as similar to a standard stepparent adoption in which the consent of the stepparent's spouse—the child's custodial parent—is essential, but termination of that parent's rights is not required.

While parental consent is, and always has been, an essential jurisdictional prerequisite for adoption, the termination of parental rights that typically occurs with respect to a biological parent who consents to the adoption of a child by a "legal stranger" is not a necessary or mandatory consequence of an adoption.

The extent to which a biological parent is relieved of parental rights and duties upon a child's adoption by others has changed considerably since the mid-nineteenth century, especially with regard to the laws of inheritance and child support. When a court finds that the essential prerequisites for a valid adoption are satisfied—parental consent, suitable adoptive parent(s), lawful placement of child—it may then conclude that it is in the best interests of a particular child to allow the child's first parent to waive one of the consequences of an adoption—namely, her right to be relieved of her parental status—and, instead, agree to co-parent with the child's new adoptive parent. In this view, the circumstances of a particular adoption and the needs of the adopted child will ultimately determine the consequences of an adoption for the child's relationship to both parents.

At least three states—California, Connecticut, and Vermont—have expressly authorized second parent adoptions in their state adoption statutes. These statutes are similar to the second parent provisions in the Uniform Adoption Act (1994), allowing same-sex "domestic partners" to use the simplified stepparent adoption procedures to adopt each other's children.

In several states, however, including Colorado, Nebraska, and Wisconsin, appellate courts have concluded that their statutes do not permit same-sex co-parent adoptions because, in their view, the "stepparent exception" to the usual rule of complete substitution of adoptive for the original biological parents cannot be applied to unmarried couples. Nonetheless, courts in these and a number of other states have applied custody laws or equitable principles to allow a legal parent's former same-sex partner to seek visitation with a child they have co-parented if the former partner can prove he or she functioned as the child's de facto or psychological parent. See, e.g., *V.C. v. M.J.B.,* 163 N.J. 200, 748 A.2d 539 (2000); *Holtzman v. Knott,* 193 Wis. 2d 649, 533 N.W.2d 419 (Wis. 1995); and other cases cited in ALI Principles of the Law of Family Dissolution §§ 2.03, 2.04, 2.21 (2002).

Several states—Mississippi, Texas, Utah—have statutes or regulations that are intended to bar lesbians and gay men from becoming either foster or adoptive parents for children in the state's public dependency system. Florida's ban on adoption by gays or lesbians, even though they can and do serve as foster parents, is being challenged in federal courts as a denial of equal treatment to these prospective parents as well as to their foster children who have few, if any, other options for permanency.

54

State Appeals Court Rulings That Deny or Approve Second Parent Adoptions by Same-Sex Couples

In the Interest of Angel Lace M. (Wis. 1994)

Steinmetz, J.

(1) Do the Wisconsin adoption statutes permit a third party to adopt the minor child of the third party's nonmarital partner?

(2) If the Wisconsin adoption statutes prohibit this adoption from taking place, do these statutes violate the constitutional rights of either the minor child or the third party? . . .

. . . We hold that this adoption is not permissible under ch. 48, Stats. We further hold that the relevant provisions of ch. 48 do not violate the constitutional rights of either the minor child or the third party.

Angel was born on March 10, 1986. On September 20, 1988, Georgina and Terry M. adopted Angel. Georgina and Terry were married at the time of the adoption. They separated in February, 1990, and divorced in June of that same year. Aside from paying court-ordered child support, Terry has played no part in Angel's life since late 1990.

In June, 1990, Georgina and Angel began living with Annette. The two women have shared equally in raising Angel since that time. . . . [In 1992] Annette filed a petition . . . to adopt Angel. Simultaneously, Georgina filed a petition to terminate Terry's parental rights and a petition for the adoptive placement of Angel with Annette. No party filed a petition to terminate Georgina's parental rights.

At the court hearing, Terry signed a statement consenting to the termination of his parental rights and testified that his consent was both voluntary and knowing. The Community Adoption Center filed a report with the court recommending the adoption. . . . [T]he circuit court determined that the proposed adoption would be in Angel's best interests. However, the court also determined that pursuant to ch. 48, Stats., Annette is not competent to adopt Angel and Angel is not competent to be adopted by Annette . . . and the court denied each of the petitions. . . .

Annette and Georgina appealed. . . . They argue that the circuit court should have granted Annette's petition for adoption because the court found that the adoption is in Angel's best interests. . . . There is no doubt that a court must find that an adoption is in the best interests of the child before the court may grant the petition for adoption. However, the fact that an adoption—or any other action affecting a child—is in the child's best interests, by itself, does not authorize a court to grant the adoption. . . .

Were we to allow a court to grant an adoption petition any time the adoption is in the best interests of the child, there would be no need for the plethora of adoption statutes . . . we reject this argument.

"Before a court may make a finding that a second parent adoption is in a child's best interests, it must first determine whether it has the power to grant such an adoption under the existing adoption statutes." [Citations omitted.] "Adoption proceedings, unknown at common law, are of statutory origin and the essential statutory requirements must be substantially met to validate the proceedings." *Estate of Topel,* 32 Wis. 2d 223, 229, 145 N.W.2d 162 (1966). . . .

In Wisconsin, a party petitioning to adopt a minor must satisfy two requirements. First, the party must be a resident of Wisconsin. Annette satisfies this first requirement. Second, the party must fit the description from either sec. 48.82(1)(a) or sec. 48.82(1)(b). Annette does not qualify under sec. 48.82(1)(a) because she is not legally "the husband or wife" of Georgina who is the "parent of the minor." However, Annette does fit the description in sec. 48.82(1)(b) because she is "an unmarried adult."

For the adoption to be valid, not only must Annette qualify as a party who may adopt Angel, but Angel must also be eligible for adoption. Section 48.81, Stats. controls who may be adopted. A minor must also satisfy two requirements to be eligible for adoption. Angel satisfies the first requirement of the statute because she was present in the state of Wisconsin at the time Annette filed the petition for adoption. See sec. 48.81(2). It is less clear whether Angel satisfies the second requirement. Pursuant to sec. 48.81(1), a minor may only be adopted if "parental rights have been terminated. . . ." Angel's adoptive father, Terry, has consented to the termination of his parental rights. Georgina's parental rights, on the other hand, remain intact.

The petitioners claim that sec. 48.81(1), Stats., is ambiguous. According to the petitioners, the statute could mean that Angel is eligible for adoption only if the rights of both of her parents have been terminated. Or, it could mean that she is eligible for adoption as long as the rights of at least one of her parents have been terminated. The petitioners ask this court to construe the statute liberally to further the best interests of Angel . . . and accept the second interpretation of the statute.

Under this second interpretation of the statute . . . a minor would be eligible for adoption when the rights of only one of her parents are terminated. The minor would be eligible to be adopted even if the remaining parent is legally fit to raise the child alone and prefers to raise the child alone. Ostensibly, a complete stranger could petition to adopt a minor who is a member of this stable family; and . . . the proposed adoption would be permissible. The legislature could not have intended to declare a minor eligible for adoption under those circumstances. This would be an absurd result. This court will not construe a statute so as to work absurd or unreasonable results. . . . Hence, we hold that pursuant to sec. 48.81(1), a minor is not eligible for adoption unless the rights of both of her parents have been terminated. Because Georgina's parental rights remain intact, Angel is not eligible to be adopted by Annette.

Section 48.92, Stats. also stands in the way of Annette's proposed adoption of Angel. This statute severs the ties between the birth parent and the adopted minor after a court enters the order of adoption. [I]f the circuit court grants Annette's petition to adopt Angel, "all the rights, duties and other legal consequences of [Georgina's relationship with Angel] shall cease to exist." . . . If the legislature had intended to sanction adoptions by nonmarital partners, it would not have mandated this "cut-off" of the "rights, duties and other legal consequences" of the birth parents in these adoptions.

The petitioners argue that, despite the use of the word "shall," this "cut-off" provision is directory, not mandatory, under Wisconsin law. . . . This interpretation ignores two basic rules of statutory interpretation. First, "shall" is presumed to be mandatory when it appears in a statute. . . . The petitioners' argument does not overcome this presumption. Second, where the legislature specifically enumerates certain exceptions to a statute, this court presumes that the legislature intended to exclude other exceptions. . . . In this case, the legislature specifically exempted stepparent adoptions by stating that the "cut-off" provision applies "unless the birth parent is the spouse of the adoptive parent. . . ." See sec. 48.92(2), Stats. This is evidence that the legislature did not intend to exempt other adoptions, including those by nonmarital partners. . . .

Therefore, we conclude that the proposed adoption does not satisfy the essential requirements of the adoption statutes and is, in fact, prohibited by these statutes. The circuit court properly denied the petitions before it despite its finding that the adoption would be in Angel's best interests. . . .

The petitioners next argue that if the relevant provisions of ch. 48, Stats., do not authorize a circuit court to grant this petition for adoption, then these statutory provisions violate the constitutional rights of either Angel or Annette or both. . . . First, the petitioners claim that the statutes deprive Angel of her right to have her best interests be the paramount factor in a court's decision regarding Annette's petition for adoption.

The requirement of due process applies only to deprivations of property or liberty interests. *Board of Regents v. Roth,* 408 U.S. 564, 569, 33 L. Ed. 2d 548, 92 S. Ct. 2701 (1972). The right to have her best interests guide our analysis in this adoption proceeding certainly does not qualify as one of Angel's property interests. . . . The right to have a child's best interests be the paramount consideration in the adoption proceedings is neither fundamental nor traditionally protected by our society. Adoption itself is not even a fundamental right. . . . It certainly follows that a legislative directive to construe adoption statutes with the child's best interests of paramount consideration is not a fundamental right. Furthermore, because adoption is a relatively recent statutory development, we cannot conclude that adoption has traditionally been protected by our society. . . .

Second, the petitioners argue that by prohibiting this adoption, the relevant statutes deprive Angel of her constitutional right to familial association. Angel's freedom to associate with Annette "receives protection as a fundamental element of personal liberty." See *Roberts v. United States Jaycees,* 468 U.S. 609, 618, 82 L. Ed. 2d 462, 104 S. Ct. 3244 (1984). However, as the petitioners acknowledge, the adoption statutes do not prevent Angel from associating with Annette. These statutes merely prevent Annette and Angel from legally formalizing their relationship. This relationship, between a child and her mother's nonmarital partner, is not one that has traditionally received constitutional protection. . . . Thus, we reject this second challenge to the constitutionality of Wisconsin's adoption statutes and hold that these statutes do not violate Angel's right to due process . . . [the court similarly rejects Angel's equal protection arguments]. . . .

We hold that Angel is not eligible for adoption under sec. 48.81(1), Stats., because her [mother's] parental rights have not been terminated. Furthermore, the proposed adoption is prohibited because sec. 48.92(2) would sever Georgina's ties with Angel. We also hold that the relevant provisions of ch. 48 do not violate the constitutional rights of either Angel or Annette. Therefore, we affirm the circuit court's order that denied the three petitions before the court.

Geske, J. (concurring).

I write separately only to encourage the Wisconsin legislature to revisit ch. 48 in light of all that is occurring with children in our society. The legislators, as representatives of the people of this state, have both the right and the responsibility to establish the requirements for a legal adoption, for custody, and for visitation. This court cannot play that role. We can only interpret the law, not rewrite it. . . .

Heffernan, J. (dissenting).

The issue addressed in this case is whether the Wisconsin statutes governing adoption allow Annette G. to adopt Angel, a child with whom she already has a functional parent-child relationship. The adoption statutes on their face do not address this issue. Therefore, this court must employ accepted canons of statutory construction to interpret the meaning of the adoption statutes. Much has been written about the nature of the canons of construction and the fact that contradictory canons exist that would lead to opposite results if applied to the same statute. [We have] helpful guidance from the legislature that . . . the adoption statutes . . . "shall be liberally construed to effect the objectives contained in this section." . . .

Sec. 48.01(2) adds: The best interests of the child shall always be of paramount consideration, but the court shall also consider the interest of the parents or guardian of the child, the interest of the person or persons with whom the child has been placed for adoption and the interests of the public. . . .

This court should interpret the adoption statutes following the approach mandated by the legislature. . . .

In the present case everyone involved agrees that the adoption is in Angel's best interests. . . . [N]one of the other interests listed in sec. 48.01(2) preclude liberal construction of the statute with the paramount consideration being the child's best interests. The interests of Angel's current parents would be furthered by allowing this adoption. Terry and Georgina are Angel's current legal parents. . . . Terry, Angel's legal father, strongly supports the adoption and has consented to termination of his parental rights. . . . Georgina, Angel's legal mother, is one of the petitioners requesting that Annette be allowed to adopt Angel and clearly believes that the adoption is consistent with her own interests.

The second interest, that of the person or persons with whom the child has been placed for adoption, is not at issue in this case. Angel is not being placed outside her present family for adoption—if the adoption is allowed she will remain with

Georgina and have a legally-recognized relationship with Annette as well. The third interest, that of the public, is also consistent with Angel's best interests. Given the shrinking percentage of children that are raised in two-parent families, and the shrinking percentage of children who receive even minimally adequate care regardless of family structure, the public interest is enhanced by granting legal recognition to two-parent families that do further the express objective in sec. 48.01(1)(g) of "providing children in the state with permanent and stable family relationships." Because the adoption in this case would further Angel's best interests while either having no effect on or enhancing the additional legislatively-recognized interests, this court should proceed to employ the legislatively-prescribed approach of interpreting the adoption statutes liberally in light of the "paramount consideration" of the best interests of the child. . . .

Justices Abrahamson and Bablitch join this dissenting opinion.

§

Matter of Jacob (N.Y. 1995)

Opinion by Chief Judge Kaye:

Under the New York adoption statute, a single person can adopt a child (Domestic Relations Law § 110). Equally clear is the right of a single homosexual to adopt (see 18 NYCRR 421.16 [h] [2]). These appeals call upon us to decide if the unmarried partner of a child's biological mother, whether heterosexual or homosexual, who is raising the child together with the biological parent, can become the child's second parent by means of adoption.

Because the two adoptions sought—one by an unmarried heterosexual couple, the other by the lesbian partner of the child's mother—are fully consistent with the adoption statute, we answer this question in the affirmative. To rule otherwise would mean that the thousands of New York children actually being raised in homes headed by two unmarried persons could have only one legal parent, not the two who want them. . . .

Limiting our analysis . . . to the preserved statutory interpretation issues, we conclude that appellants have standing to adopt under Domestic Relations Law § 110 and are not foreclosed from doing so by Domestic Relations Law § 117. . . .

Two basic themes of overarching significance set the context of our statutory analysis. First and foremost, since adoption in this State is "solely the creature of . . . statute", the adoption statute must be strictly construed. What is to be construed strictly and applied rigorously in this sensitive area of the law, however, is legislative purpose as well as legislative language. Thus, the adoption statute must be applied in harmony with the humanitarian principle that adoption is a means of securing the best possible home for a child. . . .

A second, related point of overriding significance is that the various sections comprising New York's adoption statute today represent a complex and not entirely reconcilable patchwork. . . . [A]fter decades of piecemeal amendment upon amendment, the statute today contains language from the 1870's alongside language from the 1990's. . . .

Despite ambiguity in other sections, one thing is clear: section 110 allows appellants to become adoptive parents. [It] provides that an "adult unmarried person or an adult husband and his adult wife together may adopt another person". Under this language, . . . adult unmarried persons have standing to adopt and appellants are correct that the Court's analysis of section 110 could appropriately end here. . . .

[T]he other statutory obstacle relied upon by the lower courts in denying the petitions is the provision that "[a]fter the making of an order of adoption the natural parents of the adoptive child shall be relieved of all parental duties toward and of all responsibilities for and shall have no rights over such adoptive child or to his property by descent or succession" (Domestic Relations Law § 117 [1] [a]). Literal application of this language would effectively prevent these adoptions since it would require the termination of the biological mothers' rights upon adoption thereby placing appellants in the "Catch-22" of having to choose one of two coparents as the child's only legal parent.

As outlined below, however, neither the language nor policy underlying section 117 dictates that result. . . . Both the title of section 117 ("Effect of Adoption") and its opening phrase ("After the making of an order of adoption") suggest that the section has nothing to do with the standing of an individual to adopt, an issue treated exclusively in section 110. . . . Rather, section 117 addresses the legal effect of an adoption on the parties and their property . . . [and not the legal requirements for an adoption].

Also plain on the face of section 117 is that it speaks principally of estate law. Words such as "succession," "inheritance," "decedent," "instrument" and "will" permeate the statute. Read contextually, it is clear that the Legislature's chief concern in section 117 was the resolution of property disputes upon the death of an adoptive parent or child. . . . [W]e conclude that neither subdivision of section 117 was intended to have universal application. . . .

[E]ven though the language of section 117 still has the effect of terminating a biological parent's rights in the majority of adoptions between strangers—where there is a need to prevent unwanted intrusion by the child's former biological relatives to promote the stability of the new adoptive family—the cases before us are entirely different. As we recognized in *Matter of Seaman* (78 N.Y.2d 451, 461), "complete severance of the natural relationship [is] not necessary when the adopted person remain[s] within the natural family unit as a result of an intrafamily adoption." . . .

[S]ection 117 does not invariably require termination in the situation where the biological parent, having consented to the adoption, has agreed to retain parental rights and to raise the child together with the second parent. Despite their varying factual circumstances, . . . stepparent adoptions, adoptions by minor fathers and open adoptions [all of which are permitted under New York's laws] share such an agreement as a common denominator. Because the facts of the cases before us are directly analogous to these three situations, the half-century-old termination language of section 117 should not be read to preclude the adoptions here. . . .

"Where the language of a statute is susceptible of two constructions, the courts will adopt that which avoids injustice, hardship, constitutional doubts or other objectionable results" [citations omitted]. Given that section 117 is open to two differing interpretations as to whether it automatically terminates parental rights in all cases, a construction of the section that would deny children like Jacob and Dana the opportunity of having their two de facto parents become their legal parents, based solely on their biological mother's sexual orientation or marital status, would not only be unjust under the circumstances, but also might raise constitutional concerns in light of the adoption statute's historically consistent purpose—the best interests of the child.

Judges Smith, Levine and Ciparick concur with Chief Judge Kaye.

Judge Bellacosa dissents and votes to affirm in a separate opinion in which Judges Simons and Titone concur. [Dissenting opinion, which is similar to majority opinion in *In the Interest of Angel Lace M.* (Wis. 1994), is omitted.]

§

Adoptions of B.L.V.B. and E.L.V.B. (Vt. 1993)

When social mores change, governing statutes must be interpreted to allow for those changes in a manner that does not frustrate the purposes behind their enactment. To deny the children of same-sex partners, as a class, the security of a legally recognized relationship with their second parent serves no legitimate state interest. . . . When the statute is read as a whole, . . . its general purpose is to clarify and protect the legal rights of the adopted person at the time the adoption is complete, not to proscribe adoptions by certain combinations of individuals. . . . The statute also terminates the natural parents' rights upon adoption, but this provision anticipates that the adoption of children will remove them from the home of the biological parents, where the biological parents elect or are compelled to terminate their legal obligations to the child. . . . The legislature recognized that it would be against common sense to terminate the biological parent's rights when that parent will continue to raise and be responsible for the child, albeit in a family unit with a partner who is biologically unrelated to the child. . . . Despite the narrow wording of the step-parent exception, we cannot conclude that the legislature ever meant to terminate the parental rights of a biological parent who intended to continue raising a child with the help of a partner. Such a narrow construction would produce the unreasonable and irrational result of defeating adoptions that are otherwise indisputably in the best interests of children.

§

Adoption of Tammy (Mass. 1993)

[The Massachusetts Supreme Judicial Court summarized the benefits of second-parent adoptions as follows in its decision recognizing the right under its State adoption laws of a child's custodial biological mother and her same-sex partner to jointly adopt the child:]

> Adoption will not result in any tangible change in Tammy's daily life; it will, however, serve to provide her with a significant legal relationship which may be important in her future. At the most practical level, adoption will entitle Tammy to inherit from [the second parent] Helen's family . . . and from Helen, . . . to receive support from Helen, who will be legally obligated to provide such support, to be eligible for coverage under Helen's health insurance policies, and to be eligible for social security benefits in the event of Helen's disability or death.

> Of equal, if not greater significance, adoption will enable Tammy to preserve her unique filial ties to Helen in the event that Helen and Susan [the biological mother] separate, or Susan predeceases Helen. As the case law and commentary on the subject illustrate, when the functional parents of children born in circumstances similar to Tammy separate or one dies, the children often remain in legal limbo for years while their future is disputed in the courts. . . . Adoption serves to establish legal rights and responsibilities so that, in the event that problems arise in the future, issues of custody and visitation may be promptly resolved by reference to the best interests of the children within the recognized framework of the law. [Citations omitted.]

§

In re Adoption of Two Children by H.N.R. (N.J. 1995)

[The New Jersey Supreme Court has allowed two unmarried men or women to adopt a child jointly and has also recognized second-parent adoption by the gay or lesbian partner of a child's biological parent who consents to the partner's adoption while retaining his or her own parental rights.]

. . . [Our adoption statute] requires that the "act be liberally construed to the end that the best interests of children be promoted." . . . [T]he statute is silent in respect either of joint adoption by unmarried persons or adoption by an unmarried cohabitant of his or her partner's child with the partner's consent. Since the statute does not expressly prohibit such adoptions, the question is whether it should be read as permitting them if they will serve the children's best interests. . . .

[Following the reasoning of the Massachusetts and Vermont courts, the New Jersey Court concludes that a literal reading of its adoption statute should not stand in the way of adoptions that are consensual and clearly serve children's best interests.]

55

(How) Does the Sexual Orientation of Parents Matter?

Judith Stacey and Timothy J. Biblarz

Opponents of lesbian and gay parental rights claim that children with lesbigay parents are at higher risk for a variety of negative outcomes. Yet most research in psychology concludes that there are no differences in developmental outcomes between children raised by lesbigay parents and those raised by heterosexual parents. The analysis here challenges this defensive conceptual framework and analyzes how heterosexism has hampered intellectual progress in the field. [We] discuss limitations in the definitions, samples, and analyses of the studies to date. . . . [Our analysis of] 21 studies demonstrates that researchers frequently downplay findings indicating difference regarding children's gender and sexual preferences and behavior that could stimulate important theoretical questions. A less defensive, more sociologically informed analytic framework is proposed for investigating these issues. The framework focuses on (1) whether selection effects produced by homophobia account for associations between parental sexual orientations and child outcomes; (2) the role of parental gender vis-à-vis sexual orientation in influencing children's gender development; and (3) the relationship between parental sexual orientations and children's sexual preferences and behaviors. . . .

. . . [S]ocial science research on lesbigay family issues has become a rapid growth industry that incites passionate divisions. For the consequences of such research are by no means "academic," but bear on marriage and family policies that encode Western culture's most profoundly held convictions about gender, sexuality, and parenthood. . . .

This body of research—mostly done by psychologists—almost uniformly reports findings of no notable differences between children reared by heterosexual parents and those reared by lesbian and gay parents. . . . [I]t finds lesbigay parents to be as competent and effective as heterosexual parents. . . .

In 1997, the *University of Illinois Law Review Journal* published an article by Lynn D. Wardle (833 et seq.), a Brigham Young University law professor, that impugned the motives, methods, and merits of social science research on lesbian and gay parenting. Wardle charged the legal profession and social scientists with an ideological bias favoring gay rights that has compromised most research in this field and the liberal judicial and policy decisions it has informed. He [and others] presented a harshly critical assessment of the research and argued for a presumptive judicial standard in favor of awarding child custody to heterosexual married couples. . . .

We depart sharply from the views of Wardle and [others] on the merits and morals of lesbigay parenthood as well as on their analysis of the child development research. We agree, however, that ideological pressures constrain intellectual development in this field. . . .

. . . Because anti-gay scholars seek evidence of harm, sympathetic researchers defensively stress its absence.

We take stock of this body of psychological research from a sociological perspective. We analyze the impact that this hetero-normative presumption exacts on predominant research strategies, analyses, and representations of findings. After assessing the basic premises and arguments in the debate, we discuss how the social fact of heterosexism has operated to constrain the research populations, concepts, and designs employed in the studies to date. . . .

Problems with Concepts, Categories, and Samples

. . . The means and contexts for planned parenthood are so diverse and complex that they compound the difficulties of isolating the significance of parental sexual orientation. To even approximate this goal, researchers would need to control not only for the gender, number, and sexual orientation of parents, but for their diverse biosocial and legal statuses. The handful of studies that have attempted to do this focus on lesbian motherhood. The most rigorous research designs compare donor-insemination (DI) parenthood among lesbian and heterosexual couples or single mothers. . . . To our knowledge, no studies have been conducted exclusively on lesbian or gay adoptive parents or compare the children of intentional gay fathers with children in other family forms. Researchers do not know the extent to which the comparatively high socioeconomic status of the DI parents studied accurately reflects the demographics of lesbian and gay parenthood generally, but given the degree of effort, cultural and legal support, and, frequently, the expense involved, members of relatively privileged social groups would be the ones most able to make use of reproductive technology and/or independent adoption.

Reconsidering the Psychological Findings

. . . [W]e examined the findings of 21 psychological studies . . . published between 1981 and 1998 that we considered best equipped to address sociological questions about how parental sexual orientation matters to children.

No Differences of Social Concern

The findings . . . show that the "no differences" claim does receive strong empirical support in crucial domains. Lesbigay parents and their children in these studies display no differences from heterosexual counterparts in psychological well-being or cognitive functioning. Scores for lesbigay parenting styles and levels of investment in children are at least as "high" as those for heterosexual parents. Levels of closeness and quality of parent/child relationships do not seem to differentiate directly by parental sexual orientation, but indirectly, by way of parental gender. Because every relevant study to date shows that parental sexual orientation per se has no measurable effect on the quality of parent-child relationships or on children's mental health or social adjustment, there is no evidentiary basis for considering parental sexual orientation in decisions about children's "best interest." In fact, given that children with lesbigay parents probably contend with a degree of social stigma, these similarities in child outcomes suggest the presence of compensatory processes in lesbigay-parent families. Exploring how these families help children cope with stigma might prove helpful to all kinds of families.

Most of the research to date focuses on social-psychological dimensions of well-being and adjustment and on the quality of parent/child relationships. Perhaps these variables reflect the disciplinary preferences of psychologists who have conducted most of the studies, as well as a desire to produce evidence directly relevant to the questions of "harm" that dominate judicial and legislative deliberations over child custody. Less research has explored questions for which there are stronger theoretical grounds for expecting differences—children's gender and sexual behavior and preferences. In fact, only two studies generate much of the baseline evidence on potential connections between parents' and child's sexual and gender identities. [R. Green et al., "Lesbian Mothers and Their Children," *Journal of Child Psychology and Psychiatry* 24 (1986): 551–72; Fiona L. Tasker and Susan Golombok, *Growing Up in a Lesbian Family: Effects on Child Development* (New York: Guilford, 1997)]. Evidence in these and the few other studies that focus on these variables does not support the "no differences" claim. Children with lesbigay parents appear less traditionally gender-typed and more likely to be open to homoerotic relationships. In addition, evidence suggests that parental gender and sexual identities interact to create distinctive family processes whose consequences for children have yet to be studied.

How the Sexual Orientation of Parents Matters

We have identified conceptual, methodological, and theoretical limitations in the psychological research on the effects of parental sexual orientation and have challenged the predominant claim that the sexual orientation of parents does not matter at all. We argued instead that despite the limitations, there is suggestive evidence and good reason to believe that contemporary children and young adults with lesbian or gay parents do differ in modest and interesting ways from children with heterosexual parents. Most of these differences, however, are not causal, but are indirect effects of parental gender or selection effects associated with heterosexist social conditions under which lesbigay-parent families currently live.

First, our analysis of the psychological research indicates that the effects of parental gender trump those of sexual orientation. . . .

Second, because homosexuality is stigmatized, selection effects may yield correlations between parental sexual orientation and child development that do not derive from sexual orientation itself. For example, social constraints on access to marriage and parenting make lesbian parents likely to be older, urban, educated, and self-aware—factors that foster several positive developmental consequences for their children. On the other hand, denied access to marriage, lesbian co-parent relationships are likely to experience dissolution rates somewhat higher than those among heterosexual co-parents. . . . Not only do same-sex couples lack the institutional pressures and support for commitment that marriage provides, but qualitative studies suggest that they tend to embrace comparatively high standards of emotional intimacy and satisfaction. . . . The decision to pursue a socially ostracized domain of intimacy implies an investment in the emotional regime that Giddens (1992) terms "the pure relationship" and "confluent love." Such relationships confront the inherent instabilities of modern or postmodern intimacy. . . . Thus, a higher dissolution rate would be correlated with but not causally related to sexual orientation, a difference that should erode were homophobia to disappear and legal marriage be made available to lesbians and gay men.

Most of the differences in the findings discussed above cannot be considered deficits from any legitimate public policy perspective. They either favor the children with lesbigay parents, are secondary effects of social prejudice, or represent "just a difference" of the sort democratic societies should respect and protect. Apart from differences associated with parental gender, most of the presently observable differences in child "outcomes" should wither away under conditions of full equality and respect for sexual diversity. Indeed, it is time to recognize that the categories "lesbian mother" and "gay father" are historically transitional and conceptually flawed, because they erroneously imply that a parent's sexual orientation is the decisive characteristic of her or his parenting. On the contrary, we propose that homophobia and discrimination are the chief reasons why parental sexual orientation matters at all. Because lesbigay parents do not enjoy the same rights, respect, and recognition as heterosexual parents, their children contend with the burdens of vicarious social stigma. Likewise, some of the particular strengths and sensitivities such children appear to display, such as a greater capacity to express feelings or more empathy for social diversity, are probably artifacts of marginality and may be destined for the historical dustbin of a democratic, sexually pluralist society. . . .

. . . Planned lesbigay parenthood offers a veritable "social laboratory" of family diversity in which scholars could fruitfully examine not only the acquisition of sexual and gender identity, but the relative effects on children of the gender and number of their parents as well as of the implications of diverse biosocial routes to parenthood. Such studies could give us purchase on some of the most vexing and intriguing topics in our field, including divorce, adoption, step-parenthood, and domestic violence, to name a few. To exploit this opportunity, however, researchers must overcome the hetero-normative presumption that interprets sexual differences as deficits, thereby inflicting some of the very disadvantages it claims to discover. Paradoxically, if the sexual orientation of parents were to matter less for political rights, it could matter more for social theory.

56

Single Parent Adoptions

Nancy E. Dowd

I never dreamed that I would adopt two children on my own. The two-parent hetero-sexual married model of parenthood was firmly inscribed on my consciousness at a young age, and the certainty that life would unfold this way was unshakeable. But in my late thirties, divorced, childless but still strongly desiring children, I began the process that ultimately would lead to the adoption of my daughter when I was just past my fortieth birthday, followed by the adoption of my son three years later.

"So does that mean you're an unwed mother?"

—a friend, in response to my first adoption

Probably the most difficult process for most single people who adopt is valuing and validating their decision. Choosing to create a family on one's own seems somehow selfish, although adopting a child sounds somehow more sacrificing than selfish. Nevertheless, creating a single-parent family, rather than such a family occurring as a re-sult of divorce, death, or never marrying, is a highly disfavored social choice. Single-parent families are loaded with societal stigma, and therefore a decision to voluntarily create one seems anomalous. On the other hand, the very commonality of single-par-ent families also makes the creation of such a family less remarkable and more accept-able. Two-thirds of children will spend some time before the age of eighteen in a sin-gle-parent family. A child raised by a single parent is hardly uncommon and would not be subject to special scrutiny. More important, the stigma attached to this form of family is unsupported by the data on single-parent families. It is function rather than form that matters; what families do, rather than what they look like.

"Because there are so many single-parent homes, your children won't stand out, won't feel so different."

—my social worker, during the home study in my first adoption

For me, then, as for other single parents, the critical first step is imagining this choice as one that is good for a child. The second step is determining whether it can be done. Up until fairly recently, the answer would have been no; only married couples were el-igible to adopt. But in 1988, when I began the process leading to my first adoption, I discovered that many routes were available for single people to adopt: domestic and international programs, as well as a range within each of those options. The sheer number of options is certainly not close to that available to married couples, but in many respects that makes the process of sorting out options easier, since you are not so overwhelmed.

I ultimately decided to do an independent adoption, meaning that I would connect with the child that I would adopt through an intermediary.

Regardless of legal entitlement to adopt, it is social workers and lawyers who control the adoption process, and without their support, individuals can rarely be successful in pushing against this informal bureaucratic structure. It is critical for single parents to work with a program and people who support single-parent adoption. Even with that assurance, I was sensitive to the scrutiny of me not only as an adoptive parent, but as a single adoptive parent, during the home study process. It seemed essential to establish that I had thought through the consequences of parenting a child alone, what strategies I would use for the benefit of the child and myself. Providing role models of the missing gender (in my case a male) was clearly important. Assuring the presence of help and support was also critical, because of the stress of parenting alone. The home study process can be excruciating, because you have no clear sense of exactly what the social worker is looking for, only that this person holds the key to whether you will be able to adopt. I simply saw the outcome as fated (or not), and just followed the process rather than fighting the intrusion. Ultimately, my social worker and I worked as a team rather than as adversaries.

But a critical factor in my adoption was that I am female. Single-parent male adoption is much less common than single-parent female adoption. A woman raising a child on her own seems unremarkable, reflecting common patterns of single parenthood for nonmarital couples and divorced couples. Mothers more commonly are caregivers; fathers more commonly are secondary parents, economic parents, or absent parents. Men's parenting is strongly mediated by women, particularly the presence of women in their household. Men presenting themselves as single parents, then, are likely to face more intense explicit or implicit scrutiny.

The gender issues also relate to issues of sexual orientation and sexuality. Single-parent adoptions implicitly operate on a model of presumed heterosexuality, yet sexually active single parents or cohabiting single parents are less desirable, since the role of the boyfriend or cohabiting partner is unclear and might be deemed a destabilizing factor and therefore not in the best interests of the child for placement. The question of sexual orientation may be explicit or implicit, and the consequence of revelation of gay or lesbian status may also imperil adoption unless the program and persons running the program support the adoption of children by single parents whether gay or lesbian, and by gays and lesbians whether single or in committed relationships.

In the course of my home study this issue came up in questions regarding my life preceding the home study, which included the fact that I had been married and divorced, and the question of whether I had thought about the consequences of adopting for my future social life and likelihood of marrying again. Because I fit the heterosexual norm, but was not engaged in a significant relationship at the time, I was safe and sexless at the point of adoption.

Once I was approved at the end of the home study process, the real process of connecting with my daughter began. In many forms of adoption this stage requires that you provide information about yourself to the program or to an intermediary, and again, a single person may feel a sense of needing to justify themselves, to construct themselves so that they are a good choice for placement. Because birth parents increasingly have an active or exclusive role in deciding where their child will be placed, one tries to imagine how placing a child with just one parent would seem to be a good choice. Probably the most important reassurance, however, is that everyone that I have known, single or married, who has begun and stayed with the adoption process has been successful. Even if the fears are real, they are offset by the realities of the numbers of placements with single parents.

I had decided to work with a lawyer well known for her expertise in placing children. After laboring over a letter describing myself to potential birth mothers or birth parents and sending my best picture of myself to go along with the letter, I was surprised to get a critique back from the lawyer's assistant. They suggested changes in the letter and ways I might have a picture taken, all designed to make me more desirable as a choice of a parent. This marketing aspect was very uncomfortable for me. Indeed, despite the effort to distinguish adoption from baby selling, the reality is that it feels very much like a marketplace.

There was something about the process of choosing, rather like ordering a child, that uncomfortably feels like baby selling or seeing children as property. Race is as omnipresent as money in adoption. Health factors are also present; there is a strong presumption of the desirability of a "perfect" child with no "defects" or disabilities, major or minor. And in some programs, gender is also an acceptable preference factor. Finally, I had to decide about the process of advertising and where in the country to advertise. Did I want the birth mother or birth parents to be located far away from me? Did I want them to come from a rural or urban area? What states? The questions forced me to think about my ideal birth parents as well as my concept of connection or contact with the birth parents after the adoption.

Finally I was ready to try to connect with a child. It had taken me nearly two years to get to this point. When anyone asks me about adoption, my first question is how old are you. Your age, more than anything, affects your attractiveness as an adoptive parent. It also affects how long you have to decide whether adoption might work for you, gather information, and work through the process to the point where you stand ready and available to begin the legal process of adoption. For a single parent, the time factor may be even stronger, although in the programs that work with single parents, it seems that the time factor from readiness to adopt to completion of an adoption is no longer than for married couples. Particularly because the age at which people have their first child is increasing, together with the time taken trying to become pregnant and deal with infertility, most people come to adoption in their thirties. Rarely do parents come to adoption first.

When I was ready, it was not through my chosen, well-calculated, studied, and researched path that my daughter came to me. My best friend from law school encouraged me to talk to one of her law firm partners, who had adopted three children. He put me in contact with both intermediaries, one a social worker, one a lawyer. Two months later, ten days before Christmas, the lawyer called me at work and told me that she had a baby for me, if I was willing. My heart stopped, just about. The baby was due in May or early June, and was the child of two teenagers. The parents had asked the lawyer to decide where to place the child. This lawyer had chosen me. It is a mystery and a blessing that I will never forget.

I arrived in Phoenix, where my daughter was born, five days before she was due. She was born seven days later. Waiting. Waiting. I felt like I held my breath, just waiting for her to come into being. A few days after I got to Phoenix, and before she was born, the lawyer called.

> "The birth mom knows you are in town and would like to meet you. Would you be willing to meet her?"

Of course I would meet with her. But as I prepared for that meeting, I was intensely aware that the balance of power was completely out of my hands. Indeed, this is the reality of independent adoption—the parent or parents can change their mind, since no legally enforceable commitment can be made prior to birth. Yet on the other side of adoption is an equally lopsided balance of power, totally on the side of the adoptive parents. Promises of contact and information and ongoing connection are generally not legally enforceable, only morally obligating. But what began in that meeting has continued to this day—an extraordinary connection and ongoing communication that has been one of the most amazing aspects of this whole amazing process. It defies every stereotype of adoption, the mythology of conflict between birth parents and adoptive parents, the rationale for secrecy, and the fear still generated for every adoptive parent that someday the "real" parents will reappear and somehow dissolve the bonds between them and their children.

> "You really chose to be a single parent?"   —a single divorced parent

Life as a single adoptive parent is no more difficult than it is for any single parent, or perhaps less so. Since single adoptive parents have chosen parenthood in this form, the financial aspects of single parenting are more likely not to be the challenge that single adoptive parents typically face. The most significant challenge faced by most single-mother families are economic challenges, in addition to the social stigma placed on single-parent families. The most significant challenge faced by single fathers, on the other hand, is the lack of social and cultural support for nurturing fatherhood, as well as the lack of economic structures to support fathers as nurturers rather than as breadwinners. Single-parent families nevertheless are commonplace, and that social reality makes single parenting of adoptive children easier, for both parents and children. The parents have access to the expertise of other single parents. The children do not stand out as unique or different in a world with a range of family forms.

None of this is to suggest that adoptees do not face developmental issues that are not faced by biological children raised by their biological parents. Those issues are clearly present, particularly in a world that is suffused with mythology about adoption and identity. But those issues are not significantly different for single adoptive parents as compared to couples who adopt.

The challenges facing single adoptive fathers parallel those of all single fathers, who remain in a distinct minority of all single parents who are primary caregivers. Similarly, the challenges facing gay and lesbian single parents relate to social and community acceptance and support, similar to biological parents.

The most important lesson from the data on single-parent families is that family success and good outcomes for children do not depend on form, but on function. Single-parent families can function as successfully as dual-parent families. They function similarly in the bottom line provision of care, and differently in that the structure affects how they carry out their function. But they are not second-class families any more than adopted children are second-class children. Single-parent families work, and single-parent adoptive families have a higher likelihood of functioning well because they are chosen families that lack the stress factors more common in single-parent families formed by non-marriage or divorce.

"Why didn't you have your own children?"

Life for a single adoptive parent is also not significantly different from that of couples who adopt. The biological preference is strong for both. The open acknowledgment that my children are adopted always seems to lead to the question of why I didn't simply go get pregnant. Funny how the high school anathema turns into the flip solution to a single person's childlessness. Just as couples are asked about their infertility problems, single adoptive parents are often presumed fertile and questioned for their choice of adoption over biological parenthood. Children of single adoptive parents may find that their status as adoptees comes up more frequently than is the case for children placed with couples, who may be presumed biological children and therefore have the choice of whether to be open about their adoptive status.

The diversity of family forms makes my children feel relatively unremarkable. But there is no doubt that being adopted is different, and being adopted by a single parent is different. Not worse or better, just different. Parenting alone is not for everyone, but for those who take it on with full openness to the challenges, the rewards are amazing. As all parents know, children are the challenge, and the ultimate blessing, of a lifetime. Adoption magnifies that blessing, because your children come to you through the choices and sacrifices of others who rely on you to positively support their role in your children's lives.

VII

Feminism

In presenting different feminist perspectives on adoption, this part belies any claim that there is a single or dominant feminist view of adoption. When feminists analyze the parent-child relationship, they usually focus on access to contraception and abortion, the consequences of assisted reproductive technologies (ART), male-female gender roles in parenting, or work-family conflicts, rather than adoption. As part 7 shows, however, adoption is—or should be—central to feminist concerns over the fundamental parenting choices of prospective adoptive parents as well as of the women who choose or are required to relinquish their biological children for adoption by others.

Some feminists have made the experience of mothering central to their theories, developing a jurisprudence that could be termed "biological feminism."[1] As one way of showing the differences between men and women, these feminists emphasize the distinctive connection that women feel to their children, beginning while the fetus is in utero and continuing throughout the child's life. Women's reproductive experiences and traditional role as nurturer are said to influence their capacity for connection.[2] From this perspective, mothers have a special bond with their babies that is not necessarily shared by fathers.

By contrast, other conceptions of feminism focus instead on context and relationship, and on gendered rather than merely biological differences. From this perspective feminism provides an understanding of the continuing nature of the connection between birth mother and adoptee, showing that emotional care remains even in the absence of physical care for the child; relational feminism points to the value of care as gendered, not as sex-specific.[3] Therefore, as argued here by Linda J. Lacey, an adoptive mother, feminists should be as hospitable to the adoptive mother-child nexus as to the birth mother-child nexus.

Because of its emphasis on, and challenges to, values associated with connection and caring, feminism is a particularly appropriate lens for examining adoption. Adoption in the United States has developed primarily as a woman's issue.[4] Although adoptions have often centered on ensuring adequate lines of inheritance, contemporary adoption also reflects concerns about children, child-rearing, and family formation.

Feminism can celebrate the meaning of motherhood for both biological and adoptive mothers, without denigrating either, and can examine the relationship between children and their birth and adoptive fathers, as discussed elsewhere in this reader. Adoption necessitates consideration of the multiplicity of connections among all participants in the adoptive experience, and feminism provides a focus on connections.

Part 7 begins with Katharine T. Bartlett's suggestion that parenthood be based on responsibility and connection between parents and children, rather than on the separate and individual interests of parents or children. As applied to adoption, this approach counsels respect for the decision of a mother to place her child for adoption, and specific rules that delineate the circumstances under which a father can veto the mother's decision. In the next chapter, Twila L. Perry argues that feminists must grapple with issues of hierarchy and oppression in the context of international and transracial adoption as well as surrogacy. The final several selections question the similarities and differences between adoptive and biological families, focusing on the experiences of biological mothers and adoptees. Throughout the chapters in part 7, feminists challenge accepted views of adoption.

NOTES

1. Much of this discussion is drawn from Naomi Cahn, "Birth Mothers," 17 *Wisconsin Women's Law Journal* 163 (2002).

2. Some have suggested that, because of their experiences of nurturing, women are more likely to develop an ethic of care, under which they focus on relationship rather than hierarchy. Carol Gilligan, *In a Different Voice* (Cambridge: Harvard University Press, 1982); *Mapping the Moral Domain* (Cambridge: Harvard University Press, 1988).

3. In a recent study, a birth father explored the feelings after relinquishment of a small sample of birth fathers, finding many similarities between birth mothers and birth fathers. Gary Clapton, "Birth Fathers' Lives after Adoption," 25 *Adoption and Fostering* 50 (2001).

4. See Julie Berebitsky, *Like Our Very Own: Adoption and the Changing Culture of Motherhood, 1851–1950* (Lawrence: University Press of Kansas, 2000), 8.

57

Re-expressing Parenthood

Katharine T. Bartlett

I. Introduction

. . . In this article, I argue that the law currently applied to one particular set of child custody disputes expresses a view of parenthood which is undesirable. This view is grounded in notions of exchange and individual rights, and implicitly encourages parental possessiveness and self-centeredness. I suggest how we might proceed to re-shape the law to express a better view of parenthood. This alternative view is based upon notions of benevolence and responsibility, and is intended to reinforce parental dispositions toward generosity and other-directedness. . . .

I propose that we attempt to re-direct the law applicable to disputes over parental status toward a view of parenthood based on responsibility and connection. The law should force parents to state their claims, and courts to evaluate such claims, not from the competing, individuated perspectives of either parent or even of the child, but from the perspective of each parent-child relationship. And in evaluating (and thereby giving meaning to) that relationship, the law should focus on parental responsibility rather than reciprocal "rights," and express a view of parenthood based upon the cycle of gift rather than the cycle of exchange. . . .

II. Rights and Responsibilities in the Theory of Parenthood

A. Parenthood as Exchange

Since the earliest days of the modern liberal state, parenthood has been expressed in terms of exchange: Parents have rights with respect to their children in exchange for the performance of their parental responsibilities. Sir William Blackstone, John Locke, and Samuel Pufendorf, for example, all state that the rights or powers of parents arise from their duties in caring for their offspring. . . .

The exchange view of parenthood is based upon the reciprocity of parental rights and duties. Parents have rights that create obligations and obligations that create rights. Within this circular, self-reinforcing cycle of exchange, rights are emphasized, strengthened by their justification in obligation. Indeed, the reciprocal connection to obligation seems to make rights themselves morally compelled. As a consequence, parents asserting rights to children may construe their obligations not as independent duties or expectations, but as the moral underpinning of their rights. "Having rights" means to be entitled to, to be owed, to have earned, or to deserve something in exchange for who one is or what one has done.

As is the case with other individual rights claims, parents asserting rights to children tend to emphasize what is due to them rather than what they owe to others. . . .

B. Parenthood as Responsibility within Relationship

Responsibility and relationship are difficult terms to pin down. They are evolving rather than fixed concepts, constituted by the attitudes and responses of those engaged, through practice, in living out their meanings. These attitudes and responses, of which law is a part, form a continuous, ongoing process. . . .

1. RESPONSIBILITY, RELATIONSHIP, AND IDENTIFICATION

Although some notions of social responsibility have associated duty or obligation with individual autonomy, responsibility—as I use the term here—is grounded in relationship rather than autonomy. Responsibility describes a certain type of connection that persons may experience in their relationships with one another. That connection is one of identification. Identification requires a "[r]ecognition of the other person's reality, and the possibility of putting yourself in his place. . . ." Identification must be positive and affirming; it seeks what is good for the other person.

The experience and meaning of responsibility may be quite personal and individualized. Its meaning, however, is derived within a social context that defines ideal roles for persons engaged in particular relationships. Thus, while individuals to a certain extent choose the terms of their own relationships, the choices they make and the meaning given to those choices are strongly shaped by role expectations defined by the community. At the same time, responsibility means more than fulfilling some precise set of pre-defined role requirements. A responsible person cares not only about doing "her part" (or "his part") in a limited sense, but also about outcome, and is disposed toward expanding or perhaps redefining the demands of the role as necessary to accomplish that outcome. Responsibility, in other words, is a self-enlarging, open-ended commitment on behalf of another.

Parenthood illustrates well the wide spectrum of commitments one may make in fulfilling one's role responsibility. As a parent, one may do what one thinks is expected of a person in that role, applying one's best instincts and perhaps even book-learning to guide the child from infancy into a mature and productive adulthood. But a parent who refrains from a personal commitment to how the child "turns out" has not assumed full responsibility for that relationship. The responsible, child-identified parent is inclined to interpret the role of parent broadly and flexibly, and is satisfied only when the child has "turned out" well. . . .

3. RESPONSIBILITY AND THE BEST INTERESTS OF THE CHILD

It is reasonable to ask . . . whether my focus on the law's effects on promoting parental responsibility for children represents any sort of improvement on the best interests of the child standard. Is not the concern for the responsibility of parents derived, after all, from our concern for the welfare of children? And although substitute standards that make the best interests of the child test more precise and administrable might be welcome, isn't the standard of parental responsibility urged here even more open-ended and amorphous? . . .

The best interests of the child standard represents a considerable ideological and rhetorical advancement over child custody standards that focus on the parents' interests. Forcing parents to articulate their claims to children in terms of the child's welfare expresses a societal preference for protecting children over protecting adults, a preference which, though not inevitable, is easily defended.

The best interests of the child standard, however, is not a satisfactory substitute for rights doctrine in parenthood disputes. First, in an important sense, the best interests standard merely substitutes the interests or "rights" of one party—the child—for those of others. In this sense it does not get away from rights doctrine, but rather makes the child, and not the parents, the party whose rights are paramount.

Further, the best interests of the child is a highly contingent social construction. Although we often pretend otherwise, it seems clear that our judgments about what is best for children are as much the result of political and social judgments about what kind of society we prefer as they are conclusions based upon neutral or scientific data about what is "best" for children. The resolution of conflicts over children ultimately is less a matter of objective fact-finding than it is a matter of deciding what kind of children and families—what kind of relationships—we want to have.

Finally, we care about the workings of these relationships not solely because we care about children, but also because we care about the kind of society in which we live. We want a society in which parent-child relationships are strong, secure, and nurturing. If we have to choose between children and adults, we may prefer to be a society which puts the child's interests first, but our larger concern is how the interests of both parent and child link together in relationships. . . .

IV. Unmarried Mothers Choosing to Place Their Children for Adoption

Cases in which a biological father objects to a mother's attempt to place the newborn child for adoption also present numerous issues relating to the societal meanings of responsibility within parent-child relationships. Both the current legal framework for resolving these cases, and rights claims made to break through that framework, fail to address these issues adequately. . . .

A. The Legal Background

A father's objection to a woman's attempt to relinquish their child to a third-party couple for adoption generates conflicting impulses within the law. On the one hand, giving the unwed father the full range of parental rights when the unwed mother decides to give up her rights seems only fair to the father, and serves the goal of assuring the child at least one "natural" parent. On the other hand, a newborn who is adopted into a two-parent nuclear family is presumed to have advantages over a child raised by a single parent. State laws reflect this tension. Generally speaking, when the unmarried mother gives up her child for adoption, the biological father who meets the specified statutory criteria becomes the mother's substitute, with the power to stop the adoption and take custody of the child himself. The mother's action in placing the child for adoption constitutes, in effect, a forfeiture of her otherwise superior rights. If she chooses not to exercise those rights by retaining custody of the child, the father's rights take over. . . .

B. Rights Claims

Women seeking to overcome rules giving unwed fathers veto power over adoptions, or to defend rules that allow them to make the adoption decision without interference by the father, make rights claims that, again, start with the proposition that the woman's right to place her child for adoption is compelled by her privacy interest in deciding "whether to bear or beget a child." The argument is sometimes bolstered by the claim that "since the mother had the absolute right to decide to abort and [instead] decided to allow her body to be used to bear the child, she should have priority for custody."

Both of these arguments fail to address the conflicting rights of the father. The Supreme Court has recognized the male, as well as the female, right to procreate. Supreme Court precedent establishing the constitutional rights of parents to their children also has covered men as well as women. . . .

C. Relationship, Responsibility, and Adoption of Newborns

In analyzing how we might attempt to implement the norm of responsibility in parent-child relationships, we confront two overlapping tensions. First, the goal of promoting the ideology of parental responsibility as a general matter may conflict with the goal of making evaluations based upon the ideology in individual cases. Second, the goal of protecting and enhancing the norm of responsibility within the mother-child relationship may interfere with the goal of protecting and enhancing responsibility within the father-child relationship.

The tension in the law between expressing desirable values in our general rules and reaching the "correct" results in individual cases is a recurring dilemma. Simple rules with few or no exceptions, such as those that give automatic authority to fathers to block adoptions, may send the most unequivocal messages—such as that fathers are responsible for children. The stronger the rules that both parents have responsibility, the more reinforced will be the norm that both parents should assume responsibility (reinforcement we may badly need). Yet where the result of applying such a rule in a particular situation is to allow an irresponsible father to thwart the responsible plans of a mother to provide for the care of their child, the rule seems to bring the wrong result and, in rewarding irresponsibility, send the wrong message.

The tension between promoting responsibility by fathers and promoting responsibility by mothers further complicates the matter. A rule that recognizes the biological connection between father and child by giving unwed fathers veto power over adoptions will promote, in a general way, the ideology that biological fathers should, and will, love and care for their children and be responsible parents. As a result, we might expect fathers actually to care more for their children and to provide them with material and emotional support.

Quite the opposite rule, however—one that recognizes the mother-child relationship by giving the mother authority to place the child for adoption—will support maternal responsibility. While this goal already has considerable support in our social and legal ideologies, there may be special reasons to emphasize its importance. Mothers have a kind of automatic responsibility for their children. Under current law the mother may decide whether to abort the fetus. And she must decide how to conduct herself and care for herself and the child during pregnancy. These decisions, including whether she smokes, drinks, or keeps a healthy diet, are extremely important to the child. After childbirth, too, it is almost inconceivable to us that the mother will have no part in deciding what will happen to the child. . . .

We instinctively want to transform this responsibility point into a rights or entitlement argument. Because the pregnant woman cannot avoid taking responsibility for the child, the argument would go, it is only fair to allow her to place her child for adoption. This form of argument, however, reflects the exchange view of parenthood, which in turn elevates parental rights over parental responsibility. To promote responsibility, we must focus instead on the links between responsibility, the need for freedom to act, and the circumstances under which parents will exercise this freedom.

There is an enormous range of circumstances within which conflicts over placement of children for adoption occur. The mother may wish to place the child for adoption because her economic circumstances and her family support networks make her unprepared or unable to provide properly for the child; she may conclude that although she longs to keep her child, the child would be better off with an adoptive family. In these circumstances, her decision to place her child for adoption is an act of self-sacrifice for the welfare of her child. If she is not permitted to carry out her plan, she may decide to keep the child herself, or to abort the child. Either of these two alternatives would be a choice that she might consider inferior to adoption, but necessary in her view to prevent what she perceives as an even greater harm—custody of the child by an irresponsible father.

Not all mothers, however, make decisions based on their consideration of the welfare of the child. It is conceivable that a mother may want to give up her child casually, because she concludes that having a child would interfere with her life. She may intentionally wish to frustrate the father's interest in having a child, without regard to how adequate a parent he (or she) might be. Or she may wish, simply, to act on a strongly held principle (or "right") that she, and not the father, is entitled to make the choice, because she has taken all of the mental and physical risks of pregnancy and childbirth (an attitude fostered, I have argued, by the legitimation of rights arguments).

The range of circumstances within which fathers act may also be quite varied. Some fathers will feel a strong psychological attachment to their children and wish to do well by them. These fathers will make sure that they have enough economic re-sources and family support to be able to do so. Others will react primarily to a posses-sive urge to control someone they perceive as being "theirs," or want to keep the child as an act of power over the child's mother.

In the face of the wide range of possible factual scenarios, a simple, automatic rule that assumes one particular set of circumstances—for example, that mothers always act to best promote the welfare of their children—may reinforce certain desirable as-pects of responsibility in some cases, but lead to very unsatisfactory results in others where the circumstances do not match the rule. This dilemma suggests the need for broad rules with specific, individualized application. Such rules should create a re-sponsibility-based standard that both assumes, and attempts to measure, responsible decision-making in individual, highly fact-dependent cases in which parents make competing claims to a newborn. The relevant factors may include a parent's reason for relinquishing a child for adoption (or opposing the adoption), the plan for the child, the nature of the relationship already established with the child, and so on.

Such an approach could well incorporate shorthand devices, such as presumptions or burdens of proof, that interpret society's current understanding of what constitutes responsibility, and that avoid some of the uncertainty and cost of individualized hear-ings. Thus, for example, the law might begin with a presumption that the mother's ac-tual relationship to the child established during pregnancy and childbirth makes her decision to place the child for adoption a responsible one, a presumption which the father may overcome with evidence that his plan to keep the child is more responsi-ble. Convincing and realistic plans for providing adequately for the child would be relevant evidence, as would evidence about his attitude toward the mother's preg-nancy.

Rules requiring the father to take affirmative steps to give notice of or judicially es-tablish his paternity in order to have any rights in the adoption proceeding might also be justified. These rules, however, should be based upon society's understanding of re-lationship and responsibility, rather than on what seems fair to the parents. Results should depend ultimately upon societal judgments about existing and potential op-portunities for responsible parent-child relationships, rather than upon what is due parents. Thus, for example, rules should permit distinctions between fathers who demonstrate responsibility and those who simply wish to frustrate the mother's wishes to place the child for adoption or to have what is "theirs."

An individualized, fact-specific approach may grant considerable discretion to judges. It has become routine to criticize judicial discretion on the grounds that it makes decisions too subjective and unpredictable. However, certainty or predictability of results can be overrated. Simple, easily administrable rules, while generally desir-able, almost necessarily have the effect in custody cases of disregarding, even denying, the significance of the quality of parental behavior or attention to the parent-child re-lationship in individual cases. An approach that avoids questions about responsible conduct declares that the nuanced values we may wish to advance are not important enough to warrant the bother of difficult fact-finding.

58

Transracial and International Adoption
Mothers, Hierarchy, Race, and Feminist Legal Theory

Twila L. Perry

Introduction

. . . The purpose of this article is to encourage more discussion of how transracial and international adoption might be analyzed from a feminist perspective. The subject of adoption has received little attention from feminists in general, but . . . this important subject warrants further exploration. First, much of the writing on adoption has been done by women. Women scholars are clearly interested in issues concerning motherhood, including the different ways in which women can become mothers. . . . Second, issues involving the welfare of children, who figure prominently in women's lives, also occupy a central place in feminist analysis. Finally, while much of feminist analysis addresses troubling aspects of the relationship between men and women, and the relationship between women and the government, there is a need for more feminist analysis that focuses on the relationships among women. . . .

. . . In a sense, then, this article raises the very question of what feminism is, and, perhaps, what it can or should be. It explores these issues in the context of an enterprise many women value very highly—the raising of children. While much of the focus of the discussion will be on Black women, the article also addresses issues relevant to other women of color in the context of international adoption. . . .

. . . [A] feminist analysis of adoption must view adoption as more than an individual transaction in which one or two adults legally become the parent or parents of a particular child. . . . Adoption, like marriage, involves issues of hierarchy and power; unlike marriage, however, adoption involves these issues among women. . . .

. . . I have chosen to place Black women, other women of color, and poor women at the center, rather than at the margin of my analysis. All too often, when issues are approached from a feminist perspective, it is the concerns of white, middle class women that dominate, and the concerns of women who do not fit this model are included as a variation, a footnote, or an afterthought. . . . [A] feminist analyzing adoption must take into account . . . the political and cultural meaning of motherhood and . . . must confront the possibility that women from minority groups may have ambivalent or negative feelings about transracial or international adoptions. . . . Ultimately, a feminist approach should have the goal of working toward a world in which the choice of women to place their children for adoption is not dictated by oppressive circumstances.

Writing critically about adoption is not easy. For some women . . . adoption is a first choice, and an affirmative one. For others, it may be the last resort—the only option they have left to become a parent. . . .

I. Adoption and Hierarchy

A. Adoption and Disparities in the Status of Mothers

Why is it important to focus on the disparities in status between birth mothers and adoptive mothers when race, in particular, is a factor in adoption? . . .

The answer to this question requires some background on the history of adoption in this country. . . .

After World War II, when more and more Americans sought to adopt children, and white newborns became scarce, the white, unwed mother was transformed in public consciousness from a genetically tainted individual to a person who happened to be psychologically maladjusted and was therefore unsuited to raise her own child. Society erased the stigma that white newborns previously carried and they became marketable commodities. . . .

The history of adoption among Blacks is different from that of whites. During and after slavery, Black children orphaned by the sale or death of their parents were often taken in by the families of slaves or former slaves—among Blacks, informal adoption has a very long history. At the same time, relinquishment of children for adoption because of birth outside marriage has been rare. For many years the formal adoption system utilized criteria for adoption that excluded most Black families. Also, although birth within marriage may have been considered the ideal, because of the rape and sexual exploitation of Black women by their white masters during slavery, historically, Black children born out of wedlock have never been stigmatized in the same way as the children of white women. As sociologist Joyce Ladner has observed, the Black child born out of wedlock was considered a child who had a right to live in the community without stigmatization.

There may or may not have been class differences between the Black women who surrendered their children for adoption and the Black women who adopted them. What is clear, however, is that [this] transaction was one that took place between two women both of whose lives were subordinated by the common factor of racism. Thus, a Black woman adopting a child was making a contribution not only to the life of an individual child, but also to the welfare of Blacks as a group in the sense that she was providing benefits to a future adult member of the community. Moreover, because most Black families were at the lower end of the economic ladder in this country, any economic disparity between the two women may not have been substantial. . . .

B. Black Women and Transracial Adoption

. . . Even a cursory examination of legal scholarship on transracial adoption suggests that white and Black women scholars often take very different approaches to the issue. While the work of white women scholars often focuses on the individual parent/child relationships created in adoption and tends to view the political and racial issues in transracial adoption as somewhat peripheral, the issue of race often occupies a central place in the work of Black women scholars. In the writing of the latter, the focus generally goes beyond the issue of the need for homes for individual children, or the dynamics of individual parent-child relationships. Rather, it also emphasizes the structures of subordination that destabilize Black families, the political ramifications of transracial adoption for the welfare of Black communities, and the needs of all Black children, not only those who might possibly be adopted transracially. . . .

There are probably many reasons why Black women often appear to be ambivalent or even hostile toward transracial adoption. Some of the reasons certainly involve perceptions about the needs of individual Black children—there is skepticism about whether white women can provide Black children with the skills they need to survive in a racist society. . . .

I offer two additional explanations for the feelings some Black women may have toward transracial adoption—feelings unrelated to concerns about the competence of white women to raise Black children. I argue that many Black women feel that arguments in favor of transracial adoption that minimize the role of race in parenting devalue an important part of what motherhood means to them—a historical and contemporary struggle to raise Black children successfully in a racist world. In addition, many Black women may also resent transracial adoption because they see it as part of a larger system of racial hierarchy and privilege that advantages white women while it devalues and subordinates women of color. . . .

II. International Adoption

International adoptions began primarily as a humanitarian response by North Americans to the problem of European children orphaned by World War II. After the war, when Europe was rebuilt and its economic condition stabilized, the problem of orphaned children was resolved. Since that time, birthrates have fallen in the West, abortion and reliable methods of contraception have become available, and the stigma against women bearing children outside of marriage has declined, resulting in fewer white women surrendering babies for adoption. These factors have led to a decline in the number of children available for adoption in the West. At the same time, birthrates in the Third World have increased. The result has been a rise in the adoption of children from Third World countries by Westerners. . . .

III. Transracial and International Adoption: A Comparison

To some extent, transracial adoption and the international adoption of children from Latin America and Asia raise different issues. Some of the countries involved in international adoptions, at least in the past, actively supported or promoted such activity. Many of the children adopted are infants whose mothers presumably gave them up knowing that they were to be adopted by Westerners. Indeed, some of these mothers may be pleased that their children will have a chance to have a more economically comfortable life in America than they would have been able to offer in their often impoverished circumstances. . . .

Still, international adoptions have also been subject to controversy and criticism. It has been argued, for example, that such adoptions run the risk of creating problems of adjustment in older children who must adapt to a new culture and language, and that they sometimes create problems of identity in children who are of a different ethnic group than their parents. It has also been claimed that the continued practice of intercountry adoption retards the growth of child welfare services in the sending countries. Furthermore, it has been argued that wealthy adopters come to poor countries in the wake of wars, earthquakes, and famines and take many healthy children, leaving behind older and disabled children for institutional care. . . .

IV. Towards a Feminist Analysis

. . . Identification with the women seeking children rather than with the women surrendering them might result [for some women] in a reluctance to confront some of the issues that a feminist analysis of adoption would inevitably pose, [including] procedural safeguards concerning surrender, or open adoption, that might be seen as increasing the power of birth mothers. . . .

V. Conclusion: Practical Implications

. . . [T]he debate over transracial adoption has had the unfortunate effect of deflecting attention from the welfare of the vast majority of Black children in this country who, despite the controversy over transracial adoption, will continue to be raised by Black families in Black communities. Although . . . international adoptions of children of color also raise some troubling issues that feminism should address, I do not argue that they should be discontinued. . . . Even though . . . international adoptions take, from the sending country, potentially productive adults who could assist in that country's development, the reality is that many of the children who are adopted would otherwise likely grow up in large institutions, or under even worse conditions that would severely reduce their chances of growing up to be outstanding or even productive citizens. Even the argument that money spent on intercountry adoptions might be better spent on improving services and the economic circumstances of children in the sending countries is a tenuous one because in the absence of an adoption the money would probably end up being spent in the prospective adoptive couple's own country, rather than being transferred abroad. Finally, although it is appropriate to argue that Western women should become involved in the efforts to prevent the economic exploitation of third-world women's and children's labor in factories in their countries that service Western economic interests, the goal need not be to close these factories. Rather, it should be to change their practices so as to promote economic justice for the poor women who are employed in them. . . .

Adoption is an important institution. It provides an opportunity for people to experience the joys and challenges of parenthood. More importantly, it provides the opportunity for children to have homes who otherwise might not have them. A feminist analysis should support adoption as an institution, but at the same time should be willing to question the justice of a world which often results in the transfer of children of the least advantaged women to the most advantaged. There must be some commitment to eradicating the racism, economic exploitation and patriarchy that is often a factor that affects a woman's ability or choice to raise her own children.

59

Family Issue(s)

Naomi R. Cahn

Adoption presents feminists with a series of dilemmas, but, in this Review, I will out-line only two. First are issues relating to the sameness and difference of adoptive and biological families; second are issues relating to the socially-constructed choice to be-come a mother. I contrast the right to become a biological parent with the screening process for becoming an adoptive parent, the stigma of adoption, and the parameters of the choice to become a parent at all. These issues are highly contested, and they im-plicate fundamental social norms and stereotypes about men and women, mothers and fathers. . . .

II. Rights of Parenting

Though both natural and adoptive parents face explicit as well as implicit regulation, natural and adoptive parenting represent opposite ends of a continuum of rights based on biology. . . . What rights should biological parents have? Would it be more productive to think of all parents as having responsibilities to children and, thus, do away with the strong deference to biological parents? . . .

. . . [T]he feminist concerns relating to questions of sameness and difference can be "reproduced" in the adoption/child custody area. While few theorists have explic-itly applied feminism to adoption, a rich feminist jurisprudence addresses the related issues of child custody and surrogacy. On one hand, difference theorists celebrate women's capacities for intimacy and bonding as distinct from those of men; on the other, sameness feminists emphasize the capacity of all parents for nurturing. In the adoption context, this division might mean that difference feminists would support a mother's right to keep her child under virtually any circumstances (such as in the surrogacy context), while sameness feminists might, instead, emphasize comparative parental roles and responsibilities. More fundamentally, the issues surrounding whether biological and adoptive families are the same or different, and the policy implications of any conclusion, remain unresolved. This Section explores these themes.

Some feminist writers have celebrated the intimate connection between a mother and her child. As one way of showing the differences between men and women, these feminists have emphasized the distinctive connection that women feel to their children, beginning while the fetus is in utero and continuing throughout the child's life. . . .

. . . Through this literature runs a recognition and appreciation of the mother-child-fetus interrelationship. This perspective acknowledges women's connectedness based on the biological experiences of pregnancy and motherhood. It also strongly supports the mother's right to custody as against others.

Not quite on the other side of the debate, although with a different emphasis, are feminists who either emphasize the importance of more gender-neutral values, such as nurturing or responsibility, in the parenting relationship, rather than an intuitive and natural biological bond, or who focus almost solely on the interests of the child. . . . These attempts all examine how parents perform their roles, and the impact on the child of parental performance, rather than assuming that parents will naturally fill their roles. What these various gender-neutral approaches could mean in the adoption area is that parents who have nurtured a child . . . would become legally responsible for the child, notwithstanding the interests of the biological parents. . . .

While feminist discussion of biology is comparatively well-developed as it relates to custody and even to surrogacy, only recently has it spilled over into the adoption context. Perhaps this is because feminists have never really questioned the primacy of biological parenting in the legal system, and because biological parenting is only now facing challenges as technological developments increasingly manipulate the parameters of biological parenting.

III. The Biology of Adoption

In the adoption context, this debate over biology could address many interrelated issues. First, and perhaps most simple, are issues relating to the continuing relationship between the biological parents and the child, such as how long each parent should have to change his or her mind about the adoption, and whether any adoption should be "open" (that is, allowing future contact between the biological parent(s) and the child). Existing state law varies as to how long the biological mother actually has to change her mind, ranging from three months to any time prior to the entry of the final adoption order. An emphasis on the rights of the biological mother suggests a longer time period for reconsideration of adoption, while a recognition of the rights of the adoptive parents suggests that a shorter time period may be appropriate.

As for "open adoption," this might be in the interests of all parents and the child—or it might not. While open adoption solves some issues, such as the harshness of cutting all ties between the biological parent and her child, it creates other problems as all family members search to define their new relationships. A related question concerns whether the rights of the biological mother should be the same as those of the biological father, and whether the marital status of the biological parents is relevant in determining the father's rights. Under existing law, a father who is married to the mother may possess greater rights than an unmarried biological father. . . .

A final set of issues concerns the adoptive parents and explores how people should qualify for adoption and how the stigma of adoption can be overcome. The adoption procedure is quite rigorous for would-be parents, and, in light of adoption's second-class status, yet another hurdle that the adoptive parents must overcome. Alternatively, the adoption standards can be seen as protecting children, providing them with the best environment. . . .

A. Standards of Adoption

For feminists, these issues center on the significance of biology in recognizing parental rights. At what point do biological parents lose their preference? Shouldn't biological parenting receive some protection, especially given the nine months of pregnancy, childbirth, and the ensuing child care? And what about the state's arbitrary terminations of parental rights? . . . Feminists need to recognize the child's interest in stability, the interests of the birth mother in raising the child, and the interests of the adoptive parents. This approach is illustrated by a Vermont court's resolution of an adoption case on facts similar to the DeBoer/Clausen dispute. The court awarded a biological father visitation rights while awarding custody to the adoptive family. Such a solution treats the biological and adoptive families comparably, and, perhaps, equitably.

B. The Stigma of Adoption

The sameness/difference dilemma also appears when it comes to the stigma of adoption: Are adoptive families the same as biological families? . . .

2. ADOPTION AND LAST CHANCES

. . . [T]he law values the biological part of parenting. This valuation mirrors more general societal attitudes toward biological parenting, infertility, and adoption. Here, adoption is a choice when there are no other options for becoming a parent. . . .

Underlying the stigma of adoption are issues of sameness and difference. Adoptive families are the same as non-adoptive families for some purposes and different for others. Part of the stigma may result from their deviation from the normal family, just as women's otherness has resulted from their differences from a male norm. Thinking about adoption in this manner might lead to an attempt to ignore any differences between biological and adoptive families, or to value the differences between the two types of families. Alternatively . . . it could result in changing the norm, shifting the emphasis from how families are formed and on to families and children. This would require a respect for alternative family constructions, including adoptive and gay families, that look different from the conventional middle-class nuclear family. It might help change norms that penalize families which do not conform—because of race or class—to this traditional image. Efforts to change attitudes toward adoption should be part of a more comprehensive agenda for reconceptualizing the family.

60

"O Wind, Remind Him That I Have No Child"
Infertility and Feminist Jurisprudence

Linda J. Lacey

Introduction

O wind of Tizoula, O wind of Amsoud!
Blow over the plains and over the sea,
Carry, oh, carry my thoughts
To him who is so far, so far,
And who has left me without a little child
O wind! Remind him that I have no child.

It is hard for me to imagine sadder words than the cry of the Berber woman. I am infertile and for a long period of my life, I believed that I was destined to remain childless. Like most infertile women, I spent countless hours trying to conceive, culminating in a painful operation after which I was told by my nurse that since I was 40, I was "too old to have children" anyway. When I began to try to adopt, I ran into new obstacles. There were so many things wrong with me: I wasn't Christian, I was too old and too feminist. Every aspect of my personal life was subject to intense scrutiny. As Patricia Williams describes the process: "I was unprepared for the fact that I too would be shopped for, by birth mothers as well as social workers, looked over for my age, marital and economic status, and race. All that was missing was to have my tires kicked."

My story has a happy ending. I finally found an independent lawyer and an adoption agency who accepted me as a prospective parent, and after several birthmothers changed their minds about relinquishing their babies, I was able to adopt two wonderful children who enrich my life in ways I cannot begin to describe. . . .

. . . [A]s a feminist I am constantly surprised, and often angered, at the treatment of infertility in feminist jurisprudence. There is almost no discussion of infertility as a disability or as a painful experience for women. Instead, infertility only appears as a part of extensive feminist analyses of new reproductive technologies. Feminists have constructed a "grand theory" of infertility and new reproductive techniques that has little to do with reality. Much of the discussion of reproductive technology is written in highly abstract, philosophical terms, rather than in the more experiential, narrative style which characterizes much of feminist jurisprudence. The infertile woman is generally voiceless and invisible in the telling of this story; when she does appear she is dismissed or criticized. . . .

I. The Feminist Story of Patriarchy and Reproductive Technology

A. Patriarchal Wish for Reproduction

The majority of feminist authors who discuss artificial reproductive technologies argue that these procedures are bad for women. According to their analysis, the technologies reduce women to "mother machines," breeders for the convenience of men's patriarchal desire to reproduce themselves. . . .

This picture of reproductive technology as the ultimate tool of patriarchy relies on inaccurate assumptions which permeate the discourse and make all the corollary arguments questionable. The initial problem with feminist theory in this area is the uniform usage of the term "reproduction" as the subject of the debate. Use of this term defines the exclusive goal of modern technology as an urge to duplicate oneself, an urge which may indeed have patriarchal and racial implications. The dialogue would sound markedly different if we redefined the goal as "having children." The urge to have children is very complex and not limited to a desire to see one's genetic makeup reflected in a child. People want children for a variety of reasons, selfish and not so selfish; "reproduction" is only one of those reasons. If we begin to think in terms of "having children," instead of "reproducing," it is easier to see the basic error in the dominant feminist analysis: the explicit or implicit assumption that only men wish to utilize assisted reproductive techniques. Barbara Omolade's statement is typical: "Every patriarch wants to reproduce the son."

Despite the uniformity of this assumption, none of the literature cites any authority for the proposition that men desire children more than women do, and no significant studies exist to support this contention. In fact, I believe that the opposite is true; women constitute the majority of infertile people trying to conceive or adopt a child. Evidence indicates that women generally have a stronger desire for children than men, and infertile women are therefore more likely to pursue having children through new technologies or adoption. . . .

. . . There are also indications that men and women experience infertility differently: men are concerned that something is "wrong" with them, while women mourn their lost children.

Additionally, far more single women than single men adopt children. While there may be several reasons for this phenomenon, including obstacles to adoption faced exclusively by single men, this statistic suggests that women may generally want children more than men. In the context of foreign adoption (generally the only type of adoption in which prospective parents are allowed to choose the sex of their adoptive child) girls are in much greater demand than boys. While no one knows exactly why this is true, one of the most popular theories is that women are primarily the parties who want to adopt and women want daughters. . . .

The conclusion that having children is more important to women than to men is also supported by the strand of feminist theory that recognizes that women are more emotionally connected to their children than men are. Women spend much more time taking care of their children than men and are more likely than men to want custody of their children after a divorce. Women are socialized to become mothers, while men are rarely socialized to become fathers.

While I agree with mainstream feminists that many men do try to control women through the reproductive process, it is these men that pose the real threat to women's autonomy, not reproductive technologies themselves. The technologies actually increase women's autonomy because they permit women to have children without male partners. Artificial methods of conception offer lesbian women (and gay men) a previously unheard of opportunity to have children; an opportunity they are taking in increasing numbers. As one commentator notes, "assisted reproductive technology possesses the potential to radically destabilize and disrupt the traditional conception of the family. . . ." This resulting disruption can only benefit women's autonomy.

B. The Brainwashed Mothers Theory

In the rare instances in which they discuss infertile women, feminists argue that the wish to have children is created by patriarchy and is essentially forced on women. Women are stigmatized by infertility, the theory goes, and made to feel worthless if they are childless. These feminists believe that the overemphasis on reproductive technology places a disproportionately high value on having children, and that women, barraged by messages urging them to reproduce, ultimately have no real choice in the matter. . . . Implicit in this type of statement is a suggestion that the infertile woman is fortunate to have escaped the trap of motherhood. As a result, infertile women are often dismissively told they should forget about having children. . . .

The question of whether women raised in a predominantly patriarchal society can ever act with true "free will" has generated a great deal of philosophical debate. Catharine MacKinnon argues that patriarchal culture is so universal and dominant that we cannot even imagine what our lives would be like without its influence. But just because the desire for children may be shaped by patriarchy does not make it unreal or unimportant. Regardless of the source of their wish for children, most women find having children is an extremely positive experience.

When infertile women speak about their experience, they focus on the children they want, not their failure to meet society's expectations. One woman writes, "Infertility is a silent tragedy. How do you explain to someone that you had a rough night because there was no baby to keep you awake, that your house is too clean and there are no toys cluttering the floor? Would anyone understand that you cried over Pampers commercials?" Of course it is true that some women who are ambivalent about having children are pressured into maternity. However the mainstream feminist commentators' focus on infertile women suggests that infertile women are more likely than fertile women to be brainwashed into having children against their will. Common sense suggests the reverse is true. Infertility provides a reluctant parent with a perfect excuse for childlessness. Women who persevere with artificial conception methods or adoptions are questioned and cross-examined about their desire to become parents and are necessarily highly motivated.

Some feminists argue that even if a subset of women thinks the new technologies will be beneficial to them, development of these procedures must nevertheless be restricted because their use harms the interests of women as a group. This argument relies on the premise that, in addition to serving the patriarchal wish for reproduction, alternative conception technology and adoption reinforce the stereotypical image of women as mothers. This argument is part of a continuing feminist debate about the desirability of emphasizing women's unique role as mothers. . . .

II. The Focus on Alternatives

Another common theme of feminist criticism of reproductive technology is the argument that instead of concentrating on improving reproductive technology or making it more accessible to prospective parents, we should be concentrating on alternatives such as adoption or eradication of the causes of infertility.

A. Adoption

Many feminist authors argue that the emphasis on reproductive technologies detracts from the possibility of adoption. Ruth Colker's statement is typical: "I wonder why people engage in IVF at all. . . . There are always children available to be adopted. . . . Does the use of IVF express a disrespect for the lives of poor, disabled, and often minority children who are available for adoption?" . . . I am concerned that advocates of adoption gloss over the reality of its difficulties. Each year in the United States there are approximately fifty thousand infants available for adoption, but [hundreds of thousands of] prospective parents waiting to adopt. I would certainly advise infertile women who have the chance to adopt healthy infants to do so, rather than suffer through painful infertility treatments that are likely to be unsuccessful. But that is not a realistic option for many infertile women; not everyone is as lucky as I was. I was able to find the lawyer who placed my first child because I was a "fellow" professional. In adopting my second child, I was fortunate to live in a city with an agency that would accept clients over forty. . . .

Many commentators acknowledge the difficulty of adopting healthy infants, but contend that it is necessary to restrict access to reproductive technologies, such as IVF and surrogacy, in order to encourage people to adopt hard-to-place children. . . . While adopting these children can be enormously rewarding, it requires a tremendous amount of emotional and financial commitment. Commentators never fully explain why only infertile people should be forced to make that commitment in order to have children.

Imagine a country in which a small percentage of the citizens who are blind perform a task which no one else wants to do. When the means to cure blindness appears, the sighted citizens argue that the cure should not be given to blind people, for then there would be no one left to perform the difficult task. Such an argument seems unthinkable, but it is disturbingly similar to the arguments for restricting access to cures for infertility.

Forcing infertile people to adopt hard-to-place children by removing alternatives is not only unfair to the parents, it is also unfair to the children. Some experts challenge the presumption that adoption is the best alternative for hard-to-place children, especially when it results in separating siblings from each other. In addition, numerous studies show that adoptions of these children are often disrupted when "reluctant" parents realize they are not equipped to handle the serious emotional problems of older children. These interruptions take an additional toll on the children. Unless there is careful screening of the prospective parents, hard-to-place children are at greater risk for child abuse.

The goal must be not only to find homes for hard-to-place children, but to place them with families that want them. This goal can be better met by adjusting existing policies which provide financial and other types of aid to adopting parents, rather than restricting reproductive technologies and leaving infertile parents with no other options.

For some feminist commentators, even adoption is not a desirable alternative for infertile women. While most feminists ignore the subject, the perspectives of those who do write about adoption range from approval to ambivalence to outright hostility. Early editions of *Our Bodies, Ourselves,* a classic feminist sourcebook on women's health, present a hostile image of adoption from the perspectives of both infertile women and birth mothers. In its section on infertility, the book disproportionately stresses the negative aspects of adoption, giving the benefits of adoption for infertile women only cursory treatment. The book's discussion of options for women facing unwanted pregnancies presents adoption in an even less favorable light, describing it as an alternative to abortion pushed by right-wing fundamentalists. The book presents the view that birth mothers coerced into giving up babies for adoption suffer a "'cruel, but regrettably usual, punishment that can last a lifetime,' while adoptive mothers attempt to keep birthmothers in the role of brood mares."

Our Bodies is not alone in its unsympathetic treatment of adoptive parents. . . .

It is understandable and commendable for feminists to focus on the suffering of birthmothers in the adoption process. Birthmothers are often poor, young, and single, women who are indeed vulnerable to exploitation. But a true feminist analysis should also incorporate the perspectives of adopted children, many of whom experience adoption as a chance to belong to a loving family, and of adoptive parents, who are not exploitative monsters. . . .

B. Remedies for Causes of Infertility

Other feminist commentators argue that infertility has social causes which can be remedied and that addressing infertility in conjunction with broad societal treatment of women and people of color should be our primary focus. These commentators contend that since techniques such as IVF are primarily available to middle class white women, we should concentrate on nonclassist remedies that will help everyone,

such as providing better care after childbirth and abortion and removing environmental and occupational conditions which may cause sterility. . . .

I completely agree that programs to help reduce the root causes of infertility are
desirable. But the argument that our society must choose between alternatives creates
a false dichotomy. . . . Most of the money to develop and use artificial conception
comes from private sources; the money to remedy social causes of infertility will need
to come from the government.

Infertility is not limited to the wealthy, but affects people of all classes and races.
The head of a Planned Parenthood clinic writes:

> There is a widespread belief that only upper-middle class, professional people have fer-
> tility problems. This is simply not true. Many low-income people who do not have med-
> ical insurance come to our clinic seeking treatment. They desperately want to have a
> child, but are without financial resources. I think this segment of the infertility popula-
> tion is largely ignored and forgotten.

Restricting reproductive technologies in favor of hypothetical, long-run solutions,
would effectively mean turning our backs on the people who need help the most. If
insurance companies were required to provide coverage for infertility treatments such
as IVF, then poor women would be able to use the techniques.

III. The Superiority of the Gestational Mother Theory

Certain aspects of cultural feminism have been described as "biological feminism," a
theory which emphasizes women's capacity to bear children as part of their essential
nature. A few proponents of this genre seem to suggest that a child must be biologically connected to its mother for the mother-child bond to be real or meaningful. The
argument of "biological feminists," that the gestational mother's claim of motherhood
is superior to anyone else's, supports a general conclusion that contested surrogacy
situations should be resolved in favor of gestational mothers. In the adoption context,
this approach favors the rights of the biological mother. . . .

. . . [T]here is a third possibility: the recognition that mothers are generally closer
than fathers to their children applies to all mothers, not only gestational mothers. . . .

I do not deny that pregnancy provides the first instance of intense bonding with a
child. However, there are many experiences that contribute to this bonding, most of
which are not unique to gestational mothers. I am also aware that the relationship between adoptive parents and children can pose unique problems, and that many adult
adoptees describe themselves as "incomplete" or "unfulfilled" because of lack of contact with their birthmothers. However, the adoption literature I have read indicates
that it is most often the genetic parental ties the child seeks, not the birthing ties.
Adoptees speak of the need to find someone "who has my eyes, my love of basketball,"
not the one who bore them in her womb. . . .

Conclusion

This has been the most difficult article I have ever written. . . . Infertile women deserve empathy, not scorn or dismissal. Those of us who finally become parents through nontraditional means are not imposters who only "construct" ourselves as mothers.

The dominant feminist "story" about artificial reproduction is the story of the dominant patriarchal male, who uses technology to both reproduce himself and control women. My story is written from the perspective of the childless woman who uses technology to fulfill her wish to bring children into her life. There is undoubtedly truth in both stories. Feminists who lack understanding of the infertile woman and her need for children should acquaint themselves with the previously unheard voices of the childless. Without these voices, any analysis of assisted reproduction and adoption is incomplete.

61

Adoption, Biological Essentialism, and Feminist Theory

Charlotte Witt

Feminist theorists have criticized the traditional nuclear family as a site of the invisible domination and private oppression of women by men. In addition, feminists have been among those arguing for an expansion of the way families are normatively constructed to include gay and lesbian families, single-parent families, and "blended" families. The situation is different, however, with regard to families formed by adoption. Adoptive families have been largely ignored in feminist writing on the family, which, like much nonfeminist writing on the family, assumes a biological model of the relationship between parents and children.

The biological view of the family is prevalent in feminist ethics and theorizing about the family in at least three ways. First, feminists who privilege the maternal relationship tend to do so by emphasizing its gestational and bodily aspects. This emphasis privileges a biological view of the mother-child relationship. Second, the feminist ethics of care, in some of its formulations, identifies the mother-child relationship as a model for ethical action; and the mother-child relationship in question, either explicitly or tacitly, assumes a biological and gestational tie between mother and child. And, in a related development, feminist theorizing about the self and personal identity often endorses a relational view of the self, based in some cases upon the mother-child relationship, which is again assumed to be a biological relationship.

The emphasis in feminist theory on biological and genetic ties as foundational for the mother-child relationship raises many interesting questions. One important issue concerns the question of personal identity and the role that biology and genetic ties might play in establishing an individual child's identity. I will use the term "genetic essentialism" to refer to the idea that a person's identity is determined by his or her genetic endowment. What I want to suggest is that "genetic essentialism" provides a mistaken view of personal identity, and should be rejected both in feminist ethical theory and in feminist theories of the self, and by others who theorize about what the family should or should not be like.

Genetic essentialism, if true, would provide one justification for a normative understanding of the family that endorses the biological family as better than families formed in other ways. For it is reasonable to suppose that if genetic essentialism were true, then the identity and, hence, the self-understanding of adopted children would be either blocked (in the case of closed adoptions) or complex and potentially problematic (in the case of open adoptions). These difficulties facing adoptees would support the evaluation of the biological basis of the family as better than, or more important than, other ways of creating families. In the context of feminist theory, genetic essentialism would provide one reason for thinking that the biological or gestational ties between mother and child should play a central role for both ethical theory and relational theories of the self and personal identity.

One contemporary formulation of genetic essentialism holds that a person's biological origin is essential to that person, and understands biological origin to refer to the very sperm and egg that in fact developed into that person:

> How could a person originating from different parents, from a totally different sperm and egg, be this very woman? One can imagine, given the woman, that various things in her life could have changed: that she should have become a pauper; that her royal blood should have been unknown, and so on. . . . It seems to me that anything coming from a different origin would not be this object.[1]

The philosopher Saul Kripke asks us to contrast the necessity of a woman's origins—that is, the particular sperm and egg from which she originates—with what we could imagine about her life history or the contingent events of her life. The idea is that, while genetic origins are necessary to an individual person's identity, we could imagine that person's life history altering significantly, and yet that person would remain the very same person. So, for example, an adopted child necessarily originates from the very same sperm and egg that she in fact came from, but she might have remained with her birth family (had circumstances been different) or been adopted by a family other than the one that did in fact adopt her (again, had circumstances been different). Our life stories are filled with contingency and circumstance, but our genetic origins are fixed and necessary. Surely, what is fixed and necessary about us is central to our identities, our selves, rather than the vicissitudes of our lives and fortunes. Kripke's doctrine of the necessity of origins supports genetic essentialism by articulating a principled contrast between our biological origins (sperm and egg), which are essential to our individual identity, and our life histories, which are contingent and therefore not essential to our individual identity.

To see what is wrong with genetic essentialism as a theory of personal identity, we need to distinguish between personal identity and the identity of individual members of natural kinds, like human beings and tigers. Kripke's doctrine of the necessity of origins only supports genetic essentialism on the assumption that to be an individual person is the same as to be an individual human being (a member of a natural kind or biological species). But, ever since Locke, philosophers have distinguished between persons (who have legal and ethical standing) and human beings (biological organisms). As a minimum condition, persons are beings that have some degree of self-understanding, but individual human beings need not have any self-understanding (e.g., a human infant). The identity of an individual person, which necessarily requires self-understanding, and the identity of an individual human being are governed by different criteria. Hence, while Kripke's necessity of origins might be true for individual human beings, it does not follow from that claim that it is also true for individual persons.

The relevance of genetic origins to the identity of persons, as opposed to the identity of biological organisms, is always mediated by the person's self-understanding. In making this point, I am not claiming that the genetic origins of persons could not enter into their self-understandings; they surely can and do. But it is equally possible that a contingent life event, like adoption, might be much more significant to a person's identity than a genetic predisposition to develop flat feet. For an adoptee, the process of creating a narrative of the self may well require, and be enhanced by, knowledge of genetic origins through information about and contact with the birth family (as far as these are available). But this is not because genetic endowment determines the personal identity of the adoptee. Rather, it is because knowledge of one's genetic origins, mediated by self-understanding, may be important themes in an adoptee's project of developing a narrative of the self.[2]

NOTES

1. Saul Kripke, *Naming and Necessity* (Cambridge: Harvard University Press, 1980), 113.

2. One important and possibly problematic issue in the self-understanding of adoptees concerns the topic of family resemblances. I discuss the issue of genetic essentialism in relation to family resemblances in "Family Resemblances: Adoption, Personal Identity, and Genetic Essentialism," in *The View from Home: Feminist and Philosophical Issues in Adoption* (Ithaca: Cornell University Press, forthcoming).

VIII

Other Perspectives on Adoption

In the final part of the book, we bring together a variety of readings that use the adoption process as a basis for contrast, comparison, or analogy. This part begins with alternative means of establishing parenthood, including surrogacy and reproductive interventions, continues with questions about the new reproductive technologies and genetic essentialism, and concludes with questions about the commodification of the baby market.

Analogies to Assisted Reproduction and Other Parentage Laws

62

Johnson v. Calvert (Cal. 1993)

Panelli, J.

In this case we address several of the legal questions raised by recent advances in reproductive technology. When, pursuant to a surrogacy agreement, a zygote formed of the gametes of a husband and wife is implanted in the uterus of another woman, who carries the resulting fetus to term and gives birth to a child not genetically related to her, who is the child's "natural mother" under California law? Does a determination that the wife is the child's natural mother work a deprivation of the gestating woman's constitutional rights? And is such an agreement barred by any public policy of this state?

We conclude that the husband and wife are the child's natural parents, and that this result does not offend the state or federal Constitution or public policy.

Facts

Mark and Crispina Calvert are a married couple who desired to have a child. Crispina was forced to undergo a hysterectomy in 1984. Her ovaries remained capable of producing eggs, however, and the couple eventually considered surrogacy. In 1989 Anna Johnson heard about Crispina's plight from a coworker and offered to serve as a surrogate for the Calverts.

On January 15, 1990, Mark, Crispina, and Anna signed a contract providing that an embryo created by the sperm of Mark and the egg of Crispina would be implanted in Anna and the child born would be taken into Mark and Crispina's home "as their child." Anna agreed she would relinquish "all parental rights" to the child in favor of Mark and Crispina. In return, Mark and Crispina would pay Anna $10,000 in a series of installments, the last to be paid six weeks after the child's birth....

... Mark and Crispina [filed] a lawsuit, seeking a declaration they were the legal parents of the unborn child. Anna filed her own action to be declared the mother of the child, and the two cases were eventually consolidated....

At trial in October 1990, the parties stipulated that Mark and Crispina were the child's genetic parents. After hearing evidence and arguments, the trial court ruled that Mark and Crispina were the child's "genetic, biological and natural" father and mother, that Anna had no "parental" rights to the child, and that the surrogacy contract was legal and enforceable against Anna's claims.... [Anna filed an appeal.] We granted review.

Discussion

Determining Maternity under the Uniform Parentage Act

The Uniform Parentage Act (the Act) of 1975 was [intended] . . . to eliminate the legal distinction between legitimate and illegitimate children. . . .

. . . [The Act uses] the concept of the "parent and child relationship." The "parent and child relationship" means "the legal relationship existing between a child and his natural or adoptive parents incident to which the law confers or imposes rights, privileges, duties, and obligations. It includes the mother and child relationship and the father and child relationship." . . .

Passage of the Act clearly was not motivated by the need to resolve surrogacy disputes, which were virtually unknown in 1975. Yet it facially applies to any parentage determination, including the rare case in which a child's maternity is in issue. . . .

. . . Anna, of course, predicates her claim of maternity on the fact that she gave birth to the child. The Calverts contend that Crispina's genetic relationship to the child establishes that she is his mother. Counsel for the minor joins in that contention and argues, in addition, that several of the presumptions created by the Act dictate the same result. As will appear, we conclude that presentation of blood test evidence is one means of establishing maternity, as is proof of having given birth. . . .

. . . [The Act] provides, in relevant part, that between a child and the natural mother a parent and child relationship "may be established by proof of her having given birth to the child, or under [the Act]." Apart from [that section] the Act sets forth no specific means by which a natural mother can establish a parent and child relationship. . . .

. . . [W]e are left with the undisputed evidence that Anna, not Crispina, gave birth to the child and that Crispina, not Anna, is genetically related to him. Both women thus have adduced evidence of a mother and child relationship as contemplated by the Act. Yet for any child California law recognizes only one natural mother, despite advances in reproductive technology rendering a different outcome biologically possible.

. . . ". . . It is arguable that, while gestation may demonstrate maternal status, it is not the sine qua non of motherhood. Rather, it is possible that the common law viewed genetic consanguinity as the basis for maternal rights. Under this latter interpretation, gestation simply would be irrefutable evidence of the more fundamental genetic relationship." This ambiguity, highlighted by the problems arising from the use of artificial reproductive techniques, is nowhere explicitly resolved in the Act.

Because two women each have presented acceptable proof of maternity, we do not believe this case can be decided without enquiring into the parties' intentions as manifested in the surrogacy agreement. Mark and Crispina are a couple who desired to have a child of their own genetic stock but are physically unable to do so without the help of reproductive technology. They affirmatively intended the birth of the child, and took the steps necessary to effect in vitro fertilization. But for their acted-on intention, the child would not exist. Anna agreed to facilitate the procreation of Mark's and Crispina's child. The parties' aim was to bring Mark's and Crispina's child into the

world, not for Mark and Crispina to donate a zygote to Anna. Crispina from the outset intended to be the child's mother. Although the gestative function Anna performed was necessary to bring about the child's birth, it is safe to say that Anna would
not have been given the opportunity to gestate or deliver the child had she, prior to
implantation of the zygote, manifested her own intent to be the child's mother. No
reason appears why Anna's later change of heart should vitiate the determination that
Crispina is the child's natural mother.

We conclude that although the Act recognizes both genetic consanguinity and giving birth as means of establishing a mother and child relationship, when the two
means do not coincide in one woman, she who intended to procreate the child—that
is, she who intended to bring about the birth of a child that she intended to raise as
her own—is the natural mother under California law. . . .

Anna urges that surrogacy contracts violate several social policies. Relying on her
contention that she is the child's legal, natural mother, she cites the public policy prohibiting the payment for consent to adoption of a child. She argues further that the
policies underlying the adoption laws of this state are violated by the surrogacy contract because it in effect constitutes a prebirth waiver of her parental rights.

We disagree. Gestational surrogacy differs in crucial respects from adoption and so
is not subject to the adoption statutes. The parties voluntarily agreed to participate in
in vitro fertilization and related medical procedures before the child was conceived; at
the time when Anna entered into the contract, therefore, she was not vulnerable to
financial inducements to part with her own expected offspring. As discussed above,
Anna was not the genetic mother of the child. The payments to Anna under the contract were meant to compensate her for her services in gestating the fetus and undergoing labor, rather than for giving up "parental" rights to the child. Payments were
due both during the pregnancy and after the child's birth. We are, accordingly, unpersuaded that the contract used in this case violates the public policies embodied in
Penal Code section 273 and the adoption statutes. . . .

Finally, Anna and some commentators have expressed concern that surrogacy contracts tend to exploit or dehumanize women, especially women of lower economic
status. . . . Some have also cautioned that the practice of surrogacy may encourage society to view children as commodities, subject to trade at their parents' will. . . .

We are unpersuaded that gestational surrogacy arrangements are so likely to cause
the untoward results Anna cites as to demand their invalidation on public policy
grounds. Although common sense suggests that women of lesser means serve as surrogate mothers more often than do wealthy women, there has been no proof that surrogacy contracts exploit poor women to any greater degree than economic necessity
in general exploits them by inducing them to accept lower-paid or otherwise undesirable employment. We are likewise unpersuaded by the claim that surrogacy will foster
the attitude that children are mere commodities; no evidence is offered to support it.
The limited data available seem to reflect an absence of significant adverse effects of
surrogacy on all participants.

The argument that a woman cannot knowingly and intelligently agree to gestate
and deliver a baby for intending parents carries overtones of the reasoning that for
centuries prevented women from attaining equal economic rights and professional

status under the law. To resurrect this view is both to foreclose a personal and economic choice on the part of the surrogate mother, and to deny intending parents what may be their only means of procreating a child of their own genetic stock. . . .

Kennard, J. (dissenting).

When a woman who wants to have a child provides her fertilized ovum to another woman who carries it through pregnancy and gives birth to a child, who is the child's legal mother? Unlike the majority, I do not agree that the determinative consideration should be the intent to have the child that originated with the woman who contributed the ovum. In my view, the woman who provided the fertilized ovum and the woman who gave birth to the child both have substantial claims to legal motherhood. Pregnancy entails a unique commitment, both psychological and emotional, to an unborn child. No less substantial, however, is the contribution of the woman from whose egg the child developed and without whose desire the child would not exist.

For each child, California law accords the legal rights and responsibilities of parenthood to only one "natural mother". . . . To determine who is the legal mother of a child born of a gestational surrogacy arrangement, I would apply the standard most protective of child welfare—the best interests of the child. . . .

VII. Analysis of the Majority's "Intent Test"

[I]n making the intent of the genetic mother who wants to have a child the dispositive factor, the majority renders a certain result preordained and inflexible in every such case: as between an intending genetic mother and a gestational mother, the genetic mother will, under the majority's analysis, always prevail. The majority recognizes no meaningful contribution by a woman who agrees to carry a fetus to term for the genetic mother beyond that of mere employment to perform a specified biological function. . . .

VIII. The Best Interests of the Child

. . . To break [the] "tie" between the genetic mother and the gestational mother, the majority uses the legal concept of intent. In so doing, the majority has articulated a rationale for using the concept of intent that is grounded in principles of tort, intellectual property and commercial contract law. . . .

But, as I have pointed out, we are not deciding a case involving the commission of a tort, the ownership of intellectual property, or the delivery of goods under a commercial contract; we are deciding the fate of a child. . . .

. . . The determination of a child's best interests does not depend on the parties' relative economic circumstances, which in a gestational surrogacy situation will usually favor the genetic mother and her spouse. . . . I would remand the matter to the trial court to undertake [a best interests] evaluation.

63

In re Nicholas H. (Cal. 2002)

Brown, J.

A man who receives a child into his home and openly holds the child out as his natural child is presumed to be the natural father of the child. [Uniform Parentage Act (UPA) section 7611(d).] The presumption that he is the natural father "is a rebuttable presumption affecting the burden of proof and may be rebutted in an appropriate action only by clear and convincing evidence." (section 7612(a)). The question presented by this case is whether a presumption arising under section 7611(d) is, under section 7612(a), necessarily rebutted when the presumed father seeks parental rights but admits that he is not the biological father of the child.

The answer to this question is of the gravest concern to the six-year-old boy involved in this case. While his presumed father is providing a loving home for him, his mother has not done so, and his biological father, whose identity has never been judicially determined, has shown no interest in doing so. Therefore, if, as the Court of Appeal concluded, the juvenile court had no discretion under section 7612(a) but to find that the presumption arising under section 7611(d) was rebutted by the presumed father's admission that he is not the biological father, this child will be rendered fatherless and homeless.

This harsh result, we conclude, is not required by section 7612(a) . . . [which] provides that "a presumption under Section 7611 is a rebuttable presumption affecting the burden of proof and *may be rebutted in an appropriate action* only by clear and convincing evidence." (§ 7612(a), italics added.)

The juvenile court acted well within its discretion in concluding that this case, in which no one else was a candidate for the privilege and responsibility of fathering this little boy, was not an appropriate action in which to find that the section 7611(d) presumption of fatherhood had been rebutted. . . .

Factual and Procedural Background

For the purpose of framing the narrow issue we are considering, the evidence may be summarized as follows.

When Kimberly was pregnant with Nicholas, she moved in with Thomas. Thomas is not Nicholas's biological father, as he admits, but both Kimberly and Thomas wanted Thomas to act as a father to Nicholas, so Thomas participated in Nicholas's birth, was listed on Nicholas's birth certificate as his father, and provided a home for Kimberly and Nicholas for several years.

Thomas has been the constant in Nicholas's life. . . . Thomas has lived with Nicholas for long periods of time, he has provided Nicholas with significant financial support over the years, and he has consistently referred to and treated Nicholas as his son. "In addition, there is undisputed evidence that Nicholas has a strong emotional bond with Thomas and that Thomas is the only father Nicholas has ever known."

Kimberly, on the other hand, has been a frail reed for Nicholas to lean upon. The investigation report prepared by a family services counselor stated that "information from friends and relatives of the family supported Thomas's allegations of Kimberly's drug use, transiency, lack of gainful employment and violence towards others." The juvenile court's finding that Nicholas had to be removed from her custody was based on the following grounds: "One, [Kimberly] continues to lead an unstable lifestyle, without housing or means of support of her own. . . . Number two, Nicholas has continually stated he does not wish to reside with his mother because she is mean to him; she hits and slaps him; and she smokes weed. Three, and most importantly to me as I have observed [Kimberly's] demeanor throughout this case, particularly during her testimony, I have grown increasingly concerned about [her] mental and emotional health. . . ."

Jason S., Kimberly claims, is Nicholas's biological father. However, Jason has not come forward to assert any parental rights he may have, and because the Agency has been unable to obtain enough information from Kimberly to locate Jason, his paternity could not be established.

On this record, the juvenile court found that the presumption under 7611(d) that Thomas was Nicholas's natural father had not been rebutted. The court expressly rejected the contention that Thomas's admission that he is not Nicholas's biological father necessarily rebutted the presumption. "If I were to agree with County Counsel that [Thomas's] admission that he is not Nicholas's biological father rebuts the presumption, then what we would be doing is leaving Nicholas fatherless." . . .

Discussion

[By contrast,] the Court of Appeal concluded that Thomas qualified as Nicholas's presumed father under section 7611(d), but that, under section 7612(a), his admission that he is not Nicholas's biological father necessarily rebutted that presumption. . . .

In its misreading of section 7612(a)—"that the section 7611(d) presumption is rebutted by clear and convincing evidence that the presumed father is not the child's natural father"—the Court of Appeal appears to have conflated two of the three subdivisions of section 7612. Subdivision (a) provides that "a presumption under Section 7611 is a rebuttable presumption affecting the burden of proof and may be rebutted in an appropriate action only by clear and convincing evidence." Subdivision (c), on the other hand, provides that "the presumption under Section 7611 is rebutted by a judgment establishing paternity of the child by another man." No judgment establishing the paternity of another man has been entered here. Kimberly asserts Jason is Nicholas's biological father, but Jason has not come forward to affirm that claim and, indeed, has not even been located. . . .

Our conclusion—that a man does not lose his status as a presumed father by admitting he is not the biological father—is also supported by subdivision (b) of section 7612. Subdivision (b) provides: "If two or more presumptions arise under section 7611 which conflict with each other, the presumption which on the facts is founded on the weightier considerations of policy and logic controls." As a matter of statutory construction, if the Legislature had intended that a man who is not a biological father cannot be a presumed father under section 7611, it would not have provided for such weighing, for among two competing claims for presumed father status under section 7611, there can be only one biological father. . . .

. . . Indeed, two Courts of Appeal have held that, in the words of one of them, "biological paternity by a competing presumptive father does not necessarily defeat a non-biological father's presumption of paternity" [*In re Kiana A.,* 93 Cal. App. 4th 1109, 1118 (2001)].

. . . [Our] courts have repeatedly held, in applying paternity presumptions, that the extant father-child relationship is to be preserved at the cost of biological ties. . . . This social relationship is much more important, to the child at least, than a biological relationship of actual paternity. . . . [*Susan H. v. Jack S.,* 30 Cal. App. 4th 1435, 1443 (1994)]. . . .

In a still more recent case, *Raphael P.,* . . . 97 Cal. App.4th 716 (2002) . . . the putative father contended he was entitled to presumed father status on the ground he had filed a voluntary declaration of paternity and on the ground he had received the child into his home and had openly held him out as his natural child (§ 7611(d)). The trial court rejected the former contention because it found no evidence that a voluntary declaration of paternity had in fact been filed with the required agency. With regard to the presumption under section 7611(d), the trial court, without deciding whether the facts supported application of the presumption, concluded that blood test evidence demonstrating that the putative father was not the biological father of the child "precluded [the putative father] from establishing the presumption of paternity or rebutted that presumption."

The section 7611(d) question presented by the case, the Court of Appeal in *Raphael P.* stated, was "whether biological proof of nonpaternity necessarily precludes presumed father status" (*Raphael P.,* supra, 97 Cal. App.4th at p. 724). . . .

[The Court concluded:] [T]he [trial] court should not have ordered him to undergo genetic testing, much less [have] allowed the evidence of biological nonpaternity to rebut appellant's presumed father status. . . .

. . . In such a situation, where there is a man claiming presumed father status and no indication of another man asserting paternity, we question whether paternity can rightly be considered a "relevant fact".

64

Note on the Revised
Uniform Parentage Act (UPA) of 2002

Joan Heifetz Hollinger

To resolve the difficult parentage issues in *Johnson v. Calvert* (is a child's "natural mother" the gestational mother or the genetic/intended mother?) and *In re Nicholas H.* (can a man who holds himself out as a child's "natural father" be the child's presumed legal father even though he is not the biological father?), the California Supreme Court construes various provisions of the Uniform Parentage Act (UPA). The UPA was originally promulgated by the National Conference of Commissioners on Uniform State Laws (NCCUSL) in 1973. Although only nineteen states enacted it in its entirety, the UPA has influenced the parentage laws of most states.

The primary goal of the UPA (1973) was to provide legal rules and presumptions to enable courts to recognize a parent-child relationship for all children, and more specifically, to protect nonmarital children, making them, as much as possible, legally indistinguishable from children born to married couples. The UPA was drafted in response to U.S. Supreme Court decisions that had begun to invalidate many of the historical distinctions between the legal and economic status of nonmarital ("illegitimate") and marital children as contrary to the equal protection and due process clauses of the Fourteenth Amendment (see, e.g., *Levy v. Louisiana,* 391 U.S. 68 (1968); *Stanley v. Illinois,* 405 U.S. 645 (1972)). The UPA replaces the labeling of children as "legitimate" or "illegitimate" with a concept of "legal parentage" that is intended to apply equally to all children regardless of the marital status of their biological or adoptive parents.

In the late 1990s, NCCUSL undertook to revise the UPA to take account of (1) the past quarter century's dramatic increase in the number of nonmarital children— nearly one-third of all current births, (2) federal mandates that make federal funding of state child support enforcement programs contingent on each state's implementation of simplified nonjudicial means to establish paternity, (3) advances in genetic and DNA tests of paternity and maternity, (4) developments in assisted reproductive technologies (ARTs) that are rapidly outdistancing existing laws for determining the parentage of children born as a result of ARTs.

As Justice O'Connor noted in *Troxel v. Granville,* "[t]he demographic changes of the past century make it difficult to speak of an average American family. The composition of families varies greatly from household to household. While many children may have two married parents and grandparents who visit regularly, many other children are raised in single-parent households" ((2001) 530 U.S. 57, 63–64). Although most single-parent households are headed by mothers, unwed fathers head a small but increasing percentage of these households and many others are involved in the care and support of their out-of-wedlock children (Sara McLanahan et al., "Fragile Families, Welfare Reform, and Marriage" (November 2001), available at www.brookings.edu/dybdocroot/wrb/publications/pb/pb10.pdf).

In 2000, NCCUSL proposed a new UPA—subsequently revised in 2002—that purports to address these recent developments and, especially, to facilitate the collection of child support for nonmarital children and the determination of parentage for children born as a result of ARTs. The new UPA reiterates the earlier Act's fundamental commitment to equal treatment of all children: "A child born to parents who are not married to each other has the same rights under the law as a child born to parents who are married to each other," S. 202. By eliminating the ambiguous term "natural parent" from its rules for establishing a legal "parent-child relationship," the new UPA encourages courts to focus, instead, on the precise relationship—genetic, biological, functional, adoptive—between a woman and a child or a man and a child.

The revised UPA of 2002 comes closer than any previous version to applying the same rules and presumptions for establishing legal parentage to nonmarital as well as marital children. For example, the Act fulfills federal mandates by providing a simple procedure for the voluntary acknowledgment of paternity for out-of-wedlock children. It recognizes that an ongoing relationship of care and economic support between a man or a woman and a child can be the basis for assigning parental responsibility in both nonmarital and marital contexts. It allows courts to use estoppel principles to prevent presumed marital and nonmarital parents from denying their parental status in cases where children would be seriously harmed by the denial of a legal relationship to a parental caregiver.

For children born as a result of ARTs, the UPA of 2002 precludes all "donors" of genetic materials who do not intend to parent from claiming parental rights, while allowing the recipients of donated sperm, ova, or embryos—whether single women or married or unmarried couples—to establish their parental status on the basis of their written intentions and consent to parent. Moreover, the Act's provisions "relating to determination of paternity apply to determinations of maternity," S. 106, thus enabling, albeit not requiring, courts to determine in an appropriate case that a child has two legal mothers [see also ALI Principles S. 2.03, included in this reader].

In sum, the UPA of 2002 still relies on a combination of biogenetic and marital ties to establish parentage in most cases, but also includes provisions that recognize the situations in which a biogenetic or marital connection is neither necessary nor sufficient to establish a legal parental relationship to a child.

It remains to be seen whether many states will enact the new UPA in the first decades of the twenty-first century. While paving the way for more flexible and sensible determinations of parentage for nonmarital as well as marital children, the Act will nonetheless disappoint those who want statutes to address some other complex issues, especially those raised by ARTs. Perhaps to avoid legislative battles about issues other than parentage, the drafters of the new UPA defer "to other statutes or to the common law" issues such as ownership and disposition of genetic material, insurance coverage, and procedures for collecting, preserving, and disclosing pertinent information about gamete donors to the children resulting from ARTs (see Comment to UPA S. 702 (2002)). [As indicated by many of the contributors to this reader,] however, many of us who believe adoptees should be allowed to learn more about their biogenetic origins are equally concerned about enacting laws that will provide similar information to the children resulting from ARTs.

65

Principles of the Law of Family Dissolution

American Law Institute (ALI)

Section 2.03

Definitions

For purposes of this Chapter, the following definitions apply.

(1) Unless otherwise specified, a parent is either a legal parent, a parent by estoppel or a de facto parent.

   (b) A parent by estoppel is an individual who, though not a legal parent,

     (i) is obligated to pay child support under Chapter 3 [of ALI Principles]; or

     (ii) lived with the child for at least two years and

       (A) over that period had a reasonable good faith belief that he was the child's biological father, based on marriage to the mother or on the actions or representations of the mother, and fully accepted parental responsibilities consistent with that belief, and

       (B) if some time thereafter that belief no longer existed, continued to make reasonable, good faith efforts to accept responsibilities as the child's father; or

     (iii) lived with the child since the child's birth, holding out and accepting full and permanent responsibilities as a parent, as part of a prior co-parenting agreement with the child's legal parent (or, if there are two legal parents, both parents) to raise a child together each with full parental rights and responsibilities, when the court finds that recognition as a parent is in the child's best interests; or

     (iv) lived with the child for at least two years, holding out and accepting full and permanent responsibilities as a parent, pursuant to an agreement with the child's parent (or, if there are two legal parents, both parents), when the court finds that recognition as a parent is in the child's best interests. . . .

Comment: . . . This Chapter uses the term "legal parent" to refer to any individual recognized as a parent under other state law. Individuals defined as parents under state law ordinarily include biological parents, whether or not they are or ever have been married to each other, and adoptive parents. . . .

... An individual may also be a parent by estoppel on the basis of a co-parenting agreement with the child's legal parent, or parents, when that individual has lived with the child since the child was born, holding himself or herself out as the child's parent and accepting the responsibilities thereof.

§ 2.03(1)(b)(iii). This Paragraph combines as criteria the performance of parental functions with an agreement to act as such, fully and permanently. . . .

. . . Paragraph (1)(b)(iii) contemplates the situation of two cohabiting adults who undertake to raise a child together, with equal rights and responsibilities as parents. Although adoption is the clearer and thus preferred legal avenue for recognition of such parent-child relationships, adoption is sometimes not possible, especially if one of the adults is still married to another, or if the adults are both women, or both men. Neither the unavailability of adoption, nor the failure to adopt when adoption would have been available, forecloses parent by estoppel status, although the failure to adopt when adoption was available may be relevant to whether an agreement was intended. . . .

. . . A formal, written agreement is not required to create a parent by estoppel status under Paragraph (1)(b)(iii), but the absence of formalities, like the failure to adopt when adoption is available, may affect the factfinder's determination of whether an agreement was made. The factfinder must determine whether, given the circumstances, the actions of the individual seeking status as parent and those of the legal parent or parents are sufficiently clear and unambiguous to indicate that a parent status was understood by all of them. The factfinder's determination should not turn upon whether the parties are of the same sex or different sexes, or even whether the parties are married, since these factors do not bear on whether a family relationship is intended. As a practical matter, however, the less traditional the arrangement, the greater assistance a formal agreement may be in clarifying the parties' intentions.

Paragraph (1)(b)(iii) requires the agreement of each of the child's legal parents. When the child has only one legal parent, only that parent's agreement is required. When state law recognizes more than one legal parent, each parent must agree. Agreement may be implied, and whether it is implied will depend on the particular context.

An individual may not be a parent by estoppel under this Paragraph if the agreement provides for less than a full assumption of the responsibilities as a parent. An agreement for visitation only, or one that specifically excludes obligations for financial support or for caretaking responsibility, does not serve as the basis for recognition as a parent by estoppel. However, in appropriate circumstances, a contract in which a legal parent agrees to give up some parental rights and obligations but reserve others may have some effect. . . . Parent by estoppel status is created under this Paragraph only when the court determines that the status is in the child's best interests. This inquiry should focus primarily on the costs and benefits of participation by another individual, as a parent, in the proceedings.

66

From Coitus to Commerce
Legal and Social Consequences of Noncoital Reproduction

Joan Heifetz Hollinger

[This excerpt has been modified to take account of legal and social developments since 1985.]

History's most famous infertile couple resorted to a surrogate mother. Many years before Abraham and Sarah were blessed with Isaac, the natural son of their old age, the "barren" Sarah had said to her frustrated husband: Abraham, take my slave girl Hagar and through her, I, Sarah, will have a family with you (Genesis, 16–17). Then, as now, it was not so simple. Shortly after the surrogate mother Hagar became pregnant (through coital means, of course), she began to assert her superiority over Sarah. Is it possible to anticipate, and hence, mitigate the personal and psychological rivalry between a genetic and gestational mother and an intended rearing mother? The understanding that Sarah had reached with Abraham and Hagar could not be sustained. Sarah mistreated Hagar and Ishmael, the son Hagar bore for Abraham, and eventually drove them into the wilderness. Ishmael took with him a formidable curse: "He shall be a man like the wild ass . . . at odds with all his kinsmen," the Angel of the Lord told his mother. (Id.) Abraham's name and property would descend exclusively through the biological offspring of himself and his wife Sarah and not through Ishmael, his bastard son. Hagar's compensation was God's assurance that Ishmael, although cut off from Abraham's lineage, would become the father of a separate nation.

The Biblical cast of characters found surrogacy a problematic course, even with the benefit of the Lord's guidance. Today's participants in the various scenarios for "assisting" human reproduction and creating new family relationships face their share of problems too, but with what guidance? Our society is uncertain about how to respond to the legal, ethical, and psychosocial consequences of artificial insemination, in vitro fertilization, embryo storage and transfer, and hired baby-bearers. . . .

There is an urgent need for . . . a legal framework within which contemporary efforts to produce or procure children can take place. . . . I propose a framework based on a principle of "supportive neutrality." . . . The federal and state governments should facilitate the procreative efforts of childless couples, including efforts to become adoptive parents, and should remain neutral among couples making different choices. This neutrality calls for a presumptive deference to voluntary private agreements concerning parentage and a reluctance to dictate their terms in the absence of any showing of specific harms to children's well-being.

Parties to Surrogacy Contracts

Supporting the reasonable expectations of the participants in noncoital reproduction presents greater difficulties for surrogacy arrangements than for in vitro fertilization, embryo transfers, or assisted insemination (IVF, ET, or AI). As illustrated by the experiences of the biblical Hagar, Sarah, and Abraham, the interests of the uterine hostess are potentially at odds with the interests of the intended father and mother. If the contract is fully performed, the childless couple's interests are served by their receipt of a child to raise and the gestator's interests are served by her receipt of the payments agreed upon and, presumably, by the altruistic feelings she experiences upon delivering the child to the father and his wife.

What of the feelings of loss and sorrow that may temper the altruistic rush? . . . We do not know what will be the long term experience of surrogate gestators who deliberately bear a child for others to raise. . . . What about the effect on the gestator's husband as he watches her bear a child for another man? What about her other children, who may wonder whether they, too, will be pawned off to another set of parents? Although the payments are intended, in part, to compensate the surrogate for the emotional as well as the physical consequences of her pregnancy, she may find that no matter how firm her resolve had been when she originally agreed to be a uterine hostess, she is reluctant to relinquish her baby at birth.

Specifying the Interests of the Parties

Can the principle of supportive neutrality guide private intermediaries or state courts and legislatures in efforts to protect the interests of all parties to surrogacy agreements? There may be an unavoidable tilt toward according greater protection to the interests of one party rather than to those of another. Consider, for example, what is at stake in a decision about whether the surrogate and the intended parents ought to know each other's identity. Many intermediaries who have negotiated surrogacy contracts believe that fewer difficulties will arise during the course of performance if all the parties meet and maintain contact with each other. . . .

This example suggests how difficult it is to determine which approach is "neutral"—that is, supportive of the integrity of the agreement without being unduly harmful to any of the parties. The answer depends upon which interests the law considers most essential to protect and upon what the law defines as "harm" to those interests. If the primary concern is to ensure the outcome that the intended parents end up with a baby, then this interest may be harmed unless the couple has some relationship with the uterine hostess during her pregnancy. If the primary concern is to preserve the integrity of the process by ensuring that the surrogate's consent to the original insemination and to the subsequent relinquishment is voluntary, then this interest may be harmed unless anonymity is maintained. Because, however, anonymity may in fact serve both the outcome interest and the process interest, or may in fact serve neither interest, we are unable to define it as a "harm" or as a "benefit." It is probably best for the law not to formulate any presumption with regard to anonymity, but to defer to the approach that makes the parties feel most comfortable.

The Indeterminacy of Prevailing Contract and Family Law Principles

An even more difficult test for the principle of supportive neutrality arises when the law must take sides, as, for example, when the surrogate gestator refuses to turn the child over to the father and his wife. This situation does not involve a potential clash between an outcome concern and a process concern, but a clash between two outcomes, one initially agreed upon and the other developing as a consequence of the surrogate's experience bearing the child. . . . Since a decision either way will also determine who is to raise the child, how are the child's interests to be weighed as against those of the competing adults? Prevailing contract and family law principles probably cannot yield predictable results in the dual effort to resolve the dispute between the adults and to protect the interests of the child. . . .

Consider the numerous ways in which the intended parents' breach of contract claim against the surrogate might be resolved. The court might initially declare the contract unenforceable as a violation of state laws against baby-selling. [See, e.g., *In re Baby M,* 537 A.2d 1227 (N.J. 1988).] In this event, the infant would remain with the surrogate, but the genetic father would be unable to sue for damages or other relief, and the participants in the surrogacy arrangement, including the lawyers, might be subject to criminal penalties. If the court did not find the contract unenforceable, it might award the father and his wife restitution of any sums already paid to the surrogate and reimbursement of their reasonable reliance expenses. But these would-be parents want their expectancy interest: specific enforcement of the surrogate's promises to relinquish her parental rights to the father, and to consent to the child's adoption by the father's wife. The court might decline this prayer for relief, invoking the law's traditional reluctance to order specific enforcement of personal service contracts, and, instead, might permit the surrogate to retain the child, while ordering her to pay damages to the couple to compensate for the loss of their expected child. The court might also relieve the father of any obligation to support the child, especially if the surrogate's husband were willing to assume that obligation. . . . If the court felt that money could not adequately compensate the couple for the emotional damage occasioned by the loss of "their" child, it could order the surrogate to relinquish the child in exchange for the payments originally promised her.

Because the dispute involves the fate of a child who was not a party to the contract, the court might find it inappropriate to limit its decision to the issues posed by breach of a purely commercial transaction. Assessment of the claim for specific relief would be tempered by the concern for the child's welfare. With this in mind, the couple might recast their request in family law terms, as a claim for the permanent custody of the child based on the contractual agreement to give custody to the couple and on the best interests of the child (BIC). Specific enforcement of custody agreements is not uncommon, but courts subject the request to a review under the custody standards that would operate in a particular jurisdiction in the absence of such an agreement. . . .

Under the BIC, neither the genetic mother nor the genetic father is obviously "best" as a potential nurturing parent. If the court felt that the mother's "moral fitness" was tainted by her refusal to perform the contract, the BIC standard might help the couple. Even then, the surrogate could respond by noting first, that her conduct in commercial transactions is not relevant to her fitness as a parent, and second, that she broke the contract for the sake of the infant, in order to assure the infant an opportunity to be raised by a mother in whom the genetic, gestational and rearing roles were united. If the court applied a tender years or primary caretaker presumption, the surrogate would prevail. The surrogate might similarly have an edge if the Goldstein, Freud, and Solnit (GFS) standards were invoked, because her experience as childbearer may establish her as the only contestant with at least an incipient psychological parenting relationship with the child. . . .

Some courts may have to decide whether to enforce the surrogate's promise to consent to the child's adoption by the father's wife. Here, the solicitude that courts and legislatures have shown to the right of birth mothers to withhold or revoke their consent to adoption would have to be balanced against the claims of the intended social parents that a surrogacy agreement is not a standard adoption transaction because the conception and birth of the child would not have occurred "but for" the surrogacy agreement and it is "reasonable" to enforce the expectations of the intended parents who "commissioned" the creation of the child. This argument may evoke greater judicial support in cases where the intended parents are also the genetic parents and the surrogate is simply a gestational hostess. [See, e.g., *Johnson v. Calvert*, 851 P.2d 776 (Ca. 1993).] . . .

Parents who choose to divorce have considerable control over the consequences of that decision for their children as well as for themselves. This is because the law . . . generally supports and enforces their private agreements. Parties who choose to enter surrogacy agreements have considerably less control over the consequences of their decision. The law is not only indeterminate when a dispute arises . . . it is also indeterminate when the parties agree. Surely the law owes at least as much protection to the private understandings of those who hope to create families as to those who are breaking them apart. . . .

Justifying a Presumption for Enforcing Surrogacy Contracts

To avoid these harms, contract and family law principles should be combined into a statutory presumption in favor of enforcing the terms of the private surrogacy contract, including the provisions governing the relinquishment of the child to the intended parents. . . . Any party who challenged the agreement would have to show by clear and convincing evidence either that the agreement was not freely and knowingly entered into, or that full and specific enforcement would be detrimental to the child. The presumption would thus favor the intended parents' interests in the event of a breach by the surrogate, and the surrogate's interests in the event of a breach by the genetic father.

A presumption in favor of enforcement is warranted for a number of reasons. First, because there is no way to anticipate whether a child will be better off being raised by his birth mother and her husband or by his genetic father and his wife, the child is not harmed by a presumptive allocation to the father in accord with the basic intention of the surrogacy contract. Second, placing a burden on those who would challenge the enforcement of rights and responsibilities allocated voluntarily, rather than on those who desire such enforcement, conforms with our general social, if not full constitutional, support for privately determined reproductive choices. Third, this presumption would make it considerably easier than it now is for the parties to a surrogacy arrangement that goes smoothly to obtain legal and public validation of their private conduct. Those who understand what they are doing, and do it without harming either each other or their offspring, should not have to go to court to fight for a sympathetic interpretation of their activities. Fourth, the existence of this presumption would encourage people to reflect carefully upon the consequences of a surrogacy contract before entering into one, and discourage them from initiating litigation to set aside such agreements once performance has begun. Given the special importance of avoiding the harms to children occasioned by protracted custody litigation, there is much to be said for a presumption designed to narrow the boundaries within which legal indeterminacy exists. . . .

Legislation designed to facilitate the enforcement of surrogacy contracts must, of course, ensure that both the negotiation and the performance of the contract conform to at least minimal standards of fairness. The law should require that the agreement be in writing, that the surrogate and the intended parents offer evidence of the knowing and voluntary nature of their consent, such as being represented by separate counsel, and that any party be permitted to cancel the agreement without penalty prior to the insemination of the gestational hostess.

Legislation should also provide that specific terms be included in gestational agreements to enhance the likelihood that the parties will end up with the outcome they desire so long as it is consistent with the best interests of the child. See, e.g., the provisions for judicial review and approval of gestational agreements in the proposed new Uniform Parentage Act of 2002. . . .

Minimizing Harm, Especially to the Children

What about the children who are the end product of assisted reproductive technologies? To be consistent with the principle of supportive neutrality, the state's policies for facilitating procreative choice must yield at some point to the newborn's interest in avoiding harm. In defining the parameters of the child's interest, three questions need to be addressed. Should special attention be afforded the children born through assisted reproduction? Can the kinds of harms that might befall these children be anticipated? What might be done to minimize the likelihood that these harms will occur?

No one stands at the bedside of the couple who are attempting to conceive a child through coital means to ask whether they have taken appropriate steps to protect their offspring against physical or emotional harms. Why should the children produced by noncoital means receive special treatment? With other children, we defer to parental autonomy until some actual danger looms against which the parents are by themselves unable to shield their children, or for which the parents themselves are responsible. Why should it be different here? Some kind of protection is warranted in order to identify as soon as possible the intended parents as the legal parents of children resulting from assisted reproduction. . . . Finally, these children may be at risk of certain psychosocial harms arising from their lack of information concerning their genetic heritage and family history. These harms might actually be averted or mitigated by establishing procedures to enable the children resulting from assisted reproduction to learn more about the backgrounds and identities of the genetic donors and gestational carriers who facilitated their conception and birth. . . .

A Different Kind of Harm to Children

The offspring of noncoital reproduction are not the only children who are placed at risk by the striving of men and women for procreative autonomy. There remains an altogether different category of potential harm: the risk of indifference to the hundreds of thousands of children, indeed, to the millions of children in this and other countries, who are already born but in desperate need of parents to raise them. Those who pursue some form of assisted reproduction do so in part because of the belief that they have no reasonable alternatives for obtaining a healthy child. They may believe, for example, that there are not enough infants available for adoption. While it is certainly true that there are fewer healthy white infants being placed for adoption than half a century ago, it is by no means true that a supply of adoptable children is generally lacking. . . .

In addition to the many adults eager for children to raise, there are, then, many children who need parents. What is needed is a sustained public commitment to bringing the two together. Despite recent changes in federal child welfare laws, including ASFA and MEPA, and the extension of family leave and tax benefits to adoptive families, many more legislative, financial, and other incentives are needed to overcome our longstanding societal indifference to the needs of parentless children. Without such a commitment, the worlds of adoption and of noncoital reproduction will grow farther and farther apart, and those who resort to the laboratory to conceive a child will be symbolically, if not actually, diminishing the role of adoption in our society. . . .

In our search for ways to reap the benefits and to resolve the problems raised by the new reproductive technologies, a certain skepticism about "hypergenetic" activity is in order. We would do well to remember the power of society and culture to transfer and to transform what we are from one generation to the next. Control of our genes does not, after all, provide us with very much control over the kinds of people who will carry these genes. Genes are of course relevant, but we achieve our most intimate and abiding identities as the children of the parents who raise us. As we enlist the support of the law in behalf of procreative autonomy, we should not forget that the reproduction of self that so many hope to achieve through their children is more evident in the long term relationships of rearing and nurturance than in the single act of genetic procreation.

67

Law Making for Baby Making
An Interpretive Approach to the Determination of Legal Parentage

Marsha Garrison

Current law offers little guidance on many, if not most, of the issues arising from technological conception. The legal parentage of children born through [artificial insemination (AI) and in vitro fertilization (IVF)] is often unclear, and laws governing the use of AI and IVF are largely nonexistent.

Legislatures have been slow to respond to technological conception for a variety of reasons. One is simply the speed with which the new methods of baby making have advanced. Another is the rapid shift in parenting norms that has accompanied introduction of the new technologies; while only a couple of decades ago childbirth was sought almost exclusively by married couples in their prime childbearing years, many applicants for access to the new technologies are now single, and some are postmenopausal. Nor do these new applicants necessarily wish to establish traditional family forms. Some want their children to have only one legal parent; some want their children to have no father but two mothers; some want to establish "traditional" parental relationships by conceiving with sperm from a deceased partner. The novelty and diversity of cases has inhibited the development of consensus on the best regulatory approach. . . .

. . . Existing policy analyses suffer from two large—in my view, fatal—deficiencies. First, in developing a regulatory framework, analysts have typically employed a "top-down" approach, deriving rules to govern the various issues posed by technological conception from one or another global principle: contract enforcement, reproductive autonomy, and an "anticommodification" ethic have all found proponents. But as the range of principles urged by various commentators suggests, the possibilities are many and there is no obvious reason for the unconverted to choose one over another. . . . Second, existing analyses have focused largely on the novel aspects of technological conception. As a result of this bias, they typically fail to make use of—or justify their departure from—existing legal principles. The result, all too often, is proposals that would create two inconsistent legal regimes, one for technological conception and another for sexual conception. Because inconsistent legal standards can easily produce inconsistent results, such an approach should, at the very least, be justified. But advocates of the various top-down approaches have generally failed to do so; indeed, they have often ignored the current legal regime altogether. . . .

. . . I advocate an "interpretive" approach to the law of technological conception. In contrast to the top-down methodology, this approach seeks norms in society's actual practices and beliefs. The rule-making strategy I develop thus relies heavily on the law governing sexual conception and the implicit assumptions about parentage and family on which that law is based. . . .

The interpretive approach I advocate is not novel. It is consistent with the ideal of public reason on which democratic society is based. It reflects the widely accepted principle that like cases should receive like treatment. It embodies the notion, pervasive within our legal system, that "the very concept of the rule of law" demands "continuity over time" and "respect for precedent." The common law method employed by Anglo-American courts for generations is, of course, another application of the interpretive perspective. . . .

Applying Family Law to Technological Conception

Broad Themes and Specific Principles

Contemporary parentage law offers two general themes to guide policymaking in the area of technological conception: children's interests come first and two-parent care is generally preferable to that of one parent alone. Parentage law also offers some concrete rules and principles to guide the policymaker.

First, biological relationship should be neither a necessary nor a sufficient condition for obtaining and retaining parental status: unmarried fathers who fail to act like parents can lose their parental rights; committed functional parents may displace uncommitted biological parents; and a stepfather may obtain parental rights (and trump the rights of a committed unmarried father) based on his socially preferred marital relationship with the child's mother.

Second, outside the context of marriage, parental rights should presumptively be assigned to biological parents: in no case other than that of an unmarried father does another claimant have standing to block a biological parent's assertion of parental status; and, if he promptly asserts his rights, even an unmarried father can trump the claims of a prospective adoptive parent able to offer the child greater advantages.

Third, no contracts concerning parental rights and obligations should be per se enforceable: all such contracts, whether pre-marital, post-marital, pre-conception, or post-conception, are now voidable based on the child's interests. In the adoption context—the only one in which the issue has been tested—waivers of parental rights are unenforceable, even without a showing of the child's interests, if they fail to comply with state standards.

Fourth, within limits, the state may prefer "desirable" to "undesirable" parental relationships: a committed functional parent may, in some instances, override the claims of an uncommitted biological parent; if the mother is married and plans to raise the child herself in the marital household, even a committed father might be denied his parental status in the face of a claim by her husband. Similarly, although an unmarried mother alone cannot block her child's father from asserting his parental status even if he has long failed to "act as a father" to his child, adoptive parents may deprive the father of parental rights if they can make the same showing.

Although the broad themes and specific principles that can be gleaned from contemporary family law will not resolve every question related to the parentage of technologically conceived children, they can easily resolve some of them. . . .

Surrogacy

In a case like Baby M, the "surrogate" mother is in fact no surrogate at all: she is the child's genetic and gestational parent. An agreement under which the "surrogate" transfers her interest in the child to another is thus nothing more than an adoption contract. As such, its legality should be dependent on the parties' compliance with state adoption requirements, including babyselling prohibitions and restrictions on prenatal rights transfer. States should clarify the mother's parental status, specifying that the surrogate is the child's legal mother unless and until she transfers her parental rights pursuant to state adoption law. The child's legal father should be determined under the rules applicable to sexual conception. Thus, if the surrogate mother is unmarried or state law permits an unmarried putative father to challenge the paternity of the mother's husband, the sperm donor should be able to establish his parental rights; but if the mother is married and state paternity law denies a putative father standing to challenge her husband's paternity, he should not.

A Case Based on Available Research Findings

Technologically conceived children have the same informational needs as adopted children. Both groups require information on genetically-based health risks and, as adults, may want to learn more about their biological parents or even establish contact with them. Because current adoption laws recognize the informational needs of adopted children, the informational needs of technologically conceived children should be recognized to the same extent. . . . As the Canadian Royal Commission succinctly put it: ". . . The states are beginning to move in this direction. . . ." . . .

Because the interests of children and their parents do not significantly differ depending on whether a child was adopted or technologically conceived, the argument against extending adoption registries to technologically conceived children relies primarily on the fear that loss of guaranteed donor anonymity would seriously reduce the number of AI and IVF donors. Donor decision making is not a significant issue in the adoption context because parents who relinquish children for adoption almost invariably do so because of an unplanned birth and inability to provide adequately for the baby themselves. In the case of sperm and egg donation, however, potential loss of anonymity might conceivably have a significant impact on donor decision making.

The available evidence on this point cannot be conclusively interpreted—surveys have not assessed donor attitudes in a standard manner and most rely on small samples at a single donation site—but virtually all researchers have reported that half or more of respondent donors would be willing to provide identifying information to their children at the age of majority.

68

Considerations against Donor Anonymity in Collaborative Procreation

Mary Lyndon Shanley

The practices through which we regulate the transfer of human gametes (eggs and sperm) reflect and shape our understanding of our relationship to our genetic material. I examine one such practice, anonymous transfer of sperm or eggs. While gamete transfer is like adoption in making it possible to create a family in which a parent and child are not genetically related, gamete transfer is also different from adoption. For one thing, a child conceived through gamete transfer usually has a genetic relationship with one parent (this is true for heterosexual couples, same-sex couples, and single mothers), and is carried throughout pregnancy by the woman who will be his or her mother (except when the egg donor also acts as a surrogate gestator). In addition, only genetic material, not an actual child, is transferred between adults. The genetic relation and the fact that one parent bears and gives birth to the child may make unsealed records seem less relevant in gamete donation than in adoption. I believe, however, that public policy should eliminate anonymous gamete donation. The ability of the person created with third-party genetic material to know the identity of his or her progenitors would be more attentive to the child's psychological needs and experience, and would reflect a less atomistic and more relational concept of both individuals and society than does anonymous donation.

Practices surrounding gamete transfer bear the marks of the original procedures and social context in which they developed. Initially, only sperm could be transferred, a relatively simple procedure that doctors began recommending in the 1940s. When egg transfer became possible in 1978, sperm transfer was the model (though the far more complicated procedure and scarcity of providers led to pressure to pay egg providers more).

A variety of concerns made anonymity seem appropriate when married heterosexual couples had a child using donor insemination (DI). The stigma attached to the inability to sire children due to the association of manliness with potency made many couples anxious to keep their use of DI secret. Some legal and religious authorities suggested that sperm transfer might constitute an act of adultery. Lawyers were unsure about whether the provider had any parental rights or responsibilities with respect to the child. Many psychologists counseled parents not to tell their children that they were conceived with donated sperm because the children might feel resentment if they learned that they were "different" from other children.

From the perspective of doctors and patients alike, creation of an "as if" family, one in which the children to all appearances were the biological offspring of the husband and wife, was the happy ending of infertility treatment. Both the practice of "matching" the provider and the recipient's husband in physical appearance, and anonymity, supported this goal.

With anonymity the accepted norm in adoption, it seemed all the more the case that gamete transfer, before a child existed, should be anonymous. But in the 1980s the movement towards unsealed records and open adoption, along with the greater social visibility of donor insemination as single women and lesbians began having children without a male sexual partner made some people ask whether anonymity in gamete transfer should continue.

Abolishing anonymity signifies that the child—although unambiguously and irrevocably the child of the recipients, the social parents—has come into being not only because of the parents' desire and choice, but also because of the actions of another person. The requirement to make a provider's identity available upon the request of the offspring would constitute social recognition of the fact that children come into the world through the actions of specific persons, who can now include both "intentional" parents (those who plan their conception) and genetic providers.

From the perspective of the child, and the person that child will become, knowledge of how and from whom one came to be is now being seen as part of the process of identity formation. Upon reaching the age of majority, someone created with transferred genetic material should have the right to learn, although not be compelled to learn, the identity of the provider, not simply medical facts or DNA profile. The right to learn the identity of one's genetic forebear stems from some people's desire to be able to connect themselves to human history concretely as embodied beings, not only abstractly as rational beings or as members of large social (national, ethnic, religious) groups.[1]

It is important that society as a whole affirm the right to know one's origins. Discussions of the ethics of gamete transfer have overwhelmingly centered on the choices and interests of recipients, providers, and physicians; only rarely is mention made of the person-to-be. But that person must be central to moral reasoning about procreative practices.

Some people assert that guaranteeing access to information concerning the identity of the gamete provider reflects a socially created need that comes from a patriarchal focus on genetic lineage, and others assert that it reflects a kind of genetic essentialism that downplays the importance of experience and social factors in the formation of any person. But making donor identity accessible need not promote either patriarchalism or genetic essentialism. Public policy can make sure that genes do not "trump" social identity, and that a genetic relationship will lead to legal parenthood only when the genetic parent assumes responsibility for the child's welfare.[2]

To argue that the person created by gamete transfer has a right to learn the progenitor's identity upon reaching age eighteen or twenty-one implies that the gamete provider must be prepared to have his or her identity revealed. The provider would have no legal responsibility to the child/adult beyond that; there is no obligation to meet or to provide financial support. Another implication may be that clinics should prohibit multiple donations (say, no more than three). . . . Gamete donation differs in kind and significance from blood donation to provider and recipient alike—a human being may come into existence as a result of the transfer. It seems inappropriate to distance ourselves from our gametes and the procreative potential of our body in the same way we distance ourselves from our blood or organs that can sustain, but not generate a new, life.

My suggestion that we could change the practices surrounding gamete transfer is not ivory tower imagining. Some private clinics and public agencies are already moving away from anonymous gamete transfer, as developments in the Netherlands, Sweden, the United Kingdom, Canada, and Germany illustrate.

In the United States some sperm banks give a provider the option of agreeing to the release of his name, and give recipients the option of using such a provider. Abolishing anonymity would affect how both providers and others understand the meaning of the practice of gamete transfer. New reproductive technologies introduce choice and contingency into what was long thought to be inevitable. Indeed, the ability to create families using gamete transfer requires us to frame an ethic of interpersonal and intergenerational responsibility under conditions of unprecedented choice.

Elimination of anonymous donation would lead provider and recipient alike, and indeed society as a whole, to reflect on human agency and responsibility entailed by collaborative procreation. It is possible to change both our thinking about and the policies governing the transfer of human gametes to be used in procreation, and we should frame our practices to acknowledge rather than obscure the collaborative acts necessary to bring a new life into being.

NOTES

1. Patricia Williams speaks of the significance of transgenerational history in "On Being the Object of Property," *The Rooster's Egg* (Cambridge: Harvard University Press, 1995).

2. I make an extended argument for this principle in *Making Babies, Making Families: What Matters Most in an Age of Reproductive Technologies, Surrogacy, Adoption, and Same-Sex and Unwed Parents* (Boston: Beacon Press, 2001).

69

The Jurisprudence of Genetics

Rochelle Cooper Dreyfuss and Dorothy Nelkin

I. Introduction

. . . Genetics has profoundly altered the perception of personhood within our culture. This change has, in turn, challenged many of the core principles on which current norms are based and has compelled lawmakers to reconsider the legal rules that mediate the relationships among persons and between individuals and the broader community. Thus, we see this research as influencing not only the factual answers available to the decision making process, but also the questions that are framed and the terms that are used in the debate. . . .

II. Genetic Essentialism

Anthropological studies demonstrate that personhood is a socially-defined concept. That is, the understanding of what it means to be a person and what rights are associated with personhood varies from culture to culture and, within a culture, changes over time according to external circumstances. . . .

Modern science provides support for defining personhood biologically, according to genetic characteristics. Geneticists are uncovering the inherited qualities that influence the course of life from childhood to old age. By scanning the sequences of DNA that form the basis of our inheritance, geneticists are detecting the markers that indicate predisposition to a growing number of hereditary diseases. As more markers are identified, scientists anticipate that tests will be available to indicate predisposition not only to single-gene disorders, such as Huntington's disease, cystic fibrosis, and hemophilia, but also to complex conditions and behaviors, facilitating prediction of mental illness, Alzheimer's disease, hyperactivity, heart disease, certain forms of cancer, and susceptibility to alcoholism, addiction, and even violence. Such tests yield only probabilistic information, for the relationship between predisposition and actual expression generally remains unknown. . . .

The interest in genetic identity includes a preoccupation with biological determinism. Among the traits attributed to genetics are mental illness, homosexuality, aggressive personality, dangerousness, job and educational success, exhibitionism, the tendency to commit arson, stress, risk-taking, shyness, social potency, traditionalism, and even zest for life. These complex conditions frequently are described as directly inherited, as if they were single-gene disorders. . . .

. . . With the availability of new reproductive technologies, choosing a baby can become like catalog shopping. Fertility clinics keep computer profiles of donors correlated with a list of desirable traits. Moreover, the availability of prenatal tests has encouraged new standards of perfection. The idea that genes have power and will determine the behavior and health of one's offspring has spurred a search for "the perfect baby—every parent's dream."

Observing these trends, we define a concept called "genetic essentialism." Genetic essentialism posits that personal traits are predictable and permanent, determined at conception, "hard-wired" into the human constitution. If comprehensively known and understood these inherent qualities would largely explain past performance and could predict future behavior. Standing in sharp contrast with the relational definitions of personhood observed in some societies, this ideology minimizes the importance of social context. By stressing the importance of immutable biological qualities, genetic essentialism also differs from traditions centered on the importance of life experiences in determining behavior.

III. Legal Ramifications

. . . If personal identity is no longer understood in relational terms, then doctrines dealing with community—relationships among people—must be reconsidered. Because genetic essentialism is a deterministic concept, it negates assumptions about free will, thereby putting into question much of the law concerning responsibility, intent, condemnation, and punishment. Because of the limitations that genetic understanding places on human potential, essentialism challenges the principle that equivalent opportunities should be extended to all. . . .

When the family was regarded as the primary setting for care, education, and emotional support, stability was one of the law's central goals; familial relationships were rarely disturbed. . . .

Similar considerations motivated adoption law. The principal concerns were stability, providing the adoptee with a fresh start, and protecting the integrity of ongoing relationships. States created a shield of privacy between the family and society and fostered a legal fiction of natural birth. In a majority of jurisdictions, original birth certificates and adoption records were sealed. Although some of these states permitted disclosures for "good cause"—principally medical or financial necessity—the test was usually stringent. In some states birth parents enjoyed an absolute right to anonymity.

When the person is reconceptualized as a genetic entity and forging genetic relationships becomes a goal, legal protection for these social interests weakens. For example, *Johnson v. Calvert,* a case the press described as "genetics vs. environment," was a dispute over the custody of a child conceived through in vitro fertilization (IVF). . . .

The result in *Johnson* is not remarkable; the significance of the case lies in the basis of the decision. . . .

... [T]he court defined the child as a genetic entity—a packet of genes—on the assumption that shared genes are the crucial basis of human relationships.

The same theme is discernible in other family law materials. Courts may speak of the problems created when long-term social relationships are broken, but the genetic tie increasingly receives emphasis. For example, in *Commonwealth ex rel. Coburn v. Coburn* the court dismissed an ex-husband's petition for visitation when genetic tests revealed that Angie Lee, the child he had nurtured for ten years, was not his biological daughter. Although the decision was reversed on appeal, several of the justices adopted a biological perspective. . . .

Genetic essentialism has also affected other parental relationships. Thus, legal protection generally is not accorded to the tie between a child born to a lesbian mother and her non-gestational partner no matter how long the relationship between the parties has endured. In adoption, the genetic perception of personhood is manifest in the recognition of claims of genealogical bewilderment. Despite the disruption caused in the adoptive family, and without regard to either the biological family's reliance-based interest in confidentiality or the impact on future adoptions, the essentialist view mandates that sealed adoption records be opened. Knowing one's roots is considered a prerequisite to becoming a functional adult.

Is There a Market for Adoptable Children?

70

Market-Inalienability

Margaret Jane Radin

Controversy over what may be bought and sold—for example, blood or babies—pervades our news. Although some scholars have considered whether such things may be traded in markets, they have not focused on the phenomenon of market-inalienability. About fifteen years ago, for example, Richard Titmuss advocated in his book, *The Gift Relationship,* that human blood should not be allocated through the market; others disagreed. More recently, Elisabeth Landes and Richard Posner suggested the possibility of a thriving market in infants, yet most people continue to believe that infants should not be allocated through the market. What I believe is lacking, and wish to supply, is a general theory that can illuminate these debates. Two possibilities for filling this theoretical gap are traditional liberalism and modern economic analysis, but in this Article I shall find them both wanting.

The most familiar context of inalienability is the traditional liberal triad: the rights to life, liberty, and property. To this triad, liberalism juxtaposes the most familiar context of alienability: traditional property rights. Although the right to hold property is considered inalienable in traditional liberalism, property rights themselves are presumed fully alienable, and inalienable property rights are exceptional and problematic.

Economic analysis, growing out of the liberal tradition, tends to view all inalienabilities in the way traditional liberalism views inalienable property rights. When it does this, economic analysis holds fast to one strand of traditional liberalism, but it implicitly rejects—or at least challenges—another: the traditional distinction between inalienable and alienable kinds of rights. In conceiving of all rights as property rights that can (at least theoretically) be alienated in markets, economic analysis has (at least in principle) invited markets to fill the social universe. It has invited us to view all inalienabilities as problematic.

In seeking to develop a theory of market-inalienability, I argue that inalienabilities should not always be conceived of as anomalies, regardless of whether they attach to things traditionally thought of as property. Indeed, I try to show that the characteristic rhetoric of economic analysis is morally wrong when it is put forward as the sole discourse of human life. My general view deviates not only from the traditional conception of the divide between inalienable and alienable kinds of rights, but also from the traditional conception of alienable property. Instead of using the categories of economics or those of traditional liberalism, I think that we should evaluate inalien-abilities in connection with our best current understanding of the concept of human flourishing. . . .

Market-Inalienability and Non-Commodification

Market-inalienability often expresses an aspiration for noncommodification. By mak-ing something nonsalable we proclaim that it should not be conceived of or treated as a commodity. When something is noncommodifiable, market trading is a disallowed form of social organization and allocation. We place that thing beyond supply and de-mand pricing, brokerage and arbitrage, advertising and marketing, stockpiling, specu-lation, and valuation in terms of the opportunity cost of production.

Market-inalienability poses for us more than the binary choice of whether some-thing should be wholly inside or outside the market, completely commodified or completely noncommodified. Some things are completely commodified—deemed suitable for trade in a laissez-faire market. Others are completely noncommodified—removed from the market altogether. But many things can be described as incom-pletely commodified—neither fully commodified nor fully removed from the market. Thus, we may decide that some things should be market-inalienable only to a degree, or only in some aspects.

To appreciate the need to develop a satisfactory analysis of market-inalienability, consider the deeply contested issues of commodification that confront us. Infants and children, fetal gestational services, blood, human organs, sexual services, and services of college athletes are some salient things whose commodification is contested. Our division over whether to place a monetary equivalent on a spouse's professional de-gree or homemaker services in a divorce; or on various kinds of injuries in tort ac-tions, such as loss of consortium, is another form of contest over commodification. Monetization—commodification—of clean air and water is likewise deeply contested. Moreover, debates about some kinds of regulation can be seen as contested incom-plete commodification, with the contest being over whether to allow full commodifi-cation (a laissez-faire market regime) or something less. If we see the debates this way, residential rent control, minimum wage requirements, and other forms of price regu-lation, as well as residential habitability requirements, safety regulation, and other forms of product-quality regulation all become contests over the issue of commodifi-cation.

How are we to determine the extent to which something ought to be noncom-modified, so that we can determine to what extent market-inalienability is justified? Because the question asks about the appropriate relationship of particular things to the market, normative theories about the appropriate social role of the market should be helpful in trying to answer it. We can think of such theories as ordered on a con-tinuum stretching from universal noncommodification (nothing in markets) to uni-versal commodification (everything in markets). On this continuum, Karl Marx's the-ory can symbolize the theoretical pole of universal noncommodification, and Richard

Posner's can be seen as close to the opposite theoretical pole. Distributed along the continuum are theorists we may call pluralists—those who see a normatively appropriate but limited realm for commodification coexisting with one or more nonmarket realms. Pluralists often see one other normative realm besides that of the market, and partition the social world into markets and politics, markets and rights, or markets and families; but pluralists also may envision multiple nonmarket realms. For a pluralist, the crucial question is how to conceive of the permissible scope of the market. An acceptable answer would solve problems of contested commodification. . . .

Evolutionary Pluralism Applied: Problems of Sexuality and Reproductive Capacity

I now offer thoughts on how the analysis that I recommend might be brought to bear on a set of controversial market-inalienabilities. . . . I conclude that market-inalienability is justified for baby-selling and also—provisionally—for surrogacy, but that prostitution should be governed by a regime of incomplete commodification. . . .

. . . I think we should now decriminalize the sale of sexual services in order to protect poor women from the degradation and danger either of the black market or of other occupations that seem to them less desirable. At the same time, in order to check the domino effect, we should prohibit the capitalist entrepreneurship that would operate to create an organized market in sexual services even though this step would pose enforcement difficulties. It would include, for example, banning brokerage (pimping) and recruitment. It might also include banning advertising. . . .

A different analysis is warranted for baby-selling. Like relationships of sexual sharing, parent-child relationships are closely connected with personhood, particularly with personal identity and contextuality. Moreover, poor women caught in the double bind raise the issue of freedom: they may wish to sell a baby on the black market, as they may wish to sell sexual services, perhaps to try to provide adequately for other children or family members. But the double bind is not the only problem of freedom implicated in baby-selling. Under a market regime, prostitutes may be choosing to sell their sexuality, but babies are not choosing for themselves that under current nonideal circumstances they are better off as commodities. If we permit babies to be sold, we commodify not only the mother's (and father's) baby-making capacities—which might be analogous to commodifying sexuality—but we also conceive of the baby itself in market rhetoric. When the baby becomes a commodity, all of its personal attributes—sex, eye color, predicted I.Q., predicted height, and the like—become commodified as well. This is to conceive of potentially all personal attributes in market rhetoric, not merely those of sexuality. Moreover, to conceive of infants in market rhetoric is likewise to conceive of the people they will become in market rhetoric, and to create in those people a commodified self-conception.

Hence, the domino theory has a deep intuitive appeal when we think about the sale of babies. An idealist might suggest, however, that the fact that we do not now value babies in money suggests that we would not do so even if babies were sold. Perhaps babies could be incompletely commodified, valued by the participants to the interaction in a nonmarket way, even though money changed hands. Although this is theoretically possible, it seems too risky in our nonideal world. If a capitalist baby industry were to come into being, with all of its accompanying paraphernalia, how could any of us, even those who did not produce infants for sale, avoid subconsciously measuring the dollar value of our children? How could our children avoid being preoccupied with measuring their own dollar value? This makes our discourse about ourselves (when we are children) and about our children (when we are parents) like our discourse about cars. Seeing commodification of babies as an inevitable and grave injury to personhood appears rather easy. In the worst case, market rhetoric could create a commodified self-conception in everyone, as the result of commodifying every attribute that differentiates us and that other people value in us, and could destroy personhood as we know it.

I suspect that an intuitive grasp of the injury to personhood involved in commodification of human beings is the reason many people lump baby-selling together with slavery. But this intuition can be misleading. Selling a baby, whose personal development requires caretaking, to people who want to act as the caretakers is not the same thing as selling a baby or an adult to people who want to act only as users of her capacities. Moreover, if the reason for our aversion to baby-selling is that we believe it is like slavery, then it is unclear why we do not prohibit baby-giving (release of a child for adoption) on the ground that enslavement is not permitted even without consideration. We might say that respect for persons prohibits slavery but may require adoption in cases in which only adoptive parents will treat the child as a person, or in the manner appropriate to becoming a person. But this answer is still somewhat unsatisfactory. It does not tell us whether parents who are financially and psychologically capable of raising a child in a manner we deem proper nevertheless may give up the child for adoption, for what we would consider less than compelling reasons. If parents are morally entitled to give up a child even if the child could have (in some sense) been raised properly by them, our aversion to slavery does not explain why infants are subject only to market-inalienability. There must be another reason why baby-giving is unobjectionable.

The reason, I think, is that we do not fear relinquishment of children unless it is accompanied by market rhetoric. The objection to market rhetoric may be part of a moral prohibition on market treatment of any babies, regardless of whether nonmonetized treatment of other children would remain possible. To the extent that we condemn baby-selling even in the absence of any domino effect, we are saying that this "good" simply should not exist. Conceiving of any child in market rhetoric wrongs personhood. In addition, we fear, based on our assessment of current social norms, that the market value of babies would be decided in ways injurious to their personhood and to the personhood of those who buy and sell on this basis, exacerbating class, race, and gender divisions. To the extent the objection to baby-selling is not (or is not only) to the very idea of this "good" (marketed children), it stems from a fear that the nonmarket version of human beings themselves will become impossible. Conceiving of children in market rhetoric would foster an inferior conception of human flourishing, one that commodifies every personal attribute that might be valued by people in other people. In spite of the double bind, our aversion to commodi-fication of babies has a basis strong enough to recommend that market-inalienability be maintained. . . .

Conclusion

. . . In attempting to make the hard choices in which both commodification and de-commodification seem harmful—the transition problem of the double bind—we must evaluate each contested commodification in its temporal and social context, and we must learn to see in the commodification issue the same interconnection between rhetoric and reality that we have come to accept between physical reality and our par-adigms of thought.

To the extent that we must not assimilate our conception of personhood to the market, market-inalienabilities are justified. But market-inalienabilities are unjust when they are too harmful to personhood in our nonideal world. . . .

Market-inalienability ultimately rests on our best conception of human flourish-ing, which must evolve as we continue to learn and debate. Likewise, market-inalien-abilities must evolve as we continue to learn and debate; there is no magic formula that will delineate them with utter certainty, or once and for all. In our debate, there is no such thing as two radically different normative discourses reaching the "same" re-sult. The terms of our debate will matter to who we are.

71

The Effect of Transactions Costs on the Market for Babies

Margaret F. Brinig

Introduction

Among the more controversial ideas advanced by prominent United States Circuit Court Judge and law professor Richard Posner is his suggestion that a market in babies would rectify many of the problems of the adoption system. His concept has, to say the least, provoked a tremendous reaction in various segments of American society. His critics proclaimed that sales of children would serve to demean the children and their mothers, relegating them to the status of mere commodities. Unscrupulous but wealthy parents might purchase children solely to abuse them. "Baby-selling" became a code word for the foolish extreme to which its proponents could carry law-and-economics.

The truth is that an adoption market already exists, however distasteful that may seem. As Posner aptly described it, there is already a regulated price for babies. States have set the price so low that the demand for adoptable infants vastly exceeds their supply. Because of the discrepancy between supply and demand, a black market has evolved in which the price is extremely high simply because baby selling is illegal.

Posner suggests that legalization of compensation would benefit most of the players in the adoption market, because the supply of adoptable babies will increase given a legal market price. Adoptive parents will acquire the children they so badly desire. The suffering inherent in giving a child up for adoption will decrease since natural mothers will be compensated for bearing the children. The market will provide incentives for the pregnant women to take better care of themselves so the children will be healthier. Arguably fewer women will terminate unplanned pregnancies by abortion. Finally, the children will go to the parents who value them most.

Perhaps the greatest problem with Posner's market theory remains largely unexplored. Courts, legal theorists, and economists invariably focus discussions about children upon the rights of the related adults. While child custody statutes and decisions begin with a "best interests of the child" standard, they end with choosing the interests of one parent or one set of parents. Sometimes judges and legal academic writers accomplish this sleight-of-hand by presumption. Other times the rationale is more explicit. Frequently the child suffers.

For example, although Posner briefly addresses concerns about abusive adoptive parents and a potential oversupply of older or handicapped children that may result from implementation of his ideas, he concentrates his discussions on the benefits to parents of a market price. Although the adoption market would have many buyers and sellers, it would remain regulated by the agencies screening adoptive parents. These institutions would reduce the chance that parents would acquire children to abuse them. Agencies could also match birth and adoptive parents, reducing search costs for both parties to the transaction.

Although he is keenly aware of the costs of regulation in other contexts, Posner does not spend much time discussing the welfare losses caused by adoption agency regulation. These costs are by no means unique to Posner's adoption market. They also represent part of what makes the current adoption system so frustrating. In the current system, agencies rather than price act to ration the scarce resource of adoptable children among the many potential parents who want them. In Posner's system, price would be the primary mechanism for allocating children, and agencies would serve a licensing function.

Although agencies serve to guard against abuse by adoptive parents, they also increase transactions costs for both sets of parents. Agency investigations are not only expensive and annoying, but they also greatly increase the time required for adoption. Because only the final order of adoption prevents the natural parents from revoking consent, the six-month-minimum waiting period adds uncertainty to the transaction.

The transaction costs added by legislatures to protect natural parents' custodial rights and ensure suitability of adoptive couples hurt more children than they assist. Virtually all couples trying to adopt children are suitable. Because there is no real way to predict what kind of parents most childless couples will make, agencies make both Type I (overinclusion) and Type II (underinclusion) errors. As Posner was quick to note, we have no ex ante checks on parents outside the adoption system.

The reason for the miscalculation leading to agency involvement with adoption relates to the fundamental premise of this paper. As a society, we strongly presume that natural parents are the best custodians for their children. Others, by definition, are not as qualified. Nonparents' motivations are questionable, and third party experts may judge them. The emphasis on parental right to custody is essential to the discussion. Here parents' rights, as opposed to the right of children in general to be raised by the best custodian, are stressed. This principle has led courts and legislatures to second guess the parental consent for adoption.

Birth mothers are not allowed to give binding consent until after children are born. This universal rule seems wise in light of the tremendous and overwhelming bonding between parent and child that occurs at and shortly after childbirth. But even after arrival of the child and a recovery period, courts scrutinize consent to adoption more fervently than virtually any other transaction. Looking at this judicial behavior charitably, natural parents placing children will feel tremendous regret, a loss that Posner's compensation might alleviate at least in part. It is more likely, however, that we allow revocation of this transaction despite unquestionable harm to the promisee adoptive parents, and frequently the child as well. This situation is justified by the inordinate weight accorded parental rights. Although revocation does not happen in a tremendous proportion of cases, the uncertainty it introduces into the transaction is very significant. Uncertainty creates major effects in the adoption market in much the same way that the very small risk of catastrophe dominates the insurance market and many people's thinking about nuclear power.

This paper looks at the transactions costs imposed by parental revocations and their effect on the current adoption market. The focus, therefore, veers away from natural parental rights and moves toward what is in most cases de facto, rather than preemptively, best for children. . . .

III. Rights to Revoke Consent

. . . Although adoption itself is a creature of statute (which, consequently, compels each state to spell out the requirement of parental consent), the conditions for revocation are not always explicit. In these states, the general consent law has been interpreted by judicial decisions. Some state adoption systems treat consent for adoption much like an agreement to any other contract. In these states, once a parent has given valid consent, the transaction becomes irrevocable. . . .

On the spectrum running from child's to natural parents' rights, the next group of states lists short time periods for revocation, running from ten to thirty days after valid consent is given. This gives some time for the natural parent to have a change of heart, but the time period is short enough that neither the child nor the adoptive parents will be greatly injured by revocation. . . .

Another group of states has very strict revocation requirements, but does not make consent irrevocable. These state statutes provide that there can be no revocation except in cases where consent was obtained by fraud, duress or coercion. In such cases, the consent itself is involuntary. The extent to which such states look to the best interests of children in rapid and certain placement depends upon their definition of fraud, duress or coercion. If the states require a standard similar to the commercial contracts definition of fraud, for example, the defrauding conduct would have to induce performance, would have to involve a material fact, and would have to be performed by the other party to the transaction. In adoption cases this is usually a state agency, but in direct placement cases it might be the adoptive parents themselves. This restrictive definition of the conditions in which revocation is possible tends to value children's rights as opposed to those of the natural parents. In fact, those statutes that provide for no revocation except in cases of fraud and coercion have restrictive definitions. . . .

Those states that permit revocation before the final decree lie on the opposite end of the parents' rights spectrum. Since the adoption process may take years, and usually must take at least six months, bonds between the child and adoptive parent are almost certain to form. In such states, a typical case will allow revocation in circumstances that would not suffice for revocation of a commercial contract. . . .

In between the two extremes are a number of states that allow revocation before final placement or within longer time periods following consent. Physical or psychological harm to children (and, at the same time, to adoptive parents) occurs when natural parents are permitted to revoke consent long after it has been given. In addition, there will be other, market-driven effects. Although we join those commentators and judges who have condemned lengthy revocation periods due to the harm done to the parties involved, we concentrate here on another effect of revocation. Adoptive parents have other sources of children. For example, they may resort to the black market, where, if the price is high enough, certainty can be purchased. Further, parents insecure about the stability of adoptions in their own states can look for children from other states or foreign countries. Because they are so eager to raise children, adoptive parents as a group tend to be exceptionally well informed. They will discover placements initiated in other states, and a quasi legal intermediary mechanism flourishes. Finally, although we have no way to quantify this behavior, some parents may be so wary of the market, particularly if they have gone through one unsuccessful placement, that they withdraw altogether.

Alternatively, because of the natural parent's relative market power, she can behave opportunistically, extracting consumer surplus from the adoptive parents. These additional payments might range from concessions by the natural parent to visitation after adoption, or listing in an adoption registry. Where legal, the payments might be more direct, such as greater reimbursement for prebirth expenses or loss of income.

Because there are alternatives to in-state adoptions, we can make several economic predictions about the adoption market as it is affected by the transactions cost of consent revocation. If natural parents find it relatively easy to revoke consent, there should be fewer in-state adoptions because the adoptive parents do not want to accept the increased risk. There should also be more foreign adoptions and more adoptions from out of state. This last consequence is reflected in the ratio of adoptions in-state (as revealed by court data) to the number of children born in the state whose birth certificates are altered after adoption (revealed in data kept by state bureaus of vital statistics). In fact, some states are net importers of adoptees (the numerator) while others export them (denominator exceeds numerator).

Empirical Results: Adoption and Revocation Statutes

. . . Obviously other things beside revocation legislation affect the number of adoptions that occur in states. The number of babies that are available for adoption changes with alternatives to adoption such as abortion or single parenthood. Unmarried women are more inclined to bear children as opposed to abort them if single parenthood becomes socially acceptable and if they receive adequate public assistance. . . .

The conclusion is that the number of unwed births, the revocation statutes, and the median income are the best predictors of the number of adoptions in a state.

V. Conclusion

Assuming that the uncertainty introduced by relaxed revocation statutes influences the number of adoptions, the immediate question for legislators is whether the focus on the rights of natural mothers is appropriate. Once the state guarantees that the birth mother's consent is voluntarily made, a short revocation period will suffice. As long as the emphasis is truly on "the best interests of the child," the exact wording of the statute makes little difference.

Sources

General Court of Massachusetts, An Act to Provide for the Adoption of Children, *Acts and Resolves Passed by the General Court of Massachusetts* (Boston, 1851), chap. 324, pp. 815–16.

Catherine J. Ross, "Society's Children: The Care of Indigent Youngsters in New York City, 1875–1903" (Ph.D. diss., Yale University, 1977). © 1977 by Catherine J. Ross. Excerpt reprinted by permission.

Naomi Cahn, "Perfect Substitutes or the Real Thing?" © 2003 by Naomi Cahn. An expanded version of this article will appear in *Duke Law Journal* (forthcoming). Reprinted by permission.

Julie Berebitsky, *Like Our Very Own: Adoption and the Changing Culture of Motherhood, 1851–1950* (Lawrence: University Press of Kansas, 2000). © 2000 by University Press of Kansas. Excerpt reprinted by permission.

Regina G. Kunzel, *Fallen Women, Problem Girls: Unmarried Mothers and the Professionalization of Social Work, 1890–1945* (New Haven: Yale University Press, 1993). © 1993 by Yale University Press. Excerpt reprinted by permission.

Joan Heifetz Hollinger, "State and Federal Adoption Laws," as adapted by the author, from *Adoption Law and Practice*, ed. Joan Heifetz Hollinger (New York: Matthew Bender, 1988, 2002), chaps. 1, 2, 8. Available through lexis.com. © 1988, 2002 by Matthew Bender & Co., Inc. Excerpt adapted and reprinted by permission. All rights reserved. Also adapted from the author's article "Adoption Law," *Future of Children: Adoption,* vol. 3, no. 1 (1993): 43–61. © 1993 by the David and Lucile Packard Foundation. Excerpt adapted and reprinted by permission.

American Academy of Adoption Attorneys, "Code of Ethics." Excerpt reprinted by permission of the AAAA, www.adoptionattorneys.org.

Child Welfare League of America, *Standards of Excellence for Adoption Services,* rev. ed. (Washington, D.C.: CWLA, 2000). © 2000 by the CWLA. Excerpt reprinted by permission.

In re G.C., 735 A.2d 1226 (Pa. 1999).

Rodriguez v. McLoughlin, 49 F. Supp. 2d 186 (S.D.N.Y. 1999), reversed 214 F.3d 328 (2d Cir. N.Y. 2000), cert. denied 532 U.S. 1051 (2001).

In re Jasmon O., 878 P.2d 1297 (Cal. 1994).

Marsha Garrison, "Parents' Rights vs. Children's Interests: The Case of the Foster Child," 22 *New York University Review of Law and Social Change* 371 (1996). © 1996 by the New York University Review of Law and Social Change and Marsha Garrison. Excerpt reprinted by permission.

Jill Duerr Berrick, "When Children Cannot Remain Home: Foster Family Care and Kinship Care," *Future of Children: Protecting Children from Abuse and Neglect,* vol. 8, no. 1 (1998): 72–87. © 1998 by the David and Lucile Packard Foundation. Excerpt reprinted by permission.

Elizabeth Bartholet, "Taking Adoption Seriously: Radical Revolution or Modest Revisionism?" 28 *Capital University Law Review* 77 (1999). © 1999 by Elizabeth Bartholet. Excerpt reprinted by permission. An expanded version of this article is in Elizabeth Bartholet, *Nobody's Children: Abuse and Neglect, Foster Drift, and the Adoption Alternative* (Boston: Beacon Press, 1999).

Gilbert A. Holmes, "The Extended Family System in the Black Community: A Child-Centered Model for Adoption Policy," 68 *Temple Law Review* 1649 (1995). © 1995 by the Temple University of the Commonwealth System of Higher Education and Gilbert A. Holmes. Excerpt reprinted by permission.

Session Laws of Minnesota for 1917, chapter 222. Section 1-7151-7161, amending Chapter 73, *General Statutes,* 1913, relating to adoption and change of name.

E. Wayne Carp, "The Sealed Adoption Records Controversy in Historical Perspective: The Case of the Children's Home Society of Washington, 1895–1988," *Journal of Sociology and Social Welfare,* vol. 19, no. 2 (1992): 27–57. © 1992 by the Journal of Sociology and Social Welfare. Excerpt reprinted by permission. An expanded version of this article is in E. Wayne Carp, *Family Matters: Secrecy and Disclosure in the History of Adoption* (Cambridge: Harvard University Press, 1999).

Ellen Herman, "We Have a Long Way to Go: Attitudes toward Adoption," *Boston Globe,* November 25, 1997. © 1997 by Ellen Herman. Excerpt reprinted by permission.

Elizabeth J. Samuels, "The Idea of Adoption: An Inquiry into the History of Adult Adoptee Access to Birth Records," 53 *Rutgers Law Review* 367 (2001). © 2001 by Rutgers University, The State University of New Jersey and Elizabeth J. Samuels. Excerpt reprinted by permission.

Doe v. Sundquist, 106 F.3d 702 (6th Cir. Tenn. 1997).

National Council for Adoption, "State Legislation and Mutual Consent Registries." Excerpt reprinted by permission of Tom Atwood, President, National Council for Adoption.

Janine Baer et al., "The Basic Bastard." © 2001 by Bastard Nation: The Adoptee Rights Organization. Excerpt reprinted by permission.

Child Welfare League of America, *Standards of Excellence for Adoption Services* (Washington, D.C.: CWLA, revised editions 1973, 1988, 2000). © 1973, 1988, 2000 by the CWLA. Excerpts reprinted by permission.

Naomi Cahn and Jana Singer, "Adoption, Identity, and the Constitution: The Case for Opening Closed Records," 2 *University of Pennsylvania Journal of Constitutional Law* 150 (1999). © 1999 by the University of Pennsylvania Journal of Constitutional Law. Excerpt reprinted by permission.

Joan Heifetz Hollinger, "Overview of Legal Status of Post-Adoption Contact Agreements," as adapted by the author from *Adoption Law and Practice,* ed. Joan H. Hollinger (New York: Matthew Bender, 1988, 2002), chap. 13, App. 13B–C. © 1988, 2002 by Matthew Bender & Co., Inc. Excerpt adapted and reprinted by permission. All rights reserved.

Annette Baran and Reuben Pannor, "Perspectives on Open Adoption," *Future of Children: Adoption,* vol. 3, no. 1 (1993): 119–24. © 1993 by the David and Lucile Packard Foundation. Excerpt reprinted by permission.

In re Adoption of Vito, 728 N.E.2d 292 (Mass. 2000).

U.S. Children's Bureau, "Guidelines for Public Policy and State Legislation Governing Permanence for Children," U.S. Department of Health and Human Services, Administration on Children, Youth and Families, 1999.

Child Welfare League of America, *Standards of Excellence for Adoption Services* (Washington, D.C.: CWLA, 2000). © 2000 by the CWLA. Excerpt reprinted by permission.

Annette Ruth Appell, "Increasing Options to Improve Permanency: Considerations in Drafting an Adoption with Contact Statute," 18 *Children's Legal Rights Journal* 24 (1998). © 1998 by the William S. Hein Company. Excerpt reprinted by permission.

Judith S. Modell, *Kinship with Strangers: Adoption and Interpretations of Kinship in American Culture* (Berkeley: University of California Press, 1994). © 1994 by the Regents of the University of California. Excerpt reprinted by permission.

Joan Heifetz Hollinger, "The What and Why of the Multiethnic Placement Act (MEPA)." Adapted from teaching materials developed by the author for law students, social service agencies, the American Bar Association, the U.S. Children's Bureau, and from *Adoption Law and Practice,* ed. Joan Heifetz Hollinger (New York: Matthew Bender, 1988, 2002), Appendix 3B.

Barbara Bennett Woodhouse, "'Are You My Mother?': Conceptualizing Children's Identity Rights in Transracial Adoptions," 2 *Duke Journal of Gender, Law and Policy* 107 (1995). © 1995 by the Duke Journal of Gender, Law and Policy. Excerpt reprinted by permission.

R. Richard Banks, "The Color of Desire: Fulfilling Adoptive Parents' Racial Preferences through Discriminatory State Action," 107 *Yale Law Journal* 875 (1998). © 1998 by the Yale Law Journal Company, Inc., the William S. Hein Company, and R. Richard Banks. Excerpt reprinted by permission.

Elizabeth Bartholet, "Private Race Preferences in Family Formation," 107 *Yale Law Journal* 2351 (1998). © 1998 by the Yale Law Journal Company, Inc., William S. Hein Company, and Elizabeth Bartholet. Excerpt reprinted by permission.

Sally Haslanger, "Racial Geographies." © 2004 by Sally Haslanger. Reprinted by permission.

Anita L. Allen-Castellitto, "Does a Child Have a Right to a Certain Identity?" 15 *Rechtstheorie* 109 (1993). © 1993 by Anita L. Allen-Castellitto. Excerpt reprinted by permission.

Joan Heifetz Hollinger, "Intercountry Adoption: A Frontier without Boundaries," as adapted by the author from *Adoption Law and Practice,* ed. Joan H. Hollinger (New York: Matthew Bender, 1988, 2002), chap. 11. © 1988, 2002 by Matthew Bender & Co., Inc. Excerpt adapted and reprinted by permission. All rights reserved.

Joan Heifetz Hollinger, "Who are Indian Children within the Scope of the Federal Indian Child Welfare Act (ICWA)?" as adapted by the author from *Adoption Law and Practice,* ed. Joan H. Hollinger (New York: Matthew Bender, 1988, 2002), chap. 15. © 1988, 2002 by Matthew Bender & Co., Inc. Excerpt adapted and reprinted by permission. All rights reserved.

Christine Metteer, "Pigs in Heaven: A Parable of Native American Adoption under the Indian Child Welfare Act," 28 *Arizona State Law Journal* 589 (1996). © 1996 by the Arizona State Law Journal and Christine Metteer (Lorillard). Excerpt reprinted by permission.

Joan Heifetz Hollinger, "Second Parent Adoptions Protect Children with Two Mothers or Two Fathers." © 2004 by Joan Heifetz Hollinger. Reprinted by permission.

In the Interest of Angel Lace M., 184 Wis. 2d 492, 516 N.W.2d 678 (1994).

Matter of Jacob, 86 N.Y.2d 651, 660 N.E.2d 397, 636 N.Y.S.2d 716 (1995).

Adoptions of B.L.V.B. and E.L.V.B., 160 Vt. 368, 628 A.2d 1271 (1993).

Adoption of Tammy, 416 Mass. 205, 619 N.E.2d 315 (1993).

In re Adoption of Two Children by H.N.R., 285 N.J.Super. 1, 666 A.2d 535 (1995).

Judith Stacey and Timothy J. Biblarz, "(How) Does the Sexual Orientation of Parents Matter?" 66 *American Sociological Review* 2 (2001): 159–83. © 2001 by the American Sociological Association. Excerpt reprinted by permission.

Nancy E. Dowd, "Single Parent Adoptions." © 2004 by Nancy E. Dowd. Excerpt reprinted by permission.

Katharine T. Bartlett, "Re-expressing Parenthood," 98 *Yale Law Journal* 293 (1988). © 1988 by the Yale Law Journal Company, Inc., the William S. Hein Company, and Katharine T. Bartlett. Excerpt reprinted by permission.

Twila L. Perry, "Transracial and International Adoption: Mothers, Hierarchy, Race, and Feminist Legal Theory," 10 *Yale Journal of Law and Feminism* 101 (1998). © 1998 by the Yale Law Journal of Law and Feminism, Inc, and Twila L. Perry. Excerpt reprinted by permission.

Naomi Cahn, "Family Issue(s)," 61 *University of Chicago Law Review* 325 (1994). © 1994 by Naomi Cahn. Excerpt reprinted by permission.

Linda J. Lacey, "'O Wind Remind Him That I Have No Child': Infertility and Feminist Jurisprudence," 5 *University of Michigan Journal of Gender and Law* 163 (1998). © 1998 by the University of Michigan Law School and Linda J. Lacey. Excerpt reprinted by permission.

Charlotte Witt, "Adoption, Biological Essentialism, and Feminist Theory." © 2004 by Charlotte Witt. Reprinted by permission.

Johnson v. Calvert, 5 Cal. 4th 84, 851 P.2d 776 (Cal. 1993).

In re Nicholas H., 28 Cal. 4th 56, 46 P.3d 932 (Cal. 2002).

Joan Heifetz Hollinger, "Note on the Revised Uniform Parentage Act (UPA) of 2002." © 2004 by Joan Heifetz Hollinger. Reprinted by permission. The UPA of 2002 and Comments are available from the National Conference of Commissioners on Uniform State Laws (NCCUSL), 211 East Ontario St., Suite 1300, Chicago, IL 60611 or at www.law.upenn.edu/bll/ulc/upa/final2002.htm.

American Law Institute, *Principles of the Law of Family Dissolution,* Section 2.03. © 2002 by the American Law Institute. Excerpt reprinted by permission. All rights reserved. The complete publication, *Principles of the Law of Family Dissolution: Analysis and Recommendations,* is available through the American Law Institute at www.ALI.org.

Joan Heifetz Hollinger, "From Coitus to Commerce: Legal and Social Consequences of Noncoital Reproduction," 18 *University of Michigan Journal of Law Reform* 865 (1985). © 1985 by the University of Michigan Journal of Law Reform. Excerpt adapted and reprinted by permission.

Marsha Garrison, "Law Making for Baby Making: An Interpretive Approach to the Determination of Legal Parentage," 113 *Harvard Law Review* 835 (2000). © 2000 by the Harvard Law Review Association. Excerpt reprinted by permission.

Mary Lyndon Shanley, "Considerations against Donor Anonymity in Collaborative Procreation." © 2004 by Mary Lyndon Shanley. Reprinted by permission. Adapted by the author from Mary Lyndon Shanley, *Making Babies, Making Families: What Matters Most in an Age of Reproductive Technologies, Surrogacy, Adoption, and Same-Sex and Unwed Parents* (Boston: Beacon Press, 2001). Adapted by permission of Beacon Press.

Rochelle Cooper Dreyfuss and Dorothy Nelkin, "The Jurisprudence of Genetics," 45 *Vanderbilt Law Review* 313 (1992). © 1992 by the Vanderbilt Law Review, Vanderbilt University School of Law, Rochelle Cooper Dreyfuss, and Dorothy Nelkin. Excerpt reprinted by permission.

Margaret Jane Radin, "Market-Inalienability," 100 *Harvard Law Review* 1849 (1987). © 1987 by the Harvard Law Review Association and Margaret Jane Radin. Excerpt reprinted by permission.

Margaret F. Brinig, "The Effect of Transactions Costs on the Market for Babies," 18 *Seton Hall Legislative Journal* 553 (1994). © 1994 by the Seton Hall University Law Center and Margaret F. Brinig. Excerpt reprinted by permission.

Index

Abbott, Grace, on withholding family information, 128

Abortion, 147–148, 262

Adoptees: Adoption Rights Movement (1971), 126, 128, 132, 133; benefits of open adoptive placement, 166; "best interest" of, 38, 42, 161, 170–171, 181, 196, 226, 239–243, 246–247, 250, 261, 290, 301–302, 324, 328; consent to adoption, 40; foster care and, 111–114; heterogeneity among, 2–3, 80–83; Indian Child Welfare Act (ICWA), 221, 222, 223, 224, 226–227, 230, 231; inheritance, 20, 23, 78–79, 244; Multiethnic Placement Act (MEPA), 189–193, 194; mutual consent voluntary registries, 124, 145, 154; and name change, 125; opening closed adoption records, 153–155; open records, 145, 146–148, 310; race/class and, 115–117; racial matching of, 66–67, 69, 72, 74, 192–193, 194, 198, 200–202, 205; sealed adoption records and, 5, 123, 126–133, 127, 134, 140–141, 142–144, 146–148, 315; Sibling Interaction and Behavior Study (SIBS), 85–87; transracial/transnational adoption and, 196–198, 212–214; Uniform Adoption Act (UAA) and, 63, 77. *See also* Gay/lesbian adoptions; Post-adoption contact; Psychosocial consequences of adoption; Single parent adoptions

Adoption agencies (historical), 64–71; biological family model of, 65–67; Child Welfare League of America (CWLA), 65, 66–67, 68, 69, 123, 129, 131; "defective" children and, 67–68; gender norms, 70; marriage and, 69; matching of child to adoptive parents, 66–67; normality, supposition of, 64–66, 67, 68–71; paramount value in, 70; psychology of parents and, 68–69, 71; race/religion and, 66, 67; standards for "adoptability," 67–68; uniform national standards of (1950s), 70–71

Adoption and Safe Families Act of 1997 (ASFA), 2, 118; "concurrent planning," 92; foster care, 91, 92; judicial review and, 93; and the public child welfare system, 91–92

Adoption frontiers, 185

Adoption law, 194; adoptive parents and, 38, 40, 41; adoptive relationships and, 37, 38–42, 244, 288; baby-selling and, 41; children's identity rights in, 194; contested adoption, 40–41, 50, 161; controversy in, 37; custody and parent legal standing, 40, 100–101, 102–105, 106–108, 198; financial considerations and, 41–42; gestational surrogacy and, 289–290; goals of, 42; gratuitous transfer versus bargained-for-exchange, 41–42; informal transfers of children and, 39; lack of uniformity in, 37–38; legal adoptive relationship, creation of, 1, 38, 39; parental autonomy principle and fitness presumption in, 39; parental consent, 39–40, 167–171, 325–328; placement and, 37–38, 39, 41–42; presumption of parental fitness, 39; principal elements of adoptive relationship in, 38–39, 41–42; relinquishment of children, 37, 38, 40, 42*n*; revocation of consent, 40, 160, 326–328; state and federal adoption law, 37–42, 54, 55; termination of birth parents'

About the Editors

NAOMI R. CAHN is a professor at the George Washington University Law School, where she teaches courses in family law and state regulation of the parent-child relationship. JOAN HEIFETZ HOLLINGER is a professor at the University of California, Berkeley, where she teaches courses in child welfare law and policy and sex, reproduction, and family law at Boalt Hall Law School and in the Legal Studies Program.